HIS FINAL BATTLE

Campaigning in Poughkeepsie, New York,
on the final evening of his final campaign.

JOSEPH LELYVELD

His Final Battle

THE LAST MONTHS
OF FRANKLIN ROOSEVELT

ALFRED A. KNOPF · NEW YORK
2016

THIS IS A BORZOI BOOK
PUBLISHED BY ALFRED A. KNOPF

Library of Congress Cataloging-in-Publication Data
Names: Lelyveld, Joseph, author.
Title: His final battle : the last months of Franklin Roosevelt /
by Joseph Lelyveld.
Description: First United States edition. | New York : Alfred A.
Knopf, 2016. | "This is a Borzoi Book." | Includes bibliographical
references and index.
Identifiers: LCCN 2015050730 | ISBN 978-0-385-35079-2
(hardcover) | ISBN 978-0-385-35080-8 (ebook)
Subjects: LCSH: Roosevelt, Franklin D. (Franklin Delano),
1882–1945—Last years. | Presidents—United States—Biography, |
United States—Politics and government—1933——1945. |
United States—Foreign relations—1933–1945.
Classification: LCC E807.L37 2016 | DDC 973.917092—dc23 LC
record available at http://lccn.loc.gov/2015050730.

Front-of-jacket photograph: 1944 campaign appearance at
Chicago's Soldier Field, courtesy of the Franklin D. Roosevelt
Library and Museum, Hyde Park, New York
Jacket design by Carol Devine Carson

Manufactured in the United States of America
First Edition

In memory of Ed Lelyveld, a traveling salesman, who days after FDR's death gave his grandson, just turned eight, a little book for juvenile readers on the first thirty-two presidents.

A man awaits his end
Dreading and hoping all;
Many times he died,
Many times rose again.
A great man in his pride
Confronting murderous men
Casts derision upon
Supersession of breath.

—W. B. YEATS

CONTENTS

HIS FINAL BATTLE

Plaintive

WITH EACH PASSING DAY, he extended his record as the longest-serving president in American history. As Franklin Roosevelt entered his twelfth year in office, he was a more seasoned, astute, and, sometimes, cynical reader of political mood swings than any mere two-term president. By the start of 1944, as yet another election year rolled around, he'd outlived, exhausted, or distanced the few political advisers on whom he'd relied (and even these had usually been left wondering about his intentions). Anyone was free now to float a guess about whether he'd stand for another term, based on his track record or the global crisis or both, neither of which suggested he might not. But no one could claim to know for sure. Cagey by nature, an inveterate hoarder of contradictory options in statecraft and politics, the president himself was the only political adviser he would heed when he deemed the time for decision was upon him. Those who saw him up close searched his countenance for signs of weariness and ill health. He met them with his usual charm, his practiced chattiness. Only in private, confiding in his worshipful distant cousin Daisy Suckley, who spent more time alone with him than did his bustling wife, Eleanor, would he acknowledge how very weary he felt. "He just is *too* tired, *too* often," Daisy had written in her diary the previous October.

With the most destructive military struggle in human history approaching its climax, there was no one in the White House, or his party, or the whole of political Washington, who dared stand before him in the early months of 1944 and ask face-to-face for a clear answer to the question of whether he could contemplate stepping down. All the memoirs, diaries, and caches of private letters preserved from that time reveal no such encounter. When reporters tried to insinuate this by now perennial question into his twice-weekly press conference performances, where in the pretelevision era direct quotation was usually barred, they knew they were inviting a jocular brush-off. "You're getting picayune. We're not talking about that now," the president had said in a characteristically airy response at his last such session in 1943. On that, they could quote him if they wished. Usually, they would just summarize what he said in their own words, which he might later disown, or describe his mood or appearance.

Cabinet members attempting to extract a hint of his political plans in strictest confidence, even a wink, from members of the First Family were told by his nearest and dearest that they were "completely in the dark." So Anna, the president's only daughter and eldest child, the offspring in whom he'd be most likely to confide, told Harold Ickes, the interior secretary. When an aide passed along the news that the Democratic National Committee had endorsed him for a fourth term, Roosevelt's entire comment was an uninflected, perfectly indifferent "Oh." Even Harry Hopkins, his supposed alter ego and diplomatic point man, the one messenger who'd been able to represent his thinking with absolute certitude to Churchill or Stalin—his Rasputin, some commentators and even some Democrats called him—seemed at a loss. Hopkins, who'd been sidelined after a collapse at the start of the year, was more obviously ill than his boss. "Open me up," he quipped, as he was being wheeled into an operating theater at the Mayo Clinic late in March 1944 for major intestinal surgery that would keep him out of action until July. "Maybe you'll find the answer to the fourth term. Maybe not."

Only once in the written record of that time does Franklin Roosevelt commit to paper a statement of his own feelings. It came in response to a somewhat tentative, nonetheless daring, eight-page memo from Ben Cohen, a long-serving New Deal legal draftsman and political strategist of unquestioned loyalty. Intended for the president's eyes only, Cohen's memo offered a pessimistic diagnosis of the state of the Roosevelt coalition and the prospects for an effective fourth term in the aftermath of the war, even assuming his reelection. In restrained lawyerly language, Cohen is warning his president that another term could be a failure, a barren anticlimax, a political train wreck, due to grievances and bitter antipathies that had accumulated over the years in Congress and the sclerotic administration's own ranks; such a failure, Cohen warned, could mean that "Rooseveltian ideas, like Wilsonian ideas, may be discredited for a considerable period" ("Rooseveltian," in this context, being synonymous with "liberal"). The mere mention of Woodrow Wilson might have touched a sensitive point in the psyche of this president, a member for seven years of the Wilson administration who'd lived through the eclipse of Wilsonian ideas and of the stricken leader himself.

Boldly this New Deal loyalist girds himself to ask "whether there is any practical alternative to a fourth term." Harboring ambitions for a high State Department position that would involve him in the issues facing a postwar world, Cohen might well have worried that his carefully gauged candor would not be rewarded. (It wasn't; someone else got the job he had in his sights.) After five days, he received a characteristically pithy, even tantalizing, three-sentence acknowledgment, dated March 13, 1944, showing that Roosevelt's charm and knack for concealment were both intact.

"Dear Ben," the president wrote. "That is a tremendously interesting analysis—and I think a very just one. You have left out only one matter—and that is the matter of my own feelings! I am feeling plaintive." It's signed, "As ever yours, F.D.R." The three letters of the signature are noticeably lopsided, not quite spastic in their execution, but a feeble imitation of the accustomed flourish.

"Plaintive." The word, meaning melancholy, forlorn—possibly in this context even cornered—seems well chosen, especially if we dwell on its timing. Mid-March is virtually midway in the half year separating Roosevelt's return from the summit conference in Tehran, where he allowed himself to imagine he'd established a promising personal rapport with the Soviet dictator Joseph Stalin, and the date there pledged for D-Day—the fateful, much-debated, much-delayed Anglo-American landing in Normandy. By the middle of March, a force approaching one million Americans had massed in Britain in preparation for the invasion. The outcome was by no means assured. A dubious Winston Churchill, who would have delayed it if he could, had visions of the English Channel awash in Allied corpses, body parts, and gore.

Nevertheless, the turning point of the war had already occurred. It had come the previous year, before the Tehran meeting, in the titanic, grinding battles of Stalingrad and Kursk, where Soviet forces had decimated German armies that, altogether, outnumbered the Wehrmacht units waiting to repel the Allies in France. Roosevelt certainly understood in March 1944 that the Russians were doing most of the fighting, a factor not often stressed in English-language histories. In just two months of fierce combat on the eastern front in 1943, they lost nearly as many troops as the Americans and the British, including Commonwealth nations, would lose during the entire war. By the war's end, it has been estimated, four of every five Germans killed in combat would have been taken down by the Red Army. Losses on the Soviet side, civilian and military combined, would be in the range of twenty-seven to thirty million.

Stalin had handsomely acknowledged in a banquet toast at Tehran that it was Roosevelt who'd made the rollback of Nazi forces on the eastern front possible. His decision in 1941 to rush Lend-Lease arms, planes, trucks, and machine tools to the besieged Communist regime had been questioned by key military advisers who thought the Nazis, then in striking distance of Moscow, were probably unstoppable. In their view, the equipment couldn't be spared. It had been a big gamble, a singular act of presidential foresight, intuition, leadership—call it what you will—taken at a time when the country was not yet at war; when he was widely criticized for inaction by those who passionately favored intervention, for overreaching by equally passionate anti-interventionists marching under the slogan "America first." Without that flow of American aid, the dictator said in his Tehran toast two years later, "We would lose this war."

There was an obvious symbiosis here. The historian Ira Katznelson states it plainly. Without the Russians, he writes, "the fight against Nazi Germany could not have been won."

That the outcome of the struggle was now being determined on the eastern front—where no American or British lives were at stake—was reason for gratitude and foreboding. In Roosevelt's mind, it raised questions even more pressing than that of his own political future, more pressing but not unrelated. How could there be a stable world order without some kind of understanding on basic ground rules with the Russians, who would emerge from the war as Europe's strongest power? If such an accommodation were possible, who but the

NOVEMBER 29, 1943. With Stalin in Tehran.

president could shape it? He had long regarded "the post-war set-tlement . . . as his own particular preserve." So Hopkins had found it necessary to alert British Foreign Office officials in early 1941, in case they had any ideas of their own. On this, Roosevelt was "rather touchy," Hopkins had said. This too was months before the United States actually entered the war.

Now, with D-Day looming on the horizon, he'd been advised by Admiral William Leahy and General George Marshall that the war in Europe might well be over by the end of 1944—in other words, before the next inauguration, if not the election. Such predictions of an early Nazi collapse proved to be overoptimistic by four months, a season of epic devastation and slaughter. (No one imagined that the war in the Pacific would end nearly so soon. Forecasts in early 1944 necessarily left out of consideration the war-ending potential of an atom bomb, a weapon still only a remote possibility, so top secret that military forecasters couldn't have known what the president himself had recently learned: that a nuclear device had been shown to be technically feasible; that production could now, would now, go forward with the green light he had just given.)

So there was one set of reasons for feeling plaintive, the military ones. D-Day was scheduled for May, early June at the latest, the Democratic convention for mid-July, just six weeks later. (The bomb wouldn't be ready for at least another year if it worked; Admiral Leahy, the military adviser closest at hand, predicted it never would.) If the president could contemplate for even a moment the possibility of stepping aside, when would the right moment be for making his intentions known, given those converging timetables? It wouldn't be before the as yet unlaunched invasion, nor when the invaders were still battling to break through German coastal defenses—through Hitler's vaunted Atlantic Wall, an intricate network of fortifications, machine gun nests, land mines, and booby traps thrown together by slave labor—not to mention inevitable, unanticipated obstacles such as the rural French hedgerows that soon slowed any advance inland from the beaches toward Paris. In the most optimistic scenario imaginable, it might not be before the eve of the convention, when no other plausible candidates were likely to have come to the fore, given the huge, blighting shadow he had cast over potential candidates all these years, what the *New York Herald Tribune* described as "the withering effect that Mr. Roosevelt's prolonged domination has had on his party." And who, after all, could those candidates be?

In ruminations and occasional asides, Roosevelt would speculatively, almost playfully, canvass an ever-shifting lineup of names of possible successors or running mates over these months. It was no disqualification to be something other than a politician; the industrialist Henry J. Kaiser made his list. Kaiser was a doer. He'd revolutionized American shipbuilding when "Liberty ships" were in urgent demand to send Lend-Lease arms and munitions to the British and the Russians. Nor was it necessary to be a Democrat; the American ambassador to Britain, John G. Winant, a former Republican governor of New Hampshire, made the list, too. Not on the president's list was George Catlett Marshall, his military mainstay, whose name had been floated by a Democratic senator, Edwin Johnson of Colorado, who'd come out against a fourth term for Roosevelt. Marshall instantly scotched the notion, saying he'd be in his grave before he'd be in politics.

Roosevelt didn't need political bosses like Chicago's mayor, Ed Kelly, or Jersey City's Frank Hague to tell him he was the only Democrat who could possibly win. Polls made that point plainly enough. They also told him that even he was no sure thing, that a campaign fought on domestic issues, which could happen if the war's end were heaving into view by Election Day, would most likely be won by the Republican candidate. (Unpublished figures from a Gallup survey made available to the White House had Roosevelt taking 51 percent of the vote against 32 percent for New York's governor, the forty-two-year-old former racket buster, Thomas Dewey, if the war were still raging at the time of the election. If the war were over, the percentages were almost exactly reversed, 51 to 30, with Dewey on top. If the end were "clearly in sight," the challenger was said to edge the president by a point.)

In the last congressional election, just eleven months after Pearl Harbor, the embattled nation hadn't rallied to its wartime leader's party as might have been expected. At the height of the New Deal, Democrats had held a seemingly insuperable margin in the House of Representatives that topped out in 1936 at 246 seats (insuperable until an anti–New Deal, bipartisan coalition came into being to combat Roosevelt's plan to "pack" the Supreme Court). In the 1942 congressional election, by which time that margin had already been severely reduced, Democrats lost another forty-five seats. "All the boys who went down were Roosevelt men," observed a rising congressman from Texas named Lyndon Johnson. By 1944, the margin had been whittled to an unreliable eight. Confirmed New Dealers were now a minority in their own party. Franklin Roosevelt didn't need Ben Cohen to tell him the political facts of life or chart the shoals ahead.

The country "would do anything for a change," he'd told the writer Roald Dahl, who pitched up at the Roosevelt estate in Hyde Park, New York, in the summer of 1943 as a guest of Eleanor's. (Dahl hadn't yet written *James and the Giant Peach*. Ostensibly a Royal Air Force major serving as an attaché in the British embassy, the smooth and highly gregarious officer was a sought-after Washington dinner party guest despite his comparatively modest rank; actually, he was working for British intelligence.)

On rare occasions, the hardened realist in Roosevelt allowed himself to contemplate the possibility of a Republican successor. There was only one he could imagine, if not embrace, as perhaps equal to the task. That was Wendell Willkie, his rival four years earlier whom the president had come to view with growing regard. In his view, Willkie had been a patriot, not a partisan opportunist, on key issues as the threat of war loomed. Once, when Harry Hopkins uttered something disparaging about the vanquished Hoosier, Roosevelt was quick to silence him: "Don't ever say anything like that around here again. Don't even *think* it. You of all people ought to know that we might not have had Lend-Lease or Selective Service if it hadn't been for Wendell Willkie. He was a Godsend to this country when we needed him most."

By March 1944, Willkie was back on the hustings, seeking to reclaim the mantle of Republican leadership. In early primary states in the Midwest where isolationism had flourished before Pearl Harbor, a barnstorming Willkie was fervently but recklessly presenting himself as more internationalist than Roosevelt. In *One World,* his starry-eyed, best-selling account of his wartime travels to China and Russia, he'd come on as a new Woodrow Wilson who, this time around, really saw the way to make the world safe for democracy. The president, he complained, was fumbling a historic opportunity to shape the future; he'd demonstrated no vision, unveiled no program. His administration, Willkie said, "has lost its sense of direction and is failing to carry out the great purposes for which we are fighting."

In this criticism, Willkie was echoing deep thinkers like the columnist Walter Lippmann, whose prescriptions veered toward realpolitik. In his own wartime best seller, *U.S. Foreign Policy,* Lippmann argued for a policy not unlike the one toward which the deliberately inscrutable president was actually groping, a policy based on a transformation of the wartime alliance of necessity into a consortium of three or four big powers that would design and then police a peacetime order. The columnist, a reformed Wilsonian—as a young man, he'd had a hand in drafting background papers for Woodrow Wilson's Fourteen Points, his scheme for world peace—agreed that this president was displaying no vision.

Roosevelt, a reformed Wilsonian himself, remained, characteristically, guarded about his intentions and goals. Before and after the Tehran meeting, he confined himself to what *Time* magazine aptly discounted as "round generalities" in his public statements. If asked, he'd probably have advised Willkie that he was addressing the wrong audience and that his timing was off. For Roosevelt, timing was always a key part of the art of governing. Germany and Japan still held nearly all the territory they'd seized. Though Mussolini had fallen, Rome was now in German hands, as were Athens, Warsaw, Amsterdam, Paris, and, of course, the final Nazi citadel, Berlin. MacArthur had yet to return to the Philippines. All this was on graphic display on days—becoming rarer—when the president felt well enough to be wheeled into the White House Map Room in the early months of 1944.

With brutal ground and air battles still to be fought, vast tallies of killed and wounded young Americans still to be added, voters weren't looking for a visionary, least of all Republican voters. So they would shortly show in the Wisconsin primary, where Willkie, repudiated as an apologist for the president he'd been lambasting, finished last in a field of four behind Dewey, Harold Stassen, and General MacArthur—a result so shaming that the reborn Willkie candidacy disintegrated on the spot. Defeated but unbowed, he restated a campaign theme. "The United States has no foreign policy," he said, "or a dangerously personal one known to President Roosevelt alone."

The Oxford historian of ideas Isaiah Berlin, then serving as an analyst in the British embassy in Washington, later assessed the alternative to the president that the Republicans then offered in a dispatch to the Foreign Office: "To Roosevelt's Gladstone there was no discernible potential Disraeli." Of course the president wouldn't have put it in those terms, but the don came close to expressing his view.

As winter turned to spring, his mind ranged widely over all the military and political imponderables and prospects before him. He had reason to feel plaintive, to recognize that his options and decisions were being shaped by powerful forces he could hope to influence but not control. Ben Cohen had been too wary and respectful to bring up a final set of imponderables that Roosevelt couldn't possibly ignore. That was the question of his own stamina and health, of whether he could actually survive a fourth term.

Because we read history backward, we know the answer: that the curtain would come down abruptly on the Roosevelt era on a balmy April afternoon in Warm Springs, Georgia, in what was only the twelfth week of that term (making it the third-shortest presidential term of them all, following William Henry Harrison's pathetic thirty-two days a century earlier and the mere six weeks that intervened between Abraham Lincoln's second inaugural address and his assassination). Obviously, Roosevelt's doctors must have known that this could happen, amateur historians of the period have since reasoned. Obviously, he must have had some inkling of what they knew. Obviously, there must have been a cover-up, one that continued after his death when—so it was disclosed years later—the bulk of the president's medical records had been lost and presumably destroyed. So the argument has gone in a lengthening list of books and articles, many by doctors casting themselves as medical historians and sleuths. In such studies, equally obvious nonmedical factors—political, military, also existential—are often missed.*

By existential, I don't mean anything fancy, simply that deep down, no matter how steadfastly we try to avoid the thought, we can't escape the fact that we're mortal. Mortality is the ultimate reason for feeling plaintive. In our waning hours, we get on with our tasks. Roosevelt was racing, as we all are, against time. If we want to take him in his full measure, we need to see him in his full context, in the round, not just as a dying man in what we may glibly call "denial," but as an actor playing out his role, simply because he found no alternative; in that sense, a man touched by the heroic. Of all his responsibilities as the war headed into its climactic last year, calculating the date of his own terminus was not necessarily, in that clamorous time, the most pressing. In the normal course of human events, it would be the one on which he'd be least likely to focus.

The following months would offer a telling parable from this uncomfortable perspective. That same Wendell Willkie—by all appearances a robust man, a full ten years younger than Roosevelt—would end his particular race against time a half year after his defeat in Wisconsin, felled by a heart attack on October 8. That turned out to be a half year before the death of the president whose tasks of bringing the war to a successful conclusion and building a new global order Willkie had

---

* While we're bandying the word "existential," there's an irresistible temptation to note that the author of *Being and Nothingness*, Jean-Paul Sartre himself, turned up at a White House press conference near the end of Roosevelt's life as a correspondent for *Le Figaro*. Sartre wasn't inspired on this occasion to pen a meditation on the absurd, on human transience. Instead, he wrote of the forceful impression Franklin Roosevelt made at a time when numerous later accounts describe him as barely able to function. "What is most striking," he wrote, "is the profoundly human charm of his long face, at once sensitive and strong . . . He smiled at us and talked to us in his deep, slow voice."

imagined himself completing. (Dying less than a week before Willkie was Al Smith, who was quoted as having written off Roosevelt's political future all the way back in 1928, when Roosevelt placed Smith's name in nomination for the presidency as he had four years earlier. "He won't live a year," Smith supposedly said.)

Roosevelt himself had meanwhile dreamed of forging a political alliance with Willkie that might outlast his time in the White House, a realignment of parties that could be proclaimed and bequeathed after the coming election. To that end, he'd dispatched one of his speechwriters, Samuel Rosenman, as a secret envoy to the rejected Republican to see if there was any basis for an exploration of such a project. Before Willkie's demise, he slipped into the White House for a chat with the president; the two spoke of meeting again after the election.

At the same time, as we shall see, the idea of resigning in his fourth term was never far from Roosevelt's mind in his final months; that could be an option, he would allow himself to dream, once the war had ended and a rudimentary mechanism for international peacekeeping had been set in place. That idea, too, was in the air. Senator Claude Pepper, a liberal Florida Democrat, had mentioned it to a reporter in January, saying the president had spoken of resigning once he'd completed his soldier's duty of service to the end of the war. Perhaps he would be named head of the new international security organization he was seeking to shape. That wispy thought had occurred to him as early as April 1943. So many possibilities, so little time.

The fascination of Franklin Roosevelt's final months, the home-stretch or last act of his long run, isn't that they proved final. It lies in the way his restless imagination continued to range across the oceans and battlefields to which he'd dispatched naval armadas, armies numbering millions, bombers and fighter planes by the tens of thousands; to the all-too-familiar political scene he'd dominated for so long, now waiting for his signal; to a deepening sense of isolation and exhaustion in the midst of all these storms and contests; to his cloudy hopes for an outcome worthy of the huge, immeasurable cost. Historians understandably tend to discuss these weighty preoccupations sequentially, one by one—the war, the diplomacy, the political contest, his declining health—as if they were separate subjects, for each contains its own saga, rich with complexity. But Roosevelt experienced them and brooded over them all at once, in what we now call real time, keeping a sharp eye all the while on shifting currents of American opinion, the politician's measure of the possible.

Few questions could be decided on their own merits alone. If, as he had persuaded himself, hopes for a stable order rested to some considerable degree on his personal ability to improvise a way of getting on with the Soviet dictator, that had implications for his political choices, which had implications for his own health. Such a proposition could be flipped on its head: If his party needed him to run again because it had no other candidate who could win, that had implications for relations with Moscow and also, of course, his condition. After eleven years in office, he was given not just to calculation but to constant recalculation. Entangled in a cat's cradle of contingencies bearing on the future—his and his country's—this quick-witted tactician could drive his supporters and enemies to distraction with his reluctance to limit his options by taking a major decision. Issues that were not ripe for decision should be kept "fluid," he sometimes said.

A rough parallel can be drawn between his approach to the question of a fourth term and his approach, early on, to the fraught question of intervention in the war itself. Churchill had hoped that Roosevelt's reelection to the unprecedented third term in 1940, following the Nazi invasions of Norway, Denmark, the Netherlands, Belgium, and France, would settle the matter, loosening the political constraints that had kept the president from seeking a declaration of war on Britain's side. He had similar hopes nine months later, following his first encounter as prime minister with Roosevelt, on a warship at sea off Newfoundland, only to be disappointed again. This was a leader given to hidden, sometimes baffling, subtleties. As the pressure for intervention grew, Roosevelt had to weigh the state of American rearmament and readiness against the isolationist zealotry still smoldering in Congress, and the need to rush weapons to the British and Russians; above all, the need to wait on shifting tides of sentiment in the land. Pursuing his own serpentine path, he was still laying the groundwork for intervention across the Atlantic when the Japanese crossed the Pacific and attacked Pearl Harbor on December 7, 1941.

In the ensuing years, neither the war nor his growing fatigue had changed his elusive, distinctly nonlinear pattern of thought. Contemporaries and later writers have struggled over the years to find words to describe it. Henry Wallace, the second of his three vice presidents, called it "feminine," explaining that he proceeded "by intuition and indirection." (Roosevelt could "very successfully go in two directions at almost the same time," Wallace said, elaborating.) The biographer Geoffrey Ward resorts to the word "sinuous." Frances Perkins, the first woman to serve in an American cabinet, thought him "almost clairvoyant." In her memoir, she describes her president's "four-track mind." Anthony Eden, the British foreign secretary, called him "a conjuror, skilfully juggling with balls of dynamite, whose nature he failed to understand." Roosevelt's conversation could be "perplexing," Eden wrote in a memoir, in its "cheerful fecklessness." His lively mind skipped around. He was entertaining and disconcerting at the same time, full of sudden inspirations veering off in new directions, not overly interested in contrary views. Still, few politicians, the Briton acknowledged, showed "greater artistry" in attaining their immediate objectives.

Henry Stimson, a Wall Street financier who'd served as both secretary of state and war secretary in Republican administrations, was driven to poetic metaphor in trying to describe the experience of a tête-à-tête with this president, who usually talked more than he listened: "His mind does not easily follow a consecutive chain of thought but he is full of stories and incidents and hops about in his discussion from suggestion to suggestion and it is very much like following a vagrant beam of moonshine around a vacant room." These are all ways of saying that he depended on himself more than others, trying out contradictory ideas, until they came together in a way he found convincing or, at least, helpful. Dwight Eisenhower remarked that he was "almost an egomaniac" in his "belief in his own wisdom." Summing up such impressions, the British military historian John Keegan throws up his hands and calls Roosevelt "by far the most enigmatic of the major figures" of the war.

Franklin Roosevelt had his own take on Franklin Roosevelt. Speaking in 1942 to his Hudson valley neighbor and Treasury secretary, Henry Morgenthau Jr., he cheerfully acknowledged his skill at keeping people—not excluding himself—guessing. "You know, I am a juggler," he said, "and I never let my left hand know what my right hand does . . . I may be entirely inconsistent, and furthermore I am perfectly willing to mislead and tell untruths if it will help win the war."

However it's described, his pattern of thought had grown no less elusive as he approached what would turn out to be his last year, but the number of subjects he could entertain at one time and his appetite for fresh political intelligence had both undergone discernible shrinkage. The wartime economy with its vast, new military-industrial complex (to use a phrase not yet coined) was being run from the other end of the White House, overseen by a former South Carolina senator and Supreme Court justice, James F. Byrnes—sometimes called the "assistant president"—while Roosevelt concentrated largely on the high strategy and diplomatic goals of the alliance. In his own mind, his health had to be a consideration but never one that needed to be seen, or at least could be seen, in isolation from all the other issues he faced. Like them, it needed to be finessed, cautiously.

In this, too, there was nothing really new. From its inception, the Roosevelt presidency had been founded on the finessing of any questions touching on his physical condition, his infirmity. If there was a cover-up, it was already in place in 1932, when the then governor of New York captured the White House. The writer Hugh Gallagher, himself a polio victim, called it Roosevelt's "splendid deception." Most of Roosevelt's contemporaries realized he had some residual disability from the infantile paralysis that literally laid him low in 1921, when he was five months shy of forty. But in the face of his brilliant self-portrayal, his convincing projection of verve and optimism, most assumed that, basically, he'd overcome the disease. That seemed true on the psychological plane but only there. Polio hadn't vanquished him—in that way, he was truly out of the ordinary—but it had left him completely unable to get himself into a standing position without help or walk under his own power without weighty steel braces on his useless legs, a cane to lean on with his right hand and the strong arm of one of his four sons or bodyguards to cling to with his left. As Mike Reilly, the chief of his Secret Service detail, later acknowledged, "He was a helpless cripple, incapable of walking unaided a single foot." The fact that he couldn't cross a room on his own except in one of his specially designed armless wheelchairs—or crawling, as early in his convalescence he'd taught himself to do—remained privileged information, virtually a state secret, all through his White House years. So did the fact that he regularly had to be lifted in and out of cars by the Secret Service like an infant, that he couldn't get in or out of bed or a tub, dress or undress himself, without the assistance of a valet. Each day demanded fortitude and courage, but that was all strictly off the record, not for public consumption, a barrier that neither the press nor his political enemies were normally prepared to breach.

That wasn't just courtesy. Roosevelt's handlers in the White House and the Secret Service actively policed that barrier. It was Roosevelt's own "absolute edict to the Secret Service, press photographers and the rest of us," according to his naval attaché, Admiral Wilson Brown, "that he was not to be photographed while being helped to his feet or struggling with his braces to sit down."

In 1937, an unknown photographer managed to snatch a photo of the president in his wheelchair when he was visiting the naval hospital. Stephen Early, the White House press secretary, sent a sharp rebuke to Ross McIntire, the president's physician: "Here is a picture of the President in his wheelchair—a scene we have never permitted to be photographed . . . I do think this should be investigated and steps taken to prevent any repetition." McIntire, a mere lieutenant commander in the navy then, got the message. He understood that a primary part of his job was upholding the impression of physical vitality that Roosevelt, great actor that he was, managed to convey. It was a duty at times more important to the patient than the actual treatment this ear, nose, and throat specialist gave him on an almost daily basis for his chronic sinus trouble, treatment designed to protect his highly expressive, mellifluous voice, as vital to his leadership in the age of radio as Luciano Pavarotti's would later be to opera companies that proudly engaged the tenor in lead roles.

By early 1944, the weary president had gone for nearly six months never once allowing himself to be encased in the heavy braces without which he couldn't possibly stand behind a lectern or on the back of a railway car to wave to his public. (Another half year would elapse before, as the political campaign neared, the braces were strapped on again.) News photos and newsreels shown in movie theaters—offering little more in wartime than approved footage and uplifting propaganda—almost invariably showed him seated: at his desk, in a car, at a head table, greeting foreign visitors, his head typically tilted back at a jaunty angle, his cigarette holder held aloft, an animated, hearty expression on his countenance. Jonathan Daniels, a White House assistant in Roosevelt's last year, wasn't the only one who thought he waved the cigarette holder like a scepter or magic wand.

There was no such thing as television at his press conferences, no question of a camera following him as he entered or left a room. His carefully staged public appearances were rare and grew rarer. Under wartime censorship—officially described as "voluntary" but monitored by the Office of Censorship, headed by a former Washington bureau chief for the Associated Press directly responsible to the president—his actual whereabouts were routinely deemed a state secret. He took no reporters to Tehran and would take none, later, to his second meeting with Stalin at Yalta. In the final 519 days of his life—counting from the date of his departure for Tehran, November 11, 1943—he was away from the White House more than he was in residence, spending only 208 nights there in what was not quite a year and a half. The two overseas summits accounted for 72 days, involving long sea voyages back and forth; his twenty-one trips to Hyde Park, in his special train, almost invariably by night, add up to another 95. Altogether, preferring to travel at half-normal speeds to avoid being jostled in his berth, where his useless legs made it hard for him to steady himself in bumpy stretches, he spent 60 nights on trains in this period. ("Now don't let the engineer set any speed records," he instructed the Secret Service on most of those nights.) A cross-country trip to the Pacific and back in the summer of 1944—to California by rail, then Hawaii and the remote Aleutians by ship—plus political campaigning in the autumn account for most of the remainder of his days on the rails.

In those seventeen months, Franklin and Eleanor Roosevelt were in the same place, according to a count based on the Roosevelt Library's records of their day-by-day whereabouts, only 170 days, about one-third of the time. And on the majority of those days, the two principals in the extraordinary political partnership that their marriage had long since become did not take their meals together.

Only on the completion of a journey, usually marked by his return to Washington, could any of these trips be reported in the press. In April 1944, as D-Day drew near, he was gone for a month. *The New York Times,* in one of its few references to his absence from the White House, used a subordinate clause in a brief story on his wife to reveal that the president was "somewhere in the South." Three months later, as the Democratic convention gathered in Chicago, he stopped his private train in the rail yards for a single political conversation. The fact that he had been in Chicago wasn't revealed for another eight days, by which time he was in San Diego, a fact that then remained concealed until he reached Honolulu. The first dispatches permitted on his trip out west in the summer of 1944 had to be datelined, according to White House instructions, not "SAN DIEGO" but "A U.S. NAVAL BASE ON THE PACIFIC COAST." He'd already been on the road, in his special train, for a week.

Members of his cabinet became accustomed to being unsure of the president's whereabouts. Secretary of War Stimson, who by then had responsibility for the Manhattan Project—the biggest secret of them all, aiming at the production of the first atom bombs—took it as a sign of great trust when the president told him "frankly," nearly a week in advance, the date, destination, and purpose of his trip to Tehran. In this atmosphere of secretiveness—due partly to legitimate security considerations, mostly to Roosevelt's own inclinations, suggesting a deep-seated wish to separate himself from his office—the questions of where he was and how he was increasingly ran together, overlapped. "The trouble now is that the President is almost inaccessible," the war secretary wrote in his diary, in a passing moment of frustration, not long before that meeting. "He has been sick for three or four or five days, and now when he's come out he's got such an accumulation of work it's as difficult to get at him as it would be to get at Mohammed."

The secrecy that insulated Roosevelt in wartime allowed a sense of freedom that his disability and office had tended to deny him. His loyal press secretary, Steve Early, wryly said as much in a letter to a friend just two months after Pearl Harbor: "Very confidentially, the President left Washington last Saturday. He has been resting and sleeping ever since—behaving like a free man—in seclusion somewhere within the continental boundaries of these United States."

Everyone understood that an overstressed war president was entitled to breaks, might now and then be under the weather. The concern that he might have suffered an irreversible decline in health occurred to few outside the hothouse of political Washington, and was uttered by even fewer, before the political campaign got rolling. Even then, it was hardly ever up front in the news except in the most rabid sectors of the anti-Roosevelt press, notably Colonel Robert McCormick's *Chicago Tribune* and his cousin Joe Patterson's New York *Daily News*, a tabloid with the nation's biggest circulation. Yet here, too, little of what was being said in private and implied occasionally between the lines in print was entirely new. Roosevelt health rumors—some still not laid to rest—had floated around Washington for years. Back in 1940, when speculation was rising about the possibility of an unprecedented third term, Harold Ickes wondered in his diary "whether Roosevelt, if re-elected, can stand the strain of another four years. The drain on his health has been terrific as it is. Even if he survives the ordeal, there may come a time when he feels like resigning."

By the start of 1944, it seemed clear that he'd stood the strain. But early on, following that 1940 victory, the reelected president had taken an almost immediate turn for the worse. In the first months of the third term, he'd actually been in rockier shape than he'd been at any time since. His hemoglobin count sank, and his blood pressure rose. Bleeding hemorrhoids were thought to be the root cause. They brought on anemia. Of course, none of these intimate medical details became public. When, one evening, dining at the White House, he suffered what his physician dismissed as "a very slight heart attack," not a word was spoken outside his inner circle about the president having been indisposed.

That particular bad patch was now nearly three years behind him. There had been others, but the president's health was not widely recognized as a question on December 17, 1943, the day he returned to the White House from his five-week sea-and-air voyage to Tehran and Cairo, measured in the official log at 17,443 miles, the farthest any serving president had ever traveled. Charles Bohlen, his interpreter at every meeting with Stalin, said he showed no signs of fatigue in Tehran, that his health had been "excellent." The evening of his return, Frances Perkins proclaimed him to be "in magnificent shape." To Sam Rosenman, "He looked robust and well." Here's what Henry Stimson wrote in his diary that same day: "Just as we of the cabinet arrived there, the President was wheeled in from his car. He was in his traveling suit, looked very well and greeted us all with very great cheeriness and good humor and kindness. He was at his best."

If there was any alarm over the health of a leader at that moment, it was for Winston Churchill, who was laid up in Tunisia in the aftermath of the summit meetings, near the site of ancient Carthage, with severe pneumonia and heart fibrillations. For some hours, there was

DECEMBER 17, 1943. Welcomed home
from Tehran by Frances Perkins.

even concern that the prime minister might not pull through. His
wife, Clementine, was summoned from London to his side. A week
later, Churchill was out of danger but still convalescing. A still buoyant Roosevelt, delivering a Christmas Eve fireside chat on his Mideast
travels, made a point of saying that the "heartfelt prayers" of millions
of Americans had been "with this great citizen of the world in his
recent serious illness." In the Tehran and Cairo photographs, the president himself looks much the same as he had at a get-together with
Churchill at Casablanca nearly a year earlier: full-faced, an animated,
alert public man, given to practiced expressions of delight. Then, a few
days after the radio speech, Roosevelt himself was down with the flu.

In the new year, that practiced expression would become less reliable, less convincing. It wasn't often seen outside the White House.
On January 11, a clerk had to read Roosevelt's State of the Union
address in a half-empty House chamber. The president, said to be
recovering from an infection, was not yet well enough to deliver it

in person. He summed it up in a fireside chat over the airwaves that evening. Weeks later, just before Roosevelt's sixty-second birthday, his Panglossian physician, McIntire—by then a vice admiral and surgeon general of the navy—blandly told a White House press briefing that the president's health was better than it had been at any time since 1933. "His stamina is far above average, measured by the speed with which he snaps back from extra-heavy strain or some little illness—the only kind he has had since becoming president." A few days later, he was promoted to rear admiral, a rank that would normally have come in wartime, as the *New York Herald Tribune* made a point of asserting in a front-page article, with the command of a fleet. "Put Ahead of Line Officers," a subordinate headline declared. That's as far as the newspaper dared go in suggesting that there might be something not quite right here; the article raised no questions about the president's health. McIntire held the temporary rank of captain when first assigned to the White House in 1933. He would cheerfully go on offering such roseate prognoses and testimonials, without qualifications or the slightest suggestion of concern, until the votes were counted the following November, indeed until the president died. Then he'd put his name to a ghostwritten book claiming he'd always spoken the truth.

Roosevelt spent the last week of January 1944 at Hyde Park, hoping to "snap back" from his "little illness," another eight days there late in February. He still felt tired, day after day. Though Admiral McIntire insisted he was in "robust health," the patient himself had to know he wasn't. His hands had started to shake; to disguise the tremor, he now preferred a heavy coffee mug to a cup. His signatures had become wobbly, the strokes less thick and firm. His attention sometimes wandered. Increasingly, as the election year of 1944 wore on, he found it difficult to shave or bathe himself and needed more help than ever from his black valet, a chief petty officer in the navy named Arthur Prettyman, in these and other intimate tasks of personal care. But this, too, was a matter of degree. He'd needed such help, after all, since 1921 and had long since trained himself to accept it cheerfully. At the start of April, he was complaining to Daisy Suckley that he had "sleeping sickness."

By then, he'd been shedding weight for a couple of months; it showed in his face. His loss of appetite was easily blamed on Henrietta Nesbitt, a Hudson valley neighbor whom Eleanor had installed as White House cook. The president wasn't the only one to disdain her bland offerings, but he felt powerless to replace her. Early on, some thought his new lean look an improvement, including Chicago's mayor, Ed Kelly, who seemed to have a premonition that it could be a wasting asset. In Chicago after a White House visit on February 1 at which he thought the president had looked "wonderfully well," Kelly wrote to the new Democratic chairman, Robert Hannegan, to urge that this would be a good time to take campaign photographs, now, the letter seemed to imply, rather than later. The mayor had a sharp eye for appearances. During the fall campaign, by which time Roosevelt had shed another fifteen or so pounds, he'd urge that someone rush out to buy the president a new set of shirts with a smaller neck size; he was looking scrawny.

In March, days after his reply to Ben Cohen's letter about finding "a practical alternative to a fourth term," Anna Roosevelt Boettiger, as she was then called, confronted Admiral McIntire and demanded to know what was wrong with her father. The ear, nose, and throat man doled out his standard bromides, but this time they didn't go down. The president's daughter was acting on behalf of her family. Finally, McIntire made an appointment for Roosevelt with the top cardiologist at the naval hospital in Bethesda; evidently, the admiral had known all along where the problem was likely to be found.

There are a number of things we will probably never know for certain about this transaction. The most important is what the president himself made of it. Most of his biographers have accepted the notion that his doctors never spoke frankly to him about his condition. That conclusion seems too simple to explain such a complicated character in such a complicated situation. We now know that Roosevelt knew more than he let on, thanks to the publication in 1995 of Daisy Suckley's long-hidden diary, four years after her death in her hundredth year, nearly a half century after his. The diary furnished evidence that he had more to go on than his growing weakness and sense of his own limitations, that he knew all he needed to know, which was more than he could acknowledge if he meant to follow his standard procedure and keep his options open as long as he possibly could.

His personal history points in the same direction. His own father had been stricken with a heart attack in 1890 at sixty-two, the age the son had just turned. Franklin then was eight; for the next ten years, he was a close witness of James Roosevelt's slow decline, of the measures this wealthy Hudson valley landowner and devoted family man took to eke out his life, which included plenty of rest, careful diet, and regular trips to European spas to bathe in warm mineral waters. Geoffrey Ward, the most sensitive and discerning student of Franklin Roosevelt's character, traces his "stoicism" to his sense that he could not upset his father in these, his own formative years in which—his mother's only child, her treasure—he was often kept apart from other children, not just at foreign spas, but at Hyde Park, where he was schooled by private tutors until he was fourteen.

Later, following his father's example, he was anything but indifferent to medical advice. For the better part of a decade in the 1920s, he devoted most of his energies to seeking to overcome and then work around his paralysis. In that time, he corresponded with leading polio specialists in a frustrating search for new and promising treatments and about his efforts to set up a center for other victims. This was at a Georgia hamlet called Bullochville, which was renamed Warm Springs with his enthusiastic support, in implicit tribute to the German spa Bad Nauheim, where James Roosevelt sought relief throughout the 1890s. Patience, his father had been advised, was a key to living with an ailing heart.

Patience became one of the distinctive traits of the son, who'd soon be telling the faithful Daisy about "queer" sensations in his chest. Displaying patience can also be a way of postponing, of buying time. Jonathan Daniels found his voluble chief "amazingly reticent." The playwright and presidential speechwriter Robert Sherwood captured the same quality in a memorable phrase. He wrote of Franklin Roosevelt's "heavily forested interior." In the first half of 1944, he was monitoring himself as well as the world.

CHAPTER I

Uncle Joe in Tehran

JOSEPH STALIN may have been the first person with whom Franklin Roosevelt openly discussed the likelihood that he might have to seek a fourth term. For ten days toward the end of 1943, first in Cairo, then Tehran, the president had deflected every entreaty from Winston Churchill for a private meeting in order to avoid giving any impression to the Russians that the Americans and the British were secretly cooking up negotiating tactics between themselves for the first three-power summit of the war. Once in Tehran, he seized every opportunity for private meetings with the Soviet dictator; in four days, they had three.

At the last of these, on December 1, 1943, Roosevelt said he needed to speak frankly about American politics. The coming year would be an election year, and if the war were still raging, he said, he might have to stand again, although that was not his wish. There were millions of voters of Polish background—six or seven million, he said—and if he ran, he would need their votes. There were also blocs of voters with roots in the three Baltic states, Latvia, Estonia, and Lithuania, which Moscow had absorbed into the Soviet Union. Their votes counted too. The United States would never go to war over the Baltics, the president said, and he personally understood the Soviet wish to shift the Polish border to the west for reasons of security. But until the election, then a little less than a year off, he could not, would not, enter into any negotiations on these matters.

Roosevelt was flying solo here. There were seventy persons in his delegation at Tehran, including six Filipino cooks and stewards normally assigned to the USS *Potomac,* the presidential yacht, and the new weekend retreat called Shangri-La (later, Camp David). But there wasn't a single official from the State Department in Washington and only one diplomat from the ranks of the foreign service. This was Charles Bohlen, known as Chip, a young Russia specialist who'd been summoned from the embassy in Moscow on short notice to serve as an interpreter for a president he'd never met. That president would not once turn to him for advice at the summit. The Allied foreign ministers had just gathered in Moscow, but Roosevelt's secretary of state, Cordell Hull, who was used, if not resigned, to being bypassed by his president, hadn't been invited to join him in Tehran. Vyacheslav Molotov, the Soviet foreign minister, was there. So was Anthony Eden, the British foreign secretary. This left Harry Hopkins, a social worker in his earliest days, then an administrator of key New Deal programs, as the top American fixer on the scene. When the foreign ministers gathered for lunch, it was Hopkins who sat in for the United States. Everyone understood that Hopkins—who habitually bypassed the State Department chain of command, just like his chief—wielded more power and influence than Hull. The president's right-hand man dismissed State Department specialists as "old maids" and "cookie-pushers" and "pansies," echoing the president's sentiments if not his language. But even Hopkins was not included in Roosevelt's private meetings with Stalin. What the president had to say had been brewing in his own mind since the early months of the war.

He'd long since signaled to Churchill that he saw the taming and courtship of Stalin as his personal project, a crucial step on the road to the international order that would have to be built on the ruins of war. It was a project he'd pursue all the way to Yalta, which was followed within two months by his death. In his mind's eye, Stalin was the key to victory and the postwar world. At times, it would seem, the dictator became something more than the president's project, an indispensable reason—in his own mind, the leading rationale—for his carrying on.

"I know that you will not mind my being brutally frank," he said in a handwritten letter to Churchill on March 18, 1942, "when I tell you that I think I can personally handle Stalin better than either your Foreign Office or my State Department. Stalin hates the guts of all your top people. He thinks he likes me better, and I hope he will continue to do so." Three weeks later, he was writing to Stalin to suggest a summertime meeting "near our common border off Alaska."

"The whole question of whether we win or lose the war depends on the Russians," he remarked to his Treasury secretary, Henry Morgenthau Jr., at about the same time. "If the Russians can hold out this summer and keep three and a half million Germans engaged in war, we can definitely win." The Russians held out, but Stalin stayed in the Kremlin. In December, the president pressed the dictator again, this time to join him and Churchill in a secret meeting "in some secure place in Africa that is convenient to the three of us."

To each appeal, the dictator replied tersely that he couldn't leave Moscow, given huge battles looming or under way. If satisfied with American arms deliveries and invasion plans, he expressed regrets; if impatient, he left them off. Roosevelt pressed on. By May 1943, he was again proposing Alaska "either on your side or my side of [the] Bering Straits." This time he sent Joseph E. Davies, a former ambassador to the Soviet Union, to hand deliver a letter to Stalin in the Kremlin. In it, the president raised and then ruled out Iceland as a possible rendezvous point, in part because that "would make it, quite frankly, difficult not to invite Prime Minister Churchill at the same time." Stretching the truth in a manner that can hardly be called uncharacteristic, he then wrote to Churchill denying he'd suggested a meeting that would exclude the prime minister. In June, he dispatched Averell Harriman, another of his special representatives operating outside State Department channels, to Churchill to win his approval of a Roosevelt-Stalin meeting that would do just that. Churchill had already met Stalin, Harriman pointed out, and the president should have the same opportunity to establish a personal relationship.

The prime minister wasn't persuaded. "A meeting between the heads of Soviet Russia and the United States at this juncture with the British Commonwealth and Empire excluded," he wrote to Roosevelt, would be a boon to Nazi propaganda and a "serious and vexatious" blow to Britain. In plain language, which the master stylist refrained from deploying on this occasion, it would signify the downgrading of Britain from the status of an equal partner in the alliance to a supporting role. (Roosevelt had learned the hard way that it was useless to talk to the prime minister about the end of empire, having once, in early 1942, raised the subject of India in a late-night conversation at the White House. Churchill threw a tantrum and threatened to resign if ever pressed to offer early self-determination to India as part of the war effort.) Such a slippage in Britain's imperial sway, Roosevelt clearly felt, would be not only inevitable but desirable in the postwar world he could sometimes glimpse in his mind's eye. Moreover, in his readiness to see Western colonialism rolled back, he imagined he was staking out potential common ground between himself and Stalin and thus the United States and Russia.

His fixation on Stalin from the early days, before American entry into the war—on what he personally might make of their relationship—reveals his remarkable self-confidence, crossing over now and then into realms of fantasy. It also shows his confounding, sometimes dazzling, ability to operate simultaneously on several planes as visionary, opportunist, and political schemer, as well as his readiness to test a hypothesis in politics like a scientist in a lab, or an entrepreneur with a risky business plan daring to make a deal. The hypothesis, as he put it to Hopkins in this instance, was that the dictator was "get-at-able," a potential partner in peace as well as war. His method of getting at Stalin would be to lure him into a pattern of cooperation by going to extreme lengths to prove the United States a dependable, compliant partner. "The big question which rightly dominated Roosevelt's mind," Anthony Eden wrote, describing a long evening's conversation with the president in March 1943, "was whether it was possible to work with Russia now and after the war." Even if the answer proved negative, Eden replied, "We should make the position no worse . . . by assuming that Stalin meant what he said." That, essentially, was Roosevelt's game plan.

Tehran would give him his first opportunity to see and be seen by Stalin, to discover whether a personal encounter with the dictator might yield results. His eagerness to talk about American politics and the votes of millions of Polish-Americans in his final private session with Stalin there has to be viewed in that context. On one level, Roosevelt the politician was going out on a limb to protect his domestic flanks, preserve his options. On another, the opportunist, by making a show of his own frankness, his willingness to trust, was inviting a modicum of candor, or at least flexibility, on Stalin's part, implicitly asking him to be helpful by appearing, at least, to recognize Polish aspirations. At the same time, he was withholding his formal agreement on the frontier question—finding a plausible excuse to continue stalling—knowing that Soviet forces would inevitably occupy Poland whatever he said, hoping that when that happened, he might retain some bargaining power. It had been his position for the better part of two years that territorial issues should not be settled in private by the big powers, that such negotiations should await the war's end. "Open covenants of peace, openly arrived at," had been the first of Woodrow Wilson's Fourteen Points. Wilson didn't live up to his own standard, though he tried. Roosevelt, more of a realist and more coldhearted in such matters, already knew, as he was signaling to Stalin, that he might have to bend his principles. For him, it was a question of how much, when, and what he could hope to extract in return.

In all these ways, the visionary was trying to circumvent the apparent contradictions in his rosy vision of postwar collaboration: Finessing and postponing the Polish question at a time when American forces had earned little more than a foothold on the European continent in the five months following the invasion of Sicily, he seemed to be calculating that this was no time to press territorial issues on the Russians, who had been waiting a year and a half for the invasion across the English Channel that would open the "second front." Roosevelt had first promised a landing in northwest Europe by the end of 1942 to draw away German reinforcements from the east; by the end of 1943, the promised invasion was still half a year away, at best. Until it happened, the imbalance between the Russian effort and sacrifices and those of its allies would remain huge. It was no time to expect a figure as hard-bitten as Joseph Stalin to embrace the high-sounding promises in the Atlantic Charter and the Declaration of the United Nations—documents that had set out noble goals like freedom, independence, and self-determination for the Allies without attempting to say how these would be secured.

Roosevelt himself had enumerated the Four Freedoms (of speech and religion, from fear and want) as an inspirational standard for the wartime alliance for which he'd found the name, United Nations; his hope was that it could evolve into a new world order. But he'd left the drafting of blueprints for an international organization to replace the discredited League of Nations to State Department study groups, which he then held at a distance. Determined to prove himself a realist, to avoid Wilson's self-defeating fidelity to paper accords, he focused on power, on how a hard-won peace could be maintained, by force when necessary.

So in his private musings, he dwelled more on what he called "the Four Policemen" than the Four Freedoms. These would be the United States, Britain, the Soviet Union, and China. Together they'd find a way to intervene swiftly if the peace were threatened; a threat, when they imagined it, that would most likely come from a revanchist Germany or Japan. (Neither Churchill nor Stalin saw the point of including an enfeebled, half-occupied, riven China, but, with some foresight as we can now appreciate, Roosevelt insisted. China would serve as a symbolic marker for the future; the world he imagined would not forever be dominated by whites.) The old league had proved toothless throughout the 1930s in the face of Japanese, German, and Italian aggression and flaunting of accords. In his view, before there could be agreement on a brand-new, more flexible international organization to supplant it, there needed to be agreement on how the policemen would swoop down to thwart aggression and secure the peace. It was the right question but begged the obvious next one: What would keep the powers from falling into conflict among themselves? The president's answer, no less dreamy in its way than Wilson's, seemed to amount to this: the trust he'd establish between himself and Stalin, in the context of the urgent problems a victorious but suffering and exhausted Soviet Union would be sure to face when the fighting stopped. In the midst of a hot war, he was dimly anticipating the future, trying to head off a cold war, a conflict no one had yet named and few had foreseen.

His policy making was so personal and intuitive, so seemingly off the cuff, that it's seldom reflected in documents. Its purest bureaucratic expression can be found in the files of the President's Soviet Protocol Committee, a wartime creation that Harry Hopkins, among all his other roles, chaired, which suggests that its guidelines came directly from the president. Roosevelt's alter ego had been living since 1940 in what was then called the Lincoln Study—later renamed, after redecorating, the Lincoln Bedroom—two doors down from the president's upstairs study. Most evenings found the two men together, talking politics and policies. When Hopkins married his third wife in 1942 in a White House ceremony, with Roosevelt as best man, the new Mrs. Hopkins, a former Paris editor of *Harper's Bazaar* named Louise Macy, simply moved in upstairs into a suite that had been created for the newlyweds on Roosevelt's orders.

The Soviet Protocol Committee, an offshoot of Lend-Lease, which Hopkins also oversaw, was administered by a major general, J. H. Burns. "Russia is so necessary to victory and peace," Burns wrote in a memo to Hopkins three months before the president left for Tehran, "that we must give her maximum assistance and make every effort to develop and maintain the most friendly relations with her." This was a "national policy" set by the president, he argued, yet a number of officials in regular contact with the Russians resisted it. They "do not trust Russia." (In a supplementary memo, written in longhand on the same day, Burns gave a detailed account of "vicious" infighting among Americans in Moscow. Accusations of homosexuality were being cast against the officer most in line with the supposed policy, Philip Faymonville, a brigadier general; it was assumed he was being blackmailed. The time had come, Burns advised, to "clean house of all who are not loyally carrying out the President's policies.")

"Policy making" is probably the wrong term for what Roosevelt was really about. "Policy improvisation" might be better; he was feeling his way, setting the stage. The drift of his maneuvers and hopes can be traced in an article in the magazine *The Saturday Evening Post* in April 1943, half a year before his journey to Tehran. The article, titled "Roosevelt's World Blueprint," offered an oracular, which is to say less than clear, vision based on a couple of exclusive conversations a staff writer named Forrest Davis had with a personage who could be identified as "the highest authority" but neither quoted nor named. The president, it was subsequently revealed, had read the article and approved it before publication. Its gist was that Roosevelt, "no Utopian," had the future of the world well in hand. "The President holds that a genuine association of interest on the part of the great powers must precede the transformation of the united nations military alliance into a political society of nations." Even then, such an organization would be "less ambitious and constraining" than the old league. His own approach, the oracle was apparently pleased to read, "follows more closely the path of his distant cousin, Theodore, than of Woodrow Wilson" (or, so the article also hinted, his guileless vice president, Henry Wallace, who'd recently been dreaming out loud about a global New Deal in the coming "Century of the Common Man").

Roosevelt's thinking, readers were told, was subject to change, according to circumstances. It was more opening gambit than blueprint, and it all would pivot on Moscow. "If Stalin elects to collaborate, the foundations of a post-war world can be laid with confidence," Davis wrote, with the highest authority's imprimatur. Otherwise, "the Western powers will no doubt be driven back on a balance of power system." In plain sight, it was a message to the Kremlin.

Joseph Stalin was hardly an unknown quantity in 1942 and 1943. He'd been consolidating power in the Kremlin for more than a decade. The kulaks of Ukraine had been starved and slaughtered in their millions in a forced seizure of food stocks designed to speed industrialization of the Russian heartland; much of the leadership of the Communist Party had been purged, cajoled into humiliating confessions of having conspired with the Nazis against Stalin; Trotsky, his greatest rival for power, had been driven into exile early on and assassinated in Mexico City with an ice pick; hundreds if not thousands of purged party officials, including generals and marshals of the Red Army, had been executed by the secret police in the basement of Moscow's Lubyanka prison; millions more of those classed as politically undependable had been sent to what came to be known as the Gulag to rot and die, including Poles by the tens of thousands who'd been seized during the first Soviet occupation of portions of their country in 1939 and 1940. These events had yet to be chronicled in detail by the likes of Aleksandr Solzhenitsyn or the scholar Robert Conquest (author of a searing 1968 study, *The Great Terror*). Arthur Koestler had yet to write *Darkness at Noon*, his clinical depiction of the inner workings of the terror, of the interrogations and show trials. But most of what these books describe had already happened. The broad outlines and many particulars of this dismal story were known to anyone who wanted to know them. In the United States, a panel headed by the philosopher John Dewey had dissected the testimony at the Moscow trials and concluded that they'd been stage-managed from start to finish. Of course, there'd always been those who didn't want to know. It had all been denied, wished away, or rationalized by prominent intellectuals of the Left in Europe and the United States.

After June 22, 1941, when Hitler's divisions rolled into the Soviet Union, the narrative of Stalinist repression instantly became inconvenient, out of date, not relevant to the struggle against Nazi tyranny. It was a story left on the shelf for what was called "the duration." Cultural relativism took root. If Stalin had been a tyrant, he now had to be seen as a peculiarly Russian type of tyrant, benign in his aims, though brutal in his methods; a latter-day Peter the Great, who'd ruled his vast, tumultuous domain the only way it could be ruled, with an iron hand. Stalin's ways might have been harsh, but he'd accomplished a great deal, and now, when his troops were doing most of the fighting and dying, he had to be recognized as the main bulwark standing in the way of fascism. So such thinking went. No matter that he had entered into a nonaggression pact and secret protocols with Hitler in August 1939. What choice had he, apologists reasoned, after the British and the French had bowed at Munich to Hitler's threats? A beleaguered Lenin had similarly struck a deal with imperial Germany in 1917. That Soviet troops, after the pact with Hitler, had entered Poland from the east while Germans invaded from the west was, by such reckonings, already ancient history in 1941, two years later. At the time of the pact, however, Roosevelt evidently read its meaning clearly and coolly. "The attack on Poland by Russia has depressed F.D.R., " Eleanor wrote to a friend, adding, "Stalin and Hitler are much alike, aren't they?"

When the führer had betrayed Stalin, our enemy's enemy became our friend. There appears to be no evidence in the State Department archives, the National Archive, or the Roosevelt papers at Hyde Park that the president ever sought, or was presented with, a summary of Stalin's record or an analysis of his personality. Characteristically, he gathered his impressions from people who'd had firsthand encounters with the Soviet premier. These included the fellow traveling journalist Anna Louise Strong, whom Eleanor brought to lunch to talk about the Moscow purge trials; Anthony Eden, the British foreign secretary; Roosevelt's own emissaries to Moscow in the 1930s, William C. Bullitt and Joe Davies; and, during the war, Hopkins and Harriman. Of these, it was Hopkins who knew the president best and gave him what he most wanted: a clear impression of what it would be like to deal directly with the dictator. This came in long, richly descriptive dispatches for the president's eyes only, following six hours of one-on-one talk at the Kremlin a little more than a month after the launch of Operation Barbarossa, as the German invasion was called. The United States wouldn't go to war for another four months.

For credentials, all Hopkins carried was a letter from the president asking his host to treat him "with the identical confidence you would feel if you were talking directly to me." This Stalin evidently did, judging from the impressions Hopkins relayed back to the White House:

> The questions he asked were clear, concise, direct. Tired as I was, I found myself replying as tersely. His answers were ready, unequivocal, spoken as if the man had them on the tip of his tongue for years . . . His hands are huge, as hard as his mind. His voice is harsh but ever under control. What he says is all the accent and inflection his words need . . . If he is always as I heard him, he never wastes a syllable . . . There is no small talk in him. His humor is keen, penetrating. He speaks no English but as he shot rapid Russian at me he ignored the interpreter, looking straight into my eyes as though I understood every word that he uttered.

Practically the first words out of the tyrant's mouth went to the heart of any doubts his visitor and the man to whom he reported might have had: "Mr. Stalin spoke of there being a minimum moral standard between all nations and without such a minimum moral standard nations could not co-exist." This was either a silky ruse or his way of saying that because Hitler had betrayed him, he'd now have to trust Roosevelt.

Two years later, with Roosevelt still waiting on Stalin's response to his invitation to a meeting, Harriman offered a more judgmental assessment, stiffened by a plutocrat's condescension. "We must always realize," he wrote to the president, "that Stalin's expressions are crude. I have heard him say things in a way which would be unforgivable among Anglo-Saxons." The railway heir and former investment banker went on, telling the president what he knew his chief wanted to hear:

> I am a confirmed optimist in our relations with Russia because of my conviction that Stalin wants, if obtainable, a firm understanding with you and America more than anything else—after the destruction of Hitler. He sees Russia's reconstruction and security more soundly

based on it than on any alternative. He is a man of simple purposes and, although he may use devious means in attempting to accomplish them, he does not deviate from his long-run objectives.

Refracted through his own imagination, such dispatches furnish the president with a portrait of the "get-at-able" Stalin he hoped to engage. He would not be the last president to pin his hopes on reaching a meeting of minds with an authoritarian ruler. Eisenhower would call on Franco, Nixon on Mao, Carter on the shah of Iran; more than a few lesser tyrants would be feted at the White House in the decades to come. Roosevelt, it might be argued, was setting a pattern, only he was doing so in the midst of a world war, calling on an indispensable ally, relying not on careful staff work of supposed specialists from various agencies but on his own intuitions and hopes.

The most trenchant and skeptical assessments of Stalin that reached him before Tehran had come from Bill Bullitt in three private letters, the longest of which, dated January 29, 1943, warned against "the fatal vice in foreign affairs—the vice of wishful thinking." The Soviet Union was a "totalitarian dictatorship" that ruthlessly crushed the Four Freedoms for which the Allies were supposed to stand. The notion that Stalin had been sincere in signing on to that program "implies a conversion as striking as the conversion of Saul on the road to Damascus." Yet American influence on Russia would never be greater than it was in the present, at the height of the war. So even this seasoned doubter urges the President to meet Stalin at the earliest possible date.

"No other American," Bullitt wrote, "could make the impression on him that needs to be made." And Roosevelt would have "a substantial carrot: war aid of all sorts . . . post-war aid for rebuilding." He could deliver "a greater stroke for liberty, democracy and peace," this practiced flatterer told him, "than any you have yet struck." All he had to do was to win pledges from Stalin to enter the war against Japan; forgo the annexation of European countries on which he now appeared to be bent; and dissolve the Comintern, the Moscow-based high command of Communist Parties everywhere. Whether he succeeded or failed—Bullitt plainly saw the odds stacked against success—"we should not," he wrote, "supinely accept as inevitable the irruption of the Red Army into Europe."

Roosevelt replied by saying he accepted Bullitt's "facts" and "logic" but still harbored a "hunch" that Stalin was not the cruel, expansionist despot the former ambassador had portrayed. "Harry says he's not," he wrote, referring to Hopkins, "and that he doesn't want anything but security for his country, and I think that if I give him everything I possibly can and ask nothing from him in return, *noblesse oblige,* he will not try to annex anything and will work with me for a world of democracy and peace."

Obviously, the warning against "the vice of wishful thinking" hadn't taken. Bullitt replied caustically. When it came to noblesse oblige, he wrote, Roosevelt needed to remember that he "was not dealing with the Duke of Norfolk but a Caucasian bandit, whose only thought when he got something for nothing was that the other fellow was an ass."

The president wasn't amused. "It's my responsibility, not yours," he huffed in response, "and I'm going to play my hunch." Yet he was sufficiently troubled by the Bullitt letter to mention it weeks later in his conversation with Anthony Eden. Did he think that Moscow was scheming to take over Europe? the foreign secretary was asked.

By the time the third Bullitt missive landed on his desk, in mid-August, he'd banished his most forthright adviser on Soviet affairs from his presence. This was for acts of lèse-majesté more serious than suggesting that the ruler might have allowed himself an asinine thought. The language of courtiers fits well here: Bullitt used up his White House welcome by playing an insidious role in the downfall at the State Department of Hull's deputy, Sumner Welles, to whom the president had been turning for years in preference to the aging, ailing secretary.

In 1905, at the age of twelve, Welles had been a page at the wedding of Franklin and Eleanor. He'd also gone to Roosevelt's schools, Groton and Harvard. Such social ties aside, the president thought highly of his judgment. In helping to destroy the career of Welles, the jealous Bullitt destroyed himself in the president's eyes. It was Bullitt who first brought him the story that Welles, a patrician type of impeccable manners, elegant dress, and formal bearing, had gone on a drunken binge on a Pullman train and offered sexual services along with cash to a black porter. The worldly Bullitt was no prude. He'd married the widow of the radical journalist John Reed, Louise Bryant, whose lovers had included Eugene O'Neill. With Sigmund Freud, he'd co-authored a psychological study of Woodrow Wilson, who'd sent him on his first mission to Moscow in 1919, only to spurn his report. He'd also written a slightly racy novel set in Philadelphia high society, from whence he'd come. Bullitt might have told himself—he certainly told the president—that in pursuing the Welles rumors, he was seeking only to protect the administration from scandal. What Welles had done could be construed as a criminal act; the number two man in the State Department could be blackmailed.

Roosevelt had the Federal Bureau of Investigation look into the Pullman story. J. Edgar Hoover not only confirmed it but found evidence of a second incident on a train. The president dealt with the problem by having a Secret Service guard assigned to the undersecretary to protect him from himself. He kept Welles on for two years, even as rumors reached Hull and various anti-Roosevelt senators and columnists. It was Bullitt he blamed for the leakage. When the former ambassador brought the matter up again at the end of July 1943, the president exploded in a rare burst of temper. Later, portraying himself as having played the part of Saint Peter at heaven's gate, he quoted himself as having thundered, or at least said, "Bill, you've tried to destroy a fellow human being." Daisy Suckley wrote in her diary, "The P. never wants to see Bullitt again."

George Kennan, who first served in Moscow in 1933, as an aide to Ambassador Bullitt, later rated the longest of his former chief's letters to Roosevelt as "unique" and "prophetic" in its insights into the likely tensions and shape of postwar Europe, going on to make the only slightly inflated claim that "it deserves a place among the major historical documents of the time." The president's responses earned Kennan's disdain for their flippancy. In the realm of foreign policy, the great expert on matters Soviet would later write, Roosevelt was "a very superficial man, ignorant, dilettantish, with a severely limited intellectual horizon." In Kennan's eyes also, the Welles affair was a matter of security. In Roosevelt's, it was a matter of loyalty, one that cost him two seriously flawed but seasoned advisers as he headed to the three-way summit. Before he got there, Welles had started writing columns for the *New York Herald Tribune,* and Bullitt had been trounced in a race for mayor of Philadelphia.

Loy Henderson, another alumnus of Bullitt's Moscow embassy,

read Roosevelt's attitude to Stalin differently. Tracing it back to the 1930s, he wrote that the president, "despite his distrust of Stalin and his associates, desired them to believe that he personally was friendly to them," friendlier than he expected other American officials such as Henderson himself to be. As Henderson saw it, it was a calculation that "at some time in the future the belief on their part that he was friendly to them might help him in persuading the leaders of the Soviet Union to follow courses of action beneficial to the United States."

Before Roosevelt ever set eyes on Stalin, the Soviet-American alliance was getting, with his blessing, a soft Hollywood treatment in a film from Warner Bros., a major studio. A happy ending was strongly implied. Both Roosevelt and Stalin, as portrayed by actors, were shown on-screen as natural allies, resolute and farsighted. The movie was *Mission to Moscow*, based on a book of the same title that threw together the impressions of Joe Davies, Bullitt's highly impressionable successor as ambassador to Moscow. Walter Huston, a star of that era, plays Davies, who vaingloriously insisted on playing himself in an introductory cameo. Like the best-selling book, which State Department skeptics renamed "Submission to Moscow," it was mainly notable as a whitewash of the Moscow trials and the Nazi-Soviet pact. Stalin and his colleagues come off as men of integrity and principle, even sensitivity, who have to survive in a harsh environment, challenged as they've been by Trotsky and Hitler. "There's been so much prejudice stirred up about the Soviet Union," the movie Roosevelt says in exaggerated imitation of the actual Roosevelt's cadences and pitch, "that the public haven't been given a chance to know the truth." The movie Roosevelt thus blesses the film's portrayal of the movie Stalin and the Soviet system, serving as a coming attraction for the overdue encounter of the two actual men.

A petition drawn up by the critic Dwight Macdonald debunked the film scornfully (and justly) as "the kind of propaganda movie hitherto confined to the totalitarian countries." The petition also condemned its "deification of the Leader," meaning Roosevelt. The Office of War Information meanwhile hailed it as "a magnificent contribution to the Government's motion picture program." Along with the president's letter Joe Davies had carried by hand, he'd brought the actual reels to the Kremlin for a private screening for Stalin, who, he said, then blessed the film for distribution across the country, wherever theaters still stood, all proof, in the words of the Office of War Information, that the alliance was "rooted in the mutual desire for peace of two great countries." There was nothing in it, Stalin and American wartime censors thus agreed, to offend the dictator.

The president's tacit approval of the film is a small cause for wonder. He would not have minded the deification, might even have been gratified by it. But what it presented as history, he knew, was a fairy tale. Still, in casting a warm glow on the alliance, it gave him room in which to maneuver, was useful mood music for the understandings he hoped to forge. At the war's turning point, its message was hardly unique. Winston Churchill, an ardent enemy of all things Bolshevik, had returned from his first trip to Moscow calling Stalin "a man of great sagacity." At Tehran, he'd dub the dictator "Stalin the Great." Wendell Willkie had bet on the dictator's good faith, vouched for his "hard, tenacious driving mind." He stood by his ghostwriter's conclusion in *One World:* that the Soviet Union had to be seen as "a dynamic country, a vital new society, a force that cannot be bypassed in any future world." Cordell Hull, returning from the Moscow conference in October 1943, became the first (and only) secretary of state ever invited to address a joint session of Congress, where he, a former Tennessee senator, still stood taller than any other member of the Roosevelt team. "I found in Marshal Stalin a remarkable personality, one of the great statesmen and leaders of this age," he declared from that rostrum in a carefully gauged encomium that diplomatically offered praise while avoiding any contamination, any hint of moral approval.

Ambivalence had to be repressed. In the midst of the war, Churchill, Willkie, and Hull could hardly have been expected to suggest that our most important ally might one day be portrayed as a psychopath and mass murderer. As a matter of both politics and reality, they had to acknowledge that the man they encountered in the Kremlin had moments of impressive lucidity. So like *Mission to Moscow,* they helped set the stage for the first encounter between the wartime president and the embattled, not infrequently dangerous Communist ruler.

Roosevelt was not above orchestrating optimistic expectations about the prospects for the relationship with Moscow but was guarded about what he himself had to say in public about Stalin. As his background briefing of the *Saturday Evening Post* writer showed, he wanted to be seen as keeping an open mind on how it would all turn out.

Shortly before leaving for Tehran, he received a letter from Walter Lippmann congratulating him on the positive outcome of the recently concluded foreign ministers' conference in Moscow. It was a "tremendous success," opined the columnist, who'd been looking for some sign that the president had the architecture of the coming peace on his agenda. "Moscow was a real success," Roosevelt wrote back, slightly dampening Lippmann's enthusiasm. "Sometimes, however, I feel that the world will be mighty lucky if it gets 50% of what it seeks out of the war as a permanent success. That might be a high average."

As was often the case with the many-sided Roosevelt, what he said in this note was perfectly framed for its recipient. He was assuring the columnist that he was tough-minded, realistic, not a slave of fluffy expectations. Still, as the time drew near for him to depart, he was filled with anticipation of the fateful meeting for which he had been waiting so long. "U.J. [Uncle Joe] is to meet him," Daisy wrote in her diary after receiving a confidential note from the man she called "the P," written just before his ship weighed anchor. Sensitive to his mood, as always, she wrote, "All is in the hands of God."

It almost didn't happen. For two weeks, Roosevelt and Stalin had fenced over the location of the meeting. On October 25, 1943, the president had passed the word that it would be "impossible" for him to go to Tehran because dicey communications into the Iranian capital could jeopardize his ability to fulfill his constitutional duty to act within ten days on legislation enacted by Congress. The real reason appeared to be objections from Admiral McIntire, who'd been informed that it would be necessary to fly at an altitude of sixteen thousand feet on the approach to the Iranian capital, too high in his opinion for the president's "bad heart" (as Hopkins had indiscreetly termed it in a private communication when a similar question was faced earlier in the year on his way to Casablanca). Commercial planes seldom flew over ten thousand feet in this era. McIntire ruled that an altitude of seventy-five hundred feet was tops for his patient, the first president to fly while in office. So Roosevelt recommended Basra, Iraq, to Stalin as a possible meeting place, failing that, Baghdad, Asmara, or Ankara. "I am not in any way considering the fact that from the United States territory I would have to travel six thousand miles and you would only have to travel six hundred miles from Russian territory," he wrote to Stalin, who hadn't ventured out of the Soviet Union in twenty-five years; who had since the German invasion apparently traveled out of Moscow only once, on a brief visit to the front; and who had, in fact, never flown.

The dictator, making a show of being less eager than the president, replied that the meeting could be put off to the spring and be held in Alaska, in effect saying that if it was to take place in the coming weeks as already planned, it would be Tehran or nowhere. Roosevelt didn't call his bluff. All but out the door of the White House, on his way to Cairo, where he was due to see Generalissimo Chiang Kai-shek and Churchill, he relented and sealed the deal on Stalin's terms. Without a waiver from his doctor, he'd now have to arrive in Tehran by train, an option that alarmed the Secret Service, which saw opportunities for ambushes or sabotage along the tracks. The air force pilot assigned to fly the final leg of the trip then took a trial run to Tehran and finally assured McIntire—and McIntire's patient—that he could bring the President in through mountain passes without going any higher than seven thousand feet.

En route, on November 14, his second day at sea aboard the recently launched USS *Iowa,* the second-largest battleship in the fleet, Franklin Roosevelt had a closer call than presidents are supposed to have. He was six hundred miles off the Virginia coast in the Atlantic by then, sitting on a sun-splashed deck in his wheelchair, absorbed in watching an anti-aircraft gunnery display, when an underwater explosion was detected nearby. "Torpedo on our starboard quarter! This is not a drill!" came a general announcement.

"Arthur! Arthur! Take me over to the starboard rail. I want to watch the torpedo!" an excited president called to his valet. With his ears stuffed with cotton against the rumbling of the artillery, he might have missed the warning that the torpedo, fired not by a German U-boat but, accidentally, by an accompanying U.S. destroyer, wasn't part of the drill. The great battleship, in length the equivalent of nearly three football fields end to end, swung around to present its narrowest pro-file and the missile passed at a distance of just over half a mile. Aboard were the chiefs of staff of the army, navy, and air force in addition to the president. "Had that torpedo hit the *Iowa* in the right spot," the official log noted, "it would have had an untold effect on the outcome of the war and the destiny of our country."

There remained one more scare to be surmounted before Roose-velt could finally be brought face-to-face with Stalin. The NKVD, the Soviet secret police, passed word to the Secret Service that Nazi agents, potential assassins, had parachuted into Tehran. The Soviet and British legations were next door to each other, separated by only a narrow lane that had been closed off with barbed wire and screens. The American embassy was about a mile away. The meeting was sup-posedly secret, but all Tehran knew something big was afoot. Motor-cades traveling back and forth through teeming streets would make conspicuous targets. Stalin invited Roosevelt to stay in the Soviet embassy in spacious rooms while he himself moved to smaller quar-ters in the compound. Roosevelt accepted, despite some skepticism among his advisers about the seriousness of the threat, despite also the likelihood that listening devices had been planted in the rooms so generously and eagerly being pressed on the Americans by their Rus-sian hosts. "Assume that *all* rooms and places of tete-a-tete are wired for recording," a circular from the colonel in charge of the White House Map Room had warned. "Talk in platitudes except in bi- or tripartite official conferences."

On the first morning, when the time came to make the move, a decoy motorcade departed the American embassy. The president, his spirits lifted by the intrigue and deception, followed through back-streets in an ordinary army staff car with Hopkins and his military chief of staff, Admiral Leahy. Roosevelt had given Secretary of War Stimson the impression that he was making the long journey, which Stimson called "hazardous," in order "to realize the psychological ben-efits that would come from such a meeting rather than the solution of any concrete special problems." Hull said the president thought he could talk Stalin "out of his shell." Half a century later, after the col-lapse of the Soviet Union, Sergo Beria, son of Stalin's chief hatchet man, would describe in a memoir his role in preparing daily summa-ries for the dictator from the listening devices planted in the president's chambers in Tehran. The younger Beria had Stalin wondering aloud over the apparent verbal indiscipline of Roosevelt and his aides. "Do they know that we are listening to them?" he asked.

Recalling across the decades, the Soviet eavesdropper wrote that everything the president had to say about Stalin was positive, revealing "great sympathy and respect." Not everyone in Roosevelt's entourage stayed, as we now say, on message. Crusty old admiral Leahy, whose role was to keep the president up to the minute on the war and attendant strategic issues, recorded his own first impression of the dictator in his diary: "Stalin is quick in repartee and sinister in appearance." Urged by the admiral to be tougher in one of their overheard conversations, Roosevelt was said by the young Beria to have snapped, "Do you think you can see further than I can? I am pursuing this policy because I think it is more advantageous." Was that remark, if accurately transcribed, intended for the admiral or the tape? In the case of a man at once insouciant and cunning, the answer could well have been both.

Joseph Stalin appeared in the president's quarters at the Soviet embassy shortly after three o'clock on November 28, 1943. As described by Bohlen, "It was a beautiful Iranian Sunday afternoon, gold and blue, mild and sunny." Stalin was buttoned up in a tan wool tunic with the red star of the Order of Lenin on his chest; his leather boots gleamed. He found Roosevelt waiting in his wheelchair. "I am very glad to see you," the president said. "I have tried for a long time to bring this about." It had taken nearly two years.

This initial tête-à-tête between the patrician and the commissar lasted just under an hour. A full conference session with Prime Minister Churchill and the three delegations followed, then a dinner at which the president suddenly "turned green," according to Bohlen, and collapsed with what was diagnosed as indigestion. By the next afternoon, he seemed fully restored. He thus missed a discussion between Churchill and Stalin on the location of Poland's borders.

In all, Roosevelt and Stalin would be thrown together for more than thirty hours in Tehran, giving them ample opportunity to take each other's measure. In their first encounter, Stalin let the president lead the conversation, which began with a reasonably full exchange on the military outlook as seen by each man, then detoured to a discussion of French collaboration with Germany in which the two leaders outdid each other in the severity of their judgments. Roosevelt said no Frenchman over forty should be allowed to hold office after the war. Stalin held forth on the rottenness of the French ruling classes, asserting that the Allies should do nothing to restore French colonial rule in Indochina. Roosevelt said he agreed "100%," according to Bohlen's notes. The people were worse off after a century of French rule; the territory should be placed under trusteeship for twenty or more years, leading to independence. Now it was Stalin's turn to agree "completely," according to the official summary.

It's one of history's small ironies that Roosevelt and Stalin quickly found conversational common ground in Southeast Asia, where, a generation later, the United States would sink into a bitter and hopeless struggle, carving deep political divisions at home, as it ground on twice as long as World War II. The subject never came up again between them in Tehran. (Fourteen months later, at Yalta, it would be touched on briefly, again without consequence.) The president's real purpose in this get-acquainted meeting was to test his theory that the dictator was "get-at-able."

Roosevelt craftily structured the opening discussion at the full conference in such a way as to give Stalin the decisive vote on the main issue to be resolved at Tehran—the question of how much priority to assign Overlord, the invasion across the English Channel designed to open the long-promised second front. Churchill and his commanders had consistently agreed—first at Casablanca, later at Quebec—that it would be launched in May 1944. Just as consistently, they lobbied for further operations in the Adriatic and the Aegean that would compete for supplies—in particular, landing craft—and cause Overlord to be delayed. The strictly military arguments of Sir Alan Brooke, the British chief of staff (later Viscount Alanbrooke), on the need to keep up pressure on the Germans in Italy before crossing the channel had considerable force. So did his bottomless contempt for the strategic capacity—in his view, incapacity—of most American commanders, in particular, Generals Marshall and Eisenhower. ("Stunted" and "hopeless" were among the milder epithets that leap off the pages of his diary when he's assessing their military abilities.) To the American high command, northwest Europe was the obvious place to strike if the aim was to get to the Rhineland soonest and end the war, with the lowest American casualties: the supply lines were shortest; the bulk of our forces, already massing and increasing daily in Britain, were closest; air superiority was becoming overwhelming. Further delay would be intolerable, especially to serve, as they suspected, a disguised British agenda of controlling the eastern Mediterranean for the sake of imperial suzerainty in the Middle East and India.

It had become the most abrasive issue in the Anglo-American alliance, for all the surface camaraderie, a source of deepening mistrust. A month before Tehran, Henry Stimson wrote in his diary that Churchill was determined "with all his lip service to stick a knife in the back of Overlord." Roosevelt "has been going very straight lately and has stood up to Churchill better than at any time heretofore," the secretary of war noted a week later, but with his "impulsive nature and a mind which revolts against the hard facts of logistics," it was difficult to be sure what he'd finally do. Writing to Hopkins a week before Roosevelt set out for Tehran, Stimson still sounded nervous, almost imploring. "The one prayer I make for the Commander-in-Chief is steadfastness," he said.

Addressing Stalin that first afternoon, Roosevelt evenhandedly summarized the options in the Mediterranean and the risks of a delay to Overlord, then said he and Churchill would be happy to know the marshal's views. For all his courtesy and the balance of his presentation, the next two days would show that he'd hit on a way to heighten the pressure on Churchill while simultaneously playing up to Stalin. Putting a finger lightly on the scale—and showing a hint of the steadfastness for which Stimson had prayed—the president said mildly that he himself was opposed to anything that might delay the invasion. Then he handed off to Stalin.

"This conference is over when it has only just begun," Sir Alan Brooke remarked. "Stalin has got the President in his pocket." He was right, at least, in recognizing early that his prime minister didn't. It was becoming apparent, to the dismay of the British, that Roosevelt had his own designs on Stalin.

The dictator's initial response carefully circled the central issue. He agreed with Roosevelt but didn't press his case. By the second afternoon, his tone had changed. He demanded to know who'd command Overlord. "If that is unknown, then Operation Overlord is just so much talk," he went on. Mediterranean operations would just be "diversions." The specific date of Overlord didn't matter so long as it was in May. Churchill continued to steer the conversation to the Balkans and the Aegean. In his mind, the island of Rhodes remained a tempting prize waiting to be seized. He said he couldn't commit to a date for a cross-channel invasion without further study.

Stalin pounced. "I should like to know," he said sharply, "whether the British believe in Operation Overlord or simply speak of it to reassure the Russians."

That evening, at a dinner hosted by the Russians, Stalin was relentless in teasing the prime minister, implying he harbored a secret affection for Germans. Bohlen expected his president to come to the defense of a staunch ally and friend. Instead, Roosevelt seemed to enjoy Churchill's discomfort. Finally, Churchill exploded, taking literally a remark of Stalin's that had been delivered, according to Bohlen, "in a quasi-jocular fashion, with a sardonic smile and a wave of the hand." At the war's end, the dictator said, it would be a good thing to shoot 50,000 or 100,000 Nazi officers. This left Churchill splendidly beside himself, anything but speechless.

Atrocities and war crimes should be punished, but, he fumed, the cold-blooded execution of simple soldiers who'd fought for their country would run counter to the values for which Britain was fighting. Roosevelt offered what he said was a compromise. It would be enough to shoot 49,000, he said. "There is no doubt that this was a joke, and a bad one," Bohlen later wrote. (Especially bad because both Roosevelt and Churchill were well aware of a top secret, hastily suppressed report by a British official, Sir Owen O'Malley, tending to confirm German charges that the Russians had executed thousands of Polish officers and buried them in mass graves in the Katyn Forest near Smolensk in early 1940. Churchill had passed the O'Malley report to Roosevelt at Hyde Park on August 13, 1943, with a covering note that said, "I should like to have it back when you are finished with it as we are not circulating it officially in any way." The alliance with the Soviet Union, so vital to victory in the war, could not reasonably be expected to bear the weight of such truth, if it was the truth; the fact that the Nazis were the accusers left room for doubt. Katyn might have been on Churchill's mind at that dinner in Tehran. It appears to have slipped Roosevelt's.)

After dinner, Harry Hopkins crossed the sealed-off lane to the British compound to advise Churchill privately that it was time for him to relent on Overlord. He came in the guise of a trusted friend but couldn't step out of the role that had basically defined him in the three years he'd known the prime minister, who early on had dubbed him "Lord Root of the Matter," in praise of the American's ability to get to the heart of things. Then and now, he was basically the president's messenger. On the conference's penultimate night, he performed that function again, probably without needing to say he was speaking for his chief. The United States and the Soviet Union were both insistent on May 1944 as the target date for the invasion. Stalin was promising a simultaneous offensive to keep Hitler from transferring divisions to the west. Britain, whose air force was already sending hundreds of bombers in nightly raids over Berlin, would be ill-advised to claim a veto.

When the military chiefs gathered the next morning, Brooke was ready to sign on for June 1 as the last possible date. "I thank the Lord that Stalin was there," Henry Stimson wrote in his diary after reading the Tehran minutes. "In my opinion, he saved the day."

If Roosevelt had lived to write a memoir, it's doubtful that Stalin (or, for that matter, Hopkins) would have been the hero. Most likely, he'd have felt justified in presenting himself as the director of this play, its presiding dramaturge. Stalin had been the lever he'd used to extract Britain's reluctant consent. Privately, he'd distanced himself from Churchill, but he'd avoided a painful—to his mind, unthinkable—open clash. Stalin was pleased by the outcome; so were Stimson and his military chiefs. Roosevelt had less to say in the subsequent formal sessions than the two other leaders, but on the Overlord question the commander in chief had proved "steadfast."

The president had a habit of embroidering and inflating his stories. The one he told Frances Perkins, his devoted but objective secretary of labor, on his return to Washington had him, rather than Stalin, tossing gibes at Churchill at Tehran, having first asked the prime minister not to be "sore at me for what I am going to do." In this telling, his banter and stage whispers caricaturing the cigar-chomping Churchill, how he personified John Bull, were finally rewarded with a smile and then a guffaw from the dictator. Their relations then became "personal," he boasted. "The ice was broken and we talked like men and brothers."

It's an account described only by Perkins, bearing scant resemblance to all the minutes and memoirs that came out of Tehran. Only Bohlen's depiction of Roosevelt taking too much pleasure in Stalin's baiting of his British friend comes close. Still, it's revealing of his deeper purpose. If he'd ever imagined he could make a brother of Joseph Stalin—and thereby redeem the dictator—he seemed here, in this moment of truly foolish braggadocio, to be claiming he'd succeeded. That's what he said; it's doubtful it's something he seriously believed.

Once the Overlord issue was settled, the mood of the conference eased, turning genial and optimistic. Roosevelt's second private session with Stalin had been taken up with his exposition of his still somewhat woolly thoughts about the new world organization that would be brought into being to keep the peace. Here again he portrayed the "Four Policemen" as the organization's strong arm, sitting on top of an executive committee and assembly—embryonic versions of what would become the Security Council and the General Assembly—neither of which, it seemed, would have a fixed headquarters nor any authority to get in the way of actions decided on by the Big Four. Stalin commented that the smaller nations might not embrace this arrangement. He thus "showed himself more prescient and possessed of a truer sense of values than the President," a nettled Churchill, who wasn't privy to the discussion at the time, would write in the fifth volume of his wartime memoir, showing for his part that he continued to chafe over his treatment at Roosevelt's hands in Tehran.

Roosevelt's vision of the postwar world didn't foresee one actual consequence of the war: the open-ended stationing of American forces in Europe over the ensuing seven decades (and still counting). The United States would contribute naval and air power to serious police actions but not ground troops. Congress wouldn't allow that, he told Stalin. "If the Japanese had not attacked the United States," Bohlen's minutes had him saying, "he doubted very much if it would have been possible to send any American forces to Europe." Stalin dwelled on the specter of yet another revival of German militarism.

At the last formal session, there was talk about how to dismember a vanquished Germany—Roosevelt suggesting it be divided into five pieces—but his ideas about a world organization were explored no further at Tehran. Too much war still lay ahead. Stalin reiterated what he'd already told Cordell Hull in Moscow a month earlier, that the Soviet Union would be prepared to declare war on Japan once Hitler had been crushed, but here, too, detailed discussion seemed premature. It was at his third and final private meeting with Stalin that Roosevelt used the coming American election as his excuse for opting out of the discussion on Poland's future. "This was hardly calculated to restrain the Russians," commented Anthony Eden, who didn't learn until after the conference had disbanded that the president had played the election card.

At the penultimate dinner, the leaders toasted one another, laying on thick praise that came across as heartfelt rather than contrived. Bruised though he'd been in the opening discussions on Overlord, Churchill grandly rose to the occasion, toasting Roosevelt for all he'd done to preserve "our democratic civilization" in the second of two effusive bouquets he delivered to his newly elusive ally. Then Stalin offered his handsome acknowledgment that the president's decision on Lend-Lease had made the difference between victory and defeat for his country. Roosevelt wound up the evening with a fond vision of a rainbow blending many colors "into one glorious whole. Thus," he said, "with our nations."

"We leave here friends in fact, in spirit, and in purpose," the final communiqué concluded heartily. Many would later say this marked the high tide of the alliance. Robert Sherwood went further, in his book on Harry Hopkins and his role at Roosevelt's right hand. "If there was any supreme peak in Roosevelt's career," the playwright wrote, "it might well be fixed at this moment, at the end of the Tehran conference."

The Roosevelt speechwriter Sam Rosenman chimed in: "He believed intensely that he had accomplished what he set out to do—to bring Russia into cooperation with the Western powers in a formidable organization for the maintenance of peace . . . He was indeed the 'champ' who had come back with the prize."

Roosevelt still had one major decision to make before heading home. He'd promised Stalin he'd name the Overlord commander within days after leaving Tehran. Everyone, including Churchill and Stalin, had been led to believe the huge responsibility and honor of the command on which so much would turn would be conferred on George Marshall, the army's chief of staff who'd first been brought to the president's attention by General John J. Pershing. Marshall had been the general's chief of staff during World War I, when "Black Jack" commanded the American Expeditionary Force. There was a kind of poetry in the idea that he might now fill the role of his mentor. In his diary, Stimson rated Marshall as "by far the biggest man I have met in Washington" (bigger, the war secretary clearly implied, than the president whom he expected to make the appointment). "He is selfless, tactful . . . yet capable of terrific force in carrying through a decision that he has fully made up his mind about. When he explodes he is terrific, but he very seldom explodes, and never does so in his own personal interest."

Marshall gave the president full respect as commander in chief and recognized the acuteness of Roosevelt's political instincts. ("He always had a wider point of view, of necessity, than I did," Marshall would tell his biographer.) But he kept a formal distance, avoiding jokes, small talk, and flattery, visiting the White House no more frequently than necessary, sometimes only once or twice a month, never going to Hyde Park (until the day the president was laid to rest there). Roosevelt began his notes to him, "Dear George." Marshall, who was not given to using first names, invariably signed his replies, "GMarshall." As few others dared do, he was capable of confronting his commander in chief when he disagreed with a decision. At the end of a meeting in 1940 where he'd not been given a chance to speak on an issue of military spending that seemed urgent to him, he seized the floor and deliberately stood over his president, looking down at him as he pressed his case. "A man has a great advantage, psychologically, when he stands looking down on a fellow . . . I took advantage, in a sense, of the President's condition," he'd acknowledge.

On another occasion, it was Roosevelt who took advantage of a facet of the general's condition, his innate starchiness. This was three months before Pearl Harbor when isolationist sentiment was still strong, so strong that a House vote on an extension of the draft could go either way. Marshall had sent him a ponderous memorandum, solemnly complaining that the civilian population was slow in recognizing the national emergency and "the necessity for a highly trained

Army." This was hardly news to Roosevelt. It was the biggest problem he faced. He replied by facetiously paraphrasing Marshall's note:

In effect you say:
The boys in camp are O.K.
The parental influence hurts the morale of many of them.
Please, Mr. President, do something about this weakness on the part of the civilian population.
Got any ideas?

With three sharp words, he made the point that presidents don't get to command civilian sentiment the way generals command troops.

Over time, each of these formidable figures educated the other. Roosevelt insisted on getting American troops into combat against the Germans before the end of 1942. He thought it essential for the country's morale; perhaps it would have a helpful side effect as well for the Democrats in the coming congressional elections. So overriding Marshall, he agreed with Churchill on an invasion of North Africa. Folding his hands as if in prayer, maybe partly in self-mocking jest, he then implored the general, "Please make it before Election Day." In the event, the invasion came several days too late for the Democrats. Roosevelt never uttered a word of reproach. Marshall thought that showed strength of character. Military men, he'd later reflect, weren't good at assessing political factors that "political leaders must keep in mind."

In their exchanges over the interplay between politics and global strategy, the president had taught the general something. "We fail to see," Marshall said in an interview with his biographer years later, "that the leader in a democracy has to keep the people entertained. That may be the wrong word but it conveys the thought. People demand action. We couldn't wait to be completely ready."

George Marshall had never had a field command in wartime and privately yearned to be the leading man in Overlord, but he couldn't bring himself to say so to Roosevelt or even Hopkins. He took the view that his personal wishes shouldn't count for anything; it had to be the president's decision. When rumors started to get around that he might be eased out as chief of staff, the eighty-three-year-old Pershing wrote to the president to object. "The best way I can express it," Roosevelt wrote back, "is to tell you I want George to be the Pershing of the second World War." He then thought of cabling Churchill, who'd already had to retract a promise of the command to Sir Alan Brooke, Marshall's opposite number, to suggest that Marshall be made supreme commander not only of Overlord but "of all our combined forces that are attacking the fortress of Germany." The president knew that Churchill would have a hard time swallowing that proposition. On second thought, he didn't send the message, already drafted by Hopkins.

The idea of a wider command for the American chief of staff was now in the air and Churchill got wind of it. He then swatted it down in a cable to the top British liaison officer in Washington, Field Marshal Sir John Dill. The appointment of an American supreme commander with authority over the British general staff and all British forces, the Prime Minister said, "will not occur while I hold my present office."

The two leaders thus managed an indirect exchange without giving offense on a sensitive issue. A careful word dropped in the right place would have been enough to clarify their differences.

Churchill's back-channel veto wasn't acknowledged by Roosevelt, who left the matter unresolved as he journeyed to Cairo and Tehran, where he said nothing further about his intentions. So the idea that the chief of staff would be moving out, whether to command Overlord or all Allied forces, continued to be treated as a fait almost accompli. The general and his wife quietly packed up the chief of staff's official residence at Fort Myer, Virginia, while the president pondered the question of whether his replacement as chief of staff would be temporary or permanent. Either way, Dwight Eisenhower was the name most often mentioned as a stand-in for Marshall, but Eisenhower, then commanding Allied forces in Italy, was still relatively unknown on Capitol Hill and not yet recognized as a heavyweight by the navy and air force chiefs who were privately resisting the idea that Marshall could be spared in Washington.

On the way to Tehran, Roosevelt had contrived to spend a relaxed day with Eisenhower inspecting battlefields of the North African campaign in Tunisia and musing about ancient Carthage. His real purpose, it later became clear, was to get to know and size up the general. "The President seemed in good health and was optimistic and confident," Eisenhower would later write.

Roosevelt touched only lightly on the decision about the command that was now before him. "You and I know the name of the Chief of

DECEMBER 8, 1943. With Ike in Sicily, after Tehran.

Staff in the Civil War but few Americans outside the professional services do," he remarked. He then said, "It is dangerous to monkey with a winning team." Eisenhower could have taken that as a hint, but, obviously, the president's mind wasn't yet made up. What might have settled matters was his reflection that Eisenhower hadn't been involved in the unfolding strategy for the war in the Pacific, where handling the brilliant, impossibly egotistic Douglas MacArthur was part of the chief of staff's brief. Eisenhower, Roosevelt knew, had once been MacArthur's deputy; if not disqualifying him for the chief's position, this could have been seen as a disadvantage. Or it might have been Marshall's advice that his position as chief would have to be filled on a permanent, not temporary, basis. That showed, Henry Stimson would write in his diary, Marshall's "matchless power of self-sacrifice." Roosevelt, being Roosevelt, could probably have cited half a dozen considerations and calculations. Here was an example of Eleanor's insight: "The President never thinks. He decides." After Tehran, in Cairo, he simply told George Marshall, "I didn't feel I could sleep at night if you were out of Washington."

When he chose Eisenhower as the supreme commander for the Normandy invasion, it wouldn't have occurred to him that he was elevating a man who'd one day occupy his office, becoming in less than a decade the first Republican president after the Roosevelt era, the first in twenty years.

Perhaps it's just coincidence, or a function of the calendar as 1943 turned into the election year 1944, but it's noticeable that the political tempo in and around the White House picked up in the two weeks following the president's return from his arduous five-week excursion to and from his encounter with Stalin. On the fourth day after his return, he found time to meet Robert Hannegan, who'd become commissioner of internal revenue with the strong backing of his fellow Missourian Senator Harry Truman. Hannegan was coming under consideration to be Democratic national chairman, a job on which, according to Truman's daughter, Margaret, the senator had initially been sounded out. Two days later, the president met Frank Walker, the postmaster general and incumbent chairman, who'd been eager to give up his party role. That same week, Harold Ickes, an omnivorous political gossip, mentioned in his diary that Truman would be a strong candidate for vice president (though perhaps not as strong, the diarist suggests, as Ickes himself). And Edwin Pauley, a California oilman and Democratic fund-raiser who had just seen the interior secretary, conspired with Hannegan about an important political role for Truman; what it was a subsequent note from Pauley to Hannegan doesn't say. Truman's name wouldn't be raised in press reports in connection with the coming national campaign for months. But Roosevelt's return in a positive mood had obviously inspired ferment.

The president's first remark in public about Tehran came at a press conference the day after his return. Asked to characterize Stalin, he didn't say he had become a friend, let alone a brother. "I would call him something like me—he is a realist," he said. He then waited a week, until Christmas Eve, before reporting in a fireside chat to the nation on the meetings at Tehran. The speech, which announced Eisenhower's appointment to head the invasion force, went through eight drafts before it was delivered. *Time* harshly judged it "perhaps the poorest of all the President's speeches in the past decade." It certainly wasn't packed with details of the debates at the summit. The leaders had discussed "international relationships from the point of view of big, broad objectives, rather than details," he said emptily. His account of Stalin was soothing rather than lavish. He said he "got along fine" with Marshal Stalin, a man of "relentless determination with a stalwart good humor" characteristic of his people. "I believe that we are going to get along very well with him and the Russian people—very well, indeed."

Without mentioning either Woodrow Wilson or the League of Nations by name, he spoke of the "ill-fated experiments of former years" and "tragic mistakes." He'd do all he humanly could to see they weren't repeated, he pledged. The "cheerful idiots" who'd believed Americans could avoid war by simply locking their front doors had been proved wrong. "We must be prepared to keep the peace by force," he said, making it plain in the next sentence he was speaking about Germany and Japan in the aftermath of the war. "The world is not going to let them break out again," he said.

He'd earned the right if anyone had, he thought, to speak for the world. Aiming high, he was struggling to apply the lessons of the past to a future neither he nor anyone else could clearly foresee. Inevitably, this would be the theme of his final months and days. It was also, he imagined, his job. And if he were to see it through, he'd have to be reelected.

Back in Washington on December 28, he fenced captiously with reporters over possible hidden meanings in an allegory he'd tossed out with studied casualness, in which a "Dr. New Deal" hands over his practice to a "Dr. Win-the-War." The Washington bureau chief of the *New York Herald Tribune* thought he heard a clarion call. The staunchly Republican paper, which had never supported Roosevelt, played his story on its front page under a headline that captured his conjecture: "Fourth-Term Drive Is Seen as Under Way."

"The President, now that he is back," Walter Lippmann wrote, "will find the country will respond to his leadership if he can find the energy to assert it." A week later, "Dr. Win-the-War" was down with the flu. As the election year began, Daisy wrote in her diary, the president was feeling "tired, as usual."

Also as usual, Franklin Roosevelt's innermost thoughts are hard to pin down. Perhaps with the written record we now have, we're in a slightly better position to hazard conjectures than his contemporaries. Here's one that the record doesn't contradict: The president and his advisers returned from Tehran riding a wave of optimism, as to both the final stage of the war and the chance for a stable peace, enough to renew his interest in the approaching campaign. Then, while he was bedridden for nine days, his zest for politics may have flickered. Still, in his own mind, he had a mission to complete, and part of that mission was to avoid Woodrow Wilson's fate.

If he had anything to say about it, he wouldn't be permanently side-lined, a president in name only. For four nights, when he was supposed to be recuperating in the White House, he stayed up with Sherwood and Rosenman "sitting around his bed" as they toiled together over a succession of drafts—eight of them, again—for a State of the Union address that one of his biographers would call "the most radical he ever uttered—and indeed more radical than any president before or after ever uttered." Looking beyond the war, he grandly sketched an "economic bill of rights" that would complete the architecture of a fully fledged welfare state, delivering to all citizens, "regardless of station or race or creed," a good education, a useful well-paying job, decent housing, and adequate medical care. That one address suggested that Dr. New Deal was still alive and kicking, might yet look forward to an encore. The months to come would show it was virtually his last bow.

CHAPTER 2

Wilson's Shadow

READING HISTORY BACKWARD, as we mostly do, we bring our knowledge of destinies and outcomes its actors could scarcely have imagined in the midst of all their striving. We thus open ourselves to the fallacy that they must have known or at least had some inkling of what we now think we know. Franklin Roosevelt kept his eye fixed on a far horizon, the world order that would need to be shaped at war's end. But he too was looking back. His attempt at inducting a Soviet despot into a peacetime security system had everything to do with his conviction that a stable world order would have to be based on an accommodation among major powers. That conviction in turn had everything to do with his reading of the failure of the League of Nations, the failure, from another angle, of Woodrow Wilson, a president he'd served for seven years, sometimes admiringly, sometimes impatiently, toward whom he still felt simultaneous twinges of reverence and ambivalence.

There's no documentary basis for declaring that Roosevelt had Wilson's venture to the Paris peace talks in January 1919 on his mind when he traveled to Tehran to meet Stalin twenty-four years later. There's just the striking fact that he'd been in Paris that month himself, long enough to regard himself as a witness to Wilson's attempt to make the peace conform to high-flown principles he'd unilaterally proclaimed. These threads of history are woven through Roosevelt's later ruminations and scheming about Stalin, his wishful thinking, and his fears. Roosevelt meant to succeed where Wilson had failed. Winning over Stalin now seemed to him an essential first step. This wasn't a final conclusion—Roosevelt's intuitive, pragmatic temperament didn't lend itself to final conclusions—but it was a point he'd reached on a line of thought, not without sharp turns and switchbacks, that can be traced back to 1919, when he'd yet to come of age politically.

It's a case of almost operatic foreshadowing, of leitmotifs and tragic endings. Franklin and Eleanor were on the same crossing when in February that year President Wilson sailed on the first of his two voyages home from Paris on a ship called the *George Washington,* bearing a draft of the league's covenant, portions of which Wilson had composed or edited himself. As assistant secretary of the navy—a post he'd coveted because it had once been held by his distant cousin Theodore—Roosevelt got to take his commander in chief on a formal tour of the ship. His job carried considerably more prestige than a position of the same title today; he was the immediate understudy to the secretary of the navy, a cabinet member then, head of a department that stood separate in that era from the War Department. But it was the strapping, young assistant secretary's surname, more than his title, that helped him stand out as "the Democratic Roosevelt," a potential governor or senator, or, in a few minds, including his own, something more.

Later on the *George Washington,* he was invited to the president's cabin to learn about the covenant, which had yet to be unveiled, and to lunch with Eleanor at the president's table, where Wilson, polishing a line he'd use again, said the United States had to join the league "or it would break the heart of the world for she is the only nation that all feel is disinterested and all trust." So Eleanor recorded his words.

The *George Washington* docked in Boston, where Wilson received a huge hero's welcome. Franklin and Eleanor were in the throng that turned out to hear one of only two speeches he'd make before returning to Paris ten days later for another four months of hard bargaining on the peace treaty. Governor Calvin Coolidge welcomed the president, all but promising his support for the league. However, once the draft had circulated—and the president was back on the high seas—opposition began to coalesce around the provisions promising a form of collective security. Nationalists feared that these would compromise American sovereignty, circumscribe Washington's freedom of action.

We tend to think of Woodrow Wilson and Franklin Roosevelt as existing in different eras, before and after the Great Depression, each with his own world war. But, though they were never close, their careers were intertwined from the moment the young state legislator from the Hudson valley rushed to Trenton in 1911 to throw in his lot with the reformist first-term governor of New Jersey, who seemed responsive to the presidential talk he was attracting. The distance in time between their two presidencies was the same as that between those of Jimmy Carter and Bill Clinton, or Ronald Reagan and George W. Bush, just twelve years. There were many holdovers, intellectual and personal. The Wilson connection in Roosevelt's life sheds light on his sense of his mission as a wartime president and peacemaker. Wilson for him was both a negative and a positive example, an occasional inspiration and a constant caution, less than a hero but always a touchstone. The contrasts he found in his predecessor's example become a key to Roosevelt's thinking. (Venturing into a dark parallel universe, one might recklessly add: what Lenin may have been for Stalin.)

It's easy to imagine that the Roosevelt who surprised his allies and advisers at Casablanca by unilaterally laying down "unconditional surrender" as an irreducible war aim might have harked back in his own mind to Wilson's call in 1917 for "peace without victory," a few months before the country finally went to war. He had been present in the chamber to hear that address to Congress. It hadn't gone down well with impatient interventionists like Eleanor's uncle Theodore or Henry Cabot Lodge, the Massachusetts Republican, with whom the young assistant secretary was in sometimes not-so-silent sympathy. Yet when interventionists were again beating at the White House doors in 1940 and 1941, he'd temporized the way Wilson had in 1915 and 1916 and had come to a renewed appreciation of his predecessor.

Initially, Wilson had asked Americans to be neutral in thought as well as action. Never neutral, Roosevelt felt almost from the start that the United States should go to war on Britain's side. The secretary of the navy, Josephus Daniels, later wrote that his subordinate "wished a leading role in directing it." In 1915, he sought a private meeting with Wilson to press for the creation of a war council. The president said he didn't want to "rattle the sword." The next year, with Wilson running for reelection on the slogan "He kept us out of war," the assistant secretary could hardly contain himself. "We've got to get into this war," he wrote to his chief, Daniels. Once war was declared, he begged to exchange his desk job for a commission in the navy. "Neither you nor I nor Franklin Roosevelt has the right to select the place for service," Wilson wrote to Daniels, quashing the request.

Years later—a few months before setting out for his encounter with Stalin in Tehran—Roosevelt talked about Wilson in a ruminative conversation with a remote family connection and frequent White House guest, Belle Willard Roosevelt, who was also an astute diarist. The president had plenty of time to spare for her; her troubled husband, Kermit, Theodore's second son, had only recently committed suicide at a military post in Alaska (too far from the fighting, he may have felt, for a scion of the original Rough Rider). The president said he'd been reading letters he wrote before the United States went to war in 1917 and was "horrified to find such bitter criticism and intolerance of Wilson in them."

"Because he was your chief at the time?" Belle asks.

"No, my lack of understanding . . . In view of my own experience I realize he could not have made the American people declare war then."

Wilson, he said, was a hundred years ahead of his time, a man of great vision, but he'd allowed the question of the league to become a political issue. In Roosevelt's mind, deft handling could have prevented that and saved the peace of the world. He'd imbibed a measure of Wilsonian idealism, but first and foremost he was a pragmatist. He'd have known how to slice and dice the "reservations" brought forward by opponents of the covenant, accepting enough of their language to win over the few votes needed for the treaty's approval in the Senate. What no one understood at the time, he told Belle, was that Wilson wasn't the man he'd been after that first trip to Paris, during which he'd suffered a small stroke, the precursor of larger ones to come later in the year that would sideline him and cloud his judgment over the last sixteen months of his presidency, months in which he'd remain in seclusion in the White House, giving no speeches and making few public appearances. Roosevelt implied he'd learned of the Paris stroke—which has been suspected but never confirmed—at the time from Wilson's physician, Cary Grayson, with whom he'd been friendly. "After Paris," Belle wrote, offering her synopsis of Roosevelt's monologue, Wilson "never had the same mental clarity—nor the ability of putting over his thoughts to the public."

It's a meditation stuffed with portents. But there's no hint in what Belle Roosevelt wrote that the president found any lessons for himself beyond the obvious political one, no expression of concern on his part, or hers, for his clarity, his force. He expected to succeed where Wilson failed by means of his own more sensitive political intuitions, his celebrated cunning. But his highly personalized style of policy making is recognizably Wilson's, and he depended on a support team that included many people he first encountered back in the Wilson years. Wilson took his secretary of state, Robert Lansing, to Paris but never consulted him on any significant matter, hardly spoke to him; in fact, he left Paris without showing him the draft covenant. So it was with Roosevelt and Secretary of State Hull, a devoted Wilsonian he'd first met in 1912 at the Baltimore convention that nominated Wilson. Not only was Hull not included in the delegation Roosevelt took to Tehran; he'd later complain that no one bothered to show him the Tehran minutes.

Wilson was his own secretary of state as Roosevelt would later be. He depended on a key aide and confidant who operated outside normal bureaucratic channels. This gray eminence, Colonel Edward House, regularly overnighted at the White House; only House, like Harry Hopkins after him, could pretend to have an overview of the president's policies and aims (until he fell from grace for using too confidently the broad powers Wilson lent him).

Roosevelt could hardly go through a day in the White House without encountering fellow alumni of the Wilson years. Daily battle and casualty bulletins were brought to him by his military chief of staff, Admiral Leahy, who'd been assigned to the Navy Department as a personnel officer when Roosevelt arrived there in 1913; the Roosevelts and the Leahys lived three blocks apart in Washington. By 1916, Leahy was commanding a small ship called the *Dolphin* that carried the assistant secretary and his family to and from his summer residence on the Canadian island of Campobello, across from Maine's easternmost point. When the president visited the Map Room he was usually escorted by his naval attaché, Admiral Wilson Brown, who, also in 1913, guided him on his first official visit to a naval installation, the navy yard in Brooklyn. General Edwin Watson, known as Pa, a military attaché doing double duty in 1944 as Roosevelt's appointments secretary, largely controlling access to the president, had previously been an attaché assigned to Wilson both in Paris and at the White House. Marvin McIntyre, assigned by Roosevelt to oversee sensitive relations with Congress, had handled the press for Josephus Daniels at the Navy Department. Roosevelt's White House press secretary, Steve Early, covered the Navy Department for the Associated Press in that era. Early's successor, Jonathan Daniels, was Josephus's son. Joe Davies and the financier Bernard Baruch were in and out of the White House in both the Wilson and the Roosevelt years.

Eerily, another naval officer who traveled everywhere with the president, including Tehran and Yalta as well as Hyde Park—giving him massages almost daily, checking his blood pressure, looking after his medications—had been Wilson's night nurse following his incapacitating stroke in 1919. This was Lieutenant Commander George Fox, who reported to Roosevelt's physician, Admiral Ross McIntire. The ear, nose, and throat man had been recommended for his White House post in 1933 by Wilson's physician and long-standing Roosevelt friend, Admiral Cary Grayson. The physician, assisting the second Mrs. Wilson, whom some saw as a regent, became an intermediary between the ailing president and the wider world. Grayson was named honorary chairman of Roosevelt's first two inaugurals. And then, of course, there was the singular, intrigue-filled case of Bill Bullitt, who as a young diplomat had been dispatched by Wilson in 1919 to Moscow to meet Lenin. Bullitt brought back a glowing account of the Soviet regime and a recommendation that it be recognized by the United States, which Wilson rejected. Later, he testified to the Senate Foreign Relations Committee against the Versailles Treaty, only to be resurrected in 1933 by Roosevelt and sent back to Moscow as the first American ambassador to the Soviet Union. Eventually, Roosevelt consigned Bullitt to political oblivion all over again.

Aside from Bullitt, they were a network, these old Wilsonians; they'd been playing cards and going to the races together for a generation. When Roosevelt's stream of consciousness carried him back to the example of his predecessor, he had his own trove of memories and experiences on which to draw. That example—the very idea of an American president bestriding the international scene as a peacemaker—wasn't altogether original with Wilson. Theodore Roosevelt, Wilson's rival and most persistent critic, had won a Nobel Peace Prize for negotiating an end to the Russo-Japanese War. But for a brief season in 1919, it was Wilson who embodied the role of world peacemaker as no one else, before or after. In the words of his staunch admirer Herbert Hoover, "Woodrow Wilson had reached the zenith of intellectual and spiritual leadership of the whole world, never hitherto known in history." Roosevelt, who derived his views about self-determination and colonialism from Wilson, easily slipped into the role.

His commitment to Wilson's brand of internationalism proved to be anything but consistent. He'd also wavered in Wilson's life-time in his commitment to the man. Back in February 1920—four months after Wilson's debilitating stroke, a month before the Sen-ate's burial of the Treaty of Versailles and, with it, the apparent last chance of American membership in the league—the president lost all patience with the Democratic Roosevelt. "FDR persona non grata with W," Josephus Daniels noted in his diary. After seven years as a member of the administration, the discipline and loyalty of the second-in-command at the Navy Department were once again in question. In a speech at the Brooklyn Academy of Music that month, Roosevelt had succumbed to his tendency to tell quixotic tall tales at the expense of others—in this case, the president and his immediate superior, Secretary Daniels. "I committed enough illegal acts to put me in jail for 999 years," he boasted, citing steps he'd taken against their wishes to bolster the navy's preparedness when the country was formally neutral. Word had also filtered back to the White House that he'd given a dinner for a former British foreign minister, Lord Grey, whom the secluded, embittered president was refusing to see. (One of the spurned envoy's aides was said to have joked that the second Mrs. Wilson, a widow named Edith Bolling Galt, "fell out of bed" when the president made his proposal of marriage.)

That chill was still in the air five months later on a steamy July Sunday when Roosevelt called at the White House in the company of Governor James Cox of Ohio, who'd emerged after forty-four ballots from the Democratic convention in San Francisco as the presidential nominee. Until the deciding ballot, President Wilson had entertained the fantasy that the party might nominate him for a third term despite his frailty and his evident inability to campaign or govern in any nor-mal sense. Its surprise choice for vice president now stood before him in a dark jacket over white trousers—the brash, unruly assistant secretary who, it was hoped, would add a dash of youth and verve, as well as a famous name, to the ticket. Wilson sat immobilized on the South Portico of the White House, his left side paralyzed, his eyes cast down, the Washington Monument off in the distance. At the sight of this seemingly broken man, Cox's eyes filled with tears; his running mate, who hadn't been admitted to the president's presence in the ten months since the stroke, couldn't feign his usual ebullience. Despite the heat, Wilson's left arm was covered by a shawl; it seemed incapable of moving. He never stood. Roosevelt would never again see him in the White House.

Cox said he'd admired Wilson's fight for the league. "Mr. Cox, that fight can still be won," said the president, showing just how out of touch he was. Though his voice was weak, the urgency of his conviction had not been impaired.

"Mr. President," the shaken Ohioan pledged, "we are going to be a million percent with you and your administration, and that means the League of Nations."

And they were, although Roosevelt in his campaign speeches across the country seldom mentioned Wilson, then at the nadir of his popularity. As a candidate, Roosevelt's advocacy of the league was full-throated, sometimes florid, but not dogmatic. The compromises Wilson had ruled out were by his reckoning minor adjustments of no great importance. No doubt the covenant had its imperfections, Roosevelt would say, but so did the Constitution, which had required nineteen amendments to date. He himself would be in favor of a reservation to the Versailles Treaty specifying that nothing in it could be "in any way superior to our Constitution or in any way interfere with the rights of Congress to declare war or send our troops overseas." But the covenant embodied in the treaty had been conceived with an "honest purpose" as a "practical solution of a practical problem" and the United States should still join the thirty-seven nations that had accepted it rather than stand apart with Russia's Bolsheviks. So, as he toured New England, his riff ran in speeches in Springfield, Worcester, and on the Boston Common.

The country wasn't buying; the issue had been decided in Congress, and voters had moved on. The Cox-Roosevelt ticket was crushed by Harding-Coolidge in a landslide. Roosevelt, still only thirty-eight, became a private citizen. He spoke briefly with Wilson once more the following June at a Washington funeral, updating him on one of Roosevelt's new causes. This was a campaign to endow an award named after the former president as a way of seeding his ideals. The endowment, which eventually gave rise to the Woodrow Wilson Foundation, wasn't enough to melt Wilson's coolness to his would-be but undependable disciple. A few months later, however, learning that Roosevelt had been paralyzed even more severely by polio than he'd been by his stroke, Wilson was moved to send a note of sympathy. The afflicted younger man could now, finally, be familiarly addressed as "My Dear Roosevelt" rather than with a businesslike "Dear Mr. Roosevelt." Still warmer notes followed, thanking Roosevelt for his friendship and devotion to the foundation, his "generous labors."

Though Roosevelt would continue to honor Wilson as an idealist, he started backing off his own early advocacy of the League of Nations itself. Months before Wilson's death in 1924, Roosevelt drafted a detailed "Plan to Preserve World Peace" that proposed a renaming and reconfiguration of the league, with the aim of establishing an international peacekeeping organization acceptable to the U.S. Senate. Eleanor Roosevelt saw it as a demonstration as well that he'd not allow himself to become a "self-centered invalid," sidelined by polio. Roosevelt's new Society of Nations would be initiated by the United States. "No plan to preserve world peace," he wrote, "can be successful without the participation of the United States." By 1928, writing in the journal *Foreign Affairs,* he was calling merely for "cooperation" with the league. It wasn't a time "to agitate the question" of membership, the article said. What made the question untimely was Roosevelt's own return to active politics following his seven-year effort to overcome or at least minimize the crippling effects of his disease.

Four years later, when he was launching his own campaign for president, Roosevelt slammed the door on U.S. membership in what was seen by ardent internationalists as a cynical and opportunistic response to a series of articles in isolationist newspapers, in particular those controlled by William Randolph Hearst, a potential supporter and future nemesis. Hearst papers had been ridiculing the newly fledged candidate as a starry-eyed Wilsonian.

"The League of Nations today is not the League conceived by Woodrow Wilson," he said, all but invoking the late president's blessing on the apostasy he was about to commit. Sounding more like

Warren Harding than the Franklin Roosevelt of 1920, he argued that U.S. membership "would not serve the highest purpose of the prevention of war . . . therefore, I do not favor American participation." At the height of the Great Depression, the question of membership in the league wasn't a live issue likely to sway many votes. But it was a question that could divide Democrats in the battle for the nomination. Hearst was using it to promote the candidacy of John Nance Garner of Texas, later Roosevelt's vice president.

Wilson's Colonel House, attempting a modest comeback as a Roosevelt adviser, noted the consternation among adherents to his former liege. The speech, he wrote to Jim Farley, a Roosevelt operative, had "created something akin to panic among devoted Wilson followers." Among those who were upset was Cordell Hull, the Tennessee senator and future secretary of state who'd been drawn to Roosevelt by his supposed internationalism; another was his own wife. "She hasn't spoken to me for three days," Roosevelt wrote to a friend.

The New York governor was obviously moved more by his own political self-interest than any reading of international trends. Adolf Hitler was still a year away from power. With that speech, Roosevelt hadn't really changed anything. As a new president confronted by the worst economic crisis in the nation's history, he wouldn't have had the leverage to reopen the question of membership in the league. What's striking is that eight years later—after Munich and the fall of France, after Hitler's invasion of Poland, and in the midst of the nightly air war over Britain—he was still allergic to any commitment to American participation in an international organization.

When he met Churchill on a battleship off Newfoundland in August 1941, he refused to go anywhere near it. The British had prepared a draft of the document that became the Atlantic Charter, the first broad attempt at defining Allied war aims. The draft's final provision called for an "effective international organization." When it was shown to the president, he struck out those words. American warships were patrolling the North Atlantic, but the United States still wasn't formally at war. He wasn't going to provoke isolationists into more furious resistance to the commitments he'd already made. The furthest he'd go, after debates with Churchill and his own advisers, was to endorse the eventual "establishment of a wider and permanent system of general security."

Even after the declarations of war following Pearl Harbor, Roosevelt remained leery of even the vaguest calls for a new international organization. When a prominent internationalist approached the White House seeking support for a campaign to promote the idea that this should be a key war aim, he instructed an aide, "For heaven's sake, [tell him] not to do anything at this time—as things are changing every day." When Sumner Welles, whose feeling for Wilson bordered on the religious,* proposed to the president in 1942 that other nations be drawn into a planning group "to study the future structure of the world," the idea was "summarily turned down."

The serious students Townsend Hoopes and Douglas Brinkley have interpreted Roosevelt's determined reticence, his refusal to proselytize on behalf of a faith he once preached, as "a categorical repudiation of Wilsonian idealism" by "a thoroughly disenchanted Wilsonian." Writing after the war, Sumner Welles himself took a more lenient view: "Winning the war was and had to remain the foremost objective. No step in the political realm, however beneficial it might promise to be later on, could properly be taken if it threatened to jeopardize or postpone the victory." These were, he said, "considerations by which a Commander-in-Chief must necessarily be guided."

As he pondered the choices before him, Roosevelt pondered the example of Wilson. He had long done so. In 1933, when Welles handed him a memo on Latin American policy, the new president's first question was, "How does this fit with Wilson's Mobile speech?" (It was safe for him to assume that his aide would parse the reference to a speech in Mobile, Alabama, in 1913 in which President Wilson pledged that the United States would "never again acquire a foot of territory by conquest.") Ten years later, after the Democrats had very nearly lost control of Congress, he naturally thought back to Wilson's reaction to the 1918 congressional elections in which Republicans had won both houses. "The P. ," Daisy Suckley writes in her diary on the eve of his departure for Tehran, "remembers Woodrow Wilson telling him that the public is willing to be 'liberal' about a third of the time, gets tired of new things and reverts to conservatism the other two

---

* Speaking at Wilson's tomb in the National Cathedral a month before Pearl Harbor, Welles predicted that the American people "will turn again for light and for inspiration to the ideals of that great seer, statesman, patriot and lover of his fellow men—Woodrow Wilson—whose memory we here today revere."

thirds of the time. The P. said that *if* the war is over next year, it will be impossible to elect a liberal president. He wants to get out of domestic problems & help to carry on international ones." It's a cautionary tale. Roosevelt cites Wilson for his wisdom when it comes to reading the cycles of political sentiment but blames him for failing to adjust to the new political reality sufficiently to steer the Versailles Treaty and the League of Nations Covenant through a Republican Senate.

On one level, he canonizes Wilson as a political saint. "Woodrow Wilson's whole career was a triumph of the spiritual over the sordid forces of brute strength," he said in a homily at Wilson's birthplace in Staunton, Virginia, in 1941. "At a time when world councils were dominated by material considerations of greed and of gain and of revenge he beheld the vision splendid." That doesn't sound like a "thoroughly disenchanted Wilsonian." On another level, Saint Woodrow, as interpreted by Roosevelt, was so blinded by his "vision splendid" that he bequeathed only ideals. Practical plans and workable mechanisms for the maintenance of peace formed no part of his legacy. He'd said he wanted a League of Nations that would be "virile, a reality, not a paper League," one that could, when necessary, assemble armed forces from its members to repel aggression. But that never happened.

Aiming to succeed where Wilson failed, Roosevelt focused on such issues of power, on his Four Policemen, in particular Stalin. "I am not a Wilsonian idealist," the man himself once said, in what was probably his most apt self-characterization on this point. "I have problems to solve." If he and Stalin could achieve an understanding on the proper use of force in the maintenance of order, he seemed to think, the rest of the world would fall in line, would have no choice but to allow the four powers to impose a regime of strict disarmament on all smaller states. The actual structure and charter of a new international organization were details he was ready to farm out to the State Department, which had cloaked in obscurity a committee designed to deal with just such issues. Formed before the United States had declared itself at war, it was called the Advisory Committee on Problems of Foreign Relations. Soon the committee was broken up into subcommittees, one dominated by Welles, the others answerable to Hull. This suited Roosevelt, who had "a habit," as Sam Rosenman later wrote, "of asking two different people to do the same thing at the same time . . . to have one check on the other—without either knowing it."

In this case, Roosevelt dealt more with Welles than with Hull, who tended to sulk, only occasionally pulling rank. Both the secretary and his deputy were ardent Wilsonians, each eager in his own way to renew the president's wilted commitment to the ideal of an international peacekeeping organ, so long as the other didn't get the credit. Personal enmity—exacerbated by Welles's privileged pipeline to the White House—had more to do with the tension between the secretary and his deputy than the relatively marginal issues of organizational structure over which they now and then clashed. Even after Hull brought Welles down in August 1943, thanks to Bill Bullitt's scandalmongering, Roosevelt called his favorite diplomat back to the White House for a lengthy session on the draft charter. He was leaving for Tehran the next day. Both Hull and Welles would later claim credit for the outline the president carried to his encounter with Stalin. In the recollection of the ousted deputy, recorded after the president's death, the Franklin Roosevelt of 1943 is imbued with some of the spirit of the ardent campaigner of 1920:

> The President was unusually serious. He felt deeply the import of the conferences ahead and spoke, far more than was customary, of the future after the war. At times, his face had that luminous aspect and his eyes that remote look, which struck so deeply into the hearts of those who loved him, as his life drew to a close.
>
> During the two hours I was with him, the greatest part of the conversation was devoted to international organization; how to achieve agreement with Stalin on its nature and how to establish it . . . "We won't get any strong international organization unless the Soviet Union and the U.S. work together to build it up as the years go by," he said. That to him was the key.

With Welles banished from the State Department, Secretary Hull was finally able to impose his authority on the various workshops in the department attempting to draw the blueprint of a new international organization. In practice, the Tennessean's authority was exercised by his chief aide, a native of Russia and graduate of night school in New York named Leo Pasvolsky, who'd been tactful and skillful enough to maintain Hull's confidence while working closely with Welles. No one in the department had a more complete or detailed knowledge of the League of Nations, its creation and failure, or the various ideas floating around for its replacement. Cordell Hull would eventually win the Nobel Peace Prize for the faith he lodged in Pasvolsky. President Roosevelt, still focused on a peacekeeping apparatus to be dominated by his Four Policemen, wouldn't sign off on the new blueprint, drawn up principally by Hull's aide, for half a year after his return from Tehran.

Months pass before the name Woodrow Wilson surfaces again in Daisy Suckley's diary. This time, it is in an altogether different context, having taken on a new significance. The devoted spinster, to resort to a term still in use in this era, was a literate, intelligent woman. But Franklin Roosevelt was virtually her only source of political intelligence; when it came to politics, he was her only interest as well. It's no great leap to imagine that what she wrote reflects the drift of his conversation, his concern. "I pray that the P. does not have to go through a period of disappointment and illness like Mr. Wilson," she wrote.

Was he, at this point—two weeks after D-Day, three weeks before he finally announced his availability for a fourth term—already contemplating a comparison between himself and the defeated, depleted Wilson he and Governor Cox had encountered on the South Portico of the White House in the summer of 1920, the semi-paralyzed recluse under the shawl? By this time, in June 1944, others hadn't yet started to do so. The *Daily News,* New York's anti-Roosevelt tabloid, which kept a sharp watch on the president's physical appearance, on the lookout for any sign of decline, was still principally worried on its editorial page that Roosevelt would inevitably seek a fifth term in 1948 if he managed to snatch a fourth in 1944. "It all adds up to one word: Emperor," the paper said, hammering a consistent theme.

"The same Mr. Roosevelt who fought so fiercely in 1920 is president today," the *Daily News* observed. "That he is still following in Woodrow Wilson's footsteps is evident from every action on the international front that the American people get wind of." His aim is "to trick the American people into some kind of League of Nations before they know it, then wake them up and tell them they are there, there to stay. Given a fourth term, this Administration may be able to do just that, and thereby doublecross American democracy."

Fast-forward once more, to his last bilateral conference with Churchill, Eden, and the British military chiefs the following September in Quebec. On the meeting's sixth and final night, there's a screening in the eighteenth-century French fortress overlooking the

Plains of Abraham and the St. Lawrence River of a new Hollywood biopic, which Darryl Zanuck of 20th Century Fox is lavishly promoting as "The Most Important Event in 50 Years of Motion Picture Entertainment." The movie is called *Wilson;* it might just as well have been called *The Prophet*, for it ends with the departing president, his term now concluded, leaving the Capitol in slow, painful steps on his wife's arm, straight backed and unbowed in the portrayal of an actor named Alexander Knox. "The dream of a world united against the awful wastes of war is too deeply embedded in the hearts of men everywhere," he tells his supporters. It won't die. "It may come about in a better way than we proposed." A full orchestra and chorus swell in the background with a patriotic hymn. The chorus is singing "Long may our land be bright with freedom's holy light."

"By God, that's not going to happen to me," the president was heard to grumble when the lights were switched on at the Citadel in Quebec. He'd evidently not been moved by the effort of the film-makers to portray Wilson as a prophet in his own country. Zanuck intended the film as an election year parable, but its intended beneficiary wasn't grateful. *Wilson*, as he experienced it, is the story of an enfeebled politician who went down to defeat. He doesn't appear to be thinking of Wilson's stroke. He was thinking of the beating Wilson took in the Senate, where the treaty he brought home in 1919 fell short of the necessary two-thirds vote.

Yet before Roosevelt retired that night, his worrisome blood pressure, now being taken at least once, sometimes twice daily, had shot up by about fifty points to a life-threatening 240/130.

CHAPTER 3

His "Enormous" Heart

On February 12, 1944, Franklin Roosevelt marked the birthday of his greatest predecessor by laying a wreath at the Lincoln Memorial. That afternoon, he went to the Washington Navy Yard for the ceremonial handing over of a new destroyer escort to the nascent navy of the Free French, delivering there a short speech from the backseat of his car, promising "ultimate victory." Three weeks after that, he attended the White House Correspondents' Dinner, where he heard Bob Hope crack a joke about the open-ended nature of his lease on the White House, his seeming permanence. The comedian said his father had encouraged him to dream large dreams when he was a boy. Why, his old man had said, he might even grow up to be vice president. No doubt Roosevelt threw his head back and exhibited his hearty laugh. But in the first five months of 1944, the five-minute wreath laying, the short speech at the navy yard, and the correspondents' dinner were his only public appearances outside the White House. Five months would also pass without a fireside chat, following the one at the start of the year delivered in lieu of an appearance before Congress for the State of the Union address.

Presidents don't get to recede to this degree in our own era of gaping, insatiable media maws. They have to pop up several times a week, at the least, even if it's only walking to a helicopter or stepping into the Rose Garden, to slake the thirst of cable TV and the Internet. It was easier for the Roosevelt White House to keep up appearances. He hadn't, after all, gone into as complete an eclipse as Woodrow Wilson did after his stroke in 1919. With a hiatus now and then, attributable to absence from Washington or some bothersome but transient illness, the president mostly maintained his regular schedule of twice-weekly, not-for-quotation press conferences there and once-a-week cabinet sessions as well as the hour on Monday mornings given over to meeting Democratic congressional leaders. However, he was coming in contact with a diminishing list of visitors outside his inner circle.

And that circle was itself diminished. Marguerite LeHand, known as Missy, his longtime secretary who orchestrated his days and knew his wishes before he expressed them, had been disabled in the first spring of his third term by a paralyzing stroke from which she never recovered. Marvin McIntyre, a key political aide since the Wilson era, had died while Roosevelt was traveling back from Tehran and Cairo in December. Well before his death, he'd complained that he never got to see the president alone anymore. On his return from Tehran, Harry Hopkins and his wife had moved out of the White House into their new Georgetown home, from which, soon after, he had to be rushed to the Bethesda naval hospital after collapsing with a chronic digestive disorder that severely limited his ability to absorb nourishment. In crude terms, this unique sounding board, adviser, and smoother-over was on the verge of starvation; by February, his weight was down to 128 pounds. Winston Churchill, alarmed for Hopkins's sake and even more so, perhaps, over the loss of his most reliable conduit to Roosevelt, pressed in his letters for the prognosis. On this and sometimes on strategic issues on the prolific prime minister's mind, the president's responses tended to be brief, a little vague (sometimes purposefully so), and a little slow in coming. In the first three months of the year, the Former Naval Person, as he was designated in these exchanges, batted out 102 letters and messages marked "Personal and Secret" or "Personal and Top Secret" to his American counterpart, getting a not inconsiderable, but still trailing, 76 replies, many obviously staff written, with small editing and personal touches here and there added in the president's hand.

Not long after the Hopkinses moved out, Anna Roosevelt Boettiger arrived from Seattle with her three children and moved in. At first, they were listed on the White House logs as "houseguests." Soon she'd taken up residence that would last until the end of the Roosevelt presidency, by which time she and her husband, a former *Chicago Tribune* correspondent named John Boettiger, were playing undefined, shadowy roles as occasional aides to the president, though neither occupied an official position. Tall and lissome, the president's eldest was thirty-seven and eight years into her second marriage when she landed back in the White House. She offered thoughtful evening companionship to her father, filling some of the time that had previously been reserved for Hopkins. Members of the official family came to view Anna as a potential messenger to the boss.

John Boettiger's career as a White House correspondent had to end once he became engaged to the president's daughter, with whom he'd fallen into an affair on the 1932 Roosevelt campaign train, hastening the divorces to which both were already heading. Once remarried, Colonel McCormick's former ace parlayed his new status as presidential son-in-law into a job with William Randolph Hearst, who named him publisher of the *Seattle Post-Intelligencer,* taking on Anna as an associate editor as well. As Hearst's skepticism of the New Deal congealed into antipathy, the *P-I* remained steadfast. This was not good for its publisher's career prospects in the Hearst organization. A restless, moody soul with a tendency to depressive spells—he'd end his life in a leap from a Manhattan hotel in 1950, several years after his separation from Anna—Boettiger eventually came to feel himself in exile from the center of power in the other Washington. At the start of 1943, the son-in-law asked whether he could accompany the president to his meeting with Churchill in Casablanca. "Well, you are not in uniform," Roosevelt replied, reliving perhaps the appeal he'd made to President Wilson a quarter of a century earlier to be allowed to get into uniform himself. Within six months, the Seattle publisher, with a little help from Generals Marshall and Eisenhower, had been swiftly reincarnated as an army major specializing in civil administration in newly liberated Sicily. When Roosevelt flew to Tehran toward the end of the year, Major Boettiger's wish to ride on the presidential plane finally came true. A reassignment to the Pentagon then gave Anna, languishing and lovelorn in Seattle, her initial impetus for returning to her father's side. "I crave you every minute," she wrote to her husband from their home on Mercer Island, to which she'd briefly returned after settling in the White House. "Will I love piling into that big four-poster a week from Friday night with my perfect one and only."

Anna—called Sis by her father and siblings—brought a fresh eye into the family quarters, which soon proved vital in the seemingly overdue galvanizing of concern there about her father's condition. He'd lost ten pounds in his bout with the flu in January. Only after his death the following year would Admiral McIntire, in a memoir remarkable for its false leads and contradictions, declare that this reduction had been deliberately engineered in order "to lessen the load on [his heart]." Publicly at the time, the White House physician had resisted any suggestion that the president's heart was a matter of concern.

In Roosevelt's family circle, the one consistent sentinel on his health, before Anna's return, had been his devoted friend, distant (sixth) cousin, and Dutchess County neighbor, the single and singularly undemanding, easily overlooked Daisy Suckley. For reasons that were both political and, no doubt, deeply buried in his psyche, Roosevelt habitually denied himself confidants. In general, his family and closest associates were told only what he felt they needed to know to accomplish some purpose of his own. "Of what was inside him, what really drove him, Father talked with no one," his son James would later say. Missy LeHand, who spent more time with him in the two decades she served as his secretary than any other person, on terms that verged on intimacy, came to a similar conclusion. "He was really incapable of a personal friendship with anyone," she said.

Unworldly, devoted Daisy can be counted as an exception. He felt free to think aloud in her presence when so inclined, talk to her about how he was feeling, knowing that anything he said would go no further. Over the years, he kept no journal and routinely forbade the taking of minutes at cabinet or other high-level meetings. His own words on paper, he evidently fretted, could be used against him if he needed to change course. It's unlikely he ever imagined Daisy to be keeping the intimate diary that was only discovered decades later when an old leather valise was hauled from under her bed in her family's dilapidated mansion near the Hudson. The guileless Daisy proved to be the Boswell of his rambling ruminations, recording in an uncritical, disjointed way the hopes and daydreams that occupied a portion of a mind looking for some relief from the political and strategic calculations with which it was necessarily consumed. For him, when he indulges himself in this way, it seems a comforting sort of talk therapy.

Once, long ago, there'd been a spark of romance between the two—the high point of her life, an all but forgotten episode of his—long since superseded by the cozy confidentiality of their many hours together. She fully understood and gratefully embraced her place in his life: to be one of the few people for whom he'd never have to perform. "He puts so much of himself in when talking to people . . . he uses himself up," Daisy wrote in a diary note toward the end of January 1944.

The public man felt he had always to rise to the occasion when he was with others, and he could still pull it off, not effortlessly, however. A few days after Daisy's private jotting, a *Daily News* columnist offered this description of the president as he met the press upon returning from a week's break at Hyde Park: "He was the perfect picture of the Dutchess County squire. The alert grin, the smart shift of the eyes, made it clear that Mr. Big was in top form . . . [But] the circle of the eyes are rubbed in by smokier fingers than those of yesteryear. In other words, he looked tired."

At sessions with journalists, Roosevelt only rarely allowed himself to make news. He had his own inimitable technique for sidestepping pointed or inconvenient questions. Typically, he'd soliloquize at length on a series of topics, starting off with one not altogether unrelated to the subject before him, soon shading into others of diminishing relevance, until finally he was on safe ground, reminiscing in his high-spirited, entertaining way about something light-years distant from his point of departure. Transcripts of these sessions record lots of cozy bantering, lots of compliant laughter on the part of the reporters. By his twelfth year in office, everyone knew how the game was played. Like the *Daily News* man, reporters watched to see how well he was playing it. Roosevelt himself had become the subject.

His 933rd press conference—a special gathering for black journalists, not one of whom had yet been accredited at the White House—offered an extreme example of presidential evasion raised to an art form. A challenging question had been posed: What was Roosevelt going to do about the abuse black soldiers on leave frequently encountered at the hands of white police, both civilian and military? It was a problem to be grappled with, the president acknowledged. It wasn't enough to issue orders; individuals had to be changed. He was reminded of a trip he'd taken years earlier to Chattanooga. It was easy to connect with blacks in Tennessee, where they were mostly voters. He could see their enthusiasm. In adjacent Georgia, where the

vote was denied, black onlookers stood passively. So black journalists needed to look hard at conditions, especially overseas. He's now
reminded of a trip he took to the Gambia. He goes on about squalid
conditions and disease in the Gambia for several minutes. He'd told
Churchill that colonies in West Africa should be opened to international inspection. Churchill replied that inspectors should go to the
American South, too. "I said, 'Winston, that's all right with me. Go
ahead and do it. Tell the world . . . bring it all out.'" At the end of this
long, looping aria, he'd landed back on the side of the questioner without ever having engaged the question, if anyone could still remember
what it had been.

Loquacious as ever in front of a captive audience, the president
could, in a flush of self-pity, still complain to Daisy Suckley, "I'm
either Exhibit A or left completely alone." Daisy, seldom addressed by
her given name, Margaret, proved a reliable guard against this always
lurking loneliness, content to sit in silence while the crippled object
of her devotion read or worked on his stamp collection, brooding on
one or more of his many preoccupations; on call to share a meal when
otherwise he'd have found himself alone; reliably on hand when he
was ready to speak. "He needs to have someone to count on, in the
evening," wrote Daisy, who almost never has a reason of her own to
go out. "It is so different when one can walk about, get things for
oneself, *do* something." Except when it came to his well-being, she
has few opinions of her own to advance. In this, she was the opposite
of Eleanor, who had solicitude for all the world's sufferers but little
time to indulge her husband in the "mind rest" he increasingly sought.

By 1944, there's scarcely a page in Daisy's diary without some allusion to how the president looks or feels. Plotted on a graph, these
notes would be full of ups and downs. On March 2, at the White
House, she writes, "The P. felt feverish & generally miserable & lay on
the sofa." The next week, on March 8: "Another quiet evening of work
& yawns on the part of F.D.R. I don't know that I have ever seen him
so consistently cheerful and peaceful as this week."

Other diarists—none of whom see him nearly as often as Daisy—
draw their own conclusions in these same weeks about the president's
mood and health, plot their own graphs. Vice President Wallace, who
comes across as a candid and conscientious observer in his journal,
writes at the end of January that the president "seemed unusually

well and happy." A few weeks later, in the eyes of this beholder, he still "looked quite rested" and "spoke with great animation" about a newly hatched scheme to start a four-page national newspaper after the war that would carry no opinion, only news. Obviously, Wallace isn't among those few before whom the president feels no compulsion to perform. In the same week, Daisy portrays him as leaning in two directions when he touches on his future. "The P. is tired as I have said before," she writes in Hyde Park. "He acknowledges it & wants to get out of his grueling job, but there is too much demand for him to stay in, not only from this country, but also from all the United Nations." Perhaps, she has allowed herself to think, "when the P. felt he was no longer necessary, he could resign."

Daisy's diary notes shouldn't be overinterpreted, nor undervalued. What they offer are sporadic glimpses into his mind. Less a stream than a rivulet or even trickle of consciousness, these rare incidents of private venting can be interpreted in two or more ways: as the building of a rationalization for not stepping down or for the opposite; taken together, as a frank expression of a real dilemma. There's no need, of course, to choose among alternative interpretations. Each may well have been true in one instant or the next, as we may surmise if we allow ourselves to be honest about our own experience in periods of stress; in the case of Franklin Roosevelt, in the midst of a great war, in his twelfth year in office, opportunities for true "mind rest" had to be scarce.

The war, in particular the pending invasion, and the question of the fourth term followed him wherever he went. A host of other questions too: for instance, the urgency the Nazi mass murder of Jews had lent to the Zionist project for Palestine. Roosevelt had been distantly sympathetic to the plight of Europe's Jews, not so sympathetic as to campaign for an open-door policy before what would later be called genocide had been formally adopted by Hitler's Germany at the notorious Wannsee Conference, the month after the United States entered the war. Earlier, as boatloads of refugees were turned away by officials he'd appointed, he'd looked the other way rather than leave the impression that a fight against fascism would be a fight on behalf of Jews. The immigration of aliens, in particular Jewish aliens in flight for their lives, was not a popular cause in an era in which the anti-Semitic radio preacher Father Charles Coughlin could command an audience in the tens of millions. The same calculated reticence continued in wartime. He was "politically and emotionally stingy when it came to the plight of Jews," Richard Breitman and Allan J. Lichtman conclude in a judicious study.

It was hardly the first time in his presidency that political calculations caused him to keep private moral judgments private. Ten years earlier, Roosevelt had explained to the head of the National Association for the Advancement of Colored People why he couldn't throw his support behind an antilynching bill then before Congress. With southerners controlling all the key committees, it would mean sacrificing his whole domestic program, in effect, giving up on the New Deal. He could do the tricky calculus involved in such decisions without losing sleep. That was, he believed, what the job demanded, never more so than in wartime. By 1944, the mass graves at Katyn and the domestic internment camps for Japanese-Americans had become additional ugly details in his big picture on which he found it inexpedient to focus.

On March 9, Roosevelt met two Zionist leaders, Rabbis Stephen Wise and Abba Hillel Silver, who wanted him to declare his support for a Jewish homeland in Palestine. He led them to believe he was fully behind them but wouldn't be able to say so directly until the war was won. The next afternoon, at a meeting of his cabinet, he took up the Arab cause, fully aware that some of its members were more worried about Middle Eastern oil than the survival of refugees. "Do you want to be responsible by your actions for the loss of hundreds of thousands of lives?" he claimed to have asked the rabbis. "Do you want to start a holy jihad?" Henry Wallace couldn't reconcile Roosevelt's account of the meeting with one he'd gotten from Rabbi Silver, who came away pleased by the presidential assurances that had been lavished on the two Zionists.

"The President is certainly a water-man," the vice president wrote in his diary. "He looks in one direction and rows [in] the other with utmost skill."

It was the way he operated. At key junctures, as the scholar Warren Kimball has suggested, he showed himself to be "a man with a conception but without a plan." His goals were clear, in his own mind at least; his means of attaining them were left to whatever improvisation and maneuvering circumstances might favor. Contradictions were knots to be untied, if not immediately, then in due course. In this case, he explained to Wallace, "he intends to get the Jews what they want without setting the Arabs on their ear[s]." That was a worthy goal for the future, not as pressing as winning the war or agreeing with his most powerful ally, Stalin, on a scheme for world peace and security. But it showed, for all his complaints of weariness, Roosevelt was still himself, at once high-minded and devious, well into the third month of his twelfth year as president.

With worshipful Daisy, he could dream for a few moments at a time about an escape, but, in actual practice he simply carried on, the inescapable burden always there, no matter how often he entrained secretly for Hyde Park or took to his bed with the recurring malady variously written off in early 1944 as flu, grippe, or bronchitis, nasty but commonplace, a seasonal nuisance. "It makes you feel the way an Italian soldier looks," Roosevelt wrote in January to Churchill, who was just recovering himself. Still in Marrakesh, where he'd been convalescing in a villa maintained by the American army, the prime minister laid out his plans to wrestle with the Polish problem as soon as he returned to London. Pushing the Wehrmacht back, Soviet forces were already within striking distance of the 1939 border Stalin had vowed to make permanent. D-Day was still five months away. Churchill had been consulting with Edvard Beneš, president in exile of the Czech government, who'd already sealed an agreement on frontiers with Stalin. The Czech, the prime minister wrote, "may be most useful in trying to make the Poles see reason and in reconciling them to the Russians." He felt it was the "duty" of the Poles to reach such a settlement and hoped, with heady optimism, to have it "tidied up early in February."

He made the effort and hit a wall, a Polish wall. The exile government, which had had no relations with Moscow since demanding an investigation of the Katyn slaughter by the International Red Cross, refused to pay Stalin's minimum price, which would require them to shut up about Katyn and renounce a 1921 border treaty imposed on Lenin when the Bolsheviks were too weak to resist. They'd not bought into Churchill's notion of their "duty." Roosevelt offered to mediate between the Poles and "U.J." (as before, Uncle Joe) but said his "primary concern" was to preserve the "essential unity" with the Russians achieved at Tehran.

Real territory was at stake. As Stalin tartly noted, the Poles were effectively claiming the cities of Vilnius, capital of Lithuania, and Lwów (called Lemberg when it was the capital of the Austro-Hungarian province of Galicia, Lviv after its incorporation into Ukraine). Though both had been part of the short-lived second Polish Republic, jointly smothered out of existence by the Germans and the Russians in 1939, they'd no hope of recapturing either. Churchill had already told them that the Allies couldn't support those claims. The idea, tacitly accepted by Roosevelt at Tehran when he professed not to be taking a stand on Soviet territorial claims, was to compensate Poland with a major slab of East Prussia, up to and including the Baltic coastline. No one was asking what the Lithuanians wanted, let alone the Jews who made up a large portion of multiethnic Lwów, for they'd been wiped out by SS *Einsatzgruppen* (operation groups, or less euphemistically, killing squads). Stalin eventually wrote to Churchill and Roosevelt saying that the solution of such Soviet-Polish issues "has not ripened yet." It would ripen when Soviet forces occupied Poland, an outcome the president had foreseen but one that wouldn't come for eight months. Biding his time, the cold realist in the White House wrote "No reply necessary" across the Stalin cable that had finally landed in the Map Room.

With the Polish question apparently left to simmer, the Allies found themselves bogged down in Italy, having met stiff German resistance following their landing at Anzio on January 22 and during the first of three unsuccessful assaults at Monte Cassino. Churchill, who'd championed these Mediterranean operations, now told Roosevelt he was "hardening" for the fast-approaching Normandy landings he'd tried to offset before Tehran. The president was briefed most days by Admirals Leahy and Brown but seemed, in this period of feverish anticipation, to leave military strategy and logistics to his top military planners; he encountered them face-to-face now on a less than weekly basis. According to White House logs, he conferred in person with Marshall a grand total of four times in the months of February and March, with Secretary of War Stimson three times (not counting cabinet sessions). Churchill's military chiefs, by contrast, were constantly on call, summoned to Downing Street at all hours, often nightly, which was when the prime minister preferred to work and hold forth.

If anything, the president was less in touch with the officials he'd put in charge of his domestic programs. He'd offended his "assistant president," Jimmy Byrnes, by not bothering to show him a draft of the visionary "economic bill of rights" he'd grandly incorporated into his State of the Union speech but left unmoored in any existing program. It finally resurfaced as the GI Bill of Rights later in the year, a far-reaching program of social reform repackaged as a bonus for heroes, promising training, jobs, and college educations. Now, at the start of February, Byrnes was threatening to resign because "I don't take him enough into my confidence," Roosevelt told Daisy. "Another prima donna," he scoffed. "Then he laughed," she notes, admiring his sure touch in smoothing hurt feelings.

The president was back in Hyde Park the last week of the month for another week of rest, though neither Congress nor the country had been told he'd left the White House. His last official act before boarding his special train was to veto a tax bill on grounds that it gave breaks to privileged groups while failing to raise sufficient revenue for the war. "It is not a tax bill," the veto message said in one of its opening thrusts, "but a tax relief bill providing relief not for the needy but the greedy."

That phrase, in particular, stuck in the craw of the Senate's majority leader, Kentucky's Alben W. Barkley, sometimes called the Sage of Paducah, an affable old-line Wilsonian with a Chautauqua orator's command of the spoken language who'd endured recurring derision of himself as a Roosevelt lapdog. "Dear Alben," he was sarcastically called, a reference to the salutations on brisk presidential notes that could be read as commands when they found their way into public print. Actually, it was Wilson whom Barkley revered as "the greatest statesman and greatest President under whom I ever served." Roosevelt, he would say, "had the instinct of a virtuoso for playing practical politics," a president with "a deep and penetrating insight" into how government actually worked.

In this instance, the virtuoso was out of town as cracks in his party's unity suddenly widened into a chasm. Barkley, who had reason to feel taken for granted by the president, had been told by Roosevelt himself that the veto was on its way, that it had been recommended by both the Treasury and the wartime Office of Economic Stabilization. The senator had made his case against it at the weekly leaders meeting, saying, essentially, that the bill—furnishing billions less than the president had asked for the war—was the best he could coax out of his colleagues. What he hadn't anticipated was the cutting edge of the honed-for-quotation passage ("not for the needy but the greedy") in the president's message.

The next afternoon, hours after Roosevelt's train reached Highland, New York, across the Hudson from Hyde Park, he received an urgent message from the presiding officer of the Senate, Vice President Wallace, telling him that his heretofore faithful majority leader had just jumped ship, erupting on the Senate floor in a denunciation of the veto and calling on Congress, if "it has any self-respect yet left," to override it. Among the least likely of rebels, Barkley said he'd resign the leadership he'd held for seven years rather than carry the flag for an administration that didn't appreciate his efforts. "I have carried it with little help here on the Senate floor and more frequently," he fumed, "with little help from the other end of Pennsylvania Avenue."

For the next couple of days, political insiders, Democrats especially, held their collective breaths, waiting—in some cases, with rising hope—to see whether the rebellion would gather force, whether, in fact, Barkley's tantrum signaled the beginning of the end of the Roosevelt era. There were large headlines on front pages across the nation, all but eclipsing the war. As tends to happen when journalists get excited, words like "historic" and "unprecedented" were flung about. A dispatch that landed on the front of the *New York Herald Tribune* saw Barkley's revolt against the president as "perhaps imperiling whatever ambitions he has for a fourth term." "Revolt Viewed as Sharp Check to Fourth Term," the headline declared, going a bit further. It was, the still hyperventilating paper said the next day, "the most devastating political rebuff in the twelve years of his administration." Reporters assigned to the White House had left Washington, the same article related, "in search of the President."

The president wasn't lost. Regulars in the White House press corps had known all along he was in Hyde Park, but under the "voluntary" wartime censorship rules to which they'd signed on, his whereabouts had to be treated as a state secret. Acting as if they were on a real manhunt, they now scampered off in hot pursuit from Washington to Poughkeepsie's Nelson House, a press hangout convenient to the Roosevelt estate. From there, the *New York Times* correspondent could do no better, in an article datelined "WITH PRESIDENT ROOSEVELT," than report that the president was "incommunicado." Without specifying exactly where he was, the White House then mockingly pointed out that he hadn't been with the man from the *Times*. In an adjacent article, Barkley was crowned "the outstanding Presidential possibility aside from Mr. Roosevelt" among Democrats.

New York's mayor, Fiorello La Guardia, wondered how such a repudiation of a president by his own party could be explained to our British ally. In a parliamentary system, he pointed out, the government would have been swept away. The House overrode the veto by an eye-popping margin of 204 votes, with a majority of Democrats voting against the president. In the Senate, the outcome was even more lopsided; the tax bill Roosevelt had rejected sailed through, with Democrats voting three to one in its favor. By then, Barkley had made good on his threat to resign as leader and had been unanimously, almost instantly, restored to the post he'd won in 1937 by a scant, single vote in a tooth-and-nail fight among Democrats; strong presidential backing had made the difference then. Now, at a stroke, he reemerged as indisputably his own man, not the president's. Only later would the Sage of Paducah wonder whether this hard-won boost to his prestige on Capitol Hill had done "more than any other event of my career to keep me from becoming President."

On the surface, he and Roosevelt would quickly patch up their friendship and learn to swap jokes and enjoy each other's company again. But from then on, Barkley was off the president's ever-changing list of potential running mates. Sam Rosenman, the loyal speechwriter, recounting the imbroglio in his own memoir, conceded that his boss could be "bitter, vindictive and unforgiving" toward those who thwarted him. Of course, Rosenman hastened to add, this wasn't so with "Dear Alben"—renamed "Perfidious Alben" by one of the more literate Roosevelt loyalists—for the president was genuinely fond of the senator. "Everyone's nerves had become tense and jittery in this trying wartime period of unremitting work and anxiety," he concluded, on what was meant to be a soothing note, stopping short of the obvious point that Harry Truman—who'd sided with the majority leader on the override and four years later would make Barkley his running mate, eventually a grandfatherly veep stranded in vice presidential limbo—might never have come to the fore if the wounded Kentuckian hadn't exposed how grievously overdrawn this president's account of congressional goodwill had become by the final year of his third term. (Marvin McIntyre, Roosevelt's recently deceased political operative, had been after him for a couple of years to keep up his congressional contacts, something few presidents are inclined to do and even fewer do to any advantage. The president's response was to off-load that task on McIntyre himself.)

Editorialists across the country sided with Barkley and hailed his resurrection. It was left to a home state paper, the liberal *Courier-Journal* of Louisville, to point out "the simple facts . . . that the veto [did] not deserve to be over-ridden, that neither Mr. Barkley nor anyone else can make an adequate defense of the appalling inadequacy of the tax bill, and that we still have a war to fight." Their senator, the newspaper lamented, "has caused inordinate rejoicing in the camp of the political enemies of President Roosevelt."

Several factors kept the resounding defeat on Capitol Hill from festering into something worse than an embarrassing setback, from undermining Franklin Roosevelt's political effectiveness the way the defeat of the League of Nations finally sealed the fate of Woodrow Wilson. One was Barkley's basic goodwill, his readiness once his feelings had been salved to return to the fold. As the *Courier-Journal*'s Washington correspondent wrote, "People who are looking for a champion to lead a stop-Roosevelt movement at the national convention, and who are suddenly filled with hope that they have found their leader, can look elsewhere." Kentucky's senior senator wasn't going to be their "spearhead."

More important was the swift execution of Roosevelt's retreat. By the evening of the majority leader's grand fulmination on the Senate floor, Steve Early, the White House press secretary, was at Barkley's doorstep with a personal, emollient "Dear Alben" letter from the president calling for reconciliation and throwing the senator a lifeline he would seize. Before Barkley had even resigned, it was Roosevelt who suggested that if he insisted on going through with his threat, the Democratic caucus should immediately and unanimously reelect him. Once that script had played out, the old, now new, majority leader thanked Roosevelt for his "generous and manly statement" and reaffirmed his enduring faith in the president as "a spokesman for the people," now carrying a burden "no American President has ever borne." Probably reflecting Roosevelt's true feelings, Daisy thought the senator's letter "too sweet."

A final factor that restored and kept everyone in place is almost too obvious to mention. It was Roosevelt's towering prestige at the height of the global struggle. Half a century before the total immersion in politics made possible by cable TV and the Internet, when a news cycle still lasted a minimum of twenty-four hours and nothing went viral in an instant, a president had time to recover from a setback before hair-trigger commentators rushed in to second-guess and begin a countdown to his collapse. But, though their words may not have traveled as far or fast as they would today, there were commentators aplenty in that presidential year. One of them, Arthur Krock of *The New York Times,* explained why the revolt of congressional Democrats had to be suspended. "Most of the Democrats opposed to a fourth term," he wrote, "believe no other Democrat has a chance of victory in November."

Roosevelt himself sat out the rising at Hyde Park. It's not much clearer today than it was then whether he was an active participant, masterminding the administration's response behind the scenes, or a mostly passive bystander. "When he gets off," a White House insider had said, "he acts like he hasn't even got a job here." On this occasion, he showed his customary sangfroid under pressure, revealing not a trace of irritation. Henry Wallace's first S.O.S. on the Barkley speech was rushed to him by William Hassett, a White House official whose various duties included traveling with the president, constantly on call as his liaison man. The aide came upon the president sorting through old papers with Daisy, who was employed in the presidential library he'd already bequeathed the nation. "Alben must be suffering from shell shock," was all he said. There are remarkably few accounts of this president losing his composure, giving way to rage. Wilson Brown, the naval attaché, would write that noticeable, presumably rapid, blinking was the surest sign of presidential displeasure. Bill Hassett says nothing about blinking on this occasion.

When he returned with a further bulletin from Wallace on Barkley's agitated state, he found Roosevelt and Daisy still engrossed in their archival work. "It doesn't make sense, " the president said mildly, asking no questions, still seemingly unruffled. If the majority leader had tossed a time bomb, as all Washington by then seemed to think, the president gave no sign, even to insiders, that the ticking had reached his ears. Finally, Jimmy Byrnes got to him by phone. "The thing for you to do is forget about it and just not give a damn," Roosevelt said, according to the "assistant president's" later account, which can probably be trusted because Byrnes, a onetime court stenographer, took notes in shorthand. In the end, Byrnes tells posterity, he persuaded the president to reach out to the senator and drafted the letter that was delivered in Roosevelt's name after minor changes by Roosevelt.

Byrnes portrays himself as the puller of strings, Roosevelt as an unfocused taker of his sage advice. But that's often the way counselors to powerful figures interpret events. It's the inside view, the view from below. If the president had lived to write his own account, he could have claimed to have achieved the best possible outcome with a minimum of distraction or damage to his larger purposes. He might also have pointed out that the veto message had been drafted in Byrnes's office and that the former senator and Supreme Court justice, future secretary of state and Dixiecrat governor was detailed to clean up the consequences.

Reading between the lines of Daisy's diary, we get a further hint of Roosevelt's lofty reaction to the contretemps that had momentarily seized Washington. As she saw it, he was "surrounded by a ring of children who all want his constant attention & gets mad if he sees more of one than the other . . . *He* is always supposed to be calm & collected & agreeable, no matter what everyone else does." The next day, while Barkley was going through the motions of resigning and the House was overriding the veto, Roosevelt drove Daisy in his reengineered Ford—it had hand controls and no pedals—through the woods to Top Cottage, a small stone house of his own design, which he used as a private getaway.

The hilltop on which the cottage sits is the highest point in the vicinity, affording vistas across the family estate to the highlands on the other side of the Hudson. Roosevelt had bought the land in 1937, imagining it as the site of a simple residence built to give a man confined to a wheelchair maximum mobility and ease. The fieldstones were taken from old walls on the Roosevelt lands. Wide doorways had no raised saddles that might interfere with the progress of a self-propelled wheelchair. Windows were deep enough for a seated person to take in the whole panorama. As originally conceived, living quarters were to be all on one floor, including a bedroom in which the president would never, as it turned out, spend a night. Roosevelt had once thought he'd write his memoirs at Top Cottage. Early on, before her gauziest dreams faded, Daisy called it "our house." Missy might also have thought of occupying it.

On this winter afternoon, they'd brought some books he wanted to have on hand there. Then, as weak winter sunlight streamed in, they sat by the big stone fireplace and chatted. The P said, "This flare-up in Congress by Barkley might easily have an effect on the election & might make a condition which would cause him to refuse to run." He was waiting on circumstances. Fatalism and a sense of duty had braided together; they were indistinguishable. His mood can be read either way. Weariness comes through. The ambivalence that accompanies it may be somewhat put on, but it's hard to ignore. The decision, he knew, wouldn't be entirely his.

The next day, Eleanor, who remained in Washington when Franklin left for Hyde Park, wrote in a letter to a friend that he "is more philosophical daily. He knows he only will be re-elected if they can't find someone else & I really think he doesn't care." Yet she predicted, "He'll go on as long as the people want him."

Here, finally, we discover the context for the memo sent two weeks after the Barkley revolt by the New Deal lawyer Ben Cohen asking whether there was any "practical alternative to a fourth term." Cohen, then a counsel to Jimmy Byrnes in the Office of War Mobilization, had a hand in drafting the veto message Congress had just overridden. He might have felt let down, left to wonder whether Roosevelt was up to fighting for his programs, whether they'd stand a chance on Capitol Hill after victories on the battlefields or at the polls. As Daisy Suckley's jottings show, the man to whom Cohen wrote was way ahead of him; he'd been posing such questions to himself for months.

The president was becoming increasingly impatient with committee reports, complex proposals, and programs for which he once had a considerable appetite, impatient with the usual details of governance, with all the preliminaries. He wanted events to move rapidly. In his most heartfelt letter to Churchill in this period—clearly, from beginning to end, the product of his own dictation—he rails against needless paperwork and planning:

> I have been worrying a good deal of late on account of the tendency of all of us to prepare for future events in such detail that we may be letting ourselves in for trouble when the time arrives . . . I have been handed pages and pages with detailed instructions and appendices. I regard them as prophecies by prophets who cannot be infallible . . . I am trying as hard as I can to simplify things.

Ostensibly, the letter, written on leap year's day, just before he returns from Hyde Park, has to do with postwar planning, with particular reference to Italy, France, and Germany. But it conveys a much deeper frustration. He wants to take decisions when the time is ripe; before then, he seems to be saying, he no longer wants to be bothered. Allen Drury, a young reporter with United Press, still new to his beat, went to his first White House press conference in this period and caught a whiff of the president's mood. "Underneath," he wrote in his journal, "one detects a certain lifelessness, a certain preoccupation, a tired impatience."

Too much preparation might spell trouble when it comes to presidential politics too. In the immediate aftermath of the meeting in Tehran, he hadn't demurred when party leaders told him his candidacy was a must. The lack of a demurral, the fact that he was having the conversations at all, could be taken as a nod. For ten or eleven days at the end of December after his return from meeting Stalin, before coming down with the flu, he'd been in high spirits, "at his best," Secretary Stimson had judged. The Barkley revolt two months later very nearly reopened the question of a fourth term but didn't. If we follow the White House logs, detailing the president's daily schedules, or delve into the diaries of close associates, a turning point of another sort begins to come into focus in the last two weeks of March. It has to do with his health, which had been rocky since the end of December but not, as far as his family or closest aides appeared to recognize, a matter as yet for alarm.

When he went to Hyde Park for eight days at the end of February, Admiral McIntire didn't find it necessary to accompany him. The three-star otolaryngologist, doubling as surgeon general of the navy, carried a heavy administrative burden, overseeing a system with a wartime staff of 175,000 doctors, nurses, and orderlies at 330 hospitals and medical stations around the world. As McIntire told all comers, his most important patient was getting over the flu, getting over the grippe, getting over bronchitis; the symptoms flared, faded, and flared again; Roosevelt's weakness, his weight loss, his complaints about stomach cramps and headaches, continued. On March 18, what amounts to a yellow warning signal seems to flash in the official logs. Starting on that date, Roosevelt took his dinner in bed for twenty-one consecutive evenings at the White House, usually alone, sometimes with Anna or Daisy providing bedside company. Of course this wasn't widely known beyond the family quarters. Cabinet members, congressional leaders, other top officials, had no idea. In the same period, Roosevelt managed three press conferences—which served to obscure the semi-convalescence into which he'd slipped—plus one cabinet session and a sparse calendar of official meetings including one with Secretary Hull, who'd taken over planning for the international organization that would replace the old league.

Roosevelt had sometimes teased Hull and occasionally mimicked his lisp but kept him on his team all these years, making him the longest-serving secretary of state in the nation's history, precisely for this moment, when his prestige on Capitol Hill could be redeemed in votes for a treaty that would raise the curtain on a new international order. The old Wilsonian would be his best guarantee against Wilson's sad fate. Now Hull was convening a small bipartisan panel of eight senators. He told them they needed "to keep Russia solidly in the international movement . . . and keep the entire undertaking out of domestic politics." Roosevelt was skeptical that the Republicans would take that pledge. "You'll see, they won't keep the agreement," Hull quotes him as saying.

On most days, however, there were no appointments on the president's calendar. "Every morning," Bill Hassett wrote in his diary, "in response to inquiry as to how he felt, a characteristic reply has been 'Rotten' or 'Like hell.'"

Roosevelt wouldn't have started taking dinner on a bed tray night after night of his own volition. It's a fair guess—in the absence of the mysteriously missing medical records—that he did so on doctor's orders or, rather, advice, because no one gave orders to the president. We've known such guidance was given two weeks later, following an examination by a navy cardiologist at the naval hospital in Bethesda on March 28. The hitherto-unremarked fact that the regime actually started ten days before that well-documented intervention shows how incomplete this medical history, as it has come to be understood over the decades, still remains. The conclusion that comes closest to known facts was propounded in lectures and articles by Marvin Moser, a retired Columbia University medical professor: "Roosevelt represents a textbook case of untreated hypertension progressing to [likely] organ failure and death from stroke." In the medical literature, such hypertension is sometimes called "malignant hypertension."

The idea that high blood pressure is a risk factor and precursor of coronary artery disease and strokes wasn't universally accepted in this period. Some specialists, including Dr. Paul Dudley White, who later treated President Eisenhower, had seen most forms of hypertension as an inevitable, even benign part of aging; the term "benign essential hypertension" actually appeared in medical texts. Safe and effective drugs to lower high blood pressure and prevent clots didn't begin to become available for more than ten years after Roosevelt's death. In the 1940s, only commonplace aspirin was widely recommended for this purpose. Since then, deaths from stroke have been reduced by more than 60 percent.

When it comes to Roosevelt's condition, Dr. Moser's analysis is too obvious, too easy for some. Pursuing sensational rumors that began to spread a year or more before the president's death, they've convinced themselves that he had cancer of one kind or another. (Melanoma, prostate cancer, lymphoma, and stomach cancer have all been mentioned. Of these, the theory that he might have had metastatic melanoma has been the most persistent. There's no documentary evidence to support it, but it isn't contradicted by symptoms that can be traced through his last year: weight loss, waning energy, even his periodic chest problems. Even if there were such a diagnosis then, there were no effective treatment protocols; oncology hadn't yet come into its own as a specialty.)

It's to such rumors that Dr. Frank Lahey, a renowned surgeon who figures in some of them, may have been referring when he wrote to

Admiral McIntire on December 20, 1944, two days after Roosevelt's return from a sojourn in Warm Springs: "Now that you have got the President back home, I expect that you and we will be saved from some of these extraordinary rumors." It's not clear when Lahey, the eponymous founder of the Lahey Clinic, now a major medical center north of Boston, first examined the president, but by that time he'd done so at least twice. Some of "these extraordinary rumors" turn on undocumented deductions about him or attributed to him by people long since deceased. A letter Lahey wrote on March 16, 1944, shows that he did play a significant consulting role in the case of the ailing Harry Hopkins. (The letter, a detailed review of surgical options, with a drawing illustrating a possible procedure, went to the adviser's physician brother in Tacoma.) It's a clue pointing to parallel or inconsistent possibilities: that Lahey might have meant Hopkins when he was understood years later by a colleague to be speaking about a stomach cancer in Roosevelt (for Hopkins had survived stomach cancer in the 1930s), or, if he was consulted on the aide when Hopkins was at Bethesda, that he's likely to have been brought in even earlier to see the boss. There the trail goes cold.

Much of this cloud of hearsay and speculation, giving rise to whatever controversy still hovers in corners of the Internet, can be laid to Roosevelt himself. The working hypothesis here is that the secretiveness surrounding the president's health was imposed by the patient and absolutely consistent with his character and methods, his customary slyness, his chronic desire to keep his political options open to the last possible moment. If Admiral McIntire's public testimony hadn't been so falsely reassuring, if accurate information on the president's health had been publicly disclosed in a timely way, then, obviously, the cause of truth and what's now called "transparency"—a word absent from Roosevelt's vocabulary—would have been better served. It's far less obvious, however, that this would have brought a swifter or better conclusion to the war. That's another argument without end, one no medical facts could resolve.

In any case, as the otolaryngologist well knew, Franklin Roosevelt was his commander in chief. This affable navy physician had faithfully served his patient for eleven years, mainly engaged in treatments appropriate to his specialty: spraying the presidential sinuses, nostrils, and throat, often daily. In the process, the good doctor, an Oregonian who'd enlisted on the eve of World War I, became a White House fixture, an insider. High administration officials like Harold Ickes pumped him for information, assuming he was privy to more of the president's thinking than they were. "Ross is one of the few men who are really close to the President these days," the interior secretary would write in his diary.

It was around the middle of March when daughter Anna summoned McIntire demanding to know what was ailing her father. Later, she acknowledged she already had her doubts that the White House physician was up to his job. "I didn't think McIntire was an internist who really knew what he was talking about," she said. "I felt Father needed more care, more general care." According to Geoffrey Ward, "McIntire was annoyed at what he considered her interference but made arrangements for a checkup by a specialist at the naval hospital."

Enter Howard G. Bruenn, M.D., a navy cardiologist by way of Johns Hopkins and Columbia Presbyterian hospital in New York. Four months would pass before Bruenn's central role in attending to the ailing president was first mentioned in a press report. He'd be with Roosevelt most days and on every trip, including Yalta and the final journey to Warm Springs, where he'd try to resuscitate the dying president. He'd then wait twenty-five years before writing up his personal notes in a medical journal in 1970, having been encouraged to do so by Anna Roosevelt and her third husband, a physician named James Halsted. In the final twenty years of his life, Bruenn would give at least seven interviews to historians and writers, sticking close to the restrictions he set for himself on the journal article.

In their first conversation, he'd assured Dr. Halsted he was not interested in writing a gossipy "'Lord Moran' book," a reference to Churchill's physician who in two volumes of chatty diary notes granted himself unusually broad license when it came to patient confidentiality. Even so, Dr. Halsted referred him to trusted historians—Arthur M. Schlesinger Jr. and Frank Freidel—for advice on how to avoid "adverse effects," presumably on the reputation of the long-buried president. Halsted also mentioned the possibility of depositing the cardiologist's material at the Roosevelt Library with a proviso that it be sealed for another twenty-five years. He neither pressed the suggestion nor explained why it might be desirable to bury Bruenn's account for a quarter century.

There's no further hint in his interviews or correspondence of any sensitive details Bruenn felt obliged to withhold. Always he'd insist that the president, over a period of slightly more than a year and innumerable rambling conversations, never once raised a question about his condition, prognosis, or the nature of the medications the cardiologist was prescribing. In interviews, Howard Bruenn left the impression that McIntire had decreed that conversation on medical issues with the patient would remain the admiral's exclusive prerogative. If that was the rule, it seems more likely that it was Roosevelt who laid it down, rather than his doctor. Why, otherwise, would he have adhered to it so strictly?

The timeline here is intriguing: On March 18, Roosevelt received a message from Prime Minister Churchill proposing a small-scale summit in Bermuda at Easter. That same evening, he started taking his dinners at the White House in bed. Declarations and diplomatic messages in his name still passed under his eyes for his approval. A notable one was issued on March 21, his bluntest statement to date on what would be named the Holocaust only later, after its full dimensions and horror had sunk in. ("The wholesale extermination of the Jews of Europe goes on unabated every hour," it said. "That these innocent people, who have already survived a decade of Hitler's fury, should perish on the very eve of triumph over barbarism which their persecution symbolizes, would be a major tragedy.") The words may now seem inadequate, but they marked a notable raising of consciousness.

After a week of dinners in bed, the president summoned his special train to carry him secretly, overnight, to Hyde Park. There, on March 25, he rested up, Daisy tells us, sitting outdoors in early spring sunshine, to ready himself for a special visitor due the next day.

She was Lucy Mercer Rutherfurd, dismissed by Eleanor as her social secretary long years before, during another world war, after she discovered a cache of love letters to her husband, the dashing, not yet invalided assistant secretary of the navy. If Lucy hadn't been a Catholic and if Franklin's mother, Sara Delano Roosevelt, hadn't threatened to disinherit her beloved only child, that bombshell might have led to a divorce. As it was, it blew up the conjugal relationship between Franklin and Eleanor, who learned how to stay together—for all practical purposes, living apart—as political partners and, in their distinctive ways, devoted friends and parents. As part of their armistice, Franklin had to promise never to see the soon-to-be-wed Lucy again, but before very long he instigated an intermittent, carefully superficial correspondence with her, as if between mere acquaintances, signing off his letters to his presumptive lover with a deceptively impersonal "Sincerely yours, Franklin D. Roosevelt." Presidential limousines were later put at her disposal to bring her to his inaugurations, and when she called the White House under the assumed name "Mrs. Paul Johnson," secretaries knew to put her through instantly to the president. For the sake of privacy, the old friends sometimes spoke in French, adding a touch of intrigue and romance to their conversation.

On March 19, Lucy's husband of twenty-four years, a wealthy, much older, once renowned sportsman named Winthrop Rutherfurd, had died after a long illness. Separated in age by twenty-nine years, they'd had one daughter, whom Roosevelt had welcomed to the White House and sometimes called his goddaughter. On March 26, only one week after her husband's death, the new widow paid what appears to have been her first visit to Hyde Park (all her earlier connection to the Roosevelt household having been in Washington). The ailing president, with all his burdens, couldn't easily come to her to offer his condolences so, it seems, he invited her to receive them in the privacy of his home. He could have written a heartfelt note; obviously, the invitation was more than a gesture. Early the next morning, weary but apparently still smitten, Roosevelt took the train back to Washington to resume his dinners in bed and get ready to meet the cardiologist at the Bethesda hospital on March 28.

We're left to imagine what combination of memory and melancholy filled his thoughts on this particular ride back to the capital. Political calculation may not have been foremost, despite the latest flurry of speculation, ignited over the weekend by comments by a former New Deal official named Aubrey Williams, who'd recently seen the president and had come away "with the distinct impression that he wouldn't run again, although he didn't say so directly." ("He looked so tired and worn that I was shocked," this Roosevelt loyalist told *The Atlanta Journal*.)

Also on March 28, Eleanor returned to the White House from a three-week tour of the Caribbean, starting at the Guantánamo Bay naval station, where she'd been shown quarters that her husband was expected to occupy shortly. Admiral McIntire had prescribed a vacation in the sun as a cure for his lingering infections. Now, despite these well-laid plans, it abruptly became known that Guantánamo would not, after all, be the president's destination. Though it had been all right for the First Lady—and another recent visitor from Washington, Secretary of the Navy Frank Knox—the Secret Service was said to have determined that it would not be all right for the commander in chief, who later explained at one of his off-the-record sessions with reporters that "Cuba is lousy with anarchists, murderers, etcetera, and a lot of prevaricators." Instead, his R & R would be at an unspecified location in the South, which turned out to be—by no coincidence, it seems reasonable to conclude—a long but not overly strenuous drive from Winthrop Rutherfurd's farm in the horse country around Aiken, South Carolina, where the newly widowed Lucy spent her winters.

Roosevelt had already explained to Churchill, who was trying to renew the partnership they'd had before Tehran, why he wasn't up for a meeting in Bermuda. "I am very angry with myself," he wrote, crossing out the first two paragraphs of a message drafted by his staff. "The old attack of grippe having hung on and on, leaving me with an intermittent temperature, Ross [McIntire] decided about a week ago that it is necessary for me to take a complete rest of about two or three weeks in a suitable climate . . . I see no way out and I am furious." If he was furious, it was over his need to acknowledge his own limitations. There's no other sign that he felt the need of another meeting with the prime minister at that time.

Showing that his focus was still on the cross-channel invasion over which the Americans and the British had sparred at Tehran and earlier, Roosevelt added, "I'm glad you feel hardened about OVER-LORD." He might have thought, but would never have said, he was glad the prime minister had finally come around.

Howard Bruenn made an error when he began his note taking on March 28. He set down March 27 as the date of his first diagnostic encounter with the president of the United States. In years to come, both he and Ross McIntire would slip up and say in interviews that the cardiologist had the president in his care for two years when, if

March 28, 1944, is accepted as the starting line, it was actually one year and two weeks extending over two calendar years. Some writers, who have apparently never had the experience of confusing dates and sequences after a long passage of time, have found a deep Freudian significance in these lapses: proof that these Bruenn notes—surviving outtakes from the missing medical record—are untrustworthy. Others who have lived long enough to know that confusion of that sort is anything but uncommon find no reason to doubt the authenticity of the cardiologist's personal jottings, which he deposited in the Hyde Park archive after finally writing them up and publishing his article in 1970. To a layman's eye, the notes are what would be expected on an initial examination. (A cardiologist to whom I showed them was struck by the fact that Bruenn doesn't appear to have begun by taking a standard health history as doctors are trained to do, no matter how thoroughly they've been briefed or what they've read. Of course, he could have done so without writing down his findings for reasons of presidential privacy.)

McIntire had clearly been aware of problems with Roosevelt's "ticker," as Anna would call it, but Bruenn was apparently the first cardiologist who'd ever been asked to examine the patient. That's maybe less surprising than it may seem, for cardiology was then, from today's perspective, in what might be considered its infancy. There were no tiny catheters with balloons on the ends with which to perform plaque-clearing invasive surgeries; there were no statins, beta-blockers, ACE inhibitors, effective blood thinners, echocardiograms, stents, or similar breakthrough technologies and drugs. Anna was at her father's side when, after a morning without appointments and lunch in his bedroom, he was wheeled into the electrocardiograph department at the naval hospital in Bethesda.

Years later, when Bruenn was interviewed in his seventies and eighties, he would say in layman's language that he found Roosevelt's condition "shocking" and "God awful." His contemporaneous notes sound muted, matter of fact, as they set out to list cardiovascular symptoms in a routine way. Without most of the technological short-cuts at the command of today's specialists, Bruenn was more dependent on the care and art he could muster for his physical examination of the patient. *No engorgement of vessels of neck. Apex impulse not visible. No thrills after apex beat.* Normal findings, so far. What follows isn't at all normal: *Apex beat . . . about 2 cm. outside [mid-clavicular] line. Upon percussion, heart markedly enlarged to left. Aortic arch broadened. Blowing systolic murmur at apex.* Now, as any other cardiologist would recognize, he's describing a diseased heart, one that has become enlarged and shifted away from its normal location in the chest.

More accessibly, the notes describe the patient's face as "very grey," suggesting an oxygen deficiency in the blood. The notes also say, "Moving about caused breathlessness and puffing." (Moving about could only mean changes of position on the examining table, not, obviously, walking.) Blood pressure was a worrisome 186/108. Everything pointed to an alarming enlargement of the heart, induced by chronic high blood pressure. This was confirmed by chest X-rays. "Under fluoroscopy," Bruenn wrote in a typed summary of the handwritten notes, "heart was 'enormous.' Aorta somewhat widened and tortuous."

McIntire had promised to have Roosevelt's medical records delivered to Bruenn but failed to do so, an extraordinary lapse under the circumstances; this was not just any heart patient.* Bruenn had to leave the president sitting on the examination table in order to phone the White House physician to ask where they were. As Bruenn later recalled, the admiral made excuses, said he wasn't sure he could lay his hands on them. The cardiologist had to explain why he really needed to see them. When finally the file arrived, the records showed that blood pressure readings, taken irregularly over the previous several years, had been consistently high. That confirmed Bruenn's worst suspicions. While McIntire focused on Roosevelt's nose and throat, the president's obvious cardiovascular issues hadn't been addressed in any systematic way. The sum of Bruenn's findings was a diagnosis of "acute congestive heart failure," more specifically, "left ventricular heart failure." He doesn't put those very specific medical terms in his personal notes. They only show up later in a typed, undated summary of those notes, which could have been written long after the initial exam. It's possible, if not probable, that a measure of self-censorship was involved with an eye to the huge political impact if somehow his

---

* The admiral's hesitation over the president's medical file, which was kept in a safe at the hospital, foreshadows its eventual disappearance after Roosevelt's death and strongly suggests, if there were any doubt, who might have been responsible.

diagnosis became known. What he wrote in the president's medical file, kept in the safe, vanished with the file after Roosevelt's death. Had his findings gotten out, it would have been big news. His findings didn't become public for twenty-six years.

By 1970, when Bruenn's article appeared, congestive heart failure was a treatable condition. In 1944, the best that up-to-date doctors like Bruenn were able to manage was, basically, to limit the strain on the heart by limiting the patient's activities and diet. The recommendations the cardiologist presented to Admiral McIntire the next day were essentially the following: cutting back the president's workday to two hours in the office in the morning, with "no irritation" permitted; the same in the afternoon; an hour's rest "lying down" at midday and another before dinner "in quarters" followed by ten hours of sleep. Did "no irritation" mean he couldn't be told of battlefield reversals or the myriad other instances of bad news that would normally be brought to his desk? The question is never addressed. In the event, there would be no hints of any effort to protect him from disturbing developments. But soon the sedative phenobarbital would be prescribed "as a brake on excessive activity and a cushion against possible emotional trauma." There's no evidence, one way or the other, as to whether the president had any idea that he was being sedated. If there's one secret his doctors kept to themselves, it was their conclusion that the president of the United States now needed to be drugged as a guard against "excessive activity" and "emotional trauma," which could induce palpitations.

Bruenn's initial notes go on to suggest that the patient be forbidden his customary pack and a half of Camel cigarettes. Elsewhere, perhaps after that idea has been turned down as asking too much, they concede that he can smoke "in moderation." He was to avoid his one recreation, swimming, "for present," and avoid straining during movement of his bowels. Effervescent laxatives were forbidden. So were foods producing flatulence. It was a prescription, if strictly followed, for semipermanent convalescence, for maintaining, in other words, the regime he'd more or less been following in the days leading up to the hospital visit. A wartime president was to be told that he needed to sleep half his time and reduce his workload to that of a bank teller. A random contrast hints at the difference. On March 18, 1943, his first appointment was at 9:45 in the morning; he finished dictating to his secretary Dorothy Brady at 10:30 in the evening, having met with at least fourteen official visitors in between plus a delegation of labor leaders. On the same date a year later, his first appointment was at 11:45 in the morning, and he retired at 8:30 in the evening, seeing only three official visitors and his two secretaries in the course of the day.

"Rest! with perhaps two to three months off," would be a good beginning, Bruenn suggested. "S.G. [surgeon general] somewhat unprintable when notified," he wrote in an undated note to himself. The most significant pharmaceutical intervention he suggested was a course of digitalis, an herbal drug derived from leaves of the common foxglove flower. Digitalis, also called digoxin, could be useful in reducing the size of an engorged heart, but it could also be dangerous; a little too much could prove highly toxic, leading to nausea, vomiting, anorexia, even death.

"McIntire was appalled at my suggestion," the cardiologist told Doris Kearns Goodwin decades later. "'The president can't take time off to go to bed,' he said. 'You can't simply say to him, Do this or do that. This is the president of the United States.'"

The exchange is worth pondering. It reflects the doctor-patient relationship between McIntire and Roosevelt. It, too, says Roosevelt called the shots, at least that he thought he did. Over the next two days, McIntire scheduled a series of consultations, first with a panel of navy doctors and then with two outside consultants, the Boston surgeon Frank Lahey and an Atlanta internist, James Paullin, each of whom had served as president of the American Medical Association, each an honorary consultant to the navy on medical manpower issues. At first, Paullin resisted the diagnosis of heart failure and potentially risky use of digitalis. But he reluctantly came around after Bruenn—the only heart specialist at the table—laid out the X-rays and laboratory results along with his own physical findings.

Bruenn, very likely the best cardiologist the navy had under military discipline, confronted Admiral McIntire—his superior officer, after all—with an ultimatum. In what seems likely to have been a private session, the cardiologist "told him I literally didn't want to have anything to do with the situation unless [he] agreed to digitalization."

Lahey "wanted to know condition of colon, etc." but eventually "submitted that no surgical procedure was indicated," according to Bruenn's notes. "He did, however, indicate that the situation was seri ous enough to warrant acquainting the patient with the full facts of the case in order to assure his full cooperation."

Less than an hour after his return to the White House from Bethesda on the afternoon of the twenty-eighth, the president had told his regular press conference that his problem was a lingering bronchitis. This was before he could have been "fully acquainted." An observant *Daily News* reporter wrote, "Still looking tired, though he has had no appointments since Friday noon, the President's face was overcast with a gray pallor. However he was not listless . . . and had seemingly recovered from the head cold which fogged his voice." *The New York Times* reported on its front page that he was "in a jovial mood."

A week later, responding to press inquiries about the findings of the Bethesda checkup, McIntire never used the word "heart" or "cardiologist" or admitted to any cardiac concerns. "For a man of 62-plus," he said, "we had very little to argue about." There was just the slightly debilitating, transient "residuals" of the flu and ensuing bronchitis, which enough exercise and sunshine would put right. Even for the unfailingly loyal admiral, it was a brassy performance when you consider that two days earlier the admiral had quietly passed the baton for day-to-day management of the president's health to a cardiologist. He "informed me," Bruenn wrote, "that if I were persona grata to the President, I would be in direct charge from here on in."

CHAPTER 4

Somewhere in the South

THE FOXGLOVE EXTRACT did its job efficiently and well, at least in the first few weeks. It wasn't a cure; the underlying condition remained. But day by day, Dr. Bruenn noted that the First Patient's heart sounds were improving in tone and volume, the organ's muscles again pumping effectively. The swollen heart was beginning to shrink back to normal size. His color was better, his lungs were clear, and he was sleeping through the night, complaining only that he was eating too much. He worried about getting "fat," the patient said repeatedly. In fact, he'd been put on a daily diet of twenty-six hundred calories, soon reduced to 1,800 to relieve the strain on his heart; six Camels were now supposed to be his limit. Only his blood pressure resisted treatment. Measured in the first five days of his new regime, it was never lower than 192/106, rising as high as 226/118, a level that would now be considered alarming.

On April 7, Marquis Childs, a sympathetic columnist, was ushered into the slightly cluttered, homey Oval Office, yet to be transformed into a gleaming stage set for camera crews, where he sat at close enough quarters to be able to light what Roosevelt called his "cig" after his subject had screwed it into its discolored ivory holder. Taking no notes, relying on what he termed his "trained memory," Childs had the better part of an hour to study the president's face and demeanor. This is what he heard, what he thought he saw:

> The President spoke in a firm voice without hesitation. His face was sallow but he appeared in good health. Around his eyes are innumerable fine lines. They add to the appearance of puffiness about

his eyes. Otherwise his face is little marked . . . While I was there he smoked two and perhaps three cigarettes. He is quite deaf . . . I had an impression of the man's curious aloneness.

Nowhere does Childs ask himself whether that man could survive an additional four years. Yet Roosevelt has a ready answer. When the columnist suggests that people don't appreciate the burden of the office, its occupant nonchalantly replies, "I wouldn't say burden. You see I don't work so hard any more. I've got this thing simplified . . . I imagine I don't work as many hours a week as you do."

The response, coming just ten days after the president had been diagnosed with congestive heart failure, is more telling than the columnist could have realized. We don't know whether Roosevelt ever actually heard the words "heart failure" in connection with his condition, but we do know he has been told he has to cut back drastically on his work schedule, to a level less than half what it had normally been. The proof that he takes the medical imperative seriously is in his compliance with the new regime. He seems to have processed the admonition of the physicians—however it was delivered, bluntly or softly—and to be well on the way to convincing himself that if he could survive in his office by limiting his daily expenditure of energy, it was his duty to do so. Perhaps his mind drifted back to a rare family dinner at the White House when he listened noncommittally as his third son—Franklin junior, a lieutenant commander in the navy, on brief shore leave—argued loudly for a fourth term, saying every member of the armed forces would think their commander in chief "a quitter" if he stepped down before the war's end.

He'd written to Churchill of his desire to "simplify things." Now he tells the columnist he has "this thing simplified." This thing is the presidency and the effort he puts into it. A hint that he has found a way to carry on can be seen in his seemingly carefree boast that he puts fewer hours into his job as leader of a wartime alliance battling in two hemispheres, across two oceans, than the syndicated columnist puts into his more finite labors. His medical condition—of which Marquis Childs and the rest of America knew nothing—would not deter him. "The habit of power had grown on him," the columnist afterward surmised. "He wanted to remain as commander until the war was won." At the same time, Childs found nothing insincere in the president's professed longing to exit the White House, to write and travel.

"Being an exceedingly complex individual, he doubtless believed this himself," the columnist concluded.

Childs was an astute, respected reporter. So was Turner Catledge of *The New York Times,* then the paper's top national reporter, later its managing editor in overall charge of news coverage, finally its first executive editor. In that same period, Catledge was ushered into the Oval Office, having been told by Jimmy Byrnes that the president would see him. Catledge and Childs saw two different Roosevelts. Here is how the future editor remembered his off-the-record encounter when he got around to writing his memoir a quarter of a century later:

> When I entered the President's office and had my first glimpse of him in several months, I was shocked and horrified—so much so that my impulse was to turn around and leave. I felt that I was seeing something I shouldn't see. He had lost a great deal of weight. His shirt collar hung so loose on his neck that you could have put your hand inside it. He was sitting there with a vague, glassy-eyed expression on his face and his mouth was hanging open.

Catledge's Roosevelt was as loquacious as ever but not entirely cogent. "Repeatedly," the memoirist recalled, "he would lose his train of thought, stop and stare blankly at me. It was an agonizing experience for me." Only the arrival of a waiter announcing the president's lunch allowed the reporter to make his "escape."

Do we conclude that Childs saw the president on a good day, Catledge on a bad one, or, because neither was able to write directly about these "background" sessions under the ground rules that governed such conversations, that they allowed memory to tint and reconfigure them? In Roosevelt's last months, such contrasts are not infrequent. One visitor has premonitions of the president's death, or thinks in later years, after recounting the experience on more than one occasion, that he had them. Another is struck by his force and his charm.

Turner Catledge made me a foreign correspondent. Years after his death, I succeeded to the position he held. I knew him to be a fair-minded and judicious journalist. So did Roosevelt. Yet if Roosevelt had not died in office, the journalist's later recollection might have been less stark, might have faded with time. What can't be doubted is that he was shocked by the president's appearance, just as Childs would long remember his "firm voice" and "good health."

The day after his session with Childs, Roosevelt headed south for the breather in the sun that was supposed to be restorative, to enable him to carry on. The first tangible clue that he'd been briefed on the nature of his condition comes in an undated letter he wrote to Daisy Suckley in which he introduced (and misspelled) the name of his cardiologist. "I forgot to tell you," the letter says, "that Dr. Bruin came down, too—He is one of the best heart men—Tho' my own is definitely better—does queer things still." The letter was never sent but he invited Daisy to travel south to join him and, once she was there, told her more: that "the diastole and systole are not working properly in unison," as she later transcribed what she had heard in her diary. It's not clear that she—or he—actually understood that the diastole and systole are not organs functioning on their own, that they're phases in the heart's cycle of dilations and contractions, that they're the measure of blood pressure; that in cases like his, when the heart has to strain to dispatch oxygen throughout the system, they register the dangerous abnormality known as hypertension. If they were not "in unison"—to use Roosevelt's language, reflecting a less than rudimentary layman's grasp—he may have had an irregular heart rhythm, what's called atrial flutter or fibrillation, but those terms don't show up in Bruenn's notes.

"The P.," Daisy wrote, discovered that his doctors "were not telling *him* the *whole* truth & that he was evidently more sick than they said! It is foolish of them to attempt to put something over on *him!*" The available evidence doesn't show how he made this discovery or when, whether it was before or after he left Washington on April 8 accompanied by Dr. McIntire. Dr. Bruenn joined them after a week. Neither one of these uniformed physicians could have resisted the commander in chief's insistence on learning more.

Various conjectures are possible involving not only the two navy doctors but the consultants Lahey and Paullin, who'd seen him as recently as April 2. It's not impossible that Bruenn spoke to the president about medical matters, swearing an oath of secrecy he then continued to honor until his own death half a century later, not impossible, but unlikely. If the specialist didn't feel free to speak directly to

Roosevelt, he felt no similar inhibition when it came to the president's daughter. We know of two such conversations between Bruenn and Anna, who may have served as a go-between, an amateur nurse practitioner. The historian Robert Ferrell points out that the patient could also have been kept abreast of his blood pressure readings by his longtime medical orderly George Fox, the naval officer who stood by to administer his nightly massages. (In this period and later, according to Dr. Bruenn, Roosevelt's blood pressure was taken twice a day.) Of the four doctors, Ross McIntire was the only one he could rely on to take the delicacy of the political choices he faced into account.

A conjecture, at best, is an informed guess: The most likely in this instance is that it was McIntire who introduced the terms "diastole" and "systole" into the president's vocabulary, that he did so at or about the time the patient was warned he had to make a drastic reduction in his workload, which would be before Roosevelt left Washington, before he told Childs of how he'd gotten "this thing simplified." He'd been complaining for months of the slump in his energy. He knew his own symptoms, didn't need to be informed that his right hand shook, that he was sometimes less alert than he'd normally been, that he needed more help in the most basic tasks of dressing and bathing. His daily experience told him his prognosis had the potential to be truly dire. Beyond anything McIntire might have said, it was enough for him to ratify the new schedule. He'd retreat rather than surrender; feeling that he had no obvious alternative, he'd bet on getting by.

Roosevelt seems to have had a superstition against traveling on Fridays. April 7 was Good Friday. The president left the White House after dinner the following evening, boarding his secret train as usual at a platform under the Bureau of Engraving and Printing, five blocks from the White House, where it would attract none of the attention it would inevitably have drawn at busy Union Station. His efficient and swift departures depended on elaborate coordination among the White House travel office, headed by an official named Dewey Long, the Secret Service, and the railways. A "pilot train" was always sent in advance to guard against sabotage on the line. Tunnels and overpasses were checked by railway police, train crews vetted by the Secret Service, local police and military units put on alert. Regular passenger and freight schedules were reviewed and, where necessary, revised so the presidential train could pass unimpeded.

When he traveled north to Hyde Park, he relied on the Baltimore and Ohio line to carry him to Philadelphia, where his train would transfer to tracks of the Reading Railway and, eventually, at Weehawken, New Jersey, to the West Shore line of the New York Central, running up the Hudson's less-traveled western bank to Highland, New York, across the river from Poughkeepsie and Hyde Park, thus avoiding the tunnels into Manhattan and the Hell Gate Bridge over the East River, which were considered too busy, too exposed.

This time, the overnight presidential train, already called by the enduring acronym POTUS, headed in the opposite direction on the tracks of the Southern Railway. As always on these jaunts, the president slept in his own stateroom, in his own car, a Pullman carriage called the *Ferdinand Magellan,* expensively refitted in the first year of the war with armor plating; bulletproof glass some six inches thick, formed by laying six plates of heavy glass one over another; watertight bulkhead doors and escape hatches in the roof large enough for the Secret Service to haul the crippled president out in the event of a derailment or an attack; at 285,000 pounds, the heaviest passenger car ever on U.S. rails. Confined every day to a wheelchair, he felt freer there, in the sense of being less confined, more on his own, than he did, it sometimes seemed, in the White House. "I'm in no hurry. The sooner I get where I'm going," he once said, "the sooner people will be wanting something from me."

Members of the presidential party could move from car to car on the train. The president's infirmity limited him to the perfectly maintained, comfortably deluxe *Ferdinand Magellan,* where the sitting room was approximately nine feet by twelve, matched by a paneled dining room where eight could sit at table for a meal or a conference. In between were four compartments. Roosevelt's stateroom B, in the precise middle of the Pullman car where he'd be jostled least, was a small cube, not quite seven feet wide. That he could happily spend as much as five days, even a week, in such close quarters, as happened in two coast-to-coast trips in the summer of his last year, is a poignant reminder of how immobilized he was in his everyday life. The passing scene, the forward whoosh of the train, were liberating for one whose special wheelchair was just narrow enough to clear the corridor that connected his compartment to the sitting and dining areas; the steady thrumming of steel wheels on steel rails became soothing mood music.*

His destination on this occasion, Georgetown, South Carolina, was a town in the coastal Low Country on Winyah Bay, where the Waccamaw meets the Black, Pee Dee, and Sampit Rivers. Georgetown is just across the bay from Hobcaw Barony, a sixteen-thousand-acre plantation, proud possession then of the financier Bernard Baruch, a native of the state who'd assembled the property in a series of purchases decades earlier after making his fortune as a stock picker on Wall Street. Winston Churchill, Eleanor Roosevelt, and Harry Hopkins had been among the notable figures who'd enjoyed his hospitality there. So had Clare Boothe Luce before and even after her marriage to the publisher of *Time* and *Life* magazines. The president, never averse to spicy gossip, told members of his staff of her affair with Baruch. "She was Barney Baruch's girl," he said. "Yes, he educated her, gave her a yacht, sent her to finishing school."

A perennial and persistent éminence grise, Baruch let the president know that the peace and quiet of Hobcaw could be his for the asking. Large gestures of generosity were not infrequently associated with his name; in that they tended to promote his influence, they weren't always accepted as disinterested. He'd thrown a lavish bash for Harry Hopkins's latest wedding at which champagne flowed freely, a not inconsiderable embarrassment once the elaborate menu—including caviar, pâté de foie gras, baked oysters, lobster in aspic, profiteroles—became the subject of newspaper reports, just as ration books were being issued for basic household staples like sugar, coffee, and meat. The bridegroom, whose byline had appeared that very month on a magazine article extolling austerity as a patriotic duty, was swamped with hate mail. ("No family should object to meat rationing," he'd written, "when they realize the beef and bacon they don't get is being served to their sons and brothers in the army.") A letter addressed to "Commissar Hopkins" accused the former social worker of looking on the American people as "suckers."

---

* Or so a visitor can easily imagine, walking through the restored and refurbished *Ferdinand Magellan,* now sitting in a shed at the Gold Coast Railroad Museum, just outside the gates of the Miami Zoo. In addition to the four small compartments called staterooms, there was another off the kitchen galley for the black Pullman porters who traveled with the president. His valet and the Secret Service would also have been within close call.

A couple of months later, Baruch would blame Hopkins for his big disappointment of the war years. In early 1943, Roosevelt had seemed ready to install him as czar of war production, in a post similar to one Baruch had occupied under Woodrow Wilson, but then, without explanation, changed his mind. The aging financier had taken too long to say yes. Still an imposing figure at six feet four, he was in his seventy-third year, becoming aware of a need for afternoon naps and worsening deafness that made meetings with more than one or two persons a trial; he was aware too that his prestige and influence might be greater as a freewheeling adviser outside the administration with broad access than as a heavily burdened insider. Finally arriving at the Oval Office after more than a week of reflection for what he thought would be the laying on of hands, he said, "I'm here reporting for duty." The president, with whom he lunched regularly, acted as if he hadn't taken in his visitor's words. As he was apt to do, Roosevelt held forth on unrelated matters for the better part of an hour, never mentioning the job that was supposed to be on offer, then left for a cabinet meeting. The subject never came up again, and Baruch, understandably, felt ill-used and wounded. Nevertheless, his offer of hospitality stood.

Roosevelt's wariness when it came to Baruch can't be interpreted as lack of regard. It can only be surmised. Baruch was not modest about the wisdom he had to offer. ("I am girding myself again because I want to push production and also fight for the right kind of peace . . . I know what should be done about some things . . . No odds will deter me," he wrote in a stream of letters to Pa Watson, a pal from the Wilson years, whom he believed to have the president's ear.) Nor was he likely to prove a good listener tuned in to the hints and steers—the changes in tone of voice or facial expression—habitually used by Roosevelt to communicate his wishes to subordinates. And no one was better connected in the upper reaches of the administration or the Washington press; he could be—and often was—a bearer of tales to columnists like Drew Pearson and Arthur Krock whom the president kept at arm's length.

Arriving in the Low Country on Easter Sunday, Roosevelt was there to rest and fish, mainly rest. For the first time, he was wheeled onto an elevator the Navy Gun Factory had recently installed at the rear of the *Ferdinand Magellan* for his exclusive use, obviating any need for wheeling him up or down cumbersome ramps. A bulky Secret Service man stood there with him. Roosevelt worried it wouldn't take their combined weights. It held them fine. Reporters for the three U.S. news services then accredited to the White House had accompanied him under a "voluntary" embargo barring them from mentioning his whereabouts until his return to Washington, which was expected in two or three weeks but turned out to be in four; only twice would they be allowed on the Hobcaw premises, which were guarded by sixty-two marines from Camp Lejeune plus Coast Guard patrols and planes (even a blimp) on the river and bay, in addition to the usual contingent of Secret Service men who camped out when off duty in another of the train's cars, sidetracked at a railway mail drop west of town. Yet another wagon, staffed by army signal corpsmen, served as a wartime communications center, with capabilities that included two-way radio hookups with any point on the army's global network. But urgent messages on paper still had to be hustled eight miles overland. Baruch had stubbornly resisted the intrusion of a phone line into his baronial hideaway. But two special phone lines had been installed in Roosevelt's bedroom suite for the use of the president, who could hardly have been expected to travel to the parked railway carriage if he wanted to make a call; one line was for emergency use, the other for personal calls. He spent an hour on the phone with General Mark Clark, commander of American forces in Italy. Otherwise, there's scant evidence he made much use of either line. Secretary of State Hull used the telegraph, not the phone, to brief Roosevelt on his private meetings with his bipartisan panel of senators about American plans for a new world organization, a subject high on the agenda of a president determined not to stumble where Woodrow Wilson fell. To check up on how he was getting on, Eleanor herself had to phone Admiral McIntire, who, as usual, didn't divulge much.

Roosevelt, it was understood, was not to be disturbed. When the three preceding weeks of near convalescence in the White House are added to those four, it turns out that he was partially sidelined for nearly two months in the spring of 1944 as the great invasion and a presidential campaign drew near. Discretion and wartime secrecy combined to ensure that official Washington, let alone the country, scarcely noticed. The news embargo was astonishingly effective, turning most insiders into outsiders. The citizens of Georgetown, South Carolina, soon figured out the reason for all the patrols and the railway cars parked on sidings—locally, it's still mentioned as "the worst-kept secret in Georgetown's history"—but the story stayed in the Low Country. Roosevelt had been in South Carolina more than two weeks before Harold Ickes, with his multiple contacts and networks, learned enough to record in his diary whose guest the president was and where. Henry Stimson found out a week earlier but not from the White House and not because of the crucial position he occupied as the top civilian in the War Department. Baruch, passing through Washington, happened by the secretary of war's office and proudly spilled the beans.

Now it's easily said that the clock was ticking fatefully during his sojourn on the Winyah Bay. Being only human, he wasn't ready to see it that way. In his own mind, he was recharging his batteries, storing up reserve energy for the war's crescendo and his final campaign, at the least endeavoring to convince himself that he might prove equal to whatever lay ahead. (In yet another of the compartments of a mind honeycombed with secret recesses, he may simultaneously have been trying out through this rest cure the experience of actual retirement.)

"The President felt miserable on arrival," Lieutenant William Rigdon, a White House naval aide who was in the official party, later recalled. "I never had known him to be so dispirited; he would have an early dinner and go immediately to bed." Still, that first afternoon Roosevelt had himself wheeled down the grassy bluff forming a front lawn, through a line of majestic live oaks festooned with Spanish moss just taking on a greenish springtime tint, to a dock extending over a shore where alligators occasionally lolled. There, seated in a wheelchair, he dropped a line into the water, getting plenty of sunshine but no bites. From the pier, also from the comfortable corner bedroom he'd occupy on the ground floor of Baruch's spacious mansion, his view across the salt marshes and water was perfectly unspoiled except for the smokestacks of International Paper's biggest plant on a distant horizon, dwarfing a nearby steel mill the size of a thumbnail, or so it appeared from where he sat.

The house itself, fronted by a veranda and six stately columns two stories high, was vaguely antebellum in inspiration despite a brick Georgian facade—Georgian in the sense of English style, not the neighboring Peach State—but it was only fifteen years old, commissioned after a Civil War–era structure called the Old Relick burned to the ground at the end of 1929. Baruch had lent the president more than the corner room. He had turned over the whole mansion to the commander in chief's entourage, graciously withdrawing himself to the nearby home of his daughter, Belle, an accomplished equestrian and pilot, a striking figure at six feet two, whose string of lesbian liaisons her father had learned, with some discomfort, to tolerate. By the time Hobcaw became a temporary base for the leader of the wartime alliance, Belle had taken title to most of the property, whose sandy roads she'd sometimes patrol sitting cross-legged on the hood of a jeep, hunting predatory bobcats and feral hogs. For the war's first year and a half, she and an English lover had nightly stakeouts on the shoreline, searching for German U-boats landing undercover agents, sometimes spotting flashing signals and other signs of intruders—what might have been the sound of paddles, rustling noises in the undergrowth, fleeting shadows—though no agents were apprehended. Then the Coast Guard took over the patrols, augmented by the Camp Lejeune marines for the protection of the top secret guest, though the threat along the coast was deemed to have passed.

Lieutenant Rigdon, junior as he was on the White House staff, was there substituting for the president's usual support team, a sign of how limited Roosevelt's activities at Hobcaw were meant to be. Admiral Leahy was there to relay the latest military bulletins and filter cables from London and Moscow. But the convalescing president was to be protected as much as possible from the routine business of his job that had always followed him on working vacations. The unremitting correspondence, the back-and-forth on political and congressional issues, was to be farmed out to others in Washington. So, it was reasoned, Bill Hassett, who usually traveled with him, and his secretaries Grace Tully and Dorothy Brady could all be left behind. Insofar as possible, this would be a rest cure. Roosevelt's real job now would be to unharness himself as much as a wartime president could. Even movies, a favorite diversion, would be too much. They were available to be shown every night at Hobcaw, but, according to Rigdon the president couldn't be persuaded to stay up much beyond his prescribed bedtime of 9:00.

In their very blankness, the official logs probably exaggerate the resoluteness of the president's inactivity. He was not incurious about the neighborhood, once the nation's largest producer of rice until, after abolition, it was undersold and put out of business by domestic and foreign competitors. Now the old plantations had been taken over by wealthy northerners, of whom Baruch was among the first, who turned them into hunting lodges and posh winter retreats, outposts of Yankee high society. Roosevelt is known to have dropped in on some of these on afternoon drives that are said to have taken him as well by the nearest military unit, a small rescue and recovery team the navy had stationed on the coast to deal with training flights on target practice runs when they ended badly, in the ocean. He's also believed to have driven through the several black villages on Baruch's plantation—leftover slave quarters whose inhabitants, now employees on the estate, were sequestered at Hobcaw during the president's stay as part of the Secret Service effort to keep his whereabouts and activities secret.

No photographs were taken of Roosevelt at Hobcaw. Similarly, no announcement was made of a visit by Mark Clark, who flew down to South Carolina to give him "a full report on developments and battle plans in Italy," a meeting that first surfaces in print in the general's memoir, published six years later. "As usual," Clark would write, "he showed a surprising knowledge of details and was quick to offer ideas as I explained our plans for reaching Rome."

In all likelihood, Roosevelt had been updated by Admiral Leahy on the grindingly slow progress of Allied forces in Italy. He was supposed to be undergoing a total rest, but each day brought new bulletins from the War and Navy Departments summarizing developments in all theaters of the war, usually four single-spaced pages, going theater by theater, augmented by half a dozen maps in the case of the War Department. Two or three times a week, there would be further top secret bulletins from the Office of Strategic Services, the forerunner of the CIA, with morsels of intelligence and eclectic gossip of the sort Roosevelt normally relished—everything from the prospects for an anti-Hitler coup in the upper reaches of the German high command to the deepening plight of Hungarian Jews. The OSS paid particular attention to trends in the Polish government in exile, which Roosevelt and Churchill were still hoping to prod into some sort of rapprochement with Moscow. (Many of the most influential exiles, especially military Poles, were from portions of eastern Poland that Stalin was now claiming as part of the Soviet Union, the agency noted, and therefore least likely to prove pliable.)

The State Department chipped in to this information pool with its own "Daily Telegram," dwelling on problems in the European Advisory Commission in London, where Soviet representatives were digging in and refusing to discuss Poland or any issue besides the surrender terms to be presented to the Germans. The department's daily was occasionally supplemented by long cables, marked "For the President's Eyes Only," from Ambassador Harriman in Moscow reporting on encounters with Stalin or Minister of Foreign Affairs Molotov. The Daily Telegram goes from Dignified (a code name for Hull) to Redwood (for Roosevelt). In other exchanges, the president is Zephyr.

Thus during his sojourn on the plantation, the president was hardly cut off from information. He had always been a remarkably quick study and may have absorbed much of it. We don't know. The bulletins, sitting in Map Room files at the Roosevelt archive at Hyde Park, can't tell us how closely they were read, but they contained plenty of grist for Roosevelt's ongoing, seemingly daily recalibration of prospects in the war and for the peace he still meant to shape. In this period, General Marshall was drafting most of his messages to Churchill, but they all passed before Roosevelt's eyes, with Leahy routinely reminding the general as he sent on a new missive from Downing Street that "any reply thereto must have the President's approval." When the drafts were returned, they were signed, in a noticeably shaky hand, simply "Roosevelt." Regularly the military bulletins reported on "the status and movement" of the new B-29s, long-range bombers that would carry the war to Japan's home islands. Roosevelt had no qualms about intensifying bombardment from the air; he figured it would limit American casualties.

. . .

Leahy found the quiet of Baruch's retreat "almost oppressive" from the first day. Roosevelt, who slept for twelve hours most nights and napped most days after lunch, would have next to nothing to say about how he found it. "In one word, I have rested," he said on the eve of his return to Washington to the three reporters present for what was counted as his 948th press conference. Earlier, he claimed to have made up for all the sleep he'd lost the previous twelve years. His daughter, Anna, who was there for only a day, later said that he'd brought along his stamp collection and a pile of mystery novels. According to her, he never touched the stamps and picked up only one of the mysteries. "She said he would just sit or lie down without trying to do anything," Harold Ickes wrote in his diary. "He must have been in much worse shape than I had realized." At no point in his presidency was he less active or more opaque.

Later, after his return to the White House, he'd claim in a letter to the still convalescing Harry Hopkins that there'd been a method to his inertia: "You have to lead not the life of an invalid but the life of common or garden sense . . . I had a really grand time down at Bernie's—slept twelve hours out of the twenty-four, sat in the sun, never lost my temper, and decided to let the world go hang. The interesting thing is that the world didn't hang."

It took less than a week for him to show signs of getting back to himself. On about the fifth evening, he began to linger over the dinner table, an indication that he was regaining his customary sociability, his need for an audience. For the first time, Howard Bruenn found himself a regular guest at the president's table. He was impressed. "The conversation was animated with [Roosevelt] playing the dominant role," he would write in the clinical notes he eventually published in a medical journal. When Baruch was at the table, it ranged all the way back to the Wilson era. If the cardiologist recalled any nonclinical details, he kept them to himself. Baruch remembered the president playing solitaire after dinner and showing off all the varieties of the game he'd mastered while Admiral Leahy waited patiently to go over some cables that needed replies. Roosevelt didn't wheel himself to the table when others played gin rummy but stayed close enough to follow their banter, joining in the laughter it produced. Limited to one cocktail a night, the president decreed that there would be no seconds for his companions. Pa Watson, assigned the room at Hobcaw next to the president's, started sneaking off to Bellefield, Belle's comfy residence a couple of miles distant, for nightcaps; others in the official party followed. Eventually, the president showed up for lunch on Belle's terrace, driving past her airstrip and the hangar built for her two planes.

After a week, the mail pouches from Washington resumed, and most days the president delved into them. He might not have been in top epistolary form, but he was recognizably himself. On April 23, he sent a bantering reply to Churchill, who had been pressing him to meet Charles de Gaulle, to whom Roosevelt had developed a distinct aversion (stoked, it appears, by Admiral Leahy, who'd been the last U.S. ambassador to the Vichy regime): "If he asks whether I will receive him if he comes, I will incline my head with complete suavity and with all that is required by the etiquette of the 18th century," which is more, he gibed, than Churchill's ancestor the Duke of Marlborough would have done. But he spent more time fishing than working, still getting no bites. His luck changed on April 22, on an afternoon-long cruise aboard a Coast Guard patrol boat out to the open sea, where, circling the wreck of a navy collier called the *Hector*, the presidential party started hauling in bluefish. Roosevelt was credited with seven on this, the most strenuous day of his sojourn in the Low Country. The next day he was game for an eighty-mile sightseeing drive up the coast beyond Pawleys Island to Myrtle Beach.

As traced in Dr. Bruenn's notes, encouraging signs of resilience— evidence the rest cure was having the desired effect—compete with contrary warning signals, leading the cardiologist to minor adjustments in the president's regimen. Aberrant squiggles on an electrocardiogram suggested that the digitalis dosage needed to be upped. A diuretic called Thesodate was deemed to be having no effect on his blood pressure, so it was halted. Bruenn returned to Washington for a conference with McIntire and a panel of navy doctors. "The program of rest and marked limitation of activity is to be rigidly controlled," the president's doctors concluded on April 23. Obviously, their vigilance had not been relaxed.

On April 25, the languid social pace at Hobcaw briefly quickened with the arrival of Eleanor and Anna on a plane that also brought the prime minister of Australia and the president-elect of Costa Rica. The president did his duty as host, entered into a discussion of the Pacific war with the Australian, John Curtin, but confided to Eleanor that while he was feeling better, he still didn't have any "pep." The three news agency reporters, who'd been cooling their heels in Georgetown's leading hotel, weren't summoned to Hobcaw to see Roosevelt and the prime minister together. *The New York Times* had already reported that Curtin would be meeting the president. The actual meeting was covered from Washington on the basis of a White House announcement. It was held, the *Times* said coyly, drawing attention to the news embargo, at "the Southern house where [the president] is having a holiday." The Australian flew home by way of London and apparently relayed his impression of Roosevelt to Churchill, who then passed it on to Sir Alan Brooke: "He said that Roosevelt was not well and that he was no longer the man he had been." The same could be said of himself, the weary prime minister commented.

After their overnight at Hobcaw, Roosevelt traveled to the airfield to see off his wife, daughter, and guests, passing near a supposedly upscale brothel called Sunset Lodge, a celebrated local landmark that might have been pointed out to him because its ruins are still pointed out today. Two days later, an eagerly awaited visitor arrived for a luncheon at which Roosevelt, not Baruch, acted as host. Using gas ration coupons supplied by Baruch, Lucy Rutherfurd motored over from her home in the horse country near Aiken, South Carolina, with a daughter-in-law. The president sat at the head of the dining table; at the other end sat Baruch, who almost certainly knew about the old liaison. Most of the guests, including three admirals—Leahy, McIntire, and Brown—had some connection to the Navy Department, where Franklin Roosevelt was still serving in the summer of 1917, when he was none too discreetly going on picnics and cruises with the tall, statuesque woman now seated on his right. In all probability, they would have had some inkling too, would have known enough to realize it was not a matter for present reminiscence, nor mentioning within the hearing of the president's wife. Dispelling whatever unspoken memories hovered over the table, a message was brought in during the meal with news that a third heart attack in two days had taken the life of Frank Knox, the navy secretary, a Teddy Roosevelt Rough

Rider, newspaper publisher, and running mate to Alf Landon in 1936 who'd signed on with Franklin Roosevelt in 1940 shortly before he declared his availability for a third term (saying, "I am an American first and a Republican after that").

Following Lucy's departure, the three agency reporters were finally summoned to Hobcaw to hear the president express his distress over the loss of the secretary; in his first public utterance in three weeks, he said of Knox what would be said of him in less than a year, that he was "a casualty of the war." The Associated Press dispatch carried a curious dateline, more translucent than transparent. "IN THE SOUTH WITH PRESIDENT ROOSEVELT," it said. Helpfully, the commander in chief was reported to be "bronzed and obviously in improved health."

That same evening, however, in the aftermath of Lucy's visit and the shock of Knox's passing, his blood pressure shot up to 230/120. He was also afflicted by severe abdominal pain and slight nausea, which persisted for the next two days. Dr. Bruenn attributed the pain to gallstones and twice treated him with codeine. The cardiologist waited a month to order an X-ray that confirmed the diagnosis. Obviously, he didn't consider this a crisis. And, in fact, according to a log kept by Lieutenant Rigdon, the president felt well enough to go trolling for catfish up the Black River the afternoon after the first attack. When his abdominal distress flared again, Bruenn placed him on a soft diet of buttered toast dipped in milk (a concoction known as milk toast, fed to children and convalescents), rice pudding, and custard. On May 5, his next-to-last day on Baruch's plantation, the physician was able to write in the running medical commentary he kept for his own reference that the president "appears very well. No complaints. In excellent spirits."

"After a restful four weeks," Admiral Leahy would conclude in his own private diary, "the President had regained his normal condition of health and was displaying some of his accustomed energy." Some, by no means all; still, it was reassuring.

Anyone following the news in those days wouldn't have thought of the president as trolling for catfish and sleeping long hours. His forceful leadership seemed manifest in mounting expectations of the now imminent invasion in Europe and the daily pounding by Allied planes, a minimum of one thousand in any twenty-four-hour period, of German railways, airfields, and industrial targets. In the last thirteen days of April, these round-the-clock waves of bombers were reported to have dropped sixty thousand tons of bombs. None of this suggested a passive, disengaged, out-of-action leader. His military bulletins told him what cheerleaders in the press were generally unable to report: the number of planes lost in these raids. The report on the 771 bombers of the Eighth Air Force sent over Berlin on the single night of April 29, for instance, informed Roosevelt that 63 had not returned to their bases, along with 16 of their fighter plane escorts.

On the home front, his force was felt as well, never more so than the day he was privately entertaining Lucy. That same afternoon, in one of the administration's most flagrant interventions in the domestic economy on behalf of the war effort, the Chicago headquarters and production facilities of the mail-order behemoth Montgomery Ward were taken over by the army on what were declared to be orders from President Roosevelt.

Although one of its subsidiaries was engaged in manufacturing gun mounts and airplane parts, Montgomery Ward had the overwhelming bulk of its business in domestic retail commerce—farmers accounting for 75 percent of its customers—and thus claimed immunity to wartime regulations designed to prevent interruptions of production due to strikes and lockouts. For two years, it had been stalling on collective bargaining with a union that had won the support of a majority of its seventy-five thousand employees. The union complied with a government order not to strike. The company simply ignored an order to negotiate. Attorney General Francis Biddle offered his lawyer's opinion that both the War Labor Disputes Act, a wartime measure, and the emergency powers of the commander in chief inherent in the Constitution reposed in the president ample authority to order a takeover of the company. A platoon of soldiers with fixed bayonets showed up to execute the order. The next day, with the attorney general himself in attendance, the company's crusty chairman, Sewell Avery, was bodily removed from his office by four soldiers, carried as if in a basket, and deposited in his limousine at curbside. As he was spirited away, Avery sought a nasty epithet to hurl at the AG. "You . . . New Dealer!" he cried.

Biddle, in a memoir, called the takeover an opéra bouffe, acknowledging that he may have overplayed his role. His orders came from Jimmy Byrnes, but he had little doubt that the "assistant president" had been on the phone with Roosevelt at Hobcaw and that Roosevelt had given the takeover his blessing. Subsequently, it was clear to him that the president enjoyed the whole performance. When he was hauled before a House investigating panel, Roosevelt cheered him on. "Don't let the boys get you down," he wrote in what Biddle called a "thoroughly typical note," scrawling under his typed initials a jocular battle cry, "Bite 'em!"

The monthlong news blackout on the president's whereabouts was lifted on his return to the White House on May 7. The country was finally told where he'd been sojourning, how comprehensive his rest cure in the Low Country had been, how he'd fished, sunned, and restored his customary levels of energy in time for the war's final and decisive stage. (Nary a word was said about possible gallstones or persistent high blood pressure.) No one expressed a public doubt about the cheery portrait drawn by the three news agency reporters who'd accompanied him to Georgetown (but had been in his company only twice). Standing out in a chorus of hosannas was a celebratory editorial in *The New York Times,* which had opposed his bid for a third term in 1940. Headed "The President Returns, " it began, "Tanned, refreshed and vigorous, President Roosevelt is back at his desk in Washington." His responsibilities would be "redoubled," the *Times* said, in the imminent "finish fight with a strong enemy . . . Now he is prepared for it in body and mind."

Relief, not unmixed with continuing concern, could be heard in the reflections of Roosevelt partisans and some administration insiders. Bill Hassett, the White House official who frequently served as an amanuensis, drafting much of the president's correspondence, found him "brown as a berry, radiant and happy" but wondered if he'd fully recovered. Henry Stimson, after an appointment in the Oval Office, thought the president seemed "much snappier." In contrast, David Niles, a White House political operative, confided to Jonathan Daniels, another staffer, that he thought Roosevelt looked "painted up" for his first press conference, two days after his return. Niles brought back a rumor from his native Boston that the president had undergone a

MAY 17, 1944. On his return from
South Carolina.

prostate operation during his absence, implying cancer without using
the word, then as likely to be whispered in what passed as polite conversation as spoken out loud. Daniels thought he was "not in the least
sunburned." After the passage of decades, no one of these impressions
can be taken as definitive. On balance, they indicate that in the eyes
of most beholders, following the retreat in Baruch's barony—a month
before the Normandy invasion—Franklin Roosevelt remained a convincing president, not one obviously suffering from a wasting, possibly
fatal disease.

Daisy Suckley, who returned on the presidential train from South
Carolina, may be counted as the closest observer in the circle of the
First Family. "Under his tan, he looks thin & drawn & not a bit well,"
she wrote in her diary after joining him at Hobcaw near the end of
his stay. As for the assessment that mattered most, that of Roosevelt
himself, Daisy reported, possibly repeating his own words, he "feels
good-for-nothing." Eleanor Roosevelt was at Hyde Park when her

husband reached the White House. The First Lady didn't rush back. She had appointments to keep in New York and Pittsburgh and joined him only after five days. It may have been in this period, after Hobcaw, that this usually disciplined, many-sided man, seen by most of his countrymen as an embodiment of courage and optimism, allowed himself to voice an inescapable fact of his life that he was normally loath to mention. "I can't live out the normal life span," he supposedly said. That uncharacteristically revealing remark was apparently made to Anna or relayed to her by her mother. (Years later, Anna repeated it in an interview with the writer Jim Bishop.)

As the weeks passed, the salutary effects of the Carolina rest cure began to fade. The president may have looked better to most onlookers on his return to Washington, but his own sense of well-being was at best intermittent, fragile if not feigned. "I am really practically all right," he wrote to Churchill, "though I am still having some tests done on my plumbing and keeping regular hours with much allocation to sleep." After just eight days back in the White House, he said to Admiral Leahy, "Bill, I just hate to run for election. Perhaps the war by that time will have progressed to a point where it will not be necessary for me to be a candidate." In transcribing these words into his diary and later into a memoir, Leahy didn't attempt to make military or political sense of them. What time would "that time" be? The Democrats were scheduled to nominate their candidate for president in less than ten weeks. Was Roosevelt harboring a hope that the Normandy invasion would be so successful, turn the tide of the war so swiftly, that Hitler's Reich would be in a visible state of collapse by that time? If so, where was his backup plan on a successor? Or was he trying to persuade himself that he hadn't committed himself to a decision when he was already past the point of no return? Here was Wallace's unreadable "water-man," rowing in one direction, looking in another, still keeping all his options open. Or was he merely on the downside of a mood swing?

The written record reveals only one person with a plausible claim to having directly confronted Franklin Roosevelt by this time with an argument that he lacked the stamina to carry on. That was Ed Flynn, the Democratic boss of the Bronx, a trusted consigliere since 1928, when he had a hand in persuading a coyly reluctant Roosevelt to run for governor of New York. How bluntly and fully Flynn managed to make the case for stepping aside, how willing Roosevelt was to hear it, are questions he answered only indirectly in a memoir published two years after the president's death. Invited to spend a night at the White House with his wife after the Hobcaw hiatus, Flynn found Roosevelt unnervingly disengaged. He wrote of his apparent "lack of interest in the problems facing him," of how he now lacked "the power to make decisions," finally, of his uncharacteristic irritability. "In my long acquaintance with him I had never before seen an irritable note," Flynn testified.

It's not a great leap of imagination to conclude that the problem in which Roosevelt seemed uninterested, over which he manifested indecision and irritation, was the problem of the fourth term—the only one he'd likely be discussing at this time with his friend the boss of the Bronx. Having made no discernible headway with the president, Flynn turned to Eleanor. "I spoke with Mrs. Roosevelt and begged her to use whatever influence she had to keep him from running again." The journalist Joseph Lash, Eleanor's close friend and biographer, could find no evidence that she tried.

"All of us knew that Franklin was far from well," she later wrote, "but none of us ever said anything about it—I suppose it was because we felt that if he believed it was his duty to continue in office, there was nothing for us to do but make it as easy as possible for him."

A week after his aside to Leahy about not wanting to run, Daisy Suckley ventured to ask how he'd go about selecting a running mate. "I haven't even decided if I will run myself," he again protested. Sensible Daisy replied that he was "practically nominated already."

Roosevelt's answer showed that his own doubts about his health and stamina remained at the front of his mind. "It wouldn't be fair to the American people to run for another term," he said, if he knew he couldn't serve for four years. At some length, he explained how he'd go about selling the shipbuilder Henry J. Kaiser as an eleventh-hour substitute. Beyond Daisy's diary, there's a hint in a request passed from the White House to J. Edgar Hoover at about this time that Roosevelt was half-serious. The request triggered an FBI field report, undertaken, it appears, to discern whether there were any skeletons in the industrialist's closet. The FBI found Kaiser's relations with labor unions to be generally positive. "I don't think it will be very helpful except that it shows nothing definitely unfavorable," Sam Rosenman wrote, passing it on to the president.

At the White House, a couple of days before that conversation with Daisy, Roosevelt had given Harold Ickes a baffling self-diagnosis involving a mystery hit-and-run ailment that flitted from organ to organ, then gave up its siege:

> It seemed that he had some trouble with his colon, which at first he thought might be a growth. Then suddenly it moved to his left side under his heart. It was very painful. Then, without notice, it moved over to his right side . . . This had the effect of persuading him it could not be a growth. Then suddenly it disappeared and he had no pain.

At the least, this said he was not indifferent to his condition.

Nearly a month later, toward the end of June, Roosevelt was still deluding or kidding himself, giving voice to what he had come to consider his real wish to be relieved of a job that, just two weeks after D-Day, he could not plausibly shed. Here again, like many of us, only more so, he showed himself capable of holding contradictory trains of thought in his mind, priming himself to move in different directions on parallel planes. One of the reasons he didn't step aside after realizing that his Hobcaw rest cure had produced something less than a miracle cure was surely that the opportunity, a manageable off-ramp, didn't present itself. Carrying on was a more obvious choice than getting out. Given the scope of his responsibilities and the apparent expectations of the country as expressed in polls, not to mention his constitutional obligation to stay in office for another seven months, it was hardly an expression of a death wish.

"Here we are," Daisy wrote in her diary, "less than a month before the Dem. Convention & the P. doesn't know if he will run, or not."

CHAPTER 5

Going After "Bigger Coins"

THE FIRST HALF of June 1944 would have been challenging for any president. For one under close medical supervision, coming off a long convalescence, wrestling with doubts about his ability to carry on, the crowded and eventful days might have been too much to handle. Though still trying to hew to a limited schedule, Franklin Roosevelt sailed through them with every appearance of command, breaking a silence over the airwaves of nearly five months in radio addresses to the nation on the nights of June 5 and 6: first to announce the long-anticipated fall of Rome, then to invoke the nation's prayers on the occasion of what's likely to remain for all time the greatest amphibious invasion in history, known ever after by its military designation, D-Day. While thousands were still dying on the beaches of Normandy and tens of thousands scrambling inland off those beaches under withering fire, he turned the very next day to the thorny, potentially pivotal issue of Poland's place in postwar Europe, welcoming the premier of the Polish government in exile and hosting a state dinner that kept him up past midnight. The following day, he discussed secret appropriations for the atom bomb with Secretary Stimson. In between these public and private sessions, he held five of his not-for-quotation press conferences, kept up his correspondence with Stalin and Churchill, finessed the terms for an imminent White House visit by the proud and prickly leader of the anti-Vichy French government in waiting, Charles de Gaulle, and found it possible to give his blessing to Cordell Hull's nearly finished draft of a charter for a United Nations organization, though it departed in places from models he'd previously sketched. Later in this same fateful month, after resting up in Hyde Park, he'd sign the GI Bill of Rights, which would stand as his last significant domestic achievement. Whatever his underlying condition, whatever the eventual outcome of these various initiatives, his performance that fortnight was reassuringly presidential, enough so that his own doubts about his ability to carry on could often be pushed aside.

Roosevelt had initially prepared a stern appeal to the German people, in which he proposed to tell them their defeat was now inevitable, "that this is the time to abandon the teachings of evil." His plan had been to deliver it once the Normandy beachheads had been secured. Churchill passed on it but Stalin chilled the idea with a dose of dour common sense, "taking into consideration," as he put it, "the whole experience of war with the Germans and the character of the Germans." Such an appeal would begin to register with the enemy, this practitioner of mass psychology and intimidation shrewdly reasoned, only after they'd been forced to recognize that the invasion was succeeding. Still looking for an utterance appropriate to this vast venture, the solemn occasion of its launch, the president then reached for the Book of Common Prayer, taking his copy with him to Pa Watson's gentleman's farm in rolling country outside Charlottesville, Virginia, where he spent the inevitably tense weekend before the attack. There, with the help of his daughter and her newsman husband, he drafted the prayer he'd deliver on behalf of the nation at the end of the first day in this newest chapter of the war.

Turbulent weather conditions on the English Channel then forced the delay of the launch and thus the prayer. So it was that on the evening of June 5 the president found himself speaking on the ouster of the Nazis from Rome, with only a passing allusion to "our Allied forces . . . poised for another strike at Western Europe." By dwelling on Italy, he helped reinforce conclusions drawn by German analysts—intelligence agencies, cryptographers, meteorologists—that the cross-channel attack probably wouldn't come for another two weeks or more and would most likely occur in the vicinity of Calais, where the channel is narrowest, a misapprehension the Allies had endeavored to nurture with false intelligence tips fed to known double agents and deceptive radio transmissions conveying orders for dummy military units in Scotland that never existed. Deception, combined with a low cloud cover and failed aerial reconnaissance on the German side, had preserved a measure of surprise, despite the enormous scale of the invasion. So much so that General Erwin Rommel, the dread Desert Fox, now in command of Hitler's Atlantic Wall, was on a brief home leave combined with a visit to the führer as the first wave of 130,000 troops—57,500 of them American—were cramming into 6,483 vessels, including 3,372 landing craft, carrying hundreds of Sherman tanks, bulldozers, and other heavy equipment in addition to the closely packed, heavily laden, sea-tossed troops, all bound down ten designated, mine-swept sea-lanes for Norman shores southwest of Calais. As the president began his fireside chat about the Italian campaign and the fall of Rome, he knew already that General Eisenhower's fateful attack order had finally been given, that U.S. airborne troops and gliders were taking off, that the invasion armada would soon be irreversibly on its way. "We will accept nothing less than full victory!" the general's order proclaimed.

Roosevelt's doctors had prescribed ten hours' sleep a night. He'd had fewer than four when the call came through at 3:00 on the morning of June 6, telling him that American troops had hit the Normandy beaches Rommel had strewn with heavy steel barriers—angled spikes, pyramids, polygons dubbed "Rommel asparagus"—conceived and positioned to thwart armored vehicles, tanks especially. These and nearby German bunkers and artillery positions had been under relentless bombardment from sea and air in order to clear the best possible foothold for the first serried ranks of often seasick, generally keyed-up, even desperate soldiers spilling from jammed-up landing craft into shallow water, sometimes not shallow enough. It was a scene the president could only begin to imagine, but he must have tried. "He sat up in bed and put on his sweater," Eleanor would later recall in an interview, "and from then on he was on the telephone." By 4:00, he had instructed the White House operators to summon the staff, more to experience the momentousness of the occasion than to take up pressing tasks. He was in his office before 10:00 that morning to meet congressional leaders. He then spent more than an hour with General Marshall and his other military chiefs. It's possible he got in a brief afternoon nap after a late lunch under a magnolia tree on the White House lawn. But by 4:00, he was back in his office for a crowded press conference, which he opened on a note more celebratory than solemn, although by then he had some idea of the severity of American casualties, especially on Omaha Beach, casualties that were fewer than feared but still running into the thousands. The final count for June 6 alone would be 4,649 killed, wounded, and missing GIs. By the end of the month, more than one million troops would be landed in France, a force too big to be pushed back into the channel as Hitler had demanded of his generals.

"All smiles, all smiles," the president exclaimed as the reporters filed in at an hour when Graves Registration teams were already tagging corpses on Omaha Beach some thirty-seven hundred miles away, an hour when, as one GI in the Twenty-Ninth Infantry Division recounted, "there were men crying, men moaning, and men screaming." The president was in evident high spirits himself but warned against overconfidence, spinning one of his tall tales, this one about a nameless "fellow" he claimed to know, "a welder or something like that," who quit his job in a munitions plant because he figured the war was almost won. No, the war was far from over. "You don't just land on a beach," he said, "and walk through . . . to Berlin."

A similar caution was woven that evening into the prayer he read over the airwaves, in which he beseeched a divine blessing on the "struggle to preserve our Republic, our religion, and our civilization." In its assured, direct address to the Godhead, its King James locutions, it was an appeal that harked back to the Groton chapel and his old headmaster there, Endicott Peabody. "Success may not come with rushing speed," he acknowledged, "but we shall return again and again; and we know that by Thy grace, and by the righteousness of our cause, our sons will triumph." Blessings were called on those who wouldn't return ("Embrace these, Father, and receive them, Thy heroic servants, into Thy kingdom") and the secular postwar goal of "a world unity that will spell a sure peace." Roosevelt was hardly a regular churchgoer, but the unabashed piety came easily. It had been his practice to summon his cabinet and closest advisers to a private church service of rededication on his inauguration days. In a reflective and understated editorial, *The Washington Post* asked whether his prayer exhibited the humility and contrition "necessary to all real prayer." Noting that King George VI (head, after all, of an established church) had also offered a D-Day prayer, it asked implicitly whether there wasn't something inappropriate, slightly monarchical, about the president's. An irate columnist in the anti-Roosevelt New York *Daily News* seized that faint suggestion and ran with it. The prayer implied, John O'Donnell wrote, that the Supreme Being and "the self-anointed apostle of the Prince of Peace"—that "Big Brain and Golden Voice in the White House"—were "partners in these days of death." That was heavy-handed but not entirely wide of the mark. Roosevelt had put himself forward at this climactic moment in what amounted metaphorically to a bishop's miter, expressing the sense of responsibility he felt for his numberless flock.

"Every movement of his face and hands reflected the tightly contained state of his nerves," said Grace Tully, his secretary, describing his demeanor in the hours leading up to D-Day. The restrained *Post* comment asserted that it was the first time a president had taken it on himself to lead the nation in prayer. A letter writer then pointed out that Warren Harding had tried. Otherwise, the prayer was widely accepted as a grace note, appropriate for a huge undertaking whose immediate consequences and ultimate outcome still hung in the balance. The Government Printing Office would reprint it in Gothic type on four-color scrolls and in a little prayer book that came in a slipcase. Private entrepreneurs sold it on postcards.

It was no coincidence that Roosevelt's reengagement with the unresolved issue of Poland followed swiftly—in fact, immediately—on the Normandy landings. The timing was the president's. Poland, more and more a touchstone of Soviet-American relations, remained the biggest obstacle in the way of the understanding with Stalin in which he'd invested so much time and energy, on which so many of his hopes still hinged: Soviet intervention in the war against Japan, which the Joint Chiefs still deemed critical; agreement on an enforcement mechanism to maintain the "sure peace" for which he'd just prayed; more immediately, the fulfillment of the Soviet dictator's pledge to launch an offensive that would drastically limit Hitler's ability to shift forces to the newly opened western front. The Poles and the Russians were nominally part of the same alliance, but Stalin had broken relations with the Polish exile government over Katyn—specifically, over its appeal to the International Red Cross to investigate the massacre of Polish officers there. Earlier in the year, Roosevelt had offered to mediate in the dispute between Moscow and the exile Poles. Stalin had brushed the offer aside. Now the president was determined to see if he could help heal the breach without offending the dictator. While assuring Stalin that he advanced no proposals of his own, he pressed the Polish premier to fly to Moscow and try to come to an understanding with the Kremlin. He thus offered his own good offices in place of mediation.

What was under discussion at the White House was not the suffering Poland of June 1944, a grim land of unspeakable horrors and more in store, still largely occupied by a huge German army; where Jews by the hundreds of thousands were still being gassed and thrown into industrial crematoria at previously obscure, now forever notorious locations, including Auschwitz-Birkenau, Treblinka, Majdanek, Chelmno, Sobibor; where millions of others had been forcibly displaced from their homes as ethnically unfit by both the Nazis and the Russians; where lands incorporated into the Soviet Union in 1939 were about to be reclaimed and occupied by the Russians. What was under discussion were the dimensions and nature of the Poland that would emerge from this dark age—its borders and ability to set its own course, its relation, ultimately, to its powerful eastern neighbor.

The world at large and Poles in particular didn't yet know of the territorial concessions and trades that Churchill explicitly—and Roosevelt implicitly—had agreed to at Tehran half a year earlier. Forever after, Poles would regard these as a great betrayal, a sellout. American politicians on the right would later take up the cry. But in the midst of the war, at a time when the Russians were doing most of the fighting against the Nazis, the assumptions on which Roosevelt's approach to Poland were based were widely shared. Nowhere were they stated more baldly than in a Walter Lippmann column at the start of the year. "An independent Poland can be restored only if it is allied with Russia," the columnist wrote. "This is the way things are and there's no use pretending we can make them different by talking big and making threats at the Russians."

The president had long since reached that conclusion, though he seldom voiced it. Half a year earlier, a couple of months before going to Tehran, he had a two-hour session at the White House with the

Roman Catholic archbishop of New York, Francis Spellman, later a cardinal, who wrote a detailed memorandum purporting to spell out Roosevelt's view that the Russians had the power to fulfill their territorial ambitions in Eastern Europe. The United States and Britain could not go to war with them. The countries of Eastern Europe would have to adapt to this harsh reality. But the president hoped, so the prelate wrote, "in ten or twenty years the European influences would bring the Russians to become less barbarian." The people of Eastern Europe would "simply have to endure Russian domination" until then. Evidently, this is what Franklin Roosevelt meant, at least some of the time, when he described himself as "a realist."

What was self-evident in the penultimate year of the war could be written off as weak-kneed years later when the less happy consequences of victory were there for all to see, as if set in stone, in Moscow's heavy-handed dominion over Eastern Europe. In the early months of 1944, Stalin's importance as an ally could hardly be overstated. This feeling is manifest in small matters as well as large, for example, in a three-cornered consultation among Roosevelt, Stimson, and the top British officer in the United States, Field Marshall Sir John Dill, over a sensitive question: whether General Marshall had to accept a high military honor the Soviet Union wished to give him. Regulations and custom forbade the acceptance of military honors from a foreign power without the approval of Congress. Stimson, who was torn on the question, passed along Dill's response: "He said that in view of the importance of not offending Stalin, we ought not to hesitate a moment." A deeply reluctant Marshall was ordered to accept the medal. On the very eve of the Normandy landings, Ambassador Andrei Gromyko conferred it on the embarrassed chief of staff at the Soviet embassy.

The same impulse not to offend prevailed on Katyn. The closest the United States came to an inquiry into the massacre of Polish officers involved Ambassador Harriman's daughter Kathleen. He let her go on a carefully staged tour of one of the burial sites near Smolensk that the Russians were laying on for foreign correspondents. Kathleen, then twenty-six, was allowed to peer into graves, attend autopsies, scan postmortem reports. Harriman reported to Roosevelt that she and an embassy official who accompanied her found the evidence inconclusive but came away with the impression that "in all probability the massacre was perpetrated by the Germans." That report went no further than Roosevelt's desk but may have influenced him. When another U.S. ambassador concluded that the Russians were the guilty party, the president ordered him to suppress his report. "I have noted with concern your plan to publish an unfavorable opinion of one of our allies," he wrote. In conversation, he supposedly said, "This is entirely German propaganda and a German plot." What he actually believed and what, as a devout utilitarian, he chose to believe may not have been identical propositions in this instance. It was Mikhail Gorbachev who would deliver the final verdict in 1990 as the Soviet bloc was breaking up. He acknowledged then the wholesale slaughter of fifteen thousand Polish officers in 1940 near Katyn as the handiwork of the NKVD, Stalin's secret police.

What matters here is that the issue of Katyn had crossed Roosevelt's desk at least twice in the four months preceding the hurriedly arranged June 1944 visit of the Polish premier, Stanisław Mikołajczyk, called Mick by some of his American and British interlocutors, Stan by others. The two men had met once before, in early 1941, when Stalin and Hitler were still allies and the United States still stood on the sidelines. The Pole later recalled Roosevelt's "ringing condemnation" then of the Soviet occupation of Polish lands. This time, there'd be no condemnation, ringing or otherwise. Roosevelt had his self-assigned task: reopening some semblance of a relationship between Moscow and the exile Poles in London whose limited forces, remnants of the army Hitler chased, had just a couple of weeks earlier raised a Polish flag atop the bombed-out monastery at Monte Cassino south of Rome and who would soon have units fighting the Nazis in France. Such a reopening would require shoving Katyn as far into the shadows as possible. As a matter of realpolitik, the Poles were being asked to emulate the morally dubious Anglo-American example of absolute silence on what remained for them a burning issue. It's doubtful that the word "Katyn" was uttered by Roosevelt or Mikołajczyk in their four meetings. The reasons for this restraint would have been understood on both sides.

Our best record of Roosevelt's conversation with the Polish premier comes in a memoir published by the visitor four years later, following his flight from a Poland in which the transition to outright Communist rule had been essentially sealed. On his visit to the White House, the memoir relates, an optimistic Roosevelt deployed a characterization he'd first used on his return from Tehran, cheerfully assuring his guest that Stalin was "a realist."

"We mustn't forget when we judge Soviet actions," he quoted the president as saying, "that the Soviet Union has had only two years of experience in international relations. But of one thing I am certain, Stalin is not an imperialist." (It's a judgment that might have owed something to the dictator's easy assent, at their first tête-à-tête, to his own view on Indochina.) Looking to the future, Roosevelt declared his intention to plunge in as a mediator, once the November election—in which he was still not committed to run—was behind him. He seemed sure that the dictator, whom he'd just portrayed as inexperienced, would welcome his help.

Stalin, he said confidentially, couldn't comprehend "the device known as free elections," the pressures it released. As a democrat, Mikołajczyk would. The president was out to win the Pole's trust by seeming to confide but didn't tell the whole story. Dodging the key question posed by his visitor—whether any understanding had been reached on Polish frontiers at Tehran—he promised to use his influence to bring about a free and undivided Poland. It's a response that might in a semantic stretch be classed as diplomatic but one that leaves out his own tacit acceptance at Tehran of Churchill's agreement with Stalin; he also omitted the awkward fact that the dictator had already rejected his offer of mediation.

Finally, having dwelled on his good intentions, he got down to hard facts. He ticked off a catalog of cities and regions in disputed frontier areas that he hoped to get for Poland, including Silesia, East Prussia, Königsberg, and Lwów (now known as Lviv and situated in Ukraine). Vilna, he acknowledged, would be more than he could manage. The premier was struck by his "surprising knowledge of our country." He also was immediately aware that Roosevelt's catalog described a reconfigured Poland after all, "a change from his earlier statement that he opposes partition."

Roosevelt tells him that Stalin's eagerness for a good relationship with the United States is the best guarantee of a free Poland. He also delivers an obvious, harsh truth: "On your own, you have no chance to beat Russia, and let me tell you now, the British and the Americans have no intention of fighting Russia." The president's appeal can be variously characterized as overconfident, realistic, naive, tough, subtle, shifty, insistent, friendly. No contradiction or nuance is lost on his visitor. The Pole finally allows himself to be steered. Knowing what failure to reach an accord will mean for his country, soon to be occupied by Soviet forces, he promises to seek a meeting with Stalin. Roosevelt fires off a placating, carefully drafted message to the man in the Kremlin. Mikołajczyk, he assures the dictator, is a reasonable man who'll "not allow any petty considerations to stand in the way of his efforts to reach a solution with you." Presumably, he wasn't thinking of Katyn when he reached for the word "petty."

Months later, at the end of the year, Roosevelt would dispatch another letter to Stalin, standing by his original estimate of Premier Mick, describing him as "the only Polish leader in sight who seems to offer a genuine solution of the difficult and dangerous Polish question." It had become a theme. Put another way, Mick had become a chessboard knight the president kept trying to put in play. In three months, Stalin went through two rounds of meetings with Mikołajczyk, apparently at the president's behest. But early on it became clear that the dictator had set his own course.*

Henry Stimson, who'd served as secretary of state in the Hoover years, felt strongly that the United States should keep its distance from the brutal events that he felt were sure to transpire in "the Polish corridor." But when he sits down to record in his diary his impressions of Roosevelt's performance at the White House dinner for the Polish premier, he's full of admiration. The president, he says, "made one of the most tasteful and sweet little speeches I've ever heard him make [covering] the restoration of Poland in a way which could not in any way be offensive and yet pointed out the absolute necessity of Poland being reasonable in her demands for the restoration of her territory."

Roosevelt's renewed, ultimately futile effort on Poland in the immediate aftermath of the Normandy landings was a gambit largely of his own devising. He didn't, on this round, delegate it to a subordinate. What stands out on close examination is the deftness with which he pursued it, starting with his timing. The long-promised "second front"

---

* On July 22, with the date for Mikołajczyk's visit to Moscow still to be settled, the Polish Committee of National Liberation was formed in Lublin under Soviet auspices as a Kremlin-backed substitute for the exile government in London that Roosevelt's guest nominally led.

has finally been opened. Nothing could better demonstrate the good faith of the Allies to Stalin, who immediately hailed the landings as "an unheard of achievement, the magnitude of which has never been undertaken in the history of warfare." Then, as a gesture of gratitude, the dictator sent Roosevelt a framed portrait of himself, bemedaled in full uniform, and autographed, "To President Franklin D. Roosevelt in memory of the days of the invasion of Northern France by the allied American and British liberating armies. From his friend Joseph V. Stalin." He also renewed his pledge to launch his promised offensive, which would help limit American casualties. It's a high point of the Soviet-American alliance, and it's this moment that Roosevelt, seizing the best opportunity he's likely to have, has chosen to make his move on Poland.

His conversations with Premier Mick have an orchestrated counterpoint in Moscow, where his ambassador, Averell Harriman, has been instructed to assure the Russians that Roosevelt recognizes their stand on Polish boundary issues but counts on them to deal with the Poles "in an understanding manner," for instance by letting go of Lwów. The dictator didn't rule out such a gesture when Harriman sat down with him on the evening of June 10, five days after the furious, fraught opening of the second front. He appeared pleased by the president's attitude and promised to keep him informed. "This is the first friendly talk I've had with Stalin about the Poles," the ambassador cabled, "and I get the feeling that he saw a solution in the making."

Thus when Mikołajczyk returned to the White House two days later, Roosevelt had some basis for his optimistic take on Polish-Soviet relations. But he was not swept away. "In all our dealings with Stalin we must keep our fingers crossed," he told the premier, whose life and career would be changed by his appeal.* The commonplace figure of speech injected a note of realism more telling than the big helping of optimism he'd just served up. He used it again. A couple of weeks later, Daisy Suckley, who knew little or nothing about Russia or Poland, effused for the man she revered over the wonder that

---

* Mikołajczyk, a popular politician, would return to Warsaw in June 1945 as a member of a coalition government engineered by the Russians, finally organizing a non-Communist opposition that would almost certainly have won a majority if the election hadn't been crudely rigged by the security police. In 1947, he escaped into exile for a second time, ultimately settling in Washington, where he died in 1966.

he and Stalin were now partners, working together on the coming peace.

Roosevelt turned taciturn. He was not so sure. "The P. smiled & said, he keeps his fingers crossed," Daisy wrote in her diary. Earlier he'd told the cabinet that keeping the Russians "cozy with us" was a tricky, "ticklish" affair. He was still maneuvering, looking for a way forward as the war entered its final phase, neither a spent force nor an icon: a statesman, his admirers would ever after say.

Asked at one of his press conferences whether the Soviet Union was proving to be "an active and satisfactory collaborator" in planning for the postwar world, the president betrayed no doubts. "Absolutely," he said. "Yes." He gave a more nuanced, darker response to the *Saturday Evening Post* writer he'd used a year earlier to send aloft a message to Stalin from a Washington source designated then, by mutual agreement, as the "highest authority." This time around, the writer, Forrest Davis, was denied so transparent an attribution; the most he could say, after what we can imagine was a round of hard bargaining with the White House press office, was that he found his oracle in "the highest American quarters." Having been exposed to the thinking there, he declared the president to be banking on the idea that "the Soviet Union needs peace and is willing to pay for it by collaborating with the west." Moscow's ultimate intentions were said to be "undecipherable" in Roosevelt's view, so the "soft policy" he'd chosen to pursue involved a conscious gamble, full of risks. What alternative did the president see? As expounded by the magazine writer, it was "a Russia excluded, aggrieved and driven in on itself to prepare for the inevitable war of continents." Because these are Davis's words, not Roosevelt's, the White House was not required to disown the dark vision they described.

Nor did it disown his vision of an international security organization as it was portrayed in the magazine: "He still opposes a strongly bureaucratic United Nations with a capital of its own, housed in a marble palace such as that of Geneva." It would have no supranational armed force; instead, it would rely on the great powers—his Four Policemen—who'd form an "executive committee," consulting among themselves, usually by telephone, relying mostly on airpower to suppress threats to peace. The great powers could act without prior approval by the assembly, "or whatever the general worldwide debating society might be called." The assembly would have neither a secretariat nor "a settled habitat" but would meet, regularly or irregularly, in a succession of temporary capitals. Later he'd mention the Azores and Hawaii as possible headquarter sites for the executive committee (soon renamed the executive council, finally the Security Council). There's only one word in the article that's presented as having actually been spoken by Roosevelt, who's described as "an exponent of the realistic great power theory" and, above all, a pragmatist. It has to do with the prospect of these powers, including the United States, relinquishing any measure of their sovereignty to an embryonic peacekeeping organ as advocated by hopeful neo-Wilsonians. That word was a cutting, dismissive "nonsense."

What Roosevelt chose to impart on one particular afternoon in this circuitous fashion to *The Saturday Evening Post* (and through it to American voters, Congress, and the Kremlin) cannot be taken as definitive. In describing a floating international organization of no fixed abode, he was trying to reassure several constituencies at once that there was no global superstate in the offing, no secret design involving the United States in all the affairs of the world. His aim was to get a postwar settlement that could pass the Senate by better than the required two-thirds margin, carry Stalin along, and forestall another war. It was also to keep the coming peace accord out of the election campaign on which the curtain was about to go up. As usual, he was at once calculating and visionary. As usual, he was playing for time.*

It was his ailing, aging secretary of state who kept the planning for a new international organization on track. Cordell Hull was ten years older than his president and afflicted with heart and lung disease, the reason advanced for the two months he spent resting in Florida in the wartime winters. In his mind-numbing 1,742-page doorstop of a memoir, the Tennessean would write that Roosevelt initially "did not want an over-all international organization," just the "Four Policemen" loosely tied to various regional councils and international agencies. Step by step, the president gave way, according to the secretary's

---

* When the Senate finally voted on the UN Charter, on July 28, 1945, it gave its consent by an overwhelming margin, 89–2.

version, until finally there was a design that could be shown to the British, the Russians, and the eight senators with whom Hull had been conferring. Roosevelt's studied recalcitrance served a tactical purpose. It kept planning for a new international organization under wraps until the war had taken a decisive turn. Hull had five sessions with the president following his return from South Carolina, keeping him up to date on the work of his drafting committee and the attitude of the Republicans in his bipartisan panel. At the fifth session, on June 15, a week and two days after D-Day, he brought along Leo Pasvolsky, other key aides, and a draft of a statement to which he wanted the president to attach his own name, thereby taking ownership of Hull's program. The statement was issued that afternoon without ceremony, without the president even in attendance, as a single-page White House press release. But it bore his stamp.

Unlike Woodrow Wilson, Roosevelt didn't summon a joint session of Congress or publish a draft of the charter. Few details were provided. "The maintenance of peace and security must be the joint task of all peace-loving nations," the statement said. But "threats to the peace and breaches of the peace" would be the specific responsibility of a council composed of "the four major nations" and a "suitable number" of other countries elected for limited terms by the assembly.*

The organization wouldn't have "its own police force." How its peacekeeping machinery would work was left to the imagination. No mention was made of the draft's tentative provision for a "president" of the world organization to be elected by the assembly, a position about which Roosevelt had occasionally indulged in reveries, imagining himself occupying it in a small, scaled-down office with the help of a couple of secretaries. "The P. would like to be that person if he could," Daisy had written as recently as June 4.

Nothing was said, either, about a veto, which Republican senators wanted as much as the Russians at this preliminary stage; they sought it as a guarantee of American sovereignty, and Hull, the old Wilsonian, went along with Roosevelt's backing. Senator Arthur Vandenberg, an influential Republican on the Foreign Relations Committee, referred

* It turned out to be five major nations, with the inclusion of France, which was finally raised to the status of a permanent council member at the Yalta Conference, where Roosevelt, no Francophile, gave in to British persistence on this point.

glowingly to "our American veto." Something like the "reservations" Henry Cabot Lodge had demanded in 1919 was thus built into the program, enabling Roosevelt to praise the "non-partisan nature of the consultations" on which it was based. "The national interest demands a national program," his statement said. It would be a new beginning. Opening old wounds served no useful political purpose. So there wasn't even a passing allusion to 1919, the struggle then over the now moribund League of Nations, or the ghost of Woodrow Wilson. Just three years earlier, a fierce political battle had raged in Congress and across the land over the prospect of American intervention in another world war. Now, with the release of a bland press release, it could be presented as a foregone conclusion that the United States had to lead in peace as well as war. On that basis, a *New York Times* editorial pronounced the skimpy statement "no less historic in its way than the invasion of the European continent and our vast strides in the Pacific . . . an act of statesmanship that does credit to [the president's] sense of timing and his sense of the role of the United States in one of the great crises of history."

A commentator in the *New York Herald Tribune* injected a note of skepticism, calling it "a plan in soft focus; a framework for future world cooperation so starry and nebulous as to fit almost anybody's dream." Devout internationalists, deeming themselves enlightened, felt let down by the derision of the "superstate" of their fond imagining in Roosevelt's statement, its sharp rejection of the possibility of an international police force. Sumner Welles was among those who now found fault with the dominant role for the big powers that it foreshadowed, which struck them as a departure from the Wilsonian ideal.

Playing to a broader audience, the political ringmaster in the White House could imagine he'd carry the country with him into a postwar settlement, thereby avoiding Wilson's failure. Still, he had little faith himself that tinkering with the structure of an international organization would insure the peace. Relations among the big powers, he still felt, would be decisive. At best, as the scholar Warren Kimball has written, he saw the new organization as "a convenient venue for Great Power negotiations." In simplest terms, the future would still pivot on relations between Washington and Moscow, himself and Stalin. The Soviet dictator appeared to grasp the stakes for which Roosevelt was playing. Speaking in the same period to Milovan Djilas, the Yugoslav

Communist later imprisoned as a liberal dissident, Stalin remarked, "Churchill is the kind of man who will pick your pocket for a kopek if you don't watch him . . . Roosevelt is not like that. He dips in his hand only for bigger coins." He was vaguely hoping for a transformation of the Soviet state and its hard-bitten leader, a kind of conversion; expressed in Russian terms, something like the policy of glasnost, or openness, Gorbachev would proclaim a mere forty-two years later. Seen in that light, Roosevelt was premature by two generations.

Very gradually, as June progressed, campaign politics began to claim more of the president's attention. Not always did he sound as forlorn and detached from the subject as he did in his private venting when his audience was limited to the faithful Daisy. A week after D-Day, Jonathan Daniels noted a marked change in his boss's temperament. He was now "obviously a candidate thinking politics." Earlier that same day, June 13, London had been struck by the first of what would eventually amount to more than twenty-four hundred German V-1 missiles to rain down on the British capital in the latter half of 1944. The Normandy beachhead, in the writer Rick Atkinson's words, remained "pinched and crowded." Three hundred thousand troops had been landed, thirty-four armored battalions, and two thousand tanks, but temporarily stymied by German counterattacks, they'd now "nowhere to go." Yet in Washington, Franklin Roosevelt seemed more open to political conversation and plotting than he'd been in months, having realized, perhaps, that the war's end wouldn't come as soon as he'd hoped. To his watchful aides, this signaled a revival.

On June 14, he dictated an unusually peevish yet amusing memo to Jimmy Byrnes on an issue of minuscule import that can be read as reflecting his renewed immersion in politics and eagerness to show off how much he wished it could be otherwise. The issue was whether Senate custom should be allowed to dictate the appointment of a New Hampshire Republican, Senator Charles Tobey, to the delegation to a conference on the international monetary system simply because it was to be held in his home state, at Bretton Woods, and he had seniority. "Tobey certainly has not got the capacity," he fulminated. "If this were not an election year, I would go ahead and offer the place to the best Republican . . . I feel that I am spineless and almost weak-minded . . . I am a shellfish and hereby yield in this fool situation—incidentally not for the first time. I agree to the appointment of Tobey, even though I still think that he is a moron and will do us no good."

Medical historians have speculated loosely about the damage arteriosclerosis might have done to the president's brain. The term "secondary metabolic encephalopathy" surfaces ominously in these writings. The memo shows he had no trouble expressing himself; he could be as pungent as ever. If anything had been affected, it was his customary self-control and monumental patience. Irritability now sometimes came to the surface, but cabinet members with access to Roosevelt still had to scrounge for clues to his intentions. When Harold Ickes suggested that the time had come for shutting down the internment camps in which 120,000 mostly native-born Japanese-Americans had been confined, the president agreed in principle but cautioned against doing anything "drastic or sudden." The interior secretary took that for a sign that Roosevelt's built-in political calculator was still clicking. "My expectation is that the issue will continue to be evaded until after the election," he wrote in his diary. (He was right. The "exclusion order" was finally lifted on January 2, 1945, less than two months after the nation went to the polls.) But when he asked Anna Boettiger whom her father was relying on for political advice, she replied, "I don't know. No one."

Most days Roosevelt could almost make himself believe he felt better and was operating more effectively than he had been two months earlier, prior to his long sojourn on the Baruch plantation. He had gotten past D-Day, initiated a new approach to Stalin on Poland, given a green light to the consultations on the shape of the postwar world that would soon culminate in the Bretton Woods conference and the subsequent Dumbarton Oaks gathering on the new world organization. The Manhattan Project was moving forward but claimed an amazingly scant amount of his time, in part because very few people around him knew of its existence. From time to time, he mentioned a need to bring new faces into the White House and cabinet "after November"—Daniels took this as the surest sign that he'd resolved on a fourth term—but apart from naming replacements for the discarded

Sumner Welles to a subcabinet post as undersecretary of state and the deceased navy secretary, Frank Knox, he'd done little to renew a cabinet that by now included three septuagenarians—Hull, Stimson, and Ickes—and six others who'd been in their positions for the whole of his third term or longer. Soon Thomas Dewey, now first-term New York governor and certain Republican nominee, would be pointing at "the men in the White House who have grown old, tired, stubborn and quarrelsome," a formulation that sought to make an issue of the administration's fading vigor and plainly implied that more could—might yet—be said about the president's. A Gallup poll purported to show that 34 percent of the voting public doubted Roosevelt could complete another term, a figure that pretty much matched the proportion of anti-Roosevelt respondents and might therefore have expressed more hope than concern.

In these circumstances, preserving his energy became a political as well as a medical necessity for the president. Before D-Day, he'd hinted in one of his off-the-record press sessions that he might be "apt to disappear," implying he'd seek to be as close as possible to the action at the start of a major military campaign; the previous day, he'd actually ordered Admiral Leahy to make arrangements for him to cross the Atlantic, perhaps to London or the British side of the channel. But he changed his mind overnight, presumably to avoid the strain. Sometimes the press of work forced him to skip his afternoon naps and stay up an hour or two past his prescribed bedtime. But on the whole, he kept within the boundaries his physicians had laid down. No longer did he invite guests in for his customary "children's hour," a nightly ritual at which he'd cheerfully mix martinis and old-fashioneds and entertain by gossiping and reminiscing in a lighthearted vein, putting aside anything weighty. Now the cocktails were often replaced by a sherry, and the dinners that followed were nearly always for "the household," according to White House logs; usually that meant Anna and John Boettiger, always Daisy Suckley when she'd been fetched from the Hudson valley, Eleanor if she happened to be home and available. Missing from these gatherings now was Märtha, Crown Princess of Norway, who'd become something of a fixture in the war years while her husband, Crown Prince (later king) Olav, remained in London, conferring legitimacy on his exile government. A tall and stylish brunette with large, expressive brown eyes and not much to say, she listened to the president with every appearance of rapt delight; they flirted openly. Roosevelt paid close attention to the arrangements the Secret Service made for the comfort and security of the princess and her three children, whose safety was the declared reason for her decision to put an ocean between herself and her husband. For several years, Roosevelt treated her as almost a member of the family, even asking her to call him "godfather," spending countless hours in her company. There had always been a Märtha, Eleanor said dismissively, acknowledging his need and her failure when it came to flattering her husband's ego. The problem with Märtha, as Admiral Leahy noted, was that she "never knows when to leave" (to which Roosevelt replied, according to Daisy, "She goes out so rarely and sees so few people that she can't bear to go home"). Once the president was put on a restricted schedule, she'd become an inconvenient evening guest.

Precise data on Roosevelt's health become sketchy after his return from the Baruch plantation. Daily blood pressure readings and details of his medications were kept meticulously in his medical file, the one that was removed from the safe at the naval hospital in Bethesda shortly after his death and never seen again. In all that survives of the notes kept privately by his cardiologist, Dr. Bruenn, few daily readings are given after May 2. "The time from the middle of May to the early part of August was without incident relative to the President's health," Bruenn would say in his 1970 article in a medical journal. This was the period in which Roosevelt finally had to come to grips with the long-pending question of the fourth term. On how he was actually feeling in these weeks, Daisy Suckley remains the best guide. "I noticed that he sits rather tiredly on his chair, and you can see his heart thumping beneath his shirt," she wrote in her diary on June 20. Two days later, her note says, "The P. seems definitely better to me, though he says the blood pressure is still acting queerly & against the rules."

A cardiologist's role in caring for the president from day to day had yet to be revealed. After two months, Howard Bruenn's name hadn't been mentioned in any press report or published in any manifest of the president's traveling companions. Admiral McIntire called in Drs. Lahey and Paullin, the same consultants who examined Roosevelt in early April after Bruenn's troubling diagnosis, to look him over again at the end of May. The session lasted for more than an hour. Paullin later recalled that Roosevelt was "very jovial." McIntire's ghostwritten memoir made much of an automotive analogy Paullin spun out for Roosevelt on that occasion, telling him his heart and arteries were like the tires and engine of a car that had already piled up a lot of mileage: "If you want to finish the journey, traveling the last ten thousand miles without mishap . . . you've got to slow down." As recounted, the sermonette seems redundant, almost an insult to the patient's intelligence, considering he'd long since taken the point and slowed down, so conspicuously that habitual skeptics wondered whether the real issue was his political health. Walter Trohan, the normally resourceful, sometimes mischievous White House correspondent of Colonel McCormick's *Chicago Tribune,* cited "political observers" who found something fishy in reports focusing on "the President's health, lightening of duties, checkups and the like." They thought it could all be a ruse, "paving the way for a graceful retirement, if Mr. Roosevelt should decide he would be defeated if he runs for a fourth term." According to journalistic folkways of the time, these unnamed "observers" could have included the reporter himself. He could also have been following up on a steer from his onetime newsroom pal the presidential son-in-law, John Boettiger.

It took a lively imagination, or a cultivated regard for Roosevelt's wiliness, to suggest that he might have been deliberately magnifying his own health concerns. As always, Admiral McIntire smothered legitimate questions with a bland sauce of folksy reassurance. In this regard, Dr. Lahey's reaction was more telling than that of his fellow consultant, Dr. Paullin, but it wouldn't peek into public view until 1986, when the Supreme Judicial Court of Massachusetts ordered the release of a memorandum his successors at the Lahey Clinic had strenuously sought to suppress on grounds that its publication would call into question its promise of confidentiality to its patients.

The confidentiality really at issue in this case could well have been that of a later First Family. John F. Kennedy was a Lahey patient from the age of twelve; that's to say, before Roosevelt. Joseph Kennedy, his father, was a major backer of the clinic, which has been a repository of sensitive Kennedy family medical records. The clinic's resistance to the release of Dr. Lahey's 1944 memorandum was led by Edward B.

Hanify, a Boston lawyer who was simultaneously a board member of the Lahey Clinic and the Kennedy Library. Hanify served as Senator Edward Kennedy's lead lawyer in 1969 when he managed to avoid criminal charges after driving a car off a small country bridge at Chappaquiddick, Massachusetts, an accident that notoriously cost the life of a young woman. Senator Kennedy himself was a member of the Lahey board. The National Archive, on behalf of the Franklin Roosevelt Presidential Library, was on the other side, asserting the significance of the Lahey memorandum, the possible importance to scholars of its preservation.

By the time the full text of the Lahey memorandum was finally published in 2007, Roosevelt had been dead for sixty-two years, his age on the day it was written. Left by the surgeon in the safekeeping of the clinic's office manager, the memorandum had no named recipient; in effect, it was addressed to posterity. Dr. Lahey instructed that it be made public after his death (which came from a heart attack in the midst of an operation he was performing, in 1953) should he ever be criticized for advice he gave Roosevelt. "As I see my duty as a physician, I cannot violate my professional position nor possible professional confidence, but I do wish to be on record concerning possible later criticism," it concludes.

In the record he left, there was no obvious soft-pedaling. On the basis of physical examination, X-rays, and laboratory findings, past and present, he'd told Admiral McIntire, "I did not believe that, if Mr. Roosevelt were elected President again, he had the physical capacity to complete a term"; put another way, "over the four years of another term, he would again have heart failure and be unable to complete it."

The president had been "in heart failure, or at least on the verge of it . . . [as a result of] high blood pressure he has had for a long time," which raised "a question of coronary damage," Lahey wrote. The surgeon's diagnosis makes no mention of metastatic cancer or any other disease. None of this diagnosis was in the public domain in 1944.

"Admiral McIntire was in agreement with this," the note to posterity says of its forecast that Roosevelt couldn't last four years. The surgeon goes on to repeat the advice he gave in April: that the president's physician had "a duty to inform him concerning his capacity." And Roosevelt himself, he says, has "a very serious responsibility" in light of all this to make the selection of a vice president carefully. Again, he declares, "Admiral McIntire agrees with this and has, he states, so informed Mr. Roosevelt."

The note is dated "Monday July 10, 1944." The next morning, Franklin Roosevelt announced he would accept his party's nomination for a fourth term.

On the basis of what we now know, the likeliest catalyst for the memorandum Frank Lahey addressed to posterity would have been a confidential word from the White House physician, whom he'd just seen, that the long-postponed decision had finally been made. Why else would he have been moved to write his apologia that particular Monday? A Willkie Republican who'd spoken out for intervention in the war when the president was still vacillating, Frank Lahey never considered Roosevelt a trustworthy figure. "I have never voted for you and I do not intend doing so next November," he later claimed to have told the president in a face-to-face encounter. He may have expected to see Roosevelt on his trip to Washington the weekend before the announcement, but it was already too late for the message he meant to deliver. Thus his judgment would have had to be conveyed second-hand by the White House physician, if passed on at all. Lahey appears satisfied that it was or would be. His confidence in the admiral wasn't subsequently shaken; witness the fact that they remained cordial friends after Roosevelt's death, using first names then for the first time in their correspondence. "Dear Ross" addressed the Boston surgeon, who was familiarly known by his middle name, as "Dear Howard." Lahey wrote letters of recommendation, including one to President Truman, on behalf of the surgeon general, who was about to lose his job. "I have never known a more completely selfless individual in such a high and influential position," another of those letters declared.

Yet Lahey lived long enough to read McIntire's 1946 memoir, in which the admiral is represented as having told Roosevelt "that his chances of winning through to 1948 were *good*" if he didn't exhaust himself. That's consistent with what the White House physician told all comers at the time, in particular journalists but also cabinet members, Winston Churchill, and Roosevelt's own family. It's the opposite of what the Lahey memorandum says McIntire actually believed. His complete selflessness therefore consisted in doing his best, politically as well as medically, to promote his patient's interests and well-being. If the consultant blamed anyone, it was the patient, not the doctor.

Bound by his conviction that confidentiality was fundamental in any patient-physician relationship, the consultant had to remain silent. But he was uneasy and still felt a need to establish that he himself was never a willing party to what seemed to him a plain deception by a selfless physician and a patient who happened to be commander in chief in time of war. He'd gone to Washington to urge that physician to tell his patient he lacked "the capacity" to carry on through another term. It appears to have been a self-assigned mission, but if the conduct of Roosevelt's doctors ever became controversial, he wanted his confidential advice "on record."

Evidence that the question of his "capacity" had gotten through to Roosevelt—because of either his own reading of himself or something McIntire had said, or maybe both these possibilities—can be found in Daisy's diary. Five days before the date on the Lahey memorandum, she wrote, "He is, *I think,* rather uncertain in his mind about himself: whether he really is strong enough to take on another term—whether he ought to try it . . . whether it is not his *duty* to carry on." Her underscoring of "think" says she wasn't sure; the same seems true of the president. Indecision and inertia had their inevitable effect: He became a candidate when time for a decision finally ran out, just eight days before his party's convention was scheduled to convene.

The president himself was still busy with Charles de Gaulle, who was winding up a five-day visit on the weekend Dr. Lahey made his overnight trip to Washington, possibly with the hope of seeing the First Patient. The task of softening up the proud, unbending Frenchman was one Roosevelt had been stubbornly resisting for months, refusing to extend the full recognition the general sought as head of a provisional authority for the whole of France as it stood on the verge of liberation by Allied forces. Underestimating de Gaulle's support, inclined to see his presumption as an expression of personal rather than national pride, Roosevelt declined to make his usual pragmatic adjustments. The French people, not the Allies, would choose France's leaders, he insisted. Until then, they'd be under occupation, the price of their failure to withstand Hitler, a point that was implied rather than declared. On the eve of D-Day, de Gaulle had threatened to withdraw Free French liaison officers who were supposed to be landing with the invaders. Offended that Eisenhower, as supreme commander, got to precede him in broadcasting an announcement of the invasion and that the Allies had the audacity to seek to review his text, he stalked off saying it was an offense to France that he was being told when to speak and what he could say. Finally, the liaison officers landed with the Allies and de Gaulle spoke to his countrymen, but handling him, fitting him into their plans for his now embattled country, had blown up into a major distraction for Roosevelt, Churchill, and their exasperated generals. "No sons of Iowa farmers would fight to put up statues of de Gaulle in France," an infuriated George Marshall told Anthony Eden. A month later, it was up to Roosevelt to make nice, which he succeeded in accomplishing with his accustomed aplomb, partly in French. "It was by light touches that he sketched in his notions," the visitor later wrote, "and so skillfully that it was difficult to contradict this artist, this seducer."

Invitations from the Free French mission described de Gaulle as "President" of the Provisional Government of the French Republic. Roosevelt insisted on calling him "General" instead but sent him away with more in the recognition department than he had when he landed. For the next few months, until it finally extended full recognition in October, the United States acknowledged de Gaulle's paper structure as the de facto government of France so long as it was agreed, Roosevelt specified in a note to Churchill, that its rule would be merely civil and that Eisenhower had "complete authority" within French borders "to do what he feels necessary to conduct effective military operations."

As far as Roosevelt was concerned, de Gaulle was not his most important visitor that muggy July weekend. In the all but inviolate privacy of his heart and mind, Lucy Mercer Rutherfurd got top billing and much more of the president's time than the official state guest. Eleanor was ensconced at her own Hyde Park getaway, Val-Kill cottage, freeing her husband to invite his old friend to the White House. She arrived after dinner on Friday, July 7, the first of three consecutive days in which the presumptive former lovers were able to be together. There was much to talk about if he was prepared to unburden himself. That same afternoon, he had a session with Robert Hannegan, the Democratic chairman, the last they'd have before the big anticlimax planned for Tuesday the eleventh—his announcement that although he was reluctant to stand as a candidate, he'd be standing nonetheless—so presumably the final arrangements had now been made.

Here again the timeline is tantalizing, maybe suggestive. On Saturday evening, he called for his limousine and had himself chauffeured to 2238 Q Street, where Lucy stayed with her sister, to pick her up personally and bring her back to the White House for dinner with Anna and her husband. This time, the president's guest came as Mrs. Rutherfurd; the "Mrs. Johnson" ruse that previously masked her identity had been discarded. Eleanor, it seemed, was now the only member of the household who had to be kept in the dark. Anna well knew that by merely arranging the dinner and sitting at the same table with Lucy, she was guilty of what her mother would regard as high treason. She also felt she had no choice and that it was her duty at this late date—in the lives of her parents, her own life, even the moment in history—to support, not judge, a father who carried such burdens. Beyond that, on encountering Lucy for the first time since her girlhood, she saw instantly that she was not just another of the worshipful women Roosevelt gathered around himself. "I still found Mrs. Rutherfurd to be a most attractive, stately, but warm and friendly person," she wrote some years later. "She certainly had an innate dignity and poise."

Lucy and Franklin withdrew after dinner to the president's private quarters, where they remained together until midnight or thereabouts, so late the official logs don't record her departure. On Sunday, he and Lucy had a whole day to themselves at his Shangri-La retreat in Maryland's Catoctin hills, the present Camp David.

It would be a miracle if some hidden safe-deposit box or archive were still to disgorge a summary of their private conversations at this important juncture. The absence of a record, however, doesn't mean they were trivial or unimportant. His decision made, the president might now have felt a need for validation. The other women in his life had their roles, but he was used to managing, or looking past, their reactions. Earnest, clear-eyed, hardworking Eleanor had long since concluded the decision was his and his alone; he was out of the habit of opening up his feelings to her. The ever-faithful Daisy would be uncritical, he knew, also unable to conceal her fears for his survival.

Märtha, the Norwegian crown princess, was diverting, but her opinions, if she had any, seem never to have mattered. Dutiful Anna, like her mother, had no expectation that she might be consulted by her loving, distant, unreadable father.

He didn't need to manage his old, still-secret flame. There's only one document suggesting the tenor of their conversations, and it was possibly several years old by the time they had these hours together on three consecutive days in the early summer of 1944, the longest time they'd spent in each other's company in twenty-seven years. The letter—or, possibly, draft of a letter—from Lucy to Franklin, was undated. She addresses him as "poor darling," out of sympathy for the burden he bears and signs off by writing, "The smallest sends you her love—Bless you as ever L." Judging from this one letter, Lucy is not a writer. What we have (and were never meant to read) is a loosely woven, occasionally inchoate mix of gossip, diffident requests for advice for her stepsons, and deep feeling, mostly for him. When in a long postscript she allows herself to wonder "how much hope you have," she seems to be asking not about themselves or politics but the outcome of the war, thus how much hope for the world, "if only it will be a friendly world." She imagines the "joy" of living in a small house after it's all over, growing vegetables and flowers, instead of one of the several mansions she now inhabits. That could mean they've fantasized together about his newly built Top Cottage. Or not. She ends with a kind of aria, stilted in its phrasing but not in what it conveys:

> I know one should be proud—very proud of your greatness instead of wishing for the soft life of joy [with] the world shut out. One is proud and thankful for what you have given to the world and realizes how much more must still be given this greedy world—which never asks in vain—You have breathed new life into its spirit—and the fate of all that is good is in your dear blessed & capable hands.

If Mrs. Rutherfurd expressed herself again in that vein in those two White House evenings and the long day at Shangri-La, as seems not unlikely, she deserves mention as a factor in the launching of Roosevelt's final campaign, a player in the layered drama his life had become.

CHAPTER 6

The Great Tantalizer

"I THINK YOU OUGHT TO SEE a lot of Siberia," Franklin Roosevelt
advised Henry Wallace when his vice president sought his approval
for a journey to the Soviet Union in the spring of 1944. A warier politician than the Iowan might have wondered whether the president's
suggestion carried a sinister double meaning politically, whether he
was being sent into exile, put in the deep freeze. To the extent he
was a politician at all, Wallace was an unusual one, emerging in the
war years as a tribune for vague, windy amplifications of his leader's
terse, aspirational Four Freedoms, which only contributed to his own
reputation as a "dreamer" and "mystic" among party professionals.
He'd been the influential editor of a thriving agriculture journal and
prosperous breeder of hybrid corn before coming to Washington as
agriculture secretary. The goal of "freedom from want" on a global
scale thus provided him with a congenial platform. It also opened him
to mockery, the widely repeated gibe that he was promising to give
"a quart of milk to every Hottentot."

Not given to doubting himself, he was capable of suspecting the
motives of others. Roosevelt both perplexed and inspired him. Wallace
spent much time, his diary shows, seeking to decipher the president's
nonlinear, elusive patterns of thought, which struck him as unpre-
dictable to the point of being unreliable. The vice president wasn't
altogether humorless. No one would have called him unfriendly. Nor
would anyone have called him gregarious. Somewhat remote, unfailingly earnest, inwardly self-righteous, he heard what he wanted to
hear, believed what he wanted to believe. What he wanted to believe

most of all this election year was that his president, in sending him on a mission to the Soviet Union and China—two of the Big Four that would supposedly uphold the peace to come—was singling him out for large responsibilities in a postwar era that Wallace had promoted in a widely noticed speech as the "century of the common man." Visionary or woolly, depending on the hearer—Clare Boothe Luce memorably put his uplifting discourses down as "globaloney"—he'd won Eleanor Roosevelt's regard and a following in the New Deal, liberal wing of the Democratic Party he couldn't have claimed four years earlier when Roosevelt strong-armed his selection as running mate through a convention so resistant to this former Republican, who hadn't registered as a Democrat until 1936, nor ever before stood for public office, that his acceptance speech had to be canceled.

Four years later, rather than cultivating fellow Democrats as the 1944 convention approached and the war in Europe hurtled to its climax, the vice president of the United States passed an astonishing stretch of nearly four weeks in Siberia on a seemingly endless and meaningless goodwill mission, verging on a pilgrimage. Before arriving there, he'd convinced himself that Siberia was a "new frontier" peopled by "pioneers." He stopped at eighteen places, never hearing the word "gulag" nor suspecting the stark reality of penal colonies and forced labor it describes. "Never has one man learned so little from so much travel," the critic Dwight Macdonald would later write in a scathing profile. Wallace had started studying Russian in preparation for his journey to what had become America's most important wartime ally. Roosevelt hoped the partnership could be sustained after the war with careful management but had his doubts. Wallace tended to assume it would flourish if the British and the State Department didn't sabotage it.

Initially, he'd hoped to land in Russia proper. But the president had zero interest in dispatching him to the Kremlin, in setting the stage for him to encounter Stalin. Ruling Moscow out, he said it was for Wallace's own good. "I think people will be shooting at you during the campaign as being too far to the left," he explained, inviting Wallace to conclude that his renomination was a done deal in the eyes of the one person who really mattered.

Anthony Eden used the word "artistry," and Charles de Gaulle resorted to "artful," to describe the nimble, sometimes duplicitous tactics the president deployed conversationally to achieve his ends. Visitors regularly left his office with a warm feeling they were on the same wavelength with Roosevelt, having received no commitments nor noticed the extent to which he'd deflected them. That seems to be what happened here. (Attorney General Francis Biddle had another way to describe the same phenomenon. In a memoir, he later wrote of the president's "passion for manipulation . . . [his] lack of frankness.")

Insuring that his vice president would virtually disappear from public view, Roosevelt had urged Wallace not to take any reporters on his long trip. By the time he returned from Siberia, Mongolia, and China, he'd traveled 27,132 miles and been away fifty-one days, a period in which he was completely out of touch, he later said, with political developments at home, including a scarcely concealed movement of congressional leaders and party bosses to insure he wasn't reinstated on the Democratic ticket. Just two weeks remained until the opening of the convention, and Roosevelt had already dispatched Sam Rosenman, his trusted aide, to tell the vice president at his first stop in the contiguous United States what he didn't choose to say directly himself: "that I would like to have him as my running mate, but I simply cannot risk creating a permanent split in the party by making the same kind of fight for him that I did at the convention four years ago.

"I am sure," the president added blithely, "he will understand and be glad to step down." That was his way of persuading Rosenman that the mission wouldn't be too difficult. In the end, it proved impossible. When Rosenman told the vice president's staff he would fly out to Seattle to meet him there, he was informed that Wallace would be flying via Chicago instead. When the White House aide offered to meet him in Chicago, Wallace flew directly back to the capital. When finally Rosenman, accompanied by Harold Ickes, caught up with him at his apartment at the Wardman Park Hotel in Washington on July 10, Wallace barely listened. "I have no interest now in discussing political matters," he said stiffly. "I will do so eventually with the President."

The preliminary conversations on the Siberia trip had taken place back in mid-March when the president's health was becoming a persistent worry and his doubts about his own ability to carry on were rising. Had a cardiologist not been put on his case that month, it's far from inconceivable that he might have passed away before the convention, making Henry Wallace president by constitutional fiat. The swearing-in could have taken place in some Siberian outpost such as Irkutsk, where Wallace made a sweet, soggy speech comparing Stalin's Siberia to the American frontier of the nineteenth century. That might-have-been persisted for months. Wallace could have become president any day before Election Day 1944.*

Many months later, after Roosevelt had passed from the scene, leading Democrats would claim that such a possibility had been in the forefront of their consciousness all along. There's actually little contemporaneous evidence that politicians in the first half of 1944 had as much foresight as they later claimed. The treasurer of the Democratic Party, a California oilman named Ed Pauley, deposited four prideful accounts in various archives taking credit for a "conspiracy" he claims to have led to guarantee that Henry Wallace wouldn't become the next president by succession. Pauley warned his colleagues, so he later wrote, "You are not nominating a Vice President of the United States but a President." That, he said, was his "slogan." Some were slow to recognize, Pauley also said, "that almost any minute there might not be any Roosevelt anymore." It's no wonder. Roosevelt had been in charge so long it wasn't easy to imagine a world without him. Those who could, including Pauley, didn't put their thoughts in writing at the time. None of them were privy to Dr. Bruenn's diagnosis or Dr. Lahey's conclusions.

Pauley left more of a paper trail about the succession than Roosevelt, who, characteristically, left none. That doesn't mean the oilman was as influential as he thought he was in keeping Wallace off the ticket. If we focus on Pauley's recollections, Roosevelt comes across as passive, easily influenced, too exhausted and distracted by his wartime responsibilities to concentrate on the question of a running mate. If we focus on Roosevelt himself, on what he actually did, it becomes clear he was playing his usual long game, keeping an eye on all the factions and constituencies he'd need to hold his coalition together

---

* The Twentieth Amendment to the Constitution, adopted in 1933, provides that a vice president-elect succeeds a president or president-elect who dies before the beginning of his term. Thus Wallace would have had to be reelected to retain his next-in-line status.

for one final run, provided he was able to make it: the labor movement, southern conservatives, northern liberals, the emerging black urban vote, serving soldiers. Holding his options open, as always, this grand master could still play a few political chessboards simultaneously. Wallace had become an inconvenience, a lightning rod for an ongoing struggle over the party's direction. It was Roosevelt, not Pauley and his co-conspirators, who got this inconvenience conveniently out of the way for the better part of two months. In an afternoon's conversation, which Wallace recorded in his diary, the president did it with a little flattery and gentle steering, at a time when his closest aides thought he wasn't paying attention.

Wallace wasn't the only one who thought he got a wink from the "great tantalizer," as Pauley aptly termed the president. Months earlier, on the way home from Tehran, Roosevelt had remarked to Harry Hopkins that "assistant president" Jimmy Byrnes, the former senator and Supreme Court justice, was the best qualified of all his potential running mates or successors. Hopkins carried these tidings to Byrnes, who professed little interest in second place on the ticket but followed up vigorously half a year later in conversation with Roosevelt himself at Shangri-La. Daisy Suckley, an onlooker through a long June afternoon and evening, wrote that Byrnes did most of the talking, making it impossible for Roosevelt to get into a detective story he kept picking up as a way of closing down the chat. Byrnes came away believing Roosevelt "sincere in wanting me for his running mate." Soon he was claiming he'd received a "green light" to marshal his support among convention delegates. At the same time, the White House aides Rosenman and Pa Watson were said to be speaking positively about William O. Douglas of the Supreme Court, once a New Dealer himself and a regular in White House poker games, on whom the president was said to look with favor. Harold Ickes recorded their comments in his diary. Douglas maintained the appearance of a proper judicial distance but did nothing whatsoever to discourage the efforts in his behalf by Tommy Corcoran, a former Roosevelt operative, now a key Washington fixer for hire, and other New Deal veterans. Joseph Kennedy, wealthy father of a future president, a former ambassador to London who'd never quite been cut loose by Roosevelt despite his bitter opposition to Lend-Lease, was also said to be in the justice's corner. It was Kennedy, back in his days as chairman of the Securities and Exchange Commission, who'd brought Douglas from Yale to Washington. The justice wanted to be president, Corcoran said, "worse than Don Quixote wanted Dulcinea."

Somewhere along the line, possibly after the choice was actually made, Roosevelt also told Hopkins that Senator Harry Truman of Missouri would be a useful person to have presiding over the Senate, where he was highly regarded, when the postwar treaties were presented for its advice and consent. ("The President had his eye on him for a long time," Hopkins would tell Robert Sherwood the evening of Roosevelt's funeral.) Wallace, by contrast, was deemed to be woefully lacking in influence there after four years as presiding officer, having often been an absentee from the Capitol, where he'd established close ties to only a small clique of loyal New Dealers gathered around a Pennsylvania senator, Joe Guffey. "I doubt if there are a half dozen senators all told who have been in the Vice President's office," Truman himself would remark soon after he moved in and Wallace moved out. The senator was presumed to have the backing of his fellow Missourian Bob Hannegan, the new Democratic chairman and, as such, the president's principal pipeline to the party (and the party's to him). Ed Flynn, the smooth, well-tailored boss of the Bronx who had been close to Roosevelt since he ran for governor of New York in 1928, would later write that Truman was Roosevelt's "original idea," chosen as the one candidate all factions of the party could support, the one who'd cost the least votes. Hannegan could have been the first to mention the name, but he appears not to have thought he'd made much headway. In Flynn's otherwise unsupported version, the chairman couldn't believe it when he was told Roosevelt had settled on Truman. In any case, by July 5, when Wallace landed in Alaska on his way home from Asia, the juggler had three or four plates in the air and only one of them bore the vice president's name. Clearly there was no done deal.

Flynn, Hannegan, and Pauley each believed and later claimed he'd influenced Roosevelt's slow, almost surgical extraction of Henry Wallace from the position of president-in-waiting. Frank Walker, Hannegan's predecessor as party chairman, made no such claims for himself. A self-effacing Montanan who'd been rewarded for his loyalty by being named to the cabinet as postmaster general, Walker had a clear-eyed view of his president. "Roosevelt would seldom express an opinion on anything," he would write in a memoir. He'd listen, appear to agree with whatever was being advocated, bide his time. So it went in this case, according to this seasoned lieutenant's testimony. "By 1944," he said, "quite a few of us were in doubt as to whether Roosevelt really wanted Henry . . . I don't think he did want him—I never will feel that he really wanted Wallace as a running mate." Before the decision was finally made, Roosevelt's words would occasionally contradict Walker's intuition. Not so his actions. When Eleanor tried to show her support for the vice president in one of her syndicated My Day newspaper columns, her husband blocked it. "Franklin says I must hold it to after the convention," she wrote to her young confidant and future biographer, Joseph Lash. "I wish I were free!"

Roosevelt's reservations went beyond the political price he'd have to pay to keep Wallace on the ticket: possible defections, especially in the South; the loss of swing voters already disillusioned with the New Deal. There were also his doubts about the man himself, which touched on his suitability to be president as well as his usefulness as a running mate. Considering the suitability question was difficult to do without considering his own mortality or, if that were too painful, his recurring dream of escaping the White House at the war's end by resigning, a temptation on which his imagination continued to dwell, most recently in conversations with Bob Hannegan and Ellis Arnall, the governor of Georgia. ("Hannegan said that FDR had positively stated his determination not to serve out the full Fourth Term," so Robert Sherwood wrote after a postwar interview with the Democratic chairman.) In this context, resignation could be a euphemism for dying; constitutionally speaking, there was no difference. No one could say then, let alone now, how Roosevelt parsed such fleeting reflections on himself, the human condition, and the succession, or how often they led him back to his doubts about Wallace. He kept those doubts mostly to himself, but over the previous four years they'd accumulated. It can hardly be argued that he put them out of mind as the need to choose a running mate bore down on him.

First there was an unfinished melodrama left over from the 1940 campaign. It had taken on a name, "the Guru letters," and through many twists and turns it told the story of a leading political figure with an easily ridiculed past as a wide-eyed mystical seeker he now needed to disown. That, of course, was Henry Wallace, who for several years, before and after coming to Washington, exchanged letters in stilted, coded language with a self-proclaimed spiritual "Master" of Russian origin named Nicholas Roerich and his inner circle. Wallace signed himself Galahad or Parsifal, sometimes referring to the president as "the Flaming One," sometimes as "the Vacillating One." Russia was "the Tiger." The Master had been a practicing artist, turning out tempera paintings by the thousands, rendering angular Himalayan peaks in cobalts, purples, and pinks, with Buddhas, Madonnas, or simple pilgrims hovering nearby. Often garbed in Tibetan robes, he drew a following as an inspired interpreter of Eastern spiritualism, both the Himalayan version of Buddhism and the Victorian tributary known as Theosophy. Wallace, a lapsed Presbyterian, had long dabbled in the occult. Reincarnation had struck this plant geneticist as a plausible interpretation of the cosmic order; Roerich struck him as a plausible interpreter. "Long have I been aware of the occasional fragrance from the other world which is the real world," the agriculture secretary wrote in a "Dear Guru" letter in 1934. Soon federal funds were made available to send the Master on an expedition to central Asia in search of rare drought-resistant grasses for breeding and possible propagation in the dust bowl. Wallace also nominated Roerich for the Nobel Peace Prize. The infatuation ended around the time tax evasion charges were filed against his guru, who never returned to the United States. In 1940, with Roosevelt standing for a third term, the Republican National Committee came into possession of copies of letters, typed on government stationery or handwritten, showing that his chosen running mate had been a devotee of this exotic, suspect figure. They weren't used then but were still available for use, as Roosevelt well knew, in 1944. When an important union leader mentioned the movement's support for Wallace in conversation with the president, Roosevelt quipped, "Oh, you are talking about the Yogi Man?" Strike one against the vice president.

A second, more serious basis for Roosevelt's reservations about Wallace as a potential successor arose from a series of messy, even nasty interdepartmental feuds over funding and authority in which he'd become embroiled after being named chairman of the Board of Economic Warfare, a wartime agency charged with procuring vital strategic commodities. He held the post, probably the most important executive responsibility ever given a vice president until then, for nearly two years. Wallace's rival was the commerce secretary, a conservative Texan and well-connected political infighter named Jesse Jones, who supervised the Reconstruction Finance Corporation, which held the purse strings. The vice president may have been right on the merits, but he conducted his battles in public, vehemently and sanctimoniously, all but saying Jones was sabotaging the war effort. It was the president who was responsible for the overlapping mandates of the two agencies. "Three simultaneous presidents," he'd observed dryly before the country went to war, would be required if there were any more independent agencies. The agencies only proliferated with the gigantic demands the war effort placed on the economy. Roosevelt's acceptance of a certain amount of disarray, which he tended to view as creative tension, was higher than his tolerance for open political warfare in his administration. Wallace's lack of tact and political finesse—qualities personified in the president—left a deep impression. "Those who were around the White House at the time of this disagreeable incident," so Sherwood wrote, "felt there was now no chance that Roosevelt would support Wallace at the Democratic Convention in 1944." He didn't remonstrate with his vice president—that wasn't his way—he simply disbanded the Board of Economic Warfare on July 15, 1943, instantly reconstituting it as the Office of Economic Warfare without Wallace, who was thus stripped of a major responsibility. Strike two.

A third reservation about Wallace had to do with his foggy judgment of what's possible in international affairs. Forrest Davis, the *Saturday Evening Post* writer used by Roosevelt as a mouthpiece, twice made a point of distinguishing the president's way of thinking from Wallace's gauzy promises of something like an international New Deal after the war to stand in place of the fading colonial order. In an article that went on the newsstands just as Wallace took off for Siberia, Davis wrote that Roosevelt's view of the postwar world was "essentially pragmatic . . . unlike Henry A. Wallace [he] is not primarily addicted to what the professors call welfare politics." In his diary, Wallace noted that he had it "on very high authority" that the Davis articles had been "corrected in pencil by the President himself before they were published." At least in his diary, Wallace didn't ask himself why the dismissive reference to himself had escaped the presidential pencil. Another note had Ambassador Gromyko telling him "the Soviet Union would be most happy to have me make a trip to Moscow." It didn't cause Wallace to reconsider the reasons this was not to be.

If he sensed any lack of confidence in himself on Roosevelt's part, he didn't admit it in writing; probably he drove it from his mind. Henry Wallace was a highly intelligent man. He could also be obtuse, such as when, three months before Pearl Harbor, he sent the president a private letter marked "urgent" exhorting him to take "an extremely firm stand" in dealing with Japan. The letter makes no reference to any of the pending issues of economic sanctions or military prepared- ness, to any other Asian countries or possibly endangered outposts such as the Philippines, no reference to anything specific. Floating above facts on the ground or in the Pacific, it merely preaches against "the appeasing stand or partially appeasing stand" as if the president needed shoring up or stiffening, as if Wallace had some special insight into Japanese psyches. "I'm as sure of this as anyone can be in a matter of this sort . . . any sign of weakness, concession or appeasement will be misunderstood by Japan and the Axis and will cost us, directly or indirectly, many millions of hours of man labor and much suffering," it said. This wasn't useful political intelligence of the kind Roosevelt always craved. He could read this sort of advice on editorial pages. That 1941 missive is a clue as to why Wallace's access to Roosevelt on foreign and strategic matters during the war was largely limited to cabinet meetings, where the president did most of the talking. Like most vice presidents before Dick Cheney, Wallace had little or no influence on matters of war and peace. What can be said is that Roo- sevelt didn't reach out to him for advice, didn't think to use him the way he used Harry Hopkins or Sumner Welles. He left his vice presi- dent to make speeches in periods when he wasn't disposed to making them himself.

Wallace's slippage in the president's estimation can be traced through his involvement in the most sensitive war project of them all, the development of the atomic bomb. Early on, Roosevelt named him to a small, informal board called the Top Policy Committee that was to be kept abreast of key developments and decisions on which, besides its five members, only the president was to be briefed. Roose- velt thought to include the vice president along with Secretary Stim- son, General Marshall, and two top scientists, Vannevar Bush and

James Bryant Conant. Perhaps he was thinking of Wallace's place in the line of succession; perhaps he was thinking that the plant geneticist had a scientific bent.

Bush, the president's top science adviser, provided the liaison with the physicists actually working on the project. One day, presenting the latest report to Roosevelt, he mentioned that it had the approval of all the committee members except Wallace, whom he'd been unable to reach.

"Well, Henry is out West making political speeches," Roosevelt said, with a smile that Bush took to be dismissive. "I do not think we need to worry him." In a memoir years later, Bush wrote, "That was my cue and I never went near Wallace on atomic energy matters after that."

On July 6, a frail, pasty-faced Harry Hopkins returned to the White House after an absence of half a year, breakfasting with the president in his bedroom. Having survived desperate intestinal surgery at the Mayo Clinic and the loss of an eighteen-year-old son serving as a combat marine in the Marshall Islands, he was hardly ready to revive the political role he'd played at the 1940 Chicago convention, when he was Roosevelt's point man on the scene. At best, for weeks to come, he'd only be able to work two or three hours a day. Hopkins came away from the breakfast convinced that Wallace was out and Byrnes in as Roosevelt's running mate. Before lunch, Roosevelt saw Anna Rosenberg, a well-coiffed New York publicist with ties to organized labor who found her way onto his appointments calendar more easily than most cabinet members. She came away with the impression that Byrnes was actually a long shot. Within the following week, both the vice president and the so-called assistant president— the two prospective candidates Roosevelt knew best (and who knew him best)—were strongly encouraged by the president to get into the race. Each was privately led to believe he was Roosevelt's first choice, although, as he'd then say with a perfect imitation of sincerity, the final selection would be up to the delegates. The week after that, each would leave Chicago feeling, with some justice, that he'd been treated shabbily, maybe even betrayed.

On July 10, Wallace asked Roosevelt whether he'd be willing to sign a letter saying, "If I were a delegate to the convention I would vote for Henry Wallace." The president readily agreed. They met again twice in the next three days. In his diary, Wallace described their parting after the second meeting: "As I shook hands with him he drew me close and turned on his full smile—and giving me a very hearty hand-clasp, he said, 'While I cannot put it just that way in public, I hope it will be the same old team.'"

In those same days, Roosevelt had three conversations with Byrnes. "You are the best qualified man in the whole outfit," he said on July 12, "and you must not get out of the race. If you stay in, you are sure to win." Yet the previous evening, he'd all but eliminated Wallace and Byrnes from consideration, or so the party leaders with whom he met then had thought, narrowing the choice to Truman or Douglas. It's not that the president forgot from one conversation to the next what he'd already said. It's that he wanted to be able to make the choice without being seen to have done so, without alienating any of the candidates or their supporters. "A simple pattern emerged," wrote Frank Freidel, the Roosevelt biographer who spent more years than any other chronicling his methods and personality. "The key player of the vice presidential poker game was Roosevelt himself in his efforts to control the choice. He played the game with a gusto and effective-ness that surpassed 1940." The word "gusto" seems slightly hyperbolic when applied to the chronically weary Franklin Roosevelt of 1944, but his daily schedules make clear that he was doing more meeting and maneuvering than the party leaders who thought they were steering him. He may even have been enjoying himself. Only he could have a clear picture of where the game was headed. Exercising his mastery over his party yet again was one way of convincing himself he still might be equal to the tasks ahead.

Encouraging as he was in his private sessions with Wallace and Byrnes, Roosevelt dispatched emissaries to each to deliver the mes-sage that a consensus had formed in the party that the ticket might be harmed by his candidacy. It's not a message either was willing to receive. They knew who the ultimate source had to be. But, wanting the prize so badly, feeling so entitled to it, each stubbornly insisted he'd withdraw only if the request came directly from the president himself, face-to-face. Roosevelt was ready to drop broad hints, especially to Wallace. "You have your family to think of," he said on July 10. "Think of the cat-calls and jeers, and the definiteness of rejection." And a few days later: "Even though they do beat you out at Chicago, we will have a job for you in world economic affairs." In a conversation with Roosevelt, Byrnes acknowledged that the president couldn't be the one to ask Wallace to step down, given the vice president's loyalty. He chose not to recognize that a similar inhibition might be at work in his case. Or perhaps he was counting on it, on the president not getting in the way of his effort to grasp the nomination that now seemed within reach.

Party leaders talked about which candidate would cost the ticket the most in the basic, crude currency of any election, votes. While Wallace was the bigger worry on this score, Byrnes, Ed Flynn argued, could put at risk black votes in the North, as many as 200,000 of them in New York. This was a relatively new concern in national politics, given some force by the strong civil rights section in the platform just adopted by the Republican convention that nominated Thomas Dewey, which the Democrats couldn't attempt to match without blowing the party apart. The Republicans now promised federal legislation against lynching, against the poll tax used in southern states to keep blacks off voting rolls. They also promised continuation of the Fair Employment Practices Committee set up as an emergency wartime measure.

Inevitably, as happens every four years, the question of succession, of who'd make the best president, took second place to such nuts-and-bolts considerations. Especially in the presence of the living incumbent, it was not an easy subject. On July 11, a fateful day, it was brought up most forcefully by the columnist Walter Lippmann, who put in words destined for ink and paper what others later claimed they'd been thinking all along. Roosevelt religiously began his days sitting up in bed leafing through newspapers. He wouldn't on this particular Tuesday morning have skipped a Lippmann column titled "Henry Wallace." Nothing could have been more relevant to the packed schedule he faced. In a few hours, he'd appear before a press conference to announce, at long last, his willingness to accept the nomination. This would be followed by lunch with Wallace and an off-the-record White House dinner with party leaders arranged at Roosevelt's instigation, specifically to consider alternatives for the second place on the ticket.

"The question of [Wallace's] renomination," the columnist wrote, "is by general understanding the question of visualizing him as President of the United States ... whether with the President running for a fourth term, [the Democrats] can nominate a Vice President, not unlikely to be President in this fourth term who divides the country so deeply and so sharply." Lippmann, who admired Wallace as "an exceptionally fine human being"—he sometimes played tennis with him and had once proposed him for an honorary Harvard degree—wasn't counting votes. Tactfully but forcefully, he was raising the subject of Roosevelt's mortality and the qualities of leadership that would be required to fill his place, whether these could be supplied by "a mystic and isolated man to whom the shape of the real world is not clear, in which he is not at home and at ease."

Intimations of his own mortality hovered over Roosevelt's day. That night at dinner with the party bosses summoned to serve as his privy council, he discoursed expansively on the assassination attempt he'd escaped and various plots on his life the Secret Service had uncovered over the years, including a turkey laced with poison supposedly sent to the White House as a gift and a hole drilled through the floor of a hotel room he was due to occupy, at an angle that would have delivered a bullet to his bed. Probably this wasn't his subconscious speaking. Probably it was a deliberate prologue to the subject at hand.

At that morning's press conference, reading aloud a letter from Hannegan telling him he had the support of a majority of delegates to the coming convention, his hands shook so much he couldn't light the cigarette he'd fitted into his holder. *The New York Times* described them as "atremble." Steve Early, the press secretary, lit it for him. The people, the chairman's letter said, recognized his burdens but "are determined that you must continue until the war is won and a firm basis for an abiding peace among men is established." It didn't say how long that would take.

"All that is within me," Roosevelt's said in formal response, "cries out to go back to my home on the Hudson River ... [avoiding] the publicity which in our democracy follows every step of the Nation's Chief Executive." Considering the amount of time he'd been spending at Hyde Park, spending out of the limelight generally, that part of his response rang true. The final words were more obviously contrived for political effect. The novelist John Steinbeck, it turns out, had a hand in drafting them. "Reluctantly," the president intoned, "but as a good soldier . . . I will accept and serve in this office if I am so ordered by the Commander-in–Chief of us all—the sovereign people of the United States."

"Now get out," he called cheerfully to the reporters as they scampered for the door. A bulletin on the president's declaration was soon conveyed to his previous challenger. "Is that news?" Wendell Willkie quipped, laughing. He had no further comment.

It was a hot, sticky Washington evening when the president's short list of seven Democratic operatives repaired after dinner with him and his son-in-law, John Boettiger, to his upstairs study, another oval office, adjacent to his bedroom. The convalescing Harry Hopkins hadn't been invited. No White House staffers were on hand. Perhaps Boettiger, whose presence has never been explained, saw himself as auditioning for a political role. If so, nothing came of it.

By then, the men had all gotten down to shirtsleeves, including Roosevelt, who led off the discussion with what amounted to a eulogy for Henry Wallace. He praised his vice president warmly, repeated he'd be happy to have him on the ticket again but didn't insist. That was the key point. Once Roosevelt started talking about other possibilities, it was understood that Wallace was effectively out of the picture. "It was unanimous," Pauley, the party treasurer, would recall.

In his version, Roosevelt also dwelled "at length" on Byrnes's experience and strengths before steering the talk to the question of his religion. Born a Catholic, he'd become an Episcopalian when he married. In private, the president had quoted Archbishop Spellman as saying Catholics would find it hard to vote for one of their own who'd left the church. Flynn of the Bronx and Mayor Kelly of Chicago brought up the possible loss of black votes before the Byrnes discussion drifted inconclusively toward other southerners, Speaker of the House Sam Rayburn and the Senate majority leader, Barkley. Pauley has Roosevelt saying defections in the Texas delegation put the Speaker "out of the running," dismissing Barkley "with a wave and a laugh," and mentioning an "even more impossible possibility," Ambassador Winant, the New Hampshire Republican at the London embassy. Each of these names produced rounds of further talk, and Roosevelt may have started to wilt as the meeting extended past his prescribed bedtime. Both Flynn and the former chairman Walker portray him as not having much to say. But he was the one who spoke up for Justice Douglas as a fresh, younger face, a westerner, an answer to Tom Dewey's argument that Roosevelt and his team were geriatric. Probably he knew that Dewey and Douglas were Columbia Law classmates and had, in their salad days, even discussed forming a partnership. "Bill Douglas has a nice crop of hair," he's quoted as saying, "he looks like a Boy Scout . . . plays an interesting game of poker and would appeal to the people." Only Mayor Kelly showed real enthusiasm for the idea. At forty-five, Douglas offered relative youth and a new face, but like Wallace four years earlier he'd be a neophyte in retail politics. By background, he'd been a law professor, a federal regulator, and a judge, never before a candidate. If the president wasn't prepared to go all out for him in public, he was a hard sell. In fact, his name would never be placed in nomination.

Truman's comes up last in the several accounts. Flynn wrote that Roosevelt had instructed him to raise it. As he also recalled, each of the politicians at the meeting credited himself with having suggested Truman. Each then believed "that the President had taken his suggestion." Roosevelt reacted as if he were hearing the idea for the first time. He said he hardly knew the man from Missouri but praised him for the skill with which he'd led the Senate investigating committee seeking to root out waste and corruption in wartime spending. It could have been an embarrassment to the administration. Instead, it was a credit to the Democrats. According to Ed Pauley's account, the person who came closest to addressing the unmentionable possibility of a succession was Roosevelt himself, who wondered aloud whether Truman "had the personality to be the President of the United States." It wasn't a question that could be answered in an evening. The conversation then seemed to go in circles. It ended with Roosevelt announcing the sense of the meeting, uttering some variant of the line Frank Walker later remembered: "Boys, I guess it's Truman." If Flynn is to be believed, it had actually followed the president's script.

On the way out, Walker told Hannegan he'd do well to "go back and get it in writing." The story as it has been handed down doesn't quite add up. The chairman is supposed to have gone back upstairs to the family quarters on the pretext that he'd left a coat. More likely, it was his jacket. No one would have been carrying a coat that sweltering night, not even a raincoat; weather reports spoke of continuing drought. By some accounts, Hannegan emerged with one line scrawled on an envelope: "Bob, I think Truman is the right man. FDR." Such an envelope has never been found. What does exist is a handwritten letter mentioning Douglas as well as Truman, but because it was postdated July 19, it's less than certain it was written that night.

The best evidence that Roosevelt had more or less made up his mind isn't in the memoirs and oral histories left behind by some of the participants in the July 11 meeting. It's in assignments he made before the leaders filed out of his study: Hannegan was to deliver the message to Wallace that Rosenman had failed to get across the previous day, that he couldn't be nominated; Walker to administer what he termed the "coup de grâce" to Jimmy Byrnes. It was an unavoidable "part of the game," the president said, when Walker asked to be excused. Up to this point, Roosevelt's moves had been hard but not impossible to follow. They were a cover for an obvious contradiction. His wish to be above politics, even out of politics, was genuine at some level. But with so much at stake, he couldn't leave the choice of his running mate to the convention as he was pretending to do. So he now played politics as only he could, seeming to reopen the question the party leaders thought had been settled that evening.

He'd come to the same conclusion about Wallace and Byrnes, but there was a difference in his assessment of the two men. Wallace, he told Eleanor, was not a good politician. Even if he felt closer to him politically, he had little confidence in the vice president's instincts, didn't feel he could handle the presidency if it came to that. The assistant president, a seasoned politician respected by other politicians, was more his idea of a president by a wide margin. Each of the party operatives who came to the White House on the eleventh could have accepted him easily, except Flynn. Yet Roosevelt withheld his blessing and not just over the issue of race. That wouldn't have been the only concern. After all, he'd discounted Byrnes's segregationist background when he'd appointed him to the Supreme Court in 1939. Byrnes had never been an enthusiastic New Dealer—organized labor if given a choice would oppose him—and perhaps just as important, there was a question of temperament: Roosevelt found this pillar of his wartime White House almost as touchy as he was indispensable, "a prima donna," as he'd remarked to Daisy back in February. He relied on Byrnes, but there's a suggestion here that he didn't fully trust him.

The assistant president was "hurt, angry and frankly incredulous" when Walker went to his East Wing office the next day to deliver the message that he'd been "passed over." Shrewd and combative, Byrnes pushed back, phoning from the East Wing to the West Wing to put the question bluntly: "I would like to know if you have changed your opinion about my being a candidate." Under the circumstances, it was a loaded question. Byrnes knew his president well enough to expect something other than candor. Roosevelt did not disappoint. He urged Byrnes on. This is when he said, "You are sure to win."

Thursday, July 13, was to be Roosevelt's last day in the White House for more than a month. As always, the president's travel plans were a closely held secret. He was about to leave on a rail-and-sea voyage to the West Coast, Hawaii, and the distant Aleutians on what would be characterized as a military inspection trip, covering 13,912 miles, according to the final tally. He would not return to Washington until August 17. The assistant president wouldn't see him in all that time. As the president prepared to leave, Byrnes again confronted him, this time in person. He had a surprising pitch to make for his candidacy, which Roosevelt by now had consistently encouraged and simultaneously dismissed. The once and future segregationist put himself forward as a potential champion of black civil rights.

Byrnes came armed with a photograph he'd received from his home state of South Carolina showing Eleanor addressing a black audience, which he now used to challenge the notion that Roosevelt would lose black votes if he ran with a southerner—himself, for instance. "Look at the expression on their faces. That is idolatry," he said, smoothly adding a dose of flattery to the libation he was about to serve. The Roosevelts had done more for "those Negro people" than "anybody else in the history of the world." They'd never turn against him, Byrnes argued, according to an aide who transcribed his chief's version of the conversation that day. The president thought he had a point but said he was getting contrary advice from Ed Flynn. Here is where Jimmy Byrnes made his pitch.

"Mr. President," he said, "all I have heard around the White House for the last week is 'Negro' ... Did you ever stop to think who could do the most for the Negro?" That person would have to be a white southerner. "If Mr. Wallace or Mr. Douglas says he is against the poll tax, that is not news and they cannot change the views of southerners. But if I say I am against the poll tax, that means something." Southern senators had successfully filibustered a bill designed to eliminate the poll tax. As presiding officer Henry Wallace had been powerless to do anything about it.

"Do you think I could have stopped the filibuster if I had been presiding officer?" Byrnes asked.

"I believe you could have, Jimmy," replied Roosevelt, whose quick mind would have recalibrated the political and legislative prospects Byrnes had just sought to open. He might have been given pause; his inclination to Truman was not irrevocable, wasn't even suspected outside a small circle. He could still postpone a final choice.

On the Friday, Hannegan and Walker, acting on the instructions they'd received at the White House, again told Byrnes he was not under consideration. The assistant president quoted back what Roosevelt had told him. The party chairman had to admit he was now confused; he'd heard what he'd heard. Byrnes had heard something else. The conclusion was obvious but couldn't be spoken. "I can't call the President a liar," Bob Hannegan said.

Persistent as ever, Byrnes put through a call to Roosevelt, who'd by then reached Hyde Park. The official log says his train arrived at Highland across the river at 7:30 a.m. on Friday, July 14, in time for Eleanor to serve breakfast at the big house. Jim Bishop, a best-selling writer who commissioned interviews with railway officials and Secret Service agents years later, gives a different itinerary. He says the president arranged for his train to make a long layover in Allamuchy, New Jersey, that morning so he could visit Lucy Rutherfurd. Probably that would have been his heart's desire, but if he'd made that detour, Byrnes would never have gotten through to him after lunch that same day in Hyde Park. The old court stenographer took the exchange down in shorthand. He had a secretary on an extension doing the same. Obviously, he wasn't in a trusting frame of mind. "We have to be damned careful about language," the president said, playing with words. "They asked if I would object to Truman and Douglas and I said no. That is different from using the word 'prefer' ... You know I told you I would have no preference." They talked some more, and Roosevelt said, "Will you go on and run?"

The president got to Chicago ahead of Byrnes, staying less than two hours on Saturday the fifteenth. It would be six days before the convention learned that the head of the ticket had come and gone on his secret train. Mayor Kelly and Pauley, the party treasurer, may have accompanied Chairman Hannegan when he made his way to the siding in the Fifty-First Street rail yard, where the *Ferdinand Magellan,* the president's armored Pullman car, was parked. But it's not clear that they were in on the most sensitive part of the conversation with Roosevelt. This involved the wording of two letters: the one he'd promised Wallace, saying he'd vote for the vice president if he were a delegate but pointedly leaving the delegates free to do otherwise, almost inviting them to do so; and the postdated letter Hannegan had sought and maybe gotten four nights earlier at the White House designating Harry Truman as the favored choice.

Hannegan emerged with this letter, unmistakably in the president's hand:

> July 19
> Dear Bob,
> You have written me about Harry Truman and Bill Douglas. I should, of course, be very happy to run with either of them and believe that either one of them would bring real strength to the ticket.
> Always sincerely,
> Franklin Roosevelt

Questions still hover over this document. Was it written on July 11, as Frank Walker and most historians have assumed? Or on the thirteenth, as Jimmy Byrnes came to believe? Or in the railway car on the fifteenth, as Grace Tully, Roosevelt's secretary, would seem to indicate in her ghosted memoir, which tells of a typed original in which Douglas's name came first. Her story is that Hannegan had her reverse the order—all but determining, thereby, the succession—when the letter was retyped on White House stationery. No copy survives of any version, handwritten or typed, with the justice's name first. After his death, the chairman's son would tell an interviewer that his father had kept and destroyed the originals. The holograph copy with the senator's name first now reposes in the Truman Library in Independence, Missouri. Hannegan's widow parted with it in 1960, eleven years after her husband's death. Assuming that Tully's story is essentially true, Hannegan had to persuade Roosevelt to rewrite the letter before she retyped it. An observant sleuth could conclude that Roosevelt wrote the letter we have in the Chicago rail yard on July 15. The wording suggests it was written with his previous day's commitment to Byrnes in mind: that he "would have no preference." It doesn't rule out other candidates.

Hannegan may have boarded the *Ferdinand Magellan* with the intention of nailing down the president's commitment to Truman. But he wasn't as firmly committed to his fellow Missourian as he sometimes later suggested and has since often been assumed. The friendship of the two politicians went back to 1940 when Hannegan, a party boss from St. Louis, threw his support to the man from Independence, all the way across the state, in the final stages of a closely fought primary. Truman, who then narrowly carried St. Louis and with it the state, stuck up for Hannegan a couple of years later when the *St. Louis Post-Dispatch* assailed his subsequent nomination as Internal Revenue Service collector for eastern Missouri. ("I am of the opinion that if the twelve Apostles lived in St. Louis and were members of the Democratic Party the only one the Post-Dispatch would support would be Judas Iscariot," Senator Truman wrote to a constituent in 1942.) But Hannegan may have owed Jimmy Byrnes as much for his eventual appointment as party chairman as he did Truman. In any case, by the time he and Kelly left the train that Saturday afternoon, the Truman-Douglas letter was no longer of prime importance as far as they were concerned. As they understood him, Roosevelt had just reopened the door for Byrnes in response to the mayor's report on conversations he'd had with some black leaders in Chicago, reopened it wide.

The black leaders said they preferred Wallace but would support whomever Roosevelt wanted, Byrnes included. Flynn's fears about the loss of the black vote might be exaggerated, the mayor now felt. This fitted in with the case Byrnes had made two days earlier when he showed the president the photograph from South Carolina of Eleanor's black audience. "Well, you know Jimmy has been my choice from the very first," responded Roosevelt, who may have been thinking of his aide's pledge to fight the poll tax, or trying to make a demonstration of his good faith to Byrnes, or reacting to some other, unperceived set of mixed motives and calculations. "Go ahead and name him." Unexpressed but clearly implied were the words "if you can."

Byrnes was still in Washington when Kelly called him with the news. As soon as he could, he left for Chicago, where he was met at the station by a red fire chief's car, courtesy of the mayor, which whisked him in seeming triumph to a celebratory breakfast with Hannegan and Kelly, both now convinced he was Roosevelt's choice. It wasn't until that Monday evening that they remembered something else the president had said. The instruction, "Clear it with Sidney," would later reverberate as a rallying cry for the Republican campaign. Sidney Hillman was chairman of the political action committee of the CIO, the Congress of Industrial Organizations, which was pledged to Wallace but ready to accept Truman as a second choice. Toward the end of the campaign, Dewey and the more rabidly anti-Roosevelt editorial pages would make Hillman, an immigrant as a child from Lithuania who came up in the garment trades, a target of red-baiting. "The Communists are now seizing control of the New Deal," the Republican candidate would say. In the days before the convention, several attempts, including one by Truman, to clear Byrnes's candidacy with Hillman failed. Rumbling along in his stealth train, on his way to San Diego, the president was informed that the union movement was determined to fight Jimmy Byrnes, more on account of a wartime wage freeze than on behalf of black rights. The NAACP was also taking up battle positions. Roosevelt gave no indication he was surprised or grieved. Coolly assessing the state of play, he now pronounced Byrnes a "political liability." That was the real coup de grâce. He followed it up with instructions to Walker. "Frank," he said, "go all out for Truman."

It's a tribute to Franklin Roosevelt's wiliness that the notion has persisted over the years that he was only fleetingly engaged in the selection, that he was simply oblivious when it came to the larger question of succession. In fact, as he journeyed through the Southwest at the rear of his nine-car train, cozily ensconced in the *Ferdinand Magellan*, he was pulling strings. He never used the word "succession" but cared enough about qualifications for the presidency to eliminate Wallace as a possibility and keep Byrnes's hopes alive to the last moment, when, for the sake of party unity, he returned to Harry Truman as the safe choice. The senator, who'd promised to make the nominating speech for Byrnes, had to be persuaded he wasn't just another stalking horse, that Roosevelt really wanted him. So on the Wednesday, the day the convention opened, he was brought to Hannegan's suite in the Blackstone Hotel in the afternoon to listen in on a transcontinental call between the chairman and the president, staged for his benefit.

Truman, seated on a bed, never spoke to Roosevelt that day. Hannegan extended the receiver toward him. A familiar voice boomed out. It asked whether Hannegan had gotten "that fellow" lined up. Hannegan said something about a stubborn Missouri mule. "Well, tell him," the voice said, "that if he wants to break up the Democratic Party in the middle of the war, that's his responsibility." Bang. That was all. The call had been terminated at the other end. By one account, the first words out of Truman's mouth were "Oh shit." By another, they were "Jesus Christ."

"Why the hell didn't he tell me in the first place?" asked the man who'd just been set on a path that would lead him to the White House in nine months minus a week.

By the time he delivered this epiphany, Roosevelt's train had completed its slow, circuitous journey to Camp Pendleton, a marine base near San Diego. Eleanor had been on board with her husband ever since it left Hyde Park. After lingering in San Diego for a day, she flew to New York. The six days on the rails were the longest time they'd had together in more than a year. Roosevelt made much of it in a "Dear Babs" letter after her departure. "It was grand having you come out with me," he wrote. Eleanor was less taken with the pleasures of being cut off from the world in a slow-moving railway car. "I don't know that I am being very useful on the trip as there is nothing to do," a restless First Lady wrote to a friend. "FDR sleeps, eats and works and all I do is sit through long meals which are sometimes interesting, and sometimes dull." In the close quarters of the *Ferdinand Magellan*, Doris Kearns Goodwin concluded, they were seldom alone. In fact, Eleanor spent a large portion of her waking hours several cars back, working with Malvina Thompson, her secretary.

On the morning of July 20, seated in the front seat of a limousine, the president watched from a bluff above the Pacific as five thousand marines and three thousand sailors staged a full-scale amphibious landing for his benefit. His whereabouts and itinerary were still an official secret. It couldn't yet be reported that he was headed for Pearl Harbor and Honolulu, then the remote Aleutian Islands. This was not just an exercise in how to take a beach. For the sometimes reluctant, frequently calculating candidate it was simultaneously an exercise in image making. Footage of the commander in chief on the bluff viewing a marine division as it stormed ashore in California would be made available to newsreel producers for showing in movie houses across the country, as would film of other high points of his tour. In reality, this was only his second venture outside his railway car in six days, but he's unlikely to have been wholly engrossed in the spectacle on the beaches below. Part of his mind would have been two thousand miles or so away in Chicago, where Henry Wallace was displaying surprising staying power as a candidate. Even with the announcement that Byrnes had withdrawn—"in deference to the wishes of the President," the assistant president said sourly—the convention threatened to spin out of control.

Another part of Roosevelt's mind might have been assessing his own condition, after his first health scare since Hobcaw. His eldest son, James, a marine colonel on duty as his escort, would assert years later in yet another ghosted memoir that Roosevelt had collapsed on the train moments before he was due to leave for the military exercise. On this very day, within a couple of hours, the roll of delegates in Chicago was due to be called on his renomination. "Father turned suddenly white," so this account goes, "his face took on an agonized look, and he said to me, 'Jimmy, I don't know if I can make it—I have horrible pains!'"

The son then describes how he helped his father out of his berth so he could stretch out on the floor of his small sleeping compartment; how they agreed his appointment on the bluff couldn't be canceled—possibly, though James doesn't say so, because of the pall that might be cast over the campaign and the proceedings in Chicago, on this of all days; how, after ten or so minutes, assuring each other the problem had to be digestive, they decided against calling the two doctors accompanying the president, McIntire and Bruenn. They would surely have insisted on examining him, causing a delay.

At the end of the exercise, Roosevelt canceled a lunch he was to have had at the Coronado home of a daughter-in-law, wife of his youngest son, John, then serving as a naval officer in the Pacific, and returned to his tight quarters on the presidential train. Two days later, he'd mention in a letter to Eleanor that he'd had a case of "the colly-wobbles & stayed on the train in the p.m." the day after she left. The official log says he passed the afternoon listening to the convention on the radio. By then, an observation car had been attached to the *Ferdinand Magellan* to serve as a studio for the acceptance speech he was due to broadcast to the convention that evening.

He'd already declared that he didn't intend to run "in the usual partisan, political sense." Leisurely as it had been, the trip to the Pacific on which he was now embarked was meant to stand as a fulfillment of that pledge, conveying the message that the commander in chief was now above politics. Knowing their man, supporters and opponents

JULY 16, 1944. *Chicago Tribune.*

both knew better. The *Chicago Tribune*, calling Roosevelt "the greatest master of political deception this nation has ever known," declared it "the holy duty of every American to oppose the Great Deceiver." A *Tribune* cartoonist lampooned the idea of an apolitical Roosevelt with a drawing that was revealing in more than the intended way. It showed the president full-faced, broad shouldered, clutching a bag labeled "THE NOMINATION," running so hard, racing like a Thoroughbred, that clouds of dust trailed his great, powerful strides. Beyond the obvious satire, what was revealing was this demonstration of how completely the brilliant projection of physical vigor by the crippled president had imposed itself on the imaginations of even his most rabid opponents, how hard it still was for them to conceive that his strength might now be waning.

A contrasting and damaging image would emerge from the observation car that evening. In Chicago the president's disembodied but familiar voice was effective in rousing the delegates. Again it explained why "in the usual sense" he'd not be campaigning: "In these days of tragic sorrow, I do not consider it fitting. And besides in these days of global warfare, I shall not be able to find the time." There was a standing ovation once the absent nominee ended by echoing Lincoln's second inaugural address, promising "to finish the work we are in, to bind up the Nation's wounds." Jonathan Daniels, seated in the presidential box behind Jimmy Byrnes and his wife and Ben Cohen, the Byrnes aide who months earlier had sought "a practical alternative to the fourth term," noted that they alone refrained from standing. In the observation car, Roosevelt meanwhile reenacted a portion of the speech for the sake of a newsreel cameraman and a pool photographer for the wire services. In the Associated Press picture that went out across the country, the president appeared gaunt, exhausted, slack-jawed; the overall impression was of a failing elder, a candidate for a nursing home, gasping out his last words, the opposite of the impression his confident, sonorous voice left with the party faithful in distant Chicago. (It was not the impression, either, left by newsreel footage taken at the same time, snippets of which can now be viewed online, showing a noticeably drained and uneasy but still commanding Franklin Roosevelt, with dark rings under his eyes, orating to a couple of cameramen in the photo op following the actual broadcast of his speech.) Like many news photographs, the AP shot captured

JULY 20, 1944. Observes Marines' landing exercise in Oceanside, California (*above*). Later the same day: repeating a portion of his acceptance speech for a photographer and a newsreel cameraman *(below)*.

only a fraction of a second but seemed to convey a larger meaning, making its subject's ability to carry on look questionable. The hour was already late back east; under intense deadline pressure, an AP photo editor made a snap judgment that it would be better to select an image in which the speaker's mouth was open than one in which it was closed. This went out on the wire as the single pool photo, guaranteeing it would be used by most papers in the country. Punishing what he took to be an act of lèse-majesté, if not actual sabotage, an angry Steve Early banished an AP photographer named George Skadding from the presidential train.

The real news in the photograph wasn't noticed until it was published without cropping in *Life*. A naval officer seated far to the president's right had previously been cropped out. Now he was plainly visible at the edge of the frame and subsequently identified by a doctor at the Mayo Clinic who recognized a former classmate, the cardiologist Howard Bruenn. J. Edgar Hoover was asked by the White House to trace the source of rumors that the president was receiving treatment for his heart. It took the FBI weeks, by which time Walter Trohan had already reported in the *Chicago Tribune* that Dr. Bruenn, described as "a heart specialist," was the unnamed naval officer sitting near Roosevelt as he reenacted his acceptance address. The fact that a heart specialist had been caring for the president had been kept under wraps for four months. It wasn't front-page news in Colonel McCormick's paper even now. The reporter couldn't find anyone willing to speculate on what it might mean.

If Roosevelt stayed glued to the radio that night of July 20, he'd have heard that the roars of approval that greeted his speech were soon replaced by cries of "We want Wallace!" as a full-throated floor demonstration for the vice president got under way. He'd already have had time to review the coverage of a failed attempt on Hitler's life that same fateful day by a high German officer, Colonel Claus von Stauffenberg, hoping to ignite a wider coup against the Nazis by the German high command. The first bulletin, declaring only that the führer had survived with minor injuries and burns when a bomb exploded as he was conferring with key commanders, had been read to the Chicago convention shortly before noon. The delegates were just gathering in the afternoon to hear Alben Barkley nominate Roosevelt for a fourth term when Hitler took to the airwaves to demonstrate he was still in command and blame "an extremely small clique" of "foolish, criminally stupid officers" for the attack on himself and his inner circle. These "usurpers," he promised, would soon be eliminated. A subsequent bulletin over German radio named Stauffenberg as the would-be assassin and announced that he'd already been shot.

It was the second such bulletin in two days. The previous day the convention had been electrified by news that Japan's militarist premier, Hideki Tojo, had resigned over the fall of the island of Saipan in the western Pacific after three weeks of heavy fighting, a defeat placing the Japanese heartland within range of the new B-29s, the U.S. "Superfortress" bombers. "The knockout blow was immediately credited to the standard-bearer—Roosevelt—and rightly so," a young administration official at the convention wrote in a journal entry.

In both theaters of the war, the enemy could be taken at this juncture to be in terminal disarray. In Chicago, these faraway events were processed mainly for their likely impact on the voting in November. If the war ended too early, some Democrats feared, the Republicans might yet win. Thomas Dewey made the same calculation. The end of the war was "in sight," he told a rally in Philadelphia. "This should be said over and over again," a Republican strategy document decreed.

Wallace led Truman on the first ballot for the vice presidential nomination late on the night of the twentieth, a signal for Wallace demonstrations to resume at an even more boisterous pitch. Mayor Kelly's fire officials seized the excuse to proclaim Chicago Stadium overcrowded and demand that it be cleared, thereby avoiding a second ballot in an atmosphere party leaders deemed unhelpful, which is to say out of their control. By the next afternoon, the bosses were able to orchestrate the roll call so it unfolded in the desired fashion, leading to an inevitable Truman victory as commanded by the man in the railway car next to the marine base far away. As the journalist Allen Drury sized up the result, it wasn't the president's new running mate but his old one who emerged as the hero of the convention. "Like so many others," he wrote of Henry Wallace, "he has learned what it means to be a politically dispensable friend of Franklin Roosevelt."

As the convention adjourned, a gracious telegram was delivered to the vice president to add to a stack of gracious personal messages he'd received over the years from the same source. "You made a grand fight and I am very proud of you," the telegram said. "Tell Ilo [Mrs. Wallace] not to plan to leave Washington next November." It was signed "Franklin D. Roosevelt," the carefully enigmatic, sometimes indecipherable figure Wallace had earlier described as a "water-man," capable of rowing in one direction while gazing in another. Years later, Wallace would still be trying to figure out what happened to him in Chicago.

CHAPTER 7

Commander in Chief

A few hours after Harry Truman delivered a modest, instantly for-gettable, one-minute acceptance speech to the Democratic convention in Chicago, the head of the ticket was carried in a motorcade to the Broadway pier in San Diego, where he boarded the USS *Baltimore*, a high-speed ship with a crew of one thousand, classed as a heavy cruiser, that had been recalled from combat duty in the Pacific for the primary purpose of delivering the commander in chief to Pearl Harbor and points beyond. The crossing was to be leisurely; in the four days allowed for the trip, the cruiser traveled, for the president's comfort, at little more than half its top speed. An escort force of four destroy-ers accompanied it; fighter planes kept watch overhead. At night, the convoy went dark above decks, observing combat cruising discipline; in daylight, the ships followed a zigzag course. Outgoing radio traffic was held to a minimum so as not to disclose the *Baltimore*'s location. The chief passenger, who spent afternoon hours on the flag bridge, could receive incoming messages and news but had a valid military reason for not replying. That suited his mood, which seemed to be one of contained resignation, rather than triumph. His mind remained focused on the coming months and the end of the war in Europe, not the fourth term for which he'd just been nominated, which promised relief only in 1949, a date that now seemed eons away. Meanwhile, he needed to make a showing of his simultaneous concentration on the war in the Pacific. The candidate had said he'd not campaign "in the usual sense." Sailing into Pearl Harbor in broad daylight, passing an honor guard of recently launched and refurbished warships, thousands of sailors in their navy whites in formation on their decks, the former assistant secretary of the navy basked in the display of revived power at the site of the worst debacle in the navy's history. It was a pageant fit for a monarch, nothing "usual" about it.

Supposedly, the president was traveling under a strict news embargo, his whereabouts a secret to the world. But they were no secret to Honolulu. As he cruised past the welcoming armada, the presidential flag flew conspicuously from the *Baltimore*'s mainmast, and in the ensuing three days, when his motorcade took him to Waikiki, the city center, and nearby military installations, he traveled in an open car at his own request, responding to cheering crowds. Someone specified that the car had to be red, supposedly Roosevelt himself. The choice, so the story goes, was between one belonging to the proprietress of a well-known brothel and the fire chief's; though less commodious, the fire chief's was chosen.

All Hawaii's outgoing mail was halted for those three days, and censorship remained in force to "localize" knowledge that the president was traveling by sea and was now ashore in the territory. On July 29, his last evening there, he'd hold what the White House counted as his 962nd press conference, but his remarks that day and any other news of his trip remained under official wraps until the afternoon of August 10, when, voyaging on a destroyer, he reentered U.S. territorial waters off Alaska. Thus fifteen days elapsed between the taking on July 26 of a photograph showing Roosevelt in a Panama hat on the deck of the *Baltimore,* flanked by his top two commanders in the Pacific, General Douglas MacArthur and Admiral Chester Nimitz, and its publication, on the front page of *The New York Times* and other papers across the country. The accompanying *Times* dispatch specified in its dateline that it had been "delayed." Thanking the press for its patriotic docility in time of war, the president called the blackout on his tour "a modern marvel." (Even the two Honolulu papers, the *Advertiser* and the *Star,* were required to suppress the news that the president had been a conspicuous presence in their city.) MacArthur, who grumbled about being summoned from the war zone for "a political picture-taking junket," wasn't alone in assuming that this particular snapshot was for Roosevelt the main trophy of his long voyage.

But there was another purpose: getting a handle on this brilliant, vainglorious, histrionic general who, deep into the spring, had flirted

JULY 26, 1944. With General Douglas MacArthur in Pearl Harbor. (Admiral Chester W. Nimitz was to their left.)

with Republican congressmen, showing himself susceptible to their flattery and assurances that there was a wellspring of enthusiasm for his promotion to the presidency. "If this system of left-wingers and New Dealism is continued another four years," a Nebraska representative named Arthur Miller had written to him, "I am certain that this monarchy that is being established in America will destroy the rights of the common people." The general thanked him for his "scholarly letter," agreeing, "We must not inadvertently slip into the same condition internally as the one which we fight externally." Only the release of those letters, combined with Governor Dewey's apparent grip on the Republican nomination, had forced him to disclaim any political ambitions. MacArthur would be guilty of even more flagrant indiscipline during the Korean War, provoking Harry Truman, a more straightforward executive, to send him packing. Roosevelt reacted to this foreshadowing of that climactic clash as if it had been an amusing faux pas, beneath his notice. He wasn't visibly flustered when the grandstanding general in his leather flying jacket and trademark floppy cap contrived to arrive late, sirens blaring, forty-five minutes after all the other admirals and generals, to salute the commander in chief on the *Baltimore*. In short order, Roosevelt showed he knew how to soothe and flatter the general's sensitive ego and win his adherence.

The two men hadn't met in seven years, but their acquaintance ran back to World War I, when Major MacArthur and Assistant Secretary Roosevelt consulted on mobilization plans. MacArthur was army chief of staff when Roosevelt came to the White House in 1933—in fact, led his inaugural parade astride what William Manchester describes as "a huge stallion"—and stayed on for two years. Recalled to active service in 1941 at age sixty-one, he was given at Roosevelt's instigation command of all American and Filipino forces in the Philippines, an American colony still, soon to be overwhelmed by Japanese invaders. MacArthur vowed to go down fighting with his troops, but Roosevelt ordered him to abandon his command post on the island of Corregidor and withdraw to Australia, setting the stage for his classic vow in that season of defeat: "I shall return." With all this shared history and his own proud sense of himself, MacArthur felt entitled to speak more familiarly to the president than others of his high rank would. He seems even, in casual banter, to have responded to being addressed as "Douglas" by tossing in a few "Franklins".

With the same studied casualness, it was the general who first brought up the political campaign, asking Roosevelt on one of their drives to assess Dewey's chances, a question his nominal chief, George Marshall, would have considered a breach of discipline, way out of line. The president offered a stock answer, saying he had no time for politics. Not playing along, MacArthur laughed. Finally, Roosevelt laughed too. He's then quoted as saying, "If the war against Germany ends before the election, I won't be re-elected." Having warmed to the subject of his own prospects, he asked MacArthur for his best guess. The general assured him he was "the overwhelming favorite with the troops." That seemed to clear the air. They now spoke as old comrades, not the potential rivals some partisans had imagined them to be.

When they got around to talking strategy, there was a substantial issue to be addressed, one that was dividing military planners in Washington: whether the most efficient line of assault on Japan's heartland led through Taiwan—more commonly known then by its Portuguese name, Formosa—or the Philippines. Roosevelt, unlike Churchill, wasn't given to nagging or second-guessing his generals. It was highly unusual for him to be intervening on a strategic issue of this sort before his service chiefs had reached a consensus, even more so for him to do it with none of them present. But this time, it's obvious, he didn't want the chiefs and all the planners and subordinates who followed in their train to come between him and the temperamental MacArthur. The chief of naval operations himself, Fleet Admiral Ernest J. King, had been in Honolulu consulting with Admiral Nimitz when Roosevelt sailed from San Diego. King, the staunchest advocate of the Formosa option, actually flew over the president's ship as he traveled back to Washington. He'd been discreetly led to understand his presence wasn't wanted. The whole point of the meeting was for the commander in chief to make sure he was on the same wavelength as his top general in the Pacific.

For all his complaints about political picture taking, MacArthur had been angling for months for such a chance to step outside the chain of command and argue that the highest priority had to be given to winning back the Philippines. "I do not want command of the Navy, but must control their strategy," he had declared baldly in a memo to Secretary Stimson. On occasion, the headstrong commander hinted he might have to carry his appeal to the American people. The best therapy for MacArthur, Roosevelt understood, was to take his strategic ideas seriously.

The general's most strongly felt argument was also his weakest militarily. It was that his personal honor was at stake, the country's too, given that he'd been forced in 1942 to abandon his troops when they were already on short rations on the fortified peninsula of Bataan, from which they'd eventually be marched under savage conditions to a Japanese internment camp, with hundreds of Americans and thousands of Filipinos falling by the wayside and dying from beatings, dysentery, and disease. By some accounts, traceable to MacArthur himself and possibly exaggerated by him for dramatic effect, he went so far as to warn the president in a private exchange that the American people would "register most complete resentment against you at the polls this fall" if the United States failed to liberate its prisoners and the Filipino people at the earliest opportunity.

For the absent chiefs, Admiral King and General Marshall, the issue wasn't a commander's honor but which line of attack would yield the earliest defeat of Japan, with the smallest loss of American lives. Nimitz was tasked with presenting the navy's strategic concept, more the absent admiral King's than his own, in a three-hour discussion that went on until midnight on the president's second evening in Honolulu. Roosevelt presided in a manner that seemed "entirely neutral," MacArthur would relate, as the two commanders took turns at a large map of the Pacific, stabbing it with a long pointer. Leahy later wrote that the president was "at his best as he tactfully steered the discussion from one point to another and narrowed down the disagreement." But when the general spoke of liberating Luzon—the northernmost island in the Philippines, also the largest, most populous, and site of its capital, Manila—Roosevelt broke in. "Douglas," he said, showing he'd been briefed on this issue, "to take Luzon would demand heavier losses than we can stand. It seems to me we *must* bypass it."

In what proved to be a turning point in the discussion, MacArthur replied with feeling and authority, fusing his tactical approach with his sense of a moral imperative. "My losses," he said, "would not be heavy . . . The days of the frontal attack are over. Modern weapons are too deadly and direct assault is no longer feasible. Only mediocre commanders still use it. Your good commanders do not turn in heavy losses." His approach envisioned "leap-frogging" the enemy's strongest points with an eye to severing its communications by sea and from the air. If he took Luzon, he told Roosevelt, U.S. forces would dominate the South China Sea and cut Japan off from its conquests to the south and the raw materials they supplied, notably oil and food. If Luzon were bypassed, it would remain a formidable base for Japanese naval and air strikes.

The two admirals at the Waikiki session, Nimitz and Leahy, were swayed in varying degrees, and so was the president. The bypass strategy wasn't buried that evening—the chiefs still had to be brought along—but the balance of influence had tipped decisively in MacArthur's favor. "Someday there will be a flag-raising in Manila," Roosevelt wrote to him a couple of days later, "and without question I want you to do it." He only wished, he said, that the two of them could swap roles. "I have a hunch that you would make more of a go as President than I would as General in the retaking of the Philippines." It was a perfectly gauged application of soft soap, acknowledging when it no longer mattered, except to MacArthur's ego, that he had the stature to fill Roosevelt's job but suggesting that no one else could do his.

The general had arrived full of complaints about a political junket. On his return trip, he was in a mood of elation. "We've sold it!" he exclaimed. "You know," he later told a trusted journalist, with a characteristic touch of hauteur, "the President is a man of great vision—once things are explained to him." Within three months, Douglas MacArthur had landed on the east coast of Leyte, in time to produce helpful headlines in the final days of the president's reelection campaign, along with the iconic staged photograph of himself striding through the shallows to fulfill his sacred vow. Shocked by Roosevelt's appearance in Honolulu, he'd supposedly said, "The mark of death is on him. In six months, he'll be in his grave." Yet once on Leyte, putting aside such forebodings, he wrote to Roosevelt urging him to journey to Manila for the flag raising the president had promised. MacArthur wasn't inclined to understatement. Such a gesture, he said, would "electrify the world and redound to the credit and honor of the United States for a thousand years."

Barely six months after the Waikiki meeting, MacArthur announced the fall of Manila. His campaign in Luzon had unfolded swiftly with a succession of brilliant surprise attacks leapfrogging Japanese strongpoints with, as he'd promised, surprisingly low casualties on the American side. His victory announcement, however, proved premature by several weeks; in the interval, there was ghastly bloodshed and devastation, due mainly to Japanese reprisals on Filipinos. The flag raising had to be delayed, and when it finally occurred, it wasn't the inspiring event the general had scripted for himself. As he surveyed the ruins of a city he'd thought of as home, there was too much for him to mourn.

· · ·

The six-month lease on life MacArthur had given Roosevelt in Wai-kiki had expired by the time the too early announcement of the taking of Manila reached the Crimea, where, at Yalta, the president was meeting Stalin and Churchill. From there, possibly thinking back to that last encounter, he messaged MacArthur with praise that, while also premature, was well deserved: "The celerity of movement and economy of force involved in this victory add immeasurably to our appreciation of your success." He didn't need to say it was his success too. Economy of force was a concept he appreciated. The political and military strategizing, not to mention the tact, that went into his handling of MacArthur couldn't be disentangled one from the other. At the War Department, Henry Stimson, no praise singer, would conclude that it had "smoothed the way for the final campaign against Japan." Anthony Eden's word "artistry" again comes to mind.

For a day and a half after MacArthur took off, the president followed an unusually crowded schedule around Honolulu, visiting a dozen different military installations, giving brief pep talks at most of them with the three White House news service reporters tagging along; they'd been barred from the crossing on the *Baltimore*. Their presence helped put to rest a rumor that had been relayed to Harry Hopkins back at the White House by J. Edgar Hoover: that the as yet unannounced Pacific tour was being canceled because Roosevelt was too ill to carry on. At Hickam Field, the president watched badly wounded troops from Saipan being off-loaded from ambulance planes. Several were carried over to meet him. A few hours later, he had himself wheeled slowly by a Secret Service man through all the wards that contained amputees in a large new naval hospital in the hills above Honolulu. "He had known for twenty-three years what it was to be deprived of the use of both legs," Sam Rosenman wrote. "He wanted to display himself and his useless legs to those boys who would have to face the same bitterness. This crippled man on the little wheel chair wanted to show them that it was possible to rise above such physical handicaps."

It wasn't a display he'd ever made to the nation at large, nor one he was about to make now, at the start of his final campaign. The three White House reporters got to follow his progress through the wards, but trained in self-censorship on matters attaching to the president's paralysis, they knew better than to attempt a description as complete and graphic as the one Rosenman would later set down. No pictures were allowed of "this crippled man on the little wheel chair" as, in one of his finest hours, he stopped by one bed after another to smile and offer private words of encouragement. "I never saw Roosevelt with tears in his eyes," Rosenman observed. "That day as he was wheeled out of the hospital he was close to them."

A false note in the president's press conference a couple of hours later was scarcely noticed. Asked why American forces were doing so well in jungle fighting at which the Japanese were thought to excel, he slipped into a racial chauvinism that wasn't considered politically incorrect at the height of the war but that the embattled leader had previously avoided. "It sounds like a little bit of boasting," Roosevelt said, "but it is the difference between our type of civilization and our type of fellow, and their type of civilization and fellow. We will take them on at any game, war or pleasure, and beat them at it."

Back on the *Baltimore* that evening, Roosevelt sailed for the barren, sparsely populated Aleutian Islands, extending more than twelve hundred miles west of Alaska, in which they're incorporated politically. For the next two weeks, his movements still under a blanket of secrecy, the leader of the wartime alliance would be at sea in the northern Pacific, frequently fog-bound, with only Admiral Leahy among his key advisers to assist him. Rosenman had been left in Hawaii, as had the three White House reporters. Leahy didn't see the point of the excursion. "I look forward to little of value in the remainder of our scheduled cruise," he wrote in his diary. Roosevelt didn't find it necessary to explain why he insisted on going to these remote outposts. It seems likely that he'd told the navy he wanted to sail as close as possible to a combat zone in the Pacific, in which case the Aleutians, less than a thousand miles from the nearest Japanese-held island, were what he got. Two of their more remote islands, Attu and Kiska, had actually been occupied by the enemy for nearly a year. On Attu, the outnumbered Japanese garrison, facing defeat by an American landing force in May 1943, mounted a suicidal banzai charge, one of the biggest of the war. When the smoke cleared, the onslaught had left 600 Americans dead, another twelve hundred wounded. Japanese losses were 2,315 dead, only twenty-eight enemy troops taken prisoner. Thirteen months later, the threat to U.S. territory had long since receded. Roosevelt didn't even go to Attu. On August 3, he landed on a previously uninhabited island called Adak, where an "advance" naval headquarters had been set up, having traveled 2,335 miles from Pearl Harbor in five and a half days to get there.

Speaking breezily at an officers' mess in a Quonset hut, the commander in chief strove to help his listeners believe they were fulfilling a vital role in this cold and forgotten place. There was panic on the West Coast, he recalled, when the Japanese landed in the Aleutians: "From these islands the enemy was going to come down and destroy San Francisco, Seattle and Los Angeles. The invasion was on!" No one would have guessed how many thousands of men would have to be dedicated to the task of "throwing the Japs out and, secondly, making it impossible for the Japs to come back. Live and learn . . . In the days to come, I won't trust the Japs around the corner." The Aleutians would always be part of Alaska, he promised, and Alaska would always be part of the United States.

He was then marooned there for twenty-six hours by bad weather. The ship's radio passed on encrypted War and State Department bulletins, along with personal and diplomatic messages that couldn't wait. He had plenty on which to brood as he fished off the forecastle of the *Baltimore*, catching several small fish.

Of all such messages, the hardest to digest had arrived when he was still in mid-ocean between Pearl Harbor and Adak. It reported the death at only forty-five of Missy LeHand, for the better part of twenty years his briskly efficient and totally devoted secretary, occasional hostess at White House dinners, and rare in-house second-guesser. She'd also been, by most of the usual measures, the most important woman in his life in those years with the exception of his mother and maybe—only maybe—his wife. The First Lady outranked her, but Missy spent far more time with Roosevelt, on easier, more intimate terms. How intimate, as Geoffrey Ward rightly comments, addressing the inevitable question of whether the relationship ever found physical expression, remains "unknown and unknowable." There were certainly opportunities. For months in three winters, 1924–26, when Roosevelt was trying to overcome or at least adjust to his disability, the two lived together in Florida on a houseboat called the *Larooco*, where Eleanor only once set foot; following that, they shared a cottage in Warm Springs; still later, Missy lived in the governor's mansion in Albany and the White House, entering the boss's bedroom early and late, as needed. Childhood rheumatic fever had left her with chronic heart problems, and twice she suffered what were described as nervous breakdowns. Half a year into the third term, an incapacitating stroke paralyzed her right side and severely limited her speech. Normally optimistic and humorous, she now became depressive, sometimes wept uncontrollably when the man whom she alone addressed as simply "F.D." visited her. Discomfited by such displays of naked emotion, he curtailed his visits but paid all her medical costs and rewrote his will to provide that in the event of his death, half the income from his estate would go to meet Missy's needs, the other half to Eleanor. After a frail and distraught Missy moved back to her family in Somerville, Massachusetts, he continued to write letters, but these came to sound perfunctory in their repeated promises to visit soon when he got a break from the pressures of war, especially when written from Hyde Park, where he was already taking a breather or, in one case, when the letter mentioned a six-day fishing excursion he'd just enjoyed in Canada. At the time of her death, he'd not seen her in more than a year; the call she expected the previous Christmas had never come.

With the president at sea on the *Baltimore*, it was left to his press secretary and speechwriter to draft and release an appropriate statement of grief on his behalf. It's not clear that anyone ever had the courage to describe for Roosevelt the poignant circumstances of Missy's final hours, for that couldn't easily be done without touching on his own decline. She was stricken after viewing a newsreel showing him in the railway car reading the speech in which he'd just accepted his fourth nomination for president. Not having seen recent images of the man to whom so much of her short life had been pledged, she was appalled by his apparent loss of weight, his haggard look. Once at home, she pulled out old photographs of herself and "F.D." in happier, healthier times. In the middle of the night, she suffered a seizure; by morning, she was dead; an embolism to the brain was said to have been the cause.

Roosevelt's reaction can be imagined but not described. He was alone with whatever grief he felt. If he said anything about Missy LeHand to the all-male entourage of military officers with which he was traveling, it wasn't recorded. Still, it's worth dwelling on this stark moment in the northern Pacific before passing on from the somber, windswept Aleutians. Considering the whole context of the war and the unresolved issues it still presented, the political race he now faced, and the health concerns that accounted for the daily attendance of his personal cardiologist, the way forward might momentarily have darkened; the man held to be most powerful in the world might have felt the limitations on his effectiveness, his power; more than usually, he might have considered his own vulnerability, his mortality.

"You and I lost a very good friend," Missy's onetime assistant and eventual successor, Grace Tully, said to him once he was back in the White House. "Yes, poor Missy," the president replied. As Tully describes it, that was the whole conversation. He was brimming with emotion but wouldn't, couldn't, put it into words.

The War Department bulletins landing in the days after the radiogram about Missy's sudden death seemed overwhelmingly positive, at least at first. George Patton's Third Army had broken through German defenses at Avranches in lower Normandy and was finally accelerating eastward toward Paris, presaging its fall by the end of the month. On the eastern front, the Red Army swarmed into the cities of Lwów, the former Lemberg, and Brest Litovsk, where Lenin's fledgling regime signed a humiliating pact with the kaiser's government in 1917 and which Stalin was now bent on holding; by the time Roosevelt sailed north from Hawaii, Soviet troops occupied all the Polish lands the dictator had claimed at Tehran, a fait accompli the president had fatalistically anticipated all along. There, victory over the Germans brought an undertow of issues the Allies had circled, evaded, addressed fitfully, but not resolved.

Within days, Red Army units under the command of Marshal Konstantin Rokossovsky were advancing on the Vistula River, north and south of Warsaw. It was at this moment, on August 1, that the commanders of the mainly underground Polish Home Army, the military remnant operating on the authority of the exile government in London, chose to proclaim the start of a long-planned general rising in the capital so that Poles could participate in the expulsion of the Nazis and shape their own future before the Russians shaped it for them. At that moment, too, Premier Mick—Mikołajczyk—had

just arrived in Moscow to work out the accommodation with Stalin toward which Roosevelt had prodded him in June. For his part,
inwardly grieving and literally at sea, the president was receiving
only fragmentary reports on this intricate, fast-changing situation. In
shaping his replies, he depended on drafts prepared mostly by the
Joint Chiefs of Staff, under General Marshall's supervision, rather
than the State Department. In reviewing and revising these, he had
only Admiral Leahy on whom to rely and his own instincts.

No one—neither Stalin nor Roosevelt, Premier Mick nor the
underground Poles—appears to have foreseen Hitler's ferocious response to this constellation of events. All had assumed that the reeling
Wehrmacht would soon have to fall back from Warsaw and regroup.
Rokossovsky planned to cross the Vistula by the end of the month.
But a raging führer, still recovering from the attempt on his life two
weeks earlier, wasn't interested in orderly retreat. Instead, he embraced
a psychopathic proposal from the SS chief, Heinrich Himmler, for the
total destruction of the city and dispatched reinforcements, two SS
divisions, primed for the job. In the next two months, nearly half the
insurgent force and more than 200,000 civilians would be slaughtered, and Warsaw, bombed from the air and assaulted by tanks and
heavy artillery, largely razed.

Early on, the signals reaching Roosevelt on the *Baltimore* were
mixed. Forwarding a message from Stalin on his plans to receive Premier Mick at the Kremlin, Churchill attached a hopeful preface: "This
seems to me the best ever received from U.J." Nearly two weeks later,
passing on another Stalin message on Poland, he still writes, "The
mood is more agreeable than we have sometimes met, and I think that
we should persevere."

In fact, the Soviet mood was turning darker and more disagreeable by
the day. Stalin had his own designs on Premier Mick and nothing but
contempt for the rising in Warsaw by the outmatched patriotic Poles
who'd deliberately refrained from alerting Moscow to their plans and
proudly spurned British and American pleas that they recognize, at
least tacitly, Soviet boundary claims. In the territory it had already
seized, Moscow scraped together a shadow government it named the
Polish Committee of National Liberation, made up largely of leftist

nonentities for whom its territorial demands would never be an issue. Stalin pressed Premier Mick to engage with those Poles, few of whom he'd even heard of, dangling the premiership of what the dictator was now openly calling a government rather than a committee; in effect, he was asking his guest to swap one government and premiership for another, to accept a minority stake in a provisional regime he might nominally lead but not control. Demurring, Mick returned to London, taking with him Roosevelt's hopes for a way out of the Polish impasse.

These events all transpired in only two weeks, in which the president of the United States was rendered a passive observer, more by the shifting military situation in Central Europe than his own isolation in the distant Pacific. Within another week, on the day he finally returned to the White House, Ambassador Harriman ended a cable from Moscow marked for his eyes on a note of despair. "These men are bloated with power," the ambassador concluded, and "expect they can force their decisions without question upon us and all countries."

Churchill, an optimist no longer, wanted to press the Russians further to cooperate with Allied airdrops of military supplies to the Warsaw fighters, even to the point of forcing a showdown by commandeering the use of Soviet airfields. By this time, it was clear the Red Army, still parked on the other side of the wide Vistula, would do little or nothing to aid the resistance. Told by his advisers that dropped supplies would likely fall into the hands of the Nazis, Roosevelt tersely replied that it was too late, saying he'd been informed that the resistance was abandoning Warsaw. He'd been misinformed, but that didn't matter. Without saying so, he clearly felt there was nothing to be gained from pressing Stalin further. He still counted on the dictator's cooperation on other fronts, including the Pacific and the groundwork for the international security organization on which formal consultations had just begun at Dumbarton Oaks, a Washington estate recently acquired by Harvard, with Ambassador Gromyko leading the Soviet delegation to talks involving only the first three of Roosevelt's Four Policemen. Not without an expression of distress "over our inability to give adequate support to the heroic defenders of Warsaw," the president coolly advised the prime minister, "there now appears nothing we can do to assist them."

All these years later, it's far from clear he was wrong on the tactical issue. But he has been harshly judged. "Though he held the strongest cards in the diplomatic pack," the British historian Norman Davies wrote, without specifying which cards might have made a difference, "he preferred to play none of them, and to let the tragedy of Warsaw run its course. Roosevelt's inaction was every bit as detrimental as Stalin's." That's a little wild. Roosevelt had no army standing by on the Vistula, no police primed to protect Polish fighters, no obvious way to confront the dictator effectively. At the height of the war, with the Nazi state still to be vanquished and dismantled, he didn't see the point of gestures.

Shortly before the surviving partisans surrendered to the Germans, George Orwell wrote a polemic on the Warsaw rising. "There can be no real alliance on the basis of 'Stalin is always right,'" he said. "The first step towards a real alliance is the dropping of illusions." Orwell was skewering the soft-minded fellow traveling of British intellectuals, not Roosevelt, who said nothing at this time, privately or publicly, to whitewash Stalin's insistence on determining the outcome of the "self-determination" promised the Poles. Choosing silence, he seems to have put his illusions and whatever hopes he retained for the alliance with the Soviet Union on hold. George Kennan, who'd just been reassigned to Moscow, later contended that this would have been the time to confront Stalin, to threaten a cutoff of aid. But Kennan was not consulted. His friend and fellow Kremlinologist Chip Bohlen, who'd soon be moved into the White House as an adviser, might or might not have been; his memoir doesn't say. There he concludes that although the President's understanding of Stalin's thinking and ambitions was shallow, his instincts at the time of the Warsaw rising were probably sound. If the United States had threatened to cut off aid, Bohlen said, "the outcome in Poland would have been the same, but the entire course of the negotiations would have been changed, probably for the worse." Put less diplomatically, he was saying, with all the benefit of hindsight, that Roosevelt, the cagey, inveterate dilettante, probably made the best call and that Kennan, the deep and serious expert, was wrong.

Even by the standards of that simpler era—before the advent of expensive media consultants and TV advertising, let alone Internet and cable news cacophony—the windup of this master politician's Pacific tour had to be seen, when viewed in its political context, as amateurish, really a fizzle. The tour had its serious side—notably the strategy session with MacArthur and Nimitz and the hospital visits to the wounded—but once the news embargo had been lifted on the Honolulu talks and the president had reached the mainland, sailing into Puget Sound on a destroyer called the *Cummings* to which he'd transferred from the much larger *Baltimore,* the commander in chief who'd vowed not to run again "in the usual sense" was again a candidate exploiting his office. The plan was for him to deliver a nationwide radio address from the forecastle deck of the *Cummings* as it lay at anchor in the navy yard at Bremerton, Washington.*

In the judgment of Sam Rosenman, "The speech had nothing to say, and said it poorly." Without any assistance and only minimal revision, Roosevelt himself had dictated it in snatches aboard the destroyer as a chatty, discursive chronological narrative of his tour. Lacking a theme, full of asides on subjects as extraneous as his fishing forays and the economic future of Alaska, the speech rambled on far too long, for thirty-five minutes, coming across not as an urgent pronouncement by a vigorous wartime leader but as the stray and unfocused thoughts of a weary tourist. For reasons that would only gradually be revealed, his delivery was also feeble, at least by his standard, but it was the text itself—his own considered, or unconsidered, product—that showed that something had happened in the Pacific to depress his spirit and sap his will. It could have been Missy's death, or Stalin's double-dealing, or anxiety about the coming campaign—or a sense that he'd been wasting his time and putting on a poor show in the Aleutians. Or a medley of these and similar concerns. As so often with this president in a time of brooding, one concern compounded another, sending him into verbal detours and digressions.

Listening to the speech, neither Rosenman in Washington nor the national radio audience, running into the tens of millions, had any

---

* The original plan had been for the president to address a crowd in a Seattle stadium. This was knocked down by the White House press secretary, Steve Early, in a message to his boss while he was still at sea: "May I point out that you traveled secretly across the country and presumably will follow the same procedure returning home. Therefore, if you appear before people of Seattle at ball park and conceal yourself elsewhere, reaction will certainly not be good."

AUGUST 12, 1944. Speaking from the deck of the USS *Cummings* in
Bremerton Navy Yard, with Anna, right, looking on anxiously.

way of knowing that Roosevelt was also in acute pain. To stand erect
on the deck, he had to be helped into his steel braces. It was the first
time he'd had them strapped on in at least half a year; having shed
twelve or more pounds under his restricted diet, designed to relieve
strain on his heart, he found they no longer fit properly. The steel dug
into his flanks. Not only that, the ship rocked and a strong breeze
riffled the pages of his text. Holding himself erect with his arms and
keeping the pages in order became a strain. Also disorienting were
echoes of his own words whooping back from loudspeakers placed
around the yard, where a crowd of eight thousand workers and sailors
shifted uneasily. Accustomed to taking the measure of his audiences,
he knew he was losing, in danger of alarming, this one. A photograph
unearthed by researchers for the filmmaker Ken Burns's documentary
on the Roosevelts shows his daughter, Anna, summoned to meet him
in Bremerton, standing at the rails and staring anxiously at her father.

She knows something is wrong but not what, doesn't know that the president, from almost the start of his remarks, had been suffering chest pains, a severe attack, lasting between fifteen minutes and half an hour, of "substernal oppression with radiation in both shoulders," as Dr. Bruenn would put it in his "clinical notes," not published until 1970. The cardiologist was describing an episode of angina pectoris, the only one that has come to light in this last year of Roosevelt's life. If chest pains had been acknowledged then, three weeks after his renomination for a fourth term, the incident could have upended the presidential race, even marked the end of his political career.

"This was the first time under my observation that he had something like this," Bruenn said in an interview many years later. "This was proof positive that he had coronary disease, no question about it." In yet another interview, the cardiologist would acknowledge, "It scared the hell out of us."

The thought that it might be a heart attack is likely to have crossed the president's mind too. Somehow he labored through to the end of his speech without collapsing. "I had severe pain," he exclaimed to Dr. Bruenn once he was carried belowdecks. A count of white blood cells was then taken and an electrocardiogram administered, a cardiograph being at hand by this time wherever he traveled. "No unusual abnormalities were detected," Bruenn would say, writing carefully; in other words, just the usual ones. It had not been a heart attack, Roosevelt must have been assured, though perhaps not in so many words. (In later years, Bruenn would call it a "transient episode.") His blood pressure was high but no higher than it had been. That same evening, he was wheeled onto his train in Seattle. Regular EKG tracings were taken over the next four and a half days as he traveled across the country to Washington with the security ban on disclosing his whereabouts back in force.

On his return to the White House, after an absence of five weeks, insiders generally held the president to be, as his aide Bill Hassett noted in his diary, "in fine spirits, looking fine, too, brown, a little thin." Secretary Stimson, seeing him for the first time since June, found him "in better physical form than I had imagined." His expectation would have been shaped by the photograph on the train of a slack-jawed president, the subpar Bremerton performance, and the whispers these stirred within the administration, as Rosenman would later put it, about whether "the old master had lost his touch." That his visitors were studying him so closely shows that doubts about his ability to carry on were no longer confined to his enemies.

Roosevelt's suntan gives him a sturdy appearance in a professionally styled campaign portrait taken at Hyde Park several days after his return: the light shines off his broad brow; his chin is thrust forward, leaving his neck in the shadows; his shirt and suit fit perfectly. He looks every inch the determined, commanding wartime leader. Five days later, Henry Morgenthau calls on him in his bedroom, where the president, sitting up in his pajamas and Navy cape, was accustomed to holding court before, with his valet's help, getting dressed for the office. The Treasury secretary, a faithful friend, had taken no note of Roosevelt's appearance at an office meeting the previous week. This time he writes in his diary, "I really was shocked for the first time because he is a very sick man, and seems to have wasted away."

The lighting and setting make a difference in the impressions visitors carry away. So does the acuteness of the visitor. Mary Bingham, liberal wife of the publisher of the Louisville *Courier-Journal*, recorded one of the more telling descriptions of the presidential visage and demeanor in this period after visiting the White House to bemoan the shabby treatment Vice President Wallace had received: "His face in repose looks thin, and about the jaws somewhat sunken. When he is talking, and his face is animated, one does not notice this." That sunken look, she suggests, "accounts for some of the very bad pictures," but it's offset by his voice, which remains "powerful, positive and resonant," conveying a sense of "strength and equally great control." Roosevelt was strong enough to reel off fibs about his lack of involvement in the selection of his new running mate, on whom he left a distinctly different impression.

Harry Truman saw the president only two or three times between the night of his nomination and the election. The first time was the day after Roosevelt's return, when the senator was invited for a shirt-sleeves lunch of sardines on toast, under the magnolia tree on the White House lawn, with Anna included as hostess. In the photographs taken that afternoon, Roosevelt looked "a haggard old man," so David McCullough interprets them, by comparison to his running

AUGUST 18, 1944. Lunching with his running mate.

mate, who was only two years younger. Truman couldn't help notic-
ing that the president's hand trembled so much when he tried to pour
cream into his coffee that most of it spilled into the saucer. What
might have been construed as a foray into dark humor didn't come
across as lighthearted at all. Truman mentioned he might fly between
campaign stops. Roosevelt insisted he use only trains. "One of us has
to stay alive," he said.

"He's still the leader he's always been, and don't let anyone kid you
about it," the newly anointed candidate dutifully told the press gang
on his way out. To an aide in his office, he privately offered a contrary
assessment. "Physically he's just going to pieces," he said. It's not that
the man from Independence saw more deeply than visitors like Mrs.
Bingham or insiders who'd worked with Roosevelt all along. It's that
he suddenly had the largest personal stake. His thought couldn't be
completed or uttered, but if Roosevelt was going to pieces, Harry Tru-

man could hardly help asking himself, at some level of consciousness, where he was headed.

Others from Missouri were wondering too. Charles Ross, a top reporter on the *St. Louis Post-Dispatch*, had been an old chum and valedictorian of Truman's high school class. (Later President Truman, who hated the newspaper, would name his classmate White House press secretary.) A couple of weeks after the senator's lunch with the president, Ross started asking whether Roosevelt intended to serve out a full term. A rumor had reached his paper that the president was thinking of resigning once Germany collapsed in order to devote himself to the peace settlement. A possible source was the Democratic chairman, Bob Hannegan, to whom Roosevelt said something of the sort. What's curious here and not easy to explain is that the reporter sought out Dr. Frank Lahey, the Boston surgeon, for confirmation. In the reporter's mind, the resignation story was obviously tied to the question of Roosevelt's health, his ability to serve, on which Lahey had laid down a stern warning in strictest secrecy two months earlier.

Once again, the surgeon wrote a confidential letter to the White House physician, Admiral McIntire. The man from the *Post-Dispatch* had asked if he'd seen Roosevelt professionally. "I told him," Lahey now assured the admiral, "that I thought this was something he had no right to ask, and that the only answer I could make was that you had told me, and it was my opinion, that he was now in excellent health." McIntire, of course, knew this was exactly the opposite of what Lahey really thought.

"I suppose we must expect more and more of this business," the letter concluded, "as we get nearer the election time."

August had been an exhilarating month for the Allies in France. Paris was liberated on the twenty-fifth—a "brilliant presage of total victory," in Roosevelt's words—followed by the ports of Marseille and Toulon on the twenty-eighth, opening sorely needed supply lines for forces advancing rapidly from the west and the south. Between those dates, on the twenty-sixth, the President had a potentially fateful meeting bearing on relations with both the British and the Russians in the months and years to come. The meeting was with Niels Bohr, the visionary physicist whose application of quantum theory to the structure of the atom had led to one of the key theoretical breakthroughs of the century, unlocking the secrets of the atom's nucleus and, ultimately, the possibilities of nuclear fission and fusion, as well as earning him a Nobel Prize at the comparatively early age of thirty-seven. Smuggled out of Nazi-occupied Denmark and then airlifted from neutral Sweden by the British secret service in October 1943, he arrived at Los Alamos, New Mexico, the top secret site of the Manhattan Project, at the end of the year. Within three months, he was in Washington petitioning for an audience with the president through the good offices of Vannevar Bush, Roosevelt's top science adviser, and Justice Felix Frankfurter, whom he'd met earlier.

"Do you think I will be able to understand him?" the president asked Bush when the idea of a meeting with Bohr was broached.

"No, I do not think you probably will," the scientist said he replied, having in mind Bohr's reputation for dense discourse when speaking to people outside his field.

"Never mind, I will talk with him," Roosevelt said, according to Bush, who reconstructed the exchange in a memoir.

If ever there was an illustration of Justice Oliver Wendell Holmes's well-known verdict on Franklin Roosevelt ("a second-class intellect but a first-class temperament"), it was in his encounter with the great physicist. Thinking beyond the first nuclear explosion, still more than a year away—beyond even the end of the war and the inevitable development of even more destructive thermonuclear weapons—Bohr had a profound vision he wanted to impress on Allied leaders: that the bomb, making future wars unthinkable, had to usher in a new era in diplomacy, starting at once. He didn't coin the term but was surely among the first to grasp the concept of "mutually assured destruction." Because the weapon's secrets couldn't be contained, his reasoning went, it was urgent that a framework be erected for international cooperation before the war's end to avoid a catastrophic arms race afterward. With this goal in mind, he hoped for clearance to accept an invitation he'd received from Soviet physicists to visit Moscow.

Justice Frankfurter, one of the president's few correspondents who felt entitled to address him as "Dear Frank," presented the gist of

Bohr's thinking to Roosevelt in a long afternoon meeting at the end of March. He understood Roosevelt to say that the whole problem of how to control the spread of nuclear weapons "worried him to death." So, by his own testimony, Roosevelt was sympathetic to Bohr's thinking and open to meeting him. However, he wanted the physicist to see Churchill first; he might easily have arranged such a meeting himself, but there's no sign that he tried. Dispatching Bohr to London could have been a way of putting off having to see the physicist himself. Later, Churchill would write that Roosevelt had been "startled" when Frankfurter broached the subject of nuclear weapons and blamed Bohr for the security breach. That could have seemed a reasonable deduction. How else could the government's biggest secret have reached a Supreme Court justice's ivory tower at a time when congressional leaders were still in the dark and only a strictly minimal number of administration officials had been let in on it?

Here, once again, we have a stark example of Roosevelt's protean ability to stand on two sides of a sensitive issue he has yet to decide, leaving anyone he meets with the impression that he's fully sympathetic with whatever has been said. So the justice who sought to fix a meeting between the Dane and the president went away with the uplifting feeling that he'd been entrusted with a vital secret mission: to steer Niels Bohr to Churchill. What Roosevelt is unlikely to have told him is that he already had an agreement with Churchill making the British full partners on nuclear policy, under which the United States and Britain promised not to communicate information about the project to a third party without the other's consent. Therefore Churchill had a veto, much to the dismay of Roosevelt's top advisers on nuclear policy.

It took Bohr a couple of months to get to Churchill, who gave him only half an hour and an angry dressing-down that so much as said that the issues he was attempting to raise were no business of even the most brilliant scientists. Another few months passed before the physicist made it back to the White House—with his son Aage, also a physicist and a future Nobel laureate—which he then left, like countless visitors before him, with a warm feeling that he'd finally found a fully sympathetic recipient for his case. According to Aage, Roosevelt readily agreed that there had to be an approach to the Russians. He then regaled father and son with his Tehran tales, promising that he and Stalin ("enough of a realist to understand the revolutionary importance of this scientific and technical advance") would bring Churchill along.

Niels Bohr never saw or heard from Roosevelt again. Nor was any approach on nuclear issues made to Stalin, who, at about the same time, was beginning to receive his own intelligence reports on the goings-on on a high and isolated mesa in New Mexico. He was sure to deduce that his allies, who had ample reason to complain of Soviet secrecy, were themselves being a good deal less than forthcoming with him. By then, showing how deep the layers of mistrust really reached, Roosevelt had been alerted for a year to the likelihood of Soviet espionage on the Manhattan Project.

One challenge immediately before him when he met Bohr was his need to repair a frayed relationship with Churchill, whom he was about to meet for the first time in nine months. They'd gotten together for serious, exhausting consultations in every quarter of 1943, the last of those meetings in Cairo in December, on the heels of the conference in Tehran, where Roosevelt, to ingratiate himself with Stalin, had deliberately held the prime minister at arm's length. It's impossible to know the degree to which his eventual shutting out of the eminent physicist had to do with his effort to be agreeable to Churchill after the two finally met in Quebec in September, or how much his professed readiness to approach the "realist" in the Kremlin on nuclear matters was undermined by Stalin's total lack of interest in assisting non-Communist Polish fighters in Warsaw. He'd shown that not in words but in the immobility of Soviet forces on the other side of the Vistula—plausibly ascribed by Moscow to shortages of ammunition and fuel and similar logistical issues—while the Nazis bombarded and leveled the city.

Roosevelt's habit of juggling numerous slightly related issues at once while deciding how to act on any one of them can be seen as his greatest strength and limitation. He always had a three-dimensional view of politics and policy as overlapping fields of force in constant motion. In his mind, few issues stood alone. He knew his goals, moved forward where he could, improvised when he could. He was an agile thinker, not a deep one, less interested in justifying his actions than in plotting his next move. Quite possibly this cast of mind has something to do with the judgment of James Bryant Conant, the Harvard president (and chemist) who served as Vannevar Bush's deputy: "FDR had only fleeting interest in the atom, and that program never got very far past the threshold of his consciousness." In Conant's view, his attitude was "somewhat cavalier." The Harvard president's take on his most noted alumnus was echoed by specialists in other fields after discovering that the hearty generalist had his own hidden goals and calculations. Repeated encounters could sow disillusion. Field Marshal Sir John Dill, the senior British military man in Washington, a confidant of General Marshall's, sent this scathing assessment to Alan Brooke: "The better I get to know that man, the more superficial and selfish I think him. That is for your eye only as of course it's my job to make the most and best of him."

So it went in the case of Niels Bohr. A few weeks after leaving the physicist with the impression that he grasped the urgency of his appeal, Roosevelt gave his formal assent to a British memorandum that said, "Enquiries should be made regarding the activities of Professor Bohr and steps taken to insure that he is responsible for no leakage of information particularly to the Russians." This could easily have been read as an order to put the great physicist under surveillance. A fulminating Churchill wouldn't have stopped there. "Bohr ought to be confined," he said in a note to an aide, "or made to see that he is very near the edge of mortal crimes."

James MacGregor Burns, an early Roosevelt biographer, characterizes Niels Bohr as "the prophetic voice of international science desperately seeking to forestall an international arms race." Because the physicist wasn't taken seriously, this biographer contends, the atomic age was born "in secrecy and suspicion, not as a shared adventure in scientific cooperation and world unity, but as a military means of beating the Axis and perhaps containing the Russians." No one can say what the result might have been had Roosevelt embraced Bohr's visionary analysis and told Stalin about the bomb, counting on the dictator's cooperation on nuclear issues just then coming into focus. The president had once talked of taking an attitude of noblesse oblige in dealings with the Kremlin, meaning he hoped, by allaying Russian suspicions, to coax Stalin into a more cooperative posture on issues such as Poland. Now, it seems, he'd begun to lose confidence in that approach.

Richard Rhodes, in his history of the making of the bomb, eloquently expresses the insight Bohr struggled to convey: "Nuclear fission and thermonuclear fusion are not acts of Parliament; they are levers embedded deeply in the physical world, discovered because it was possible to discover them, beyond the powers of men to patent or hoard." That cuts against the grain of Churchill's strongest inclinations, his deepest loyalties. He was fighting to preserve Britain's influence and power in the postwar world, to restore an empire. His claim to a share of an atomic duopoly can be seen as part of that fight. So was a deepening grievance against the Americans, not excepting Roosevelt, for tending to demote Britain to the status of junior partner.

A low point in the Anglo-American alliance—and the prime minister's personal relationship with a president he now couldn't count on swaying—came in the immediate aftermath of the Normandy invasion, by far its greatest joint venture. Churchill wanted to cancel, or at least delay further, the already delayed invasion of southern France, which would inevitably draw troops, landing craft, and other resources from the ongoing struggle in Italy. "Let us resolve not to wreck one great campaign for the sake of winning another," he wrote in a supplicating appeal to Roosevelt, who replied by insisting that plans for the invasion hew to the agreed timetable: "Nothing has occurred to require any change . . . My dear friend, I beg you to let us go ahead with our plan."*

Churchill couldn't accept that as the last word. His next message to Roosevelt, labeling the plan as it stood "an absolutely perverse strategy," was never sent. Cooler heads in Whitehall prevailed. It was quickly replaced by one that started, "We are deeply grieved." The

---

* To this message, Roosevelt attached a fillip that was seen by some on the British side as showing him up as narrow and self-interested. "For purely political considerations over here," he wrote, "I could never survive even a slight setback in OVERLORD [the operation in Normandy] if it were known that fairly large forces were diverted to the Balkans." This was more a debating point than a serious argument. Neither Roosevelt nor his military strategists ever considered sending forces to the Balkans.

substitute was only slightly toned down. It all but said Roosevelt was being misled by his generals, that if the two leaders could only meet face-to-face, he'd soon be persuaded to revise the plan. "If you still press upon us the directive of your Chiefs of Staff to withdraw so many of your forces from the Italian campaign and leave all our hopes there dashed to the ground, his Majesty's Government . . . must enter a solemn protest." It was, as the discerning British historian David Reynolds has written, Churchill's "most passionate" dispute with the Americans of the war.

"Winston is very bitter about it and not so sure he really likes FDR," the private secretary to King George VI wrote in his diary. General Alan Brooke wrote of Churchill "wanting to fight the President." The prime minister himself fumed at a meeting with his military chiefs. "If we take this lying down," he said, "there will be no end to what they will put on us."

Roosevelt's response was all tact and firmness. "I appreciate deeply your clear expression of your feelings and views on this decision we are making," he began his reply to Churchill's eruption. That "we" might as well have been italicized. It referred not to the alliance but to the United States, flexing its undeniable primacy. Brooke got the point, his prime minister was resisting. "The Americans now begin to own the major strength on land, in the air and on the sea," he wrote. "They, therefore, consider that they are entitled to dictate how their forces are to be employed."

That was July. The debate went on up to and beyond the actual invasion, which had originally been planned for May in hopes that it would ease the assault on Normandy by drawing off German troops. What was to be the prelude would now be a follow-through. By August, Churchill traveled to the Mediterranean intending to watch the landings he'd sought to postpone from a destroyer off the coast near Cannes. But the destroyer was four miles offshore, and, according to Lord Moran, he didn't hear a shot.

Franklin Roosevelt granted himself a five-day Labor Day weekend at Hyde Park, resting up for his second summit in Quebec with Churchill, due to start the following week. But his mind was clearly elsewhere. It was at the start of this break, traveling up from Washington, that the presidential train made its secretly scheduled stop in Allamuchy, New Jersey, at the edge of the Rutherfurd estate, called Tranquillity, so he could visit the former Lucy Mercer. The three pool reporters were told simply that the president was paying a call on a friend whose husband recently died. From Daisy Suckley, who was along to bear her witness, we learn that the supposed condolence call lasted a full seven hours, from 8:30 in the morning to 3:30 in the afternoon. "She came on the train hatless and stockingless, in a black figured dress, & black gloves," Daisy begins her detailed account, which betrays no hint that Roosevelt, in all their chats over the years, had ever confided to her the nature, history, or consequences of this very special friendship. "She is tall & good-looking rather than beautiful or even pretty," she writes. Daisy had met Lucy once before, twenty-two years earlier, and remembered she looked sad then. "She does not look sad now, but then," she observes, "how little we know about the inner life of others." Even the president "sometimes, in repose, looks really sad."

A fine lunch of jellied soup, squab, salad, and ice cream was served by "two negro waiters" in an English-style manor house to a table-ful of Rutherfurds, their children, and their spouses. Of the dozens of officials, Secret Service men, signal corps operators, and sundry attendants on the train, only Roosevelt and Daisy are mentioned as being among the guests. The rest just waited, it appears, for this royal progress to be resumed. It hadn't been a tryst, but somehow a warning was passed along that it had to be kept from one person—Eleanor, of course—who was "waiting on the platform" when the train pulled in to the station in Highland, New York, at 6:45. That tableau, Eleanor on the platform, made a sad, telling scene from a marriage. "Mrs. Rutherfurd becomes more lovely as one thinks about her," Daisy writes, looking back on her day. "The whole thing was out of a book—a complete setting for a novel."

Winston Churchill boarded the *Queen Mary,* en route to the Quebec summit, with a touch of pneumonia and a mean disposition. In a flash of paranoia, he angrily accused his military chiefs of engaging in a conspiracy against him with their American counterparts; a "frame-up," he called it. But the late summer Atlantic breezes and some chapters by Trollope mellowed him, and soon he was telling Lord Moran that he didn't plan to "beat up" the Americans over Mediterranean strategy.

In the event, the five days at the Château Frontenac in Quebec were the most amicable the two teams of military chiefs would have, largely because they coincided with hard-fought Allied advances in all theaters of the war, on practically all fronts. For their part, the two leaders acted as if there had never been any strain in their partnership. When Churchill offered the British fleet for service in the Pacific, Roosevelt was quick to reply, "I should like to see the British fleet wherever and whenever possible."

His navy chief, Admiral King, was visibly upset. He foresaw British ships crowding already overcrowded ports, straining already overstrained logistics, getting in the way of his fleet. Stalling, King said the matter was under study. "The offer of the British fleet has been made," persisted Churchill, who was focused on reestablishing colonial rule in Singapore, Malaya, and Hong Kong. "Is it accepted?"

"It is," said the president, plainly eager to please, putting aside his own dreams of guiding such colonies to independence under international auspices. "No sooner offered than accepted."

Little time was spent on Poland for want, it seems, of anything new to say, or options to exercise while Warsaw burned. Stalin would briefly relent and allow American bombers to land at Soviet bases after dropping ammunition and arms to hard-pressed Polish forces on the night of September 18, two days after the end of the meeting in Quebec between his two Western allies. The airfields were then closed to American planes.

Hardly any time, either, was spent on the gestation of the new international organization Roosevelt had already named the United Nations, which was left to the attending State Department and Foreign Office specialists at the Dumbarton Oaks conference then heading into its final two weeks, with Moscow's representatives no longer pressing their demand that each of its sixteen so-called republics be recognized as a voting member. In a letter to Stalin before leaving for Quebec, Roosevelt had tactfully urged that the issue—no hint of which had leaked into public view—be put off until after the international organization was up and running, his way of saying that it was more than the United States could swallow.

What absorbed more attention was a proposal for the deindustrial-ization of a defeated Germany—stripping the Ruhr of its steel mills, manufacturing centers, especially its munitions plants—and turning Hitler's fatherland back into an agrarian and pastoral country made up, as Conrad Black wryly draws the picture, of "70 million shep-herds, apple cultivators and poultry farmers." This vision emerged from the U.S. Treasury Department, headed by Roosevelt's neigh-bor Henry Morgenthau Jr. In its draft form, it was titled "A Program to Prevent Germany from Starting a World War III." There were those who thought it threatened to accomplish the opposite. Some of them tended to mention the Treasury secretary's Jewish origins. Henry Stimson, for instance, would call it "Semitism gone wild for vengeance." But Roosevelt, who brought Morgenthau to Quebec, had egged him on. "Germany should be allowed no aircraft of any kind, not even a glider," he said at a White House meeting prior to the conference, according to Morgenthau's diary. On the basis of his experience as a schoolboy in Germany half a century earlier when his father was taking the waters at Bad Nauheim, he regularly presented himself as an expert on German militarism. Uniforms and marching would have to be banned too, he told Morgenthau in an off-the-cuff remark that could be taken as fanciful, or as thinking out loud, or sol-emn policy making, depending on the listener. This had always been his way. Now there were few in his immediate circle with an instinct for when or how to ask whether he was serious.

The Morgenthau Plan was effectively shelved within weeks of the conclusion of the Quebec gathering but not before getting the formal endorsement there of both Roosevelt and Churchill. The prime min-ister in less than twenty-four hours overcame his first reaction, which had been a principled objection. "The English people will not stand for the policy you are advocating," he said combatively, responding to the Treasury secretary's presentation. "I agree with Burke. You cannot indict a whole nation."

That was at a state dinner on September 15. In his diary that night, Morgenthau wrote, "I have never had such a verbal lashing in my life." But before lunch the next day, Churchill had reversed himself. What intervened that morning was an American pledge to extend Lend-Lease beyond Germany's surrender, to the tune of $3 billion in nonmilitary aid to revive a battered, nearly prostrate British economy.

It had all the appearance of a transaction. Only on his return to Washington would Roosevelt heed the counsels of Stimson and Hull, who argued that a prosperous Europe could not be reconstructed on the basis of a plan even more vengeful than the one imposed on the Germans at Versailles twenty-five years earlier, promising further eruptions and "blowbacks," as we'd now say, of nationalism and war. From a vantage point on the other side of the Cold War, then in its earliest stages of gestation, Roosevelt's punitive approach to the question of postwar Germany may appear impulsive and unsteady but hardly more so than Churchill's. With Allied casualty lists lengthening by the thousands each week, V-1 rocket assaults on London in their third month of wanton destruction, Auschwitz no longer a rumor, few could foresee that the reunification of Germany would be hailed, decades later, as a triumph for democracy.

A final topic at Quebec was Franklin Roosevelt himself, the quality of his leadership, the state of his health. It didn't get discussed openly, of course, so it's hard to be sure of what was really said in private. Some of the most widely repeated judgments appeared in print years after the president's death. Lord Moran, Churchill's physician, kept a diary, but it was added to, revised, and rewritten over a score of years before its eventual publication in 1966. In its passage on Quebec, we read, "I wonder how far Roosevelt's health impaired his judgment and sapped his resolve to get to the bottom of each problem before it came up for discussion." That remains a pertinent question, but the sequence of tenses indicates the comment was written after the conference, possibly years after. Noting the president's obvious weight loss, the diary declares in a retrospective voice, "I said to myself then that men at his time of life do not go thin all of a sudden just for nothing." That's an apt observation, too, but Roosevelt might have been long in his grave when it was written, so it was not necessarily prescient.

In a note appended to a diary not published until 1985, Churchill's private secretary, Sir John Colville, who was meeting Roosevelt for the first time, describes being addressed "in flowery language as if I were a public meeting." At Quebec, the note goes on, "I heard him say nothing impressive or even memorable and his eyes seemed glazed." Striking memories, not to be dismissed, but here again, there's no telling when they were set down. On the other hand, General Alan Brooke, often acerbic and unrestrained in his diary jottings on American generals, transcribed no such reflection after dinner at the Citadel. "I sat on the President's right and found him very pleasant and easy to talk to," he wrote.

Winston Churchill appears to be the only person in all the accounts of the Quebec gathering to open the supersensitive question of Roosevelt's life expectancy. As the conference was wrapping up, the prime minister summoned Roosevelt's physician, the resolutely upbeat admiral McIntire, to his room and asked for a "confidential report" on the president's condition. As related in his ghostwritten memoir, the doctor summarized the results of the last checkup "proving there was nothing organically wrong" but "not hesitating to stress the President's age"—seven years less than that of Churchill, who was closing in on seventy—or the "constant strain" he'd been under, a condition also not unknown to the prime minister.

Omitting the finding of congestive heart failure, the daily attendance of a cardiologist, or Roosevelt's alarmingly high blood pressure—which the previous evening, after the screening of the movie *Wilson*,* had soared to its second-highest reading—McIntire blandly repeated his usual assurance that the president could "win through."

"With all my heart I hope so," he has Churchill saying. "We cannot have anything happen to this man. His usefulness to the world is paramount."

---

* *Wilson* wasn't the only movie screened in Quebec. According to the White House log, the previous evening's feature had been Preston Sturges's *Hail the Conquering Hero*. A spoof on patriotism and valor, it ends as a reaffirmation of both and plain old American small-town virtues embodied by its "hero," one Woodrow Lafayette Pershing Truesmith. Not everyone appreciated its sparkling wit. Churchill's secretary dismissed it as "a shockingly bad film chosen by the President." The prime minister walked out "halfway through, which on the merits of the film was understandable," Jock Colville wrote, "but which seemed bad manners to the President." Roosevelt's reaction, to the movie or Churchill's exit, wasn't recorded.

CHAPTER 8

Staying on the Job

THE WEEKEND BEFORE he left for Quebec, the president confessed to Daisy Suckley that he was feeling "logy," meaning sluggish or dull. "He won't be at all surprised if he is beaten in the election," she wrote in her diary on September 4. A couple of days later, he was no cheerier. Phoning from the White House, he said he felt "like a boiled owl." Members of his staff took note of his listlessness, his apparent lack of interest in the looming campaign. Polls were showing a small but worrisome narrowing of his lead. It was down to five points, substantial but not unassailable. "He just doesn't seem to give a damn," Pa Watson, his appointments secretary, told the playwright Robert Sherwood, who'd been summoned back to the White House for speechwriting duties. Harry Hopkins concurred in the diagnosis. Sherwood hadn't seen Roosevelt in eight months. He found him "ravaged" in appearance but—to his surprise after those disheartening in-house reviews—"more full of humor and fight than ever."

That revival in his spirits had come virtually overnight. Credit for it belonged to his Republican opponent, Governor Thomas Dewey, who'd set off on his first major campaign swing just two days before the president left for Canada. Roosevelt, it seemed, had been one of the millions in the former prosecutor's radio audience as he hopped from Philadelphia to Louisville. Dewey's speeches were relentless in building an effective case against the "Fourth-termites" inhabiting the "old, tired, quarrelsome administration." Carefully drafted and packaged, forcefully delivered in a deep and resonant voice that registered as vigorous, they were meant to showcase the energy the candidate—two decades younger than his apparently fading rival—would bring to Washington. In the pretelevision age, Dewey's stiffness, his brittle sense of his own dignity, the lack of pleasure in his forced smiles, were conspicuous only to those who saw him up close. One of these was the journalist Richard Strout, who wrote that the Republican candidate displayed "all a speaker should have except warmth, humor and fellow feeling."

The Republican's speeches had a worse drawback. They irritated Franklin Roosevelt, got under his normally thick skin. "You ought to hear him," the president said to Sherwood. "He plays the part of the heroic racket-buster in one of those gangster movies. He talks to the people as if they were the jury and I was the villain on trial for his life."

The Roosevelt who'd last spoken to a national audience from Bremerton could have lost the election if he'd continued in the same vague, meandering vein that he manifested there. The Roosevelt encountered by Sherwood a month later was focused and primed for a fight. Told at one of his off-the-record press conferences that Dewey had charged him with having a "defeatist" attitude, with believing America was past its prime, he snapped, "Do you believe that?"

"No, sir," came the journalist's reply.

"Neither do I," the president said.

"Beginning about the time I went to Quebec," he revealed moments later, he'd started dictating what he called "scraps," possible responses and riffs for the single campaign speech he had on his schedule for the month, an address to a Teamsters dinner in Washington he was due to make a week after his return. One of those "scraps," a single paragraph in a relatively lengthy text, became the most memorable flight of speechifying of the whole campaign, often cited as its turning point, one of the best-known passages of this spellbinder's long career.

It wasn't about his record as a leader in wartime, which Dewey had been cautiously questioning. Nor was it about his vision of the challenges at home and abroad in the postwar period that was already in the offing, no longer seeming far off. The Republican's basic point was that the president and the worn-out administration he led were now unequal to those challenges, even as he promised implicitly to preserve New Deal programs and follow through on the creation of an international organization to maintain a permanent peace. Roosevelt spent most of his speech to the Teamsters ridiculing and belittling such verbal pirouettes, echoing and sounding much like the Roosevelt of yore, the one who'd sailed to the greatest landslide in the country's history eight years earlier, in 1936. This time around, at his sardonic best, he characterized the Republicans as saying, "Don't leave the task of making the peace to those old men who first urged it and who have already laid the foundations for it, and who have had to fight all of us inch by inch during the last five years to do it. Why, just turn it all over to us." Republicans had mastered the "propaganda techniques" of Hitler and Goebbels, he said.

Tying his opponents however loosely to the fascist enemy could be considered, in the war's last year, a low blow but not by a partisan audience primed to welcome fireworks. Only then, having shown how much fight he still had in him, did he get to the inspired "scrap" that would have the most impact, performing his bravura aria about "my little dog, Fala." He was responding not to Dewey, whose name he'd never once pronounce in public that night or in the whole campaign, but to one Harold Knutson, a Republican congressman from Minnesota, who'd gone public with a sensational accusation—that a destroyer had been ordered back to the Aleutian Islands at huge taxpayers' expense to rescue the president's stranded Scotch terrier. Faced with the navy's categorical denial that any ship had been diverted or the pooch lost, Knutson had already backed down by the time Roosevelt addressed the Teamsters. But the opportunity to discourse on Republican falsehoods was too good for him to pass up.

"These Republican leaders have not been content with attacks on me, or my wife, or on my sons," a deadpan Roosevelt began in his slowest cadence, squeezing pathos out of every line, practically every word. "No, not content with that, they now include my little dog, Fala." His pet's "Scotch soul was furious," he went on mournfully. "He has not been the same dog since." By the time he reached the end of this rollicking aside, shaking his head over "the libelous statements against my dog," the Teamsters were on their feet, bent over with laughter, cheering raucously. One was said to have clanged a ladle against a silver tray, another to have smashed glasses with a wine bottle as a way of punctuating the president's sallies.

In truth, the Fala riff had been a blatant digression from the campaign's main themes and issues, shamelessly over the top. As rendered by this peerless political thespian, it had also been wonderfully entertaining and did the job it was designed to do: announce that a restored Roosevelt was back, fully engaged in the campaign, determined to win, full of that warmth, humor, and fellow feeling his opponent found hard to muster. The Oxford historian of ideas Isaiah Berlin described it in one of his confidential dispatches from Washington to the Foreign Office as "a return to the best and most ruthless of his old fighting days . . . by turns fierce and gay." Possibly taking his cue from the don, Churchill would cable that he'd read the speech and, finding "much gusto" in it, was "delighted to see you in such vigorous form." Evidently, the prime minister drew more reassurance about the president's readiness to carry on from the Fala speech than he had from Admiral McIntire's carefully hedged reassurances at Quebec a week earlier.

Roosevelt's feisty performance helped draw attention away from a notable, less reassuring feature of his delivery—that he'd spoken from a seated position at the dinner's head table. He hadn't given up on his braces; he'd later wear them speaking from the rear of his special train on brief whistle-stop tours. But the miserable Bremerton experience had left him so mistrustful of the cumbersome steel underpinning and his own uncertain stamina that he'd never in the final seven months of his life risk a formal full-length speech standing up.

Finally, the speech to the Teamsters did to his rival what Dewey had done to him. It nettled the humorless Republican, who hammered back point by point before an aroused anti-Roosevelt throng in Oklahoma City two nights later. "It was a speech of mud-slinging, ridicule and wisecracks," the candidate said of Roosevelt's first campaign fling. "It plumbed the depths of demagogy by dragging into the campaign the names of Hitler and Goebbels."

Berating Roosevelt as "the man who wants to be President for sixteen years," Dewey said he'd not only failed to end "seven years of New Deal depression" but also failed to prepare the nation for war, costing "countless American lives" and "untold misery." What the New Deal now amounted to, the indignant governor said in his sharpest prosecutorial vein, was "an ill-assorted power-hungry conglomeration of city bosses, Communists and career bureaucrats."

Roosevelt, in Dewey's accounting, was no longer merely tired and stale. "The simple truth," he now charged, "is that my opponent's record is desperately bad. The price the American people have had to pay for it is desperately high."

Hot stuff—a tribute in its excess, it might be said, to the openness of the American system at the height of the war. At the same time, it represented a change in course by a candidate who only two weeks earlier had been pledging to pursue the same goals in war and peace—international security and full employment—as an exhausted president who he clearly implied was well past his prime. That had been an appeal onetime Roosevelt supporters—independents and even some Democrats—might heed. Now, with Roosevelt having shown a flash of his old form in a single taunting speech, the challenger had been goaded into an openly partisan counterattack. Throwing roundhouse punches, giving his most convinced supporters what they craved, he ran the risk of making himself less palatable to wavering Roosevelt backers uncertain about the president's ability to carry on. So convinced was the Republican National Committee that this was the way to go that it literally doubled down on the speech, purchasing radio time on 170 more stations than originally planned.

Dewey's counterattack in Oklahoma City failed to throw Roosevelt on the defensive. Leaving day-to-day jousting to his little-known running mate, Senator Truman, "the Champ," as his speechwriters privately dubbed him, waited a month before going on the campaign trail in any overt way. Like earlier and later occupants, he could use the White House as his platform. In the first three weeks of October, he gave two radio addresses, two other talks there to invited audiences, and four of his off-the-record press conferences, augmented by a stream of statements on such matters as the liberation of Athens and the completion of the negotiations at Dumbarton Oaks. Even on days when he was silent and out of sight, or away in Hyde Park, he had a palpable presence. In that bygone, now ancient era in which most voters still got their news from newspapers, banner headlines made the case for him on a daily basis as leader of the wartime alliance, trumpeting relentless advances in Europe and the Pacific. Taken together, the headlines conveyed the message that victory was now inevitable, even when the gains they proclaimed one day proved to have been illusory the next. Reports in September that the Allies had pierced Hitler's West Wall and that the fortress city of Aachen, just forty miles from the Rhine, was soon to fall proved weeks premature, as bitter combat continued in sometimes muddy terrain. The war in Europe, it gradually became clear, wouldn't be over by Christmas as Marshall had hoped. But as the campaign entered its final weeks, a ruined Aachen would finally be surrendered against Hitler's orders, the first German city to be picked off by the Allies, and MacArthur would land in Leyte in the Philippines; a few days later, with ten days to go to the balloting, the Japanese fleet would be intercepted north of Luzon and decimated by the U.S. Third Fleet. It couldn't easily be argued then that these gains were happening in spite of the commander in chief, or that they were overstated.

Early on, it had seemed Dewey would know better than to try. In his first foreign policy address, in Louisville two weeks before that slashing Oklahoma City rejoinder, he'd spoken in soft, high-minded terms of the need for unity in the waging of war and peace. "I am deeply convinced that our peace efforts can and must become a non-partisan effort," he said. He'd named John Foster Dulles, a future secretary of state, his liaison to Cordell Hull on the ongoing talks at Dumbarton Oaks with Britain and Russia over the mechanisms for international peacekeeping, enabling him to say, "Both parties are working together in this great effort" as a result of what he proudly termed his own "unprecedented action" as a challenger in agreeing to keep the associated issues of war and peace out of politics. He thus claimed more credit than he has gotten for standing against the isolationist tendency in his party. Red-baiting would become his campaign's last desperate gambit, but the candidate had himself already called, in that Louisville speech, for "continued close cooperation" with Russia after the war. "Only with unity of effort," he said, "can America influence the rest of the world in the manner in which its real strength has entitled and equipped it." If bipartisanship, a foreign policy commandment later left in the dust by the Vietnam and Iraq misadventures, ever stood for an unambiguous value, it has to be acknowledged that Thomas Dewey was there at its birthing. Roosevelt could give that credit to Willkie but not to Dewey, whom he was learning to loathe.

He might have felt a little differently had he heard in a timely way of his opponent's greatest contribution to the war effort—and, it might even be argued, Roosevelt's own reelection. The campaign was nearly over before the president learned of a highly sensitive negotiation that George Marshall had undertaken with the Republican candidate behind his back. The general's purpose wasn't to protect Roosevelt's political flank but rather to persuade Dewey to lay off charges that the War Department—and, therefore, the president—should have known days before the attack on Pearl Harbor that the Japanese fleet was on the move. It was a fact that American cryptographers had broken a key diplomatic code used by the Japanese, but the charge couldn't be substantiated without mentioning that fact. Marshall was right in suspecting that Dewey was preparing to do just that. The problem for American military planners was that the code in question was still being used three years later in high-level Japanese communications, including messages from the Japanese ambassador in Berlin to Tokyo, still being harvested, so Marshall maintained, for vital intelligence on military strategies in Europe as well as the Pacific.*

The day after Dewey's Oklahoma City speech, the chief of the army's cryptographic section called on him in Tulsa bearing a three-page letter from the army chief of staff stamped "Top Secret." The letter began by insisting that the governor refrain from communicating any of its contents to any member of his staff and that he read no further himself if he couldn't make that pledge. An outraged Dewey, sure that he was being manipulated for political ends—that this was some plot, an example of Roosevelt's most devious tendencies—read no further.

Two days later, the chief cryptographer called on him again at the Executive Mansion in Albany, bearing a second missive from Marshall, a redrafting of the first with easier conditions, asking him not to relate anything he was hearing for the first time. Richard Norton Smith, Dewey's biographer, notes that the letter "took pains" to convince the governor that Roosevelt had nothing whatever to do with the general's démarche. He was writing solely on his own initiative, Marshall said, because of "the utterly tragic consequences" that could flow from any disclosure that would lead "the enemy, German or Jap . . . [to] any suspicion of the vital sources of information we now possess."

---

* As Rick Atkinson shows in *The Guns at Last Light*, the Japanese ambassador had only recently reported from Berlin on Hitler's plan to launch a desperate counteroffensive in the West by the end of the year, foreshadowing what came to be known as the Battle of the Bulge, the biggest and costliest engagement American troops would face in Europe. The full significance of that timely intelligence wouldn't be grasped until the massive surprise attack was under way.

Still, Dewey wasn't convinced. Roosevelt deserved to be impeached, he groused, for failing in the days leading up to the day of infamy to make use of the intelligence at his command. Finally, recognizing he had no choice but to accept General Marshall's word—no way to use the issue without wounding himself, probably fatally—he shelved Pearl Harbor as a potential campaign issue for Republicans while the war continued. It was a calculated political decision, but it could be counted a patriotic one as well. Marshall ultimately thanked him.

October 3 was a day crowded with news, mostly having to do with the war. Once again, the Supreme Headquarters in Europe declared that Germany's West Wall had been pierced, imperiling Nazi control of Aachen. "Our Men Triumph," a subordinate headline on the front page of *The New York Times* cheered. The Red Army was reported to be closing in on Belgrade from two directions. British Flying Fortress bombers had opened a large gash in a Dutch dike in order to disable German batteries there that had been blocking access to the vital Belgian port of Antwerp. In Washington, Roosevelt signed an industrial reconversion bill designed to usher in the postwar era but said it didn't go far enough to protect jobless benefits. In Albany, Dewey promised federal tax cuts. A dispatch from London, occupying the least amount of space on the front page the next morning, sounded a dirge for the Warsaw rising against the Germans: "After sixty-three days of bitter resistance, the patriots of Warsaw have been forced to surrender and the Germans again are in control of the shattered Polish capital."

President Roosevelt didn't get to his office until noon on the morning of the third. By no coincidence, it was Poland that had detained him. As was his custom, he'd sat up in bed over breakfast, going through newspapers and overnight cables, the most important of which had come from 10 Downing Street. With seeming casualness, Churchill mentioned that he'd be leaving for Moscow in a few days to see Stalin. "Of course," the prime minister wrote blithely, "the bulk of our business will be about the Poles but you and I think so much alike about this that I do not need any special guidance as to your views." Between the lines was a clear bid to exercise Roosevelt's proxy on anything touching Poland.

Maybe because his focus was on Dewey and the campaign, the president didn't mention the Poles in the response Admiral Leahy drafted, evidently with his guidance. "I wish you every success in your visit to U.J.," he told Churchill. The diplomatic issue uppermost in his mind at that moment, it seemed, was an impasse looming in the three-power talks at Dumbarton Oaks on forming an international organization. These were now stalled on a demand by the Soviet Union that the permanent members of what would become the Security Council have power to block debate on matters touching their own conduct. As we've seen, it had previously requested assembly votes for all sixteen of its constituent "republics." The United States and Britain considered the quashing of debate an unacceptable overreach and the demand for sixteen votes an outrageous opening bid in a round of bargaining. Agreement on these issues was "a must for all three of us," Roosevelt now said, sounding like himself, not his draftsman.

The message was on its way to the Map Room for transmission to London when Hopkins, who'd been mostly sidelined in the three months since his return to part-time duty, got wind of its contents. Now, acting as if he retained all the authority he'd wielded previously as Roosevelt's principal adviser, he ordered that the president's high-priority message be held up, then worked out with Chip Bohlen terms for a substitute draft that would, tactfully but firmly, make it clear to the prime minister—and Stalin—that Churchill couldn't speak for the United States on Poland or anything else. That accomplished, he hurried upstairs to Roosevelt's bedroom suite, where he found the president shaving, to explain his intervention.

Roosevelt was not a man to cede authority easily. On the contrary, he could normally be expected to react sharply when he thought others were encroaching on his powers. This time he became "somewhat agitated," according to Bohlen, when Hopkins pointed out that he'd overlooked Churchill's presumption. He was second-guessing himself, not Hopkins. Roosevelt was "relieved when Hopkins told him he'd taken the liberty to hold [the message to Churchill]," Bohlen later wrote. He'd not meant to give the prime minister carte blanche to act in his behalf on Poland. It had been an uncharacteristic fumble, a warning sign, perhaps, that his concentration and the breadth of his strategic vision weren't what they'd been.

In the revised messages, he asked that his ambassador, Averell Harriman, be invited to sit in on the talks as his observer but made it clear Harriman would have no authority to commit the United States on any issue. "You, naturally, understand," he wrote to Stalin, "there is literally no question, political or military, in which the United States is not interested." In other words, he wasn't going to be bound by any decision taken in the bilateral Kremlin talks. On this, writing to Harriman, he was categorical. He wanted "complete freedom of action," he said, when the Anglo-Soviet talks were done. The voting issues at Dumbarton Oaks, which had seemed so urgent an hour or so earlier, could now be postponed, he told Churchill in the revised message, until he could join the prime minister and Stalin at a later meeting, in other words, until after the election. They involved matters "so directly related to public opinion in the United States" that they needed to be handled at the highest level. His reasoning is fuzzy, but his intention is clear. The political tactician was in command. He wouldn't let himself be pinned down now.

Asked that afternoon at his 971st press conference to comment on the failure of the Warsaw rising, he said he'd "set a good example" by saying nothing. "I suppose I know as much about the particular thing as any American," he went on, "and I don't know enough to talk about it." The comment, not for quotation then, is open to interpretation now. Warsaw was still under the Nazis' control. It would be up to Stalin's forces to expel them. The Soviet dictator already occupied all the Polish territory he claimed. He insisted on a Polish government that would, at a minimum, swallow the deal on a new eastern border that had been conceded at Tehran, explicitly by Churchill, tacitly by himself. None of this had been made clear to the American people, let alone the exile Polish government in London whose Warsaw forces had just been brutally routed by the Germans without the Red Army, just across the Vistula, bestirring itself on their behalf.

In the midst of a political campaign, Roosevelt wasn't about to acknowledge any of that. He'd foreseen the problem nearly a year earlier and explained as much to Stalin in Tehran. Saying he didn't yet know enough to talk about it was his way of saying he couldn't pretend to have hit on a face-saving middle ground that could be said to reconcile the Soviet advance into Eastern Europe with the Wilsonian principles of self-determination embedded in the Atlantic Charter. He'd been hoping for months for some kind of patch-up in the ruptured relations between the Kremlin and the exile Poles in London—

a little more flexibility and readiness to bargain on both sides—for the sake of appearances at least. Each side had resisted his broad hints.

Historians have the luxury of viewing the political campaign, the military battles, and the diplomatic maneuvering as films running in parallel on different screens in some scholarly multiplex. In Franklin Roosevelt's mind, they seem to have been superimposed, running simultaneously on a single screen. I strain for a metaphor again on this point to underscore the interconnectedness of disparate issues in Roosevelt's mind. To advance on the question of an international peacekeeping organization, he needed the assent of both the Russians and the Republicans. A solution for Poland, not to mention the three Baltic states, would take even more. It would take the London Poles, recognized by Britain and the United States as the legitimate government, and they weren't about to accept the secret territorial deal the Allies had struck in Tehran. If he had his way, he might well have preferred to come to a broad understanding with Stalin that would render the Polish question and the future of Eastern Europe manageable before moving forward on the United Nations. He searched for some sign that such an understanding was as important to Stalin as it seemed to him, that they'd be able to communicate on sensitive issues after the war. But if he couldn't have that, he'd take the most practical outcome he could get, a new international organization that might yet be an improvement on the impotent, easily paralyzed League of Nations. If relations with the Russians were to remain difficult, it would still provide a forum for engagement. None of this could be plainly spelled out either.

Four days after the surrender in Warsaw, Thomas Dewey found a way to tug the pivotal, scarcely understood question of Poland's eastern border into the campaign. Speaking from the reviewing stand of the annual parade in Manhattan honoring Casimir Pulaski, the Polish nobleman who fought and perished in the American Revolution, the Republican candidate went as far as he dared go, demanding to know "the results of the private deliberation of those who now discuss Poland's future in dim secrecy." He spoke of the "justice" of Polish territorial claims, given Polish sacrifices in the war. Responding on Roosevelt's behalf, Senator Robert F. Wagner, a Democratic stalwart, said that "the complete restoration and protection of Polish boundaries" was "one of the things for which we are fighting this war." Roosevelt himself still didn't "know enough to talk about it," precisely because he knew that the restoration of Polish boundaries would remain an impossible dream. Now that Poland is a member of NATO, its eastern boundary remains the one on which the Soviet dictator insisted.

It wasn't, after all, his fears for the future of Poland that propelled Winston Churchill to Moscow a couple of days later. He'd take up the subject with Stalin again once Stanisław Mikołajczyk—Premier Mick, still titular chief of the London-based Poles—returned to Moscow to join the talks. But his main aim on this trip was to strike a deal that would preserve British influence in the eastern Mediterranean and the Middle East, a strategic objective with which he'd been preoccupied since before the Normandy invasion. Now, finally, British troops were about to land in Greece. Churchill was bent on insuring that the Soviet Union would stand aside and discourage a rising by local Communists. If Stalin would concede that British interests were paramount in Greece, he was ready to concede that Romania and Bulgaria would inevitably wind up in a Soviet sphere of influence.

Opposition to such side deals on spheres of influence had been a stated cornerstone of American policy. So Churchill had said nothing to Roosevelt about the central purpose of his trip. When the subject of Poland finally came up, Stalin again dangled the premiership before Mikołajczyk as he had in August. He said he didn't expect Poland to turn Communist. "Communism does not fit the Poles," the dictator told Premier Mick. "They are too individualistic, too nationalistic." A compromise of uncertain duration briefly seemed possible. Molotov hinted that the Russians were prepared to bargain over the number of seats Mikołajczyk's party might have in a coalition in which it would still be outnumbered by Soviet-backed Poles based in the city of Lublin, already on their way to being installed as a government by the Russians. The Kremlin's Poles could be relied on to accept the new boundary in the east as a fait accompli. All Premier Mick had to do was go along, tacitly putting a respectable face on the excision of the disputed territory, which could be swapped for territory to the west taken from the Germans. The future of Poland could then be represented as settled, at least for the present.

Mick was tempted in the name of what Roosevelt would have called realism to ask Stalin if he'd consider adjustments to the border on which he was insisting. The dictator was adamant. Knowing he couldn't carry Polish nationalists in London in any case, the Polish leader then concluded a compromise was beyond his reach, causing the British prime minister to erupt. "I wash my hands of this!" Churchill roared. "We are not going to wreck the peace of Europe because of quarrels between Poles. In your obstinacy you don't see what is at stake . . . Unless you accept the frontier, you're out of business forever!"

Harriman wasn't there to witness that exchange, and Churchill didn't report it to Roosevelt, nor did he include it in his massive World War II memoir. Premier Mick had seen the silky side of Roosevelt and the rough side of Churchill, whom he'd regarded as a friend. On the Polish question, the president was determined to remain the good cop for as long as possible, at least for the duration of his reelection campaign. When Harriman flew to Washington to report on the Kremlin talks, the president confirmed that he "felt helpless to do anything constructive" on Poland before the election. Roosevelt struck Harriman as "vigorous and determined in spirit," but there was no suggestion in their conversation that he counted on finding something constructive to do about Poland after the votes were in. The dreamer in Franklin Roosevelt, Harriman recognized, seldom, if ever, outdistanced the realist. "The President does a lot of dreaming," he would say, "but when it comes down to hard decisions, his judgment is good and tough."

It's possible to wonder whether the outcome of these Anglo-Soviet talks would have been any different had Roosevelt been there but hard to make a case that it might have been. Timothy Snyder has put the fundamentals of the situation starkly as no Western statesman could or would at the time. "Stalin was a more important ally than any Polish government," he wrote. That was still an overwhelming military fact. Therefore, writes Snyder, "the western Soviet border accorded Stalin by Hitler was confirmed by Churchill and Roosevelt."

The future of Central Europe would remain a fringe issue in the campaign, for Dewey wasn't prepared to come out and argue, while the war against Nazi Germany still raged, that the United States needed to stand up to its Soviet ally on Poland. That would only beg the question of how this could be managed, given the pressure the Red Army was putting on the Germans. The best the Republican nominee could do was rail against secret diplomacy.

He was similarly constrained on what was gradually emerging as a central issue—discussed mainly through roundabout allusion and insinuation—the ultrasensitive question of Roosevelt's health. A flattering profile of Admiral McIntire, the official White House physician, had appeared in *Life* magazine after the Democratic convention in which he repeated his soothing, well-practiced bromides. ("The President's health is excellent," he said. "I can say that unqualifiedly.") Yet the issue lingered in the shadows.

A journalist who'd seen Roosevelt at Quebec told Dewey flatly that the president was a dying man. It was the candidate's "absolute duty," the unnamed scribbler said, to tell the voters, thus giving the journalist a basis he apparently still lacked for writing the story. Richard Norton Smith, Dewey's biographer, declares that Republican strategists "sweated blood" on the issue. "There wasn't a single night that went by we didn't argue that one out," Smith was told by Herbert Brownell, the campaign manager. Ultimately, it was concluded that any attempt to make political capital out of the president's health, without any firm evidence or diagnosis to back it up, would likely backfire.

For most of the campaign, Republican newspapers were hardly more forthright. The New York *Sun* ran a front-page editorial that began with the arresting exhortation "Let's not be squeamish," then raised the issue of presidential health indirectly, only by implication—that's to say, squeamishly—not once mentioning the president by name or questioning his stamina or life expectancy in any overt way. It was enough to point out that six presidents had died in office. At the time, that might have seemed daring. As we now know, the newspaper was onto something: The president that day had exactly six months to live. Obviously, *The Sun* couldn't have known that then. Never to be outdone in anti-Roosevelt polemics, Colonel McCormick's *Chicago Tribune* didn't shrink from putting the health argument bluntly as the campaign entered its final days. "In view of Mr. Roosevelt's age and brittle health," it asserted, "a vote for Roosevelt is very likely to be a vote for Truman." Roosevelt was only sixty-two; as of 1944, the last president to start a term in office at that age or older was James Buchanan in 1857. But, clearly, the question was health, not age.

What struck the cardiologist Howard Bruenn that autumn of 1944 was a discernible improvement in his patient's appetite and blood pressure levels despite "a complete disregard of the rest regimen." The campaign seemed to be giving him a booster shot.*

Roosevelt's own reaction was nonchalant and dismissive when at a White House press conference he was asked about journalists who dared mention doubts about his health. "I know more about their health than they know about mine," he said. "I think it's pretty good health."

Finally, as if accepting a dare, Roosevelt resolved to meet the submerged but persistent issue of his mortality head-on. Three weekends before Election Day, he resumed his campaigning with a determined display of vigor and fortitude, calculated to silence doubters and gossipmongers. The biographer Frank Freidel would call this eleventh-hour spurt "the most spectacular campaign performance of his career." At a White House press conference the day before traveling to New York for a four-hour, fifty-one-mile tour in an open car through four of the city's five boroughs (replicating a New York tour he'd made in his previous campaign four years earlier), he challenged the gods to come through with the cold downpour forecasters had been promising. Asked about his campaign plans, he seemed almost gleeful, saying, "It looks like rain tomorrow . . . rain and a fifty-mile gale in New York, which is not cheerful."

Would he be wearing his navy cape? a reporter asked. "I suppose so," he said in his customary bantering tone. "About the best garment I've got." He'd had three since 1913, he noted to the indulgent laughter

---

* The Democratic chairman, Bob Hannegan, wasn't above using doubts about Roosevelt's health to win support—or, in the toughest cases, neutralize opposition of anti-Roosevelt Democrats. Prominent among these was the former ambassador to Britain Joseph Kennedy. Twice in the closing days of the campaign, Hannegan called on Kennedy, each time conveying the impression that the president was sicker than party leaders had known and would likely be succeeded by Harry Truman, whom he brought along on the second visit to back him up. According to Kennedy's notes, the senator allowed the father of Truman's successor's successor to hear what he wanted to hear: that his influence would be restored after such a succession.

with which this least adversarial White House press corps regularly egged him on. "I hope you don't get wet, those who are going," the old campaigner said.

His travel plans on October 21 were an open book for the first time since Pearl Harbor, not blanketed by censorship restrictions. Newspaper accounts were later divided on whether it had actually poured or merely drizzled along the motorcade's long route. The anti-Roosevelt *Sun* noticed only "a light drizzle" that merely "threatened to turn into a heavy rain." The *Times* had a different meteorological take, describing the president "driving through a wet and windswept New York City . . . letting the elements have their way as he had his." Roosevelt, the newspaper reported, "was soaking wet almost from the start of his journey until the end."

Hearst's *Journal-American* reported "disappointingly small crowds" and "intermittent downpours," findings that were somewhat belied by the headline on an immediately adjacent article: "High Wind, Rain Lash City."

The *Ferdinand Magellan,* having traveled overnight from the capital, delivered the president to an army depot in Brooklyn where Roosevelt was lifted into a black Packard with bulletproof windows and Secret Service agents riding the running boards. The roof had been rolled back, leaving the occupants at the mercy of the elements. By the time the limousine reached Ebbets Field, the home of the Brooklyn Dodgers baseball team, it had toured the Brooklyn Navy Yard, and the commander in chief was drenched. Outside the stadium, a woman held up a handmade poster proclaiming "F.D.R. OUR MESSIAH." Inside, the limousine carried him up a ramp to a rostrum constructed over the infield where he was shifted from the car and set on his feet.

Preparing for that moment, he'd gotten into his braces before leaving his train. Untying his cape and removing a battered fedora he'd now worn in each of his four campaigns, he stood tall and bareheaded in the rain and spoke for only a few minutes while a crowd of fewer than ten thousand huddled in the grandstand, rewarding them with his "best smile," so described by Bill Hassett, his traveling secretary, as "dynamic, radiant . . . giving the lie to his detractors who have carried on unremittingly a whispering campaign, a vendetta, against his health." Previously unscreened newsreel footage rescued by the Ken Burns team shows him then sinking backward into the arms of Secret

Service men, who swiftly and smoothly landed him in the back of the Packard.

After a stop at a nearby Coast Guard station to be changed into dry clothes—something, of course, he couldn't manage on his own—he was whisked to the Bronx to review a detachment of female naval recruits in an armory, then driven through Harlem, down Broadway to Times Square, down Seventh Avenue through the garment district, where union members and shoppers crowded the sidewalks, standing twelve or so deep at Herald Square as confetti whipped about in the wind overhead. By the time he reached Greenwich Village for the only visit he'd ever make to Eleanor's modest fifteenth-floor apartment at 29 Washington Square East, he was drenched again. The police commissioner generously estimated he'd been seen by more than 1.5 million people, maybe 3 million. A hot bath and a bourbon neat—actually three that afternoon by Grace Tully's tally—a fresh change of clothes, and a two-hour nap were all he needed to ready himself for a forty-five-minute speech he was due to deliver that evening at the Waldorf. The White House would later announce triumphantly that he'd not had a sniffle after his long ride in the rain.

What younger, healthier men might have experienced as an obstacle course, the old campaigner had cruised through with seeming ease. Could he have been reasonably described that Saturday as a dying man as some later writers have done, working backward from the cold fact that he died in less than half a year? That wasn't apparent to onlookers at the time—including reporters on the scene who, of course, had no insight into his cardiovascular problems, known then to only a small number of physicians (possibly no more than six). The dominant impression was the one he was striving to make—that he retained the stamina to face the challenges ahead. It was then broadcast and echoed across the land, deflating but not banishing the hovering health question.

An editorial in the *Herald Tribune*, which strongly backed Dewey, attempted a fair-minded assessment. "The President has sought to testify in his own favor by public appearances in fair weather and foul," it acknowledged. "He has demonstrated again his courage and his stamina." It was clear too, from his speeches and press conferences, that "the alertness of his mind has been unaffected." But he had "aged greatly and suddenly in the last few months," raising a legitimate question as to "his basic physical condition," which remained "shrouded in mystery."

Time offered its readers an attentive, close-up look at the fourth-term candidate at the Waldorf dinner as he prepared to deliver an address to the Foreign Policy Association on which he'd toiled with his speechwriters to nearly midnight through several evenings and six drafts. Now he was at the banquet, seated at the dais:

> He smoked only two cigarettes all evening—one before the speech, one after. Silently, engrossed, unsmiling, he passed rapidly through his crabmeat, turtle soup, breast of chicken, then pulled out his speech text and went to work. Pencil in hand, wetting his big thumb from time to time as he turned the pages, he read the speech over to himself, speaking softly, gesturing slightly. In the unflattering light of the little reading lamp, his weary face looked seamed and haggard. As he read, he would jot down little interpolations, asides and personal stage directions. This was the old experienced actor going through the final rehearsal. Much depended on this speech.
>
> Suddenly the floodlights came up; the hard-working craftsman disappeared. In an instant the President was his old broad-smiling self, waving gaily as the diners applauded.

What he then delivered was the most comprehensive and visionary statement he was ever to permit himself on the thinking that had guided his foreign policy through the war. It was not without a partisan edge. He reminded his audience that Republicans with impeccable isolationist records—having voted against Lend-Lease, the repeal of the Neutrality Act, the extension of selective service on the eve of war—would hold key chairmanships and leadership positions if their party captured Congress two and a half weeks hence. He recalled, too, that they'd condemned his recognition of the Soviet Union in 1933, sixteen years after the Bolsheviks seized power. "Today," he went on, "we are fighting with the Russians against common foes—and we know that the Russian contribution to victory has been, and will continue to be, gigantic."

That was his only reference to that most powerful ally by name. The words "Soviet" and "Russian" and "Stalin" were missing from the remainder of the speech. So too did Woodrow Wilson and the League of Nations go unnamed. But that older history, through which he'd lived in the formative years of his public life, was obviously on his mind. "A quarter of a century ago," he said, "we helped to save our freedom, but we failed to organize the kind of world in which future generations could live—with freedom. Opportunity knocks again. There is no guarantee that opportunity will knock a third time."

He then brought the two themes together:

> The very fact that we are now at work on the organization of the peace proves that the great nations are committed to trust each other. Put this proposition any way you want, it is bound to come out the same way. We either work with the other great nations, or we might some day have to fight them. And I am against that . . . If we fail to maintain that relationship in the peace—if we fail to expand it and strengthen it—then there will be no lasting peace.

The language was elliptical, but his meaning was clear. Obviously, he wasn't talking about fighting Britain.

His peroration was at once soaring and measured. "I speak to the present generation of Americans," he said, "with a reverent participation in its sorrows and hopes . . . We are not fighting for, and we shall not attain, a Utopia. Indeed, in our own land the work to be done is never finished. We have yet to realize the full and equal employment of our freedom. So, in embarking on the building of a world fellowship, we have set ourselves a long and arduous task, which will challenge our patience, our intelligence, our imagination, as well as our faith . . . [a task] for a seasoned and mature people . . . a mature nation . . . [ready to] bear our full responsibility, exercise our full influence."

He came across as a leader who, in that moment, felt he could still lead. No one heard it as a last will and testament. The following weekend, he was off to Philadelphia and Chicago, speaking again in the rain and cold and again in stadiums—Shibe Park in Philadelphia, Soldier Field in Chicago—with whistle-stops in Delaware, Indiana, and West Virginia. At the train stations, he stood at the back of the *Ferdinand Magellan;* at the stadiums, he was driven up a ramp and delivered unabashedly partisan speeches from a seated position, his voice booming out over the crowds, which were enormous, as large as 110,000 in the Windy City. The weekend after that, the last of the campaign, he barnstormed through Connecticut and Massachusetts, making speeches on the final Saturday, in Bridgeport, Hartford, and Springfield from his train before arriving at Boston's Fenway Park, where four years earlier, declaring he'd said it "again and again and again," he'd promised America's "mothers and fathers . . . your boys are not going to be sent to any foreign wars." That 1940 Fenway pledge had come at the climax of what was also supposed to be his final campaign. Pearl Harbor was still thirteen months in the future, the start of World War II in Europe already fourteen months in the past. Now here he was again on another final campaign. As needling Republicans had reminded him ever since, his barefaced deceit from the previous one still needed explaining. The old master made it look easy. "Any real, red-blooded American," he said, "would have wanted to fight when our own soil was made the object of a sneak attack." Under those circumstances, he said, "I would choose to do the same thing—again and again and again." The refrain was recognized. It brought the partisan throng to its feet. No apologies were deemed necessary.

Between Chicago and Boston, he was back at the White House, where, on October 31, his last decision of the war on a major military command was made known. It involved the withdrawal of Joseph W. Stilwell, a driven, cantankerous four-star general known as Vinegar Joe, from his position as the senior American officer on the Asian mainland.*

Stilwell, who'd arrived in the wartime capital of Chungking less than three months after Pearl Harbor, had conspicuous strengths as a commander, a courageous leader of men, a fighter. His fluency in Chinese and deep experience of the country made him an obvious choice for the several overlapping, sometimes contradictory missions that would be piled on his shoulders: to keep open the supply of arms and fuel to Chiang Kai-shek's forces after the loss of the Burma Road; to oversee, as Lend-Lease administrator for China, their distribution; to modernize a sufficient portion of the vast, half-starved, underpaid, poorly led Chinese army so it could resist and eventually roll back the Japanese force occupying China's coastal provinces; and through the achievement of these goals, to enable the generalissimo to fulfill the destiny Franklin Roosevelt had initially scripted for China as one of the Big Four powers that would serve as cornerstones of a new world order.

* There were as yet no five-star generals in the U.S. Army. Generals Marshall, MacArthur, and Eisenhower were all advanced to that rank—named generals of the army—in December 1944.

Offsetting Stilwell's strengths as a commander were his glaring deficiencies as a diplomat and courtier. He was candid to a fault and didn't easily suffer, let alone flatter, fools—in his mind, most heads of state and other politicians, Chiang in particular and even Roosevelt. In formal encounters, he was appropriately restrained, but his caustic private views spilled not only into his diary, published after the war and his death, but also into his conversations with staff officers and Chungking-based journalists such as Theodore White of *Time* and Brooks Atkinson of *The New York Times*. Roosevelt would never have known that Stilwell put him down as "old rubber legs" and a "gasbag" and finally "old softy" in the diary, but it was no great secret in Chungking that "Peanut" was the general's honorific of choice for the generalissimo. More than once, General Marshall had to admonish him to button his lip. And Marshall was his staunchest supporter.

In the army chief's view, the president had "undercut" Stilwell by allowing other officers in the theater (notably General Claire Chennault, commander of the U.S. Fourteenth Air Force, and Roosevelt's own distant cousin the columnist Joseph Alsop, who sought and got a commission on Chennault's staff) to submit their dissenting views directly to the White House, in flagrant violation of the military chain of command. The dissenters told the president what he was inclined to believe, that Chiang was a worthy ally in danger of being undermined by Stilwell, with his obsessive drive to improve the combat readiness of Chinese ground forces so they could fight the Japanese and his constant complaint that the generalissimo had no stomach for that fight. The argument—Chennault versus Stilwell, airpower versus ground forces—had gone on for the better part of two years; twice Marshall and Secretary Stimson had intervened to prevent Stilwell's replacement. By the spring of 1944, Chennault's raids on Japanese positions had helped provoke a Japanese offensive, and Chiang's forces were retreating.

Disillusioned by now with Chiang but not with his own vision of China's role in the postwar order, Roosevelt signed his name to a series of stiff notes to the generalissimo that had been drafted in Marshall's office, softening the language only slightly. In the estimation of the popular historian Barbara Tuchman, the last of these "adopted the tone of a headmaster to a sullen and incorrigible schoolboy." Not for the first time, it demanded that Stilwell be given "unrestricted command of all your forces." Stilwell himself delivered the letter person-ally to Chiang. "I handed this bundle of paprika to the Peanut and then sat back with a sigh," the general wrote in his diary. "The har-poon hit the little bugger in the solar plexus, and went right through him. It was a clean hit."

"I understand," was all Chiang managed to say while the audience lasted. In his own diary, he would call it "the most severe humiliation I have ever had in my life."

It proved to be among the least effective of Roosevelt's wartime messages to an ally. Far from becoming unrestricted, Joe Stilwell's command—his whole mission in China—was abruptly terminated. Within days, the G'mo, as he was called, had responded with a formal request that his nemesis be relieved, saying he could no longer work with him. Hopkins quickly let the Chinese know, through a back channel, that the request would be honored. It took several weeks, long enough to insure that China would never be an issue in the cam-paign, left even more in the background than Poland, which was men-tioned only in front of audiences of Polish-Americans. Speaking off the record at a press conference a week before the election, Roosevelt downplayed the significance of his reversal on Stilwell. It had simply been a personality clash between Stilwell and Chiang, he said, "just one of them things."

"You have to remember," he continued, "that Generalissimo Chiang Kai-shek is head of the Chinese Republic of 450 million people—head of the state. He is also head of the government. And he is commander-in-chief of the army."

He was saying that one commander in chief could understand the feelings of another. He refrained from mentioning his secret letter demanding that Stilwell's authority be expanded to include effective command of Chiang's army, the despair over China's contribution to the war effort that had led him to sign it, the dawning realiza-tion that China couldn't be expected to matter much militarily in the final struggle against the Japanese, or the consequent agreement he'd just reached with General Marshall that Stilwell's successor wouldn't be expected "to assume responsibility for the operations of Chinese forces."

Nor was there any mention of the Chinese Communists or their leader Mao Zedong, whom American officers and diplomats had been visiting at their base in remote Yenan since the summer in hopes that their rapidly growing forces might prove useful against the Japanese. This was an enemy Chiang Kai-shek rightly considered an even greater threat to his rickety regime than Japan.

Roosevelt had grown disillusioned with that regime, realized it was ridden with intrigue and corruption but still hoped to avoid a civil war in China after the defeat of Japan, still insisted on China being recognized as a major power. His immediate military goal of a swift victory with the loss of the fewest possible American lives and his long-range vision of a world order in which four major powers effectively kept the peace were as much in tension, even contradiction, in a divided, partly occupied China as they were in the burned-over "bloodlands" of Central Europe.

If he meant to treat China as a sovereign nation, a great power in its own right, he could hardly insist that an American general have "unrestricted command" of its forces. That would imply advancing Chinese generals on the basis of their effectiveness as leaders in the field rather than their loyalty to the generalissimo; it could undermine Chiang. But if the Nationalist army wasn't reorganized and reformed along lines similar to those laid down by Vinegar Joe, it was hard to imagine that same Chiang playing the role in which Roosevelt had cast him. Similar dilemmas and contradictions would be faced in the decades ahead as Americans labored to prop up failing regimes in South Vietnam, Iraq, and Afghanistan, endowing their leaders with our values and goals, which regularly proved to be subordinate to theirs.

In one of his final campaign speeches, Roosevelt spoke airily of "a world of awakened peoples . . . struggling everywhere to achieve a higher cultural and material standard of living." He could hardly have pictured the rising China of the early twenty-first century when he uttered those phrases. But he was sure China would matter. Unlike Churchill, he was facing in the right direction, looking further into an unknowable postcolonial future than any other wartime leader.

He also found again, in those final political speeches, the obvious rationale for carrying on with his leadership and an administration that had built, as he proudly boasted, "the greatest war machine in all history," producing 300,000 military planes, putting eleven million Americans in uniform, landing nearly two million of them on the European continent within ten weeks of D-Day, along with two million tons of equipment, including half a million vehicles. "I am in the middle of a war. And so are you," he said in Fort Wayne, Indiana. "We are all in it . . . It is quite a job but I am perfectly able to take it, and you are too, until we win." In his self-presentation, he was at one with the country as the war headed into its "final, decisive phase." If reelected, he'd "wear the same size hat." Victory was certain, but the fighting was far from over. "You and I—all of us who are war workers—must stay on the job!"

It all blended into a single theme. The duty of fighting men and presidents and voters was to continue to victory. In broad terms, he also spoke of the economic renewal that would follow when the boys came home. But those passages were sketchy, outlines to be filled in later.

November 7 was Election Day. It was also the twenty-seventh anniversary of the Bolshevik Revolution, which Joseph Stalin had marked the previous evening with a rare radio address surveying in detail the mammoth victories of the Red Army but also, more briefly, paying what could be read as ungrudging tribute to the Allies for their battlefield achievements. In 1943, he said, the Soviet Union had struggled "without serious support from our allies." But this year, they'd finally come through with landings in France that were "unprecedented in history as regards organization and scale," a "brilliant" fulfillment of commitments made at the Tehran summit, "carried out with astonishing exactitude." In the alliance of "our country, Great Britain and the United States," he said, lay the world's best hope for peace. The international organization they were now forming would have at its disposal armed forces capable of snuffing out aggression and punishing aggressors "without delay." If there were still some point on which the Allies were not yet agreed, "one should not be surprised because differences exist, but because there are so few of them."

In speaking of aggressive nations, Stalin mentioned not only Germany but Japan, a country with which the Soviet Union wasn't yet in a state of war. That amounted, as Roosevelt would have noted when he perused the speech at Hyde Park that Election Day morning, to a public affirmation of Stalin's private commitment to enter the war in the Pacific following Hitler's defeat. That was the news in the dictator's speech, the part that led the lead article in *The New York Times*, on which the big front-page headline was based. As usual, the president left no record of his own reaction to Stalin's soothing choice of words in the remainder of the speech on the outlook for postwar unity among the victors, a choice likely to have been made with Roosevelt himself in the dictator's mind above all others. The best guess may be that he was neither taken in nor discouraged. He might have paused to wonder about the motive behind Stalin's words, but cool realist that he was, he isn't likely to have accepted them at face value. On a scale between finding them empty and finding them encouraging, he might have gone no further than to say they weren't empty.

Roosevelt's Election Day schedule, the fourth time around, was shaped in large measure by rituals he associated with past victories. He voted around noon in the Hyde Park firehouse, listing his occupation as "tree farmer." He spent the late afternoon at Top Cottage in front of a roaring fire, accompanied by Daisy, Anna Boettiger and her husband, and the two admirals, Leahy and McIntire. For dinner, back at the mansion in which he'd been raised, he had scrambled eggs, his "lucky dish." Then the dining table was cleared so he could start tabulating the returns on long sheets as he always had, with a Teletype machine clacking away in the next room and aides running in with the latest radio bulletins. Soon after 11:00, he was wheeled out front to the portico to greet a torchlight parade—another ritual—made up of local well-wishers, Vassar girls, and a fife-and-drum corps playing "Hail, Hail, the Gang's All Here." There he reminisced over the first election night parade he could remember, for Grover Cleveland's second election in 1892; ten years old then, he'd wrapped himself in an old buffalo robe. This frigid night he wore only his cape over a suit. "It looks like I will have to come back here on a train from Washington for four more years," he said. "I am glad to be here on this Election Day again. I might say again and again and again! But I'll be perfectly happy to come back here for good, as you all know. I don't have to tell you that."

The results were close only by Roosevelt standards. The "Champ" took 53.8 percent of the popular vote with a margin of nearly 3.6 million over Dewey, healthy even by today's standards when the electorate is more than twice as large as it was that wartime year but much the narrowest in his four runs for the White House (1.3 million votes fewer than his lead over Wendell Willkie four years earlier). In Electoral College terms, it was another landslide, 432 to 99 (considerably more lopsided than Roosevelt's modest, private forecast of 335 to 196).

It proved to be the last election in which the racially segregated South—the solid South, as it was then termed—was solid for Democrats. Perhaps Roosevelt's consciousness of that compromise with his own professed principles had something to do with his choice of a prayer sent to him by an Anglican bishop to conclude his radio address to the nation on the eve of the voting. "Enable us to grant the least among us," the prayer implored, "the freedom we covet for ourselves; make us ill-content with the inequalities of opportunity which still prevail among us. Preserve our union against all the divisions of race and class which threaten it." Attaching no particular significance to those sentiments, the overwhelmingly white electorate of Mississippi cast 93.6 percent of its votes for Roosevelt.

The president didn't get to sleep until four in the morning. The election result was clear, but Governor Dewey made it a long night, waiting until 3:12 before making a concession statement to the last remaining reporters in an empty hotel ballroom. He waited another three days before bowing to custom and sending a personal message to the victor. Roosevelt chose not to wait. To wrap up the evening, he sent Dewey a terse response to the graceless concession that may or may not have been intentionally pointed: "I thank you for your statement which I have heard over the air a few minutes ago." By then, it was nearly four. Wheeled to his bedroom, he offered a final assessment to an aide who'd just called out congratulations. "I still think he is a son of a bitch," Franklin Roosevelt said.

The next day, he issued a suitably elevated statement to the whole country, ever so faintly echoing Lincoln. It said that by going to the polls in the midst of a war for the first time in "fourscore years" (since 1864, that is), it had "demonstrated to the world that democracy is a living, vital force, that our faith in American institutions is unshaken; that conscience and not force is the source of power in the government of man. In that faith, let us unite to win the war and achieve a lasting peace."

Early Friday morning on the *Ferdinand Magellan*, he returned to the capital he'd dominated for nearly twelve years, not slipping back into town in secrecy as he'd routinely done in the war years but arriving in undisguised triumph at Union Station, where eight marching bands and a formation of motorcycle police were waiting in a steady, cold rain to accompany him down Constitution Avenue toward the White House. A police band led off with the inevitable "Hail to the Chief." The president chose once again, reprising his New York motorcade, to ride in an open car through a downpour, flanked on this occasion by Vice President Wallace and Wallace's newly anointed successor, Harry Truman. With the election over, Wallace had already been taken out of the line of succession under the terms of the Twentieth Amendment, which provides for a vice president-elect to become president-elect should the original president-elect expire before the date fixed for the inauguration. Government employees and schoolchildren had this morning off in the closest thing to an inaugural celebration that the election of 1944 would produce. Thousands stood in the rain to watch the leader glide by.

Wallace had some interesting, slightly dour reflections to jot in his diary that evening. One had to do with Mrs. Roosevelt, who made a point of telling him that day that he was now recognized as "the outstanding symbol of liberalism in the United States." The First Lady hoped he'd now devote himself to forming a broadened political action committee—something even more ambitious and far-reaching than the one Sidney Hillman had led for the CIO, which Dewey had lambasted as a Communist front in the campaign just ended. He said he wanted to continue working through the Democratic Party. "I turned the proposition down flatly and nicely. I can't help wondering," he added, "whether Franklin D. inspired his wife to put [it] up to me." His experience at the Democratic convention still preyed on Wallace's mind. It's clear he'd now expect such a tricky maneuver from the president.

After attending a cabinet meeting, the vice president brooded further, as he had so often in the past, on the character of the man who had chosen to ease him out of the line of succession. "He has lots of vitality left in his system," he wrote. "Just the same, I would judge from the character and quality of his remarks [that afternoon] that his intellect—but not his prejudices—will now begin to fade pretty rapidly. He will have to take awfully good care of himself to last out the four years in a state of competent leadership."

. . .

"May I be the first to ask you, Mr. President," a reporter ventured at his first postelection press conference that same day, "whether you are going to run in '48?" The transcript notes "laughter," probably uproarious as the journalists mocked their own practices, their own obsessive pursuit of the political hunt. In a moment of celebration, it was a lighthearted exchange. "That's a question I was asked in 1940, isn't it?" Roosevelt replied jauntily, taking it as an old joke. "It's hoary—absolutely hoary."

January 20, 1949—the date prescribed for the expiration of the term he'd just won and not yet even begun—might have seemed impossibly distant to Roosevelt, as it did to Wallace, had he allowed himself to look that far ahead. But that was not his way. He'd long since armored himself against dire fate with the notion that he could always resign. The thought might well have occurred to some at the press gathering that the laughing reporters and the laughing president could be whistling past the graveyard. But at a time like this, after a decisive win, that wasn't the prevailing mood. Once again, he'd juggled his ticket, masterminded his campaign, and carried the country. Whatever his prognosis, half a year now after a health crisis that had effectively been veiled, he'd managed to renew his lease on the residence and his leadership. It was a victory all right but only a small step toward the larger victory, in the war, on which he remained focused.

CHAPTER 9

Gallant, and Pitiable

THERE WERE MOMENTS, as related by Roosevelt, when Joseph Stalin displayed unexpected sensitivity and consideration. In their first encounter in Tehran, the president was already seated when the dictator entered the room. It was immediately evident to him that Stalin hadn't been told he'd be unable to rise for a greeting. Over the years, he'd seen that same moment's hesitation in countless visitors, revealed in a slight nod of the head or widening of the eyes, as the extent of his disability dawned on them. "We shook hands and he sat down," he told Daisy Suckley months later, "and I caught him looking curiously at my legs and ankles." At dinner, Roosevelt was again waiting in a seated position, as was his custom, when his guests filed into the room. This time, Stalin, taking his place on the president's right, gave voice, through an interpreter, to his thoughts. "Tell the President that I now understand what it has meant for him to make the effort to come on such a long journey," so Roosevelt recalled his words. "Tell him that the next time I will go to him."

"F.D.R. can, if *anyone* can, bring to the surface any fineness & softness in one who has chosen to call himself 'Steel,'" ever-wishful Daisy commented in her diary, amplifying perhaps some faint leitmotif in the P. 's constant churn of hope and doubt, scheming and calculation.

But Stalin's moment of sensitivity soon passed. He never came to Roosevelt. When discussions began weeks before the 1944 election on the time and place for a second three-power summit, the initial thought was that it might be held at the end of November. That proved to be too soon for Roosevelt. As for place, the fencing over who would travel where consumed more than two months. In a conversation with Harriman at the Kremlin in September, Stalin insisted he couldn't possibly leave Soviet territory. These were doctor's orders; he'd had ear trouble for two weeks after his flights to and from Tehran. Later he'd say the Politburo had ordered him not to travel abroad.

The conversations were reported directly to the president, who might well at this late stage have asked, "What about *my* health?" had he not been concentrating all his efforts at that time on demonstrating to voters and himself that his stamina was equal to the tasks ahead. Instead, as he had in the prelude to Tehran a year earlier, he stressed his constitutional responsibility to act in a timely way on Congress's bills. Though he was advised that Stalin was unyielding, Roosevelt clung to the hope that the dictator might yet be tempted to venture to the Mediterranean, variously mentioning Jerusalem, Alexandria, Athens, Rome, and Taormina in Sicily as plausible destinations. Possibly, he thought, this might be after a German collapse. As late as December 6, he wrote to Harriman, "I am still hoping for a Mediterranean port." Such mentions evoked the same response: Stalin could, or would, go no farther than the coast of the Black Sea. Lord Moran, Churchill's dyspeptic physician, instantly claimed the region to be rife with "dysentery and Bubonic plague."

The prime minister, meanwhile, was hoping to lure Roosevelt to London in December, even if that would mean having Molotov sit in as understudy for an absent Stalin. But, once again, Roosevelt was more eager to confer with Stalin than with Churchill, whom he'd seen in Quebec just a couple of months earlier. He wanted to tie up the loose ends on the Dumbarton Oaks accord, thereby launching the international organization with the Russians aboard; firm up the understanding on Soviet entry into the Pacific war; find a way forward on Poland and the occupation of Germany—more generally, on the postwar relationship. But he had other plans for December. "I can, under difficulties, arrange to go somewhere now in order to get back here by Christmas but, quite frankly," he wrote to Stalin on November 18, "it will be more convenient if I could postpone it until after the Inauguration." It wasn't until December 27 that he finally authorized Harriman to convey his willingness to journey by ship and plane to Yalta in the Crimea, site of Czar Nicholas II's summer palace on the

Black Sea, only recently evacuated—and looted—by the Nazis, who comprehensively sacked nearby towns.

Possibly Roosevelt's fertile imagination found some tactical advantage in delaying the conference, though the anticipated advance of the Red Army after a lull on its northern front could easily have suggested the opposite, inspiring a sense of urgency over all the unresolved postwar issues. More likely, he just didn't feel up to it. As is often the case with this self-immured character, it's easy to imagine a stew of motives, difficult to pin any single one down. Perhaps he now sensed a change in himself, a further slackening on the physical level, in his spirit as well, as he faced a steep, seemingly impossible ascent, the prospect of four more years in office. Maybe he was feeling the toll of the strenuous demands he'd placed on himself in the last days of the campaign, though his actual time on the stump then had been limited to the final three weekends.

What seems apparent is that the president, now thrice reelected, wasn't basking in any glow of triumph. Rather, he was allowing himself to recline into a brief passive phase as he seemed to do following his 1940 win at the polls. In this season, suspended between one term and the next, he was more disposed to wait on events than shape them. With the war approaching its climax, shaping events was a task best left to his generals. As for his new administration, it soon became obvious that he wanted it to be as little different as possible from the old one. Tom Dewey's campaign barbs notwithstanding, "old" was not going to be a disqualification.

Back in the White House, Roosevelt spent most of his efforts on the personnel front trying to persuade senior cabinet members that he couldn't spare them. An exhausted Cordell Hull, just turned seventy-three and on the verge of entering the naval hospital in Bethesda with diabetes and lung complaints left over from an old case of tuberculosis, told the president in October he couldn't stay on as secretary of state. Roosevelt dispatched Admiral McIntire to tell him all he needed was a brief rest. Hull eventually agreed to withhold his resignation until after the election. Roosevelt then asked him to hang on until the inauguration. Finally, with the secretary still in the naval hospital at the end of November, he accepted the inevitable. (Hull would remain there until after the president's death, more than four months later. "I should be where you are," Roosevelt had observed on his last visit, so Hull later wrote in his memoir.)

Harold Ickes, about to turn seventy-one, and Henry Stimson, seventy-seven, also asked if their resignations were wanted. In each case, Roosevelt wouldn't hear of it. "Of course I want you to go along at the Old Stand where you have been for 12 years," he wrote to Ickes. "We must see this thing out together." Hopkins, as intermediary, told Stimson that Roosevelt "absolutely" wanted him to stay, that his willingness to speak frankly when they differed was "good for him." John Winant, the ambassador in London, dropped a glancing allusion in a letter to his possible replacement. "It goes without saying," Roosevelt shot back, "that I want you to keep right on . . . I need you just where you are." Frances Perkins waited for the eve of the inauguration to press her case for stepping down as secretary of labor after twelve years. "Frances," she would quote him as saying, "you can't go now. You mustn't put this on me now. I just can't be bothered now. I can't think of anybody else. I can't get used to anybody else. Not now!"

In picking a new secretary of state, an appointment he'd sought to avoid, Roosevelt took what was for him the easiest way out, naming Edward Stettinius Jr., a former president of U.S. Steel who'd been serving as undersecretary since the departure of Sumner Welles. He'd never had a strong secretary of state; he didn't want one now. Handsome, white-haired, custom tailored, Stettinius was a magnet for slighting remarks. Chip Bohlen rated him "a decent man of considerable innocence." Senator Walter George put him down as "a nice enough lad if not too bright." Henry Morgenthau wrote him off as "a good clerk." Some just called him "Junior."

Washington tended to view the Stettinius appointment as a power play by Harry Hopkins, intent on his restoration to his old role as principal adviser. The columnist Marquis Childs wrote that Hopkins's influence was "perhaps greater than it ever was." Ickes, a perennial antagonist, wrote in his diary that it was "becoming frightening."

But Hopkins told Harriman he thought Jimmy Byrnes, for whom there was strong support on Capitol Hill, would make the best successor to Hull. He had no obvious reason to mislead the ambassador. Ultimately, it was Roosevelt who nixed Byrnes as "too independent." Besides, if he moved his mobilization czar to State, he'd have to find a replacement. This would bring on more turmoil, more change, than this seasoned minimalist was now willing to tolerate. Stettinius's malleability, his lack of an independent base, became qualifications in the president's eyes.

Roosevelt's resistance to change in his administration seems by this point to be a conditioned reflex. It can be interpreted as a reluctance to engage new people who might bring forward new issues in policy and personnel, new demands on his time and energy; a reluctance, in turn, derived from his sense that he needed to store up energy, recharge his batteries, as he had, more or less, at Baruch's plantation half a year earlier; in other words, regain his force and so, he may even at moments have allowed himself to think, stay alive. At Hobcaw, he was readying himself for D-Day and a seemingly unavoidable presidential campaign. Now the first challenge of his new term would be the looming summit with Stalin and Churchill, which he'd chosen to delay for a couple of months in the hope that the slippage of time might clarify issues and restore his stamina.

Of the ten weeks between the election and the inauguration, the president spent only five at the White House. Back under the comfortable cloak of wartime censorship, after traveling in the open during the campaign, he divided the rest of his time between Hyde Park and Warm Springs, to which he paid his first extended visit since Pearl Harbor—three weeks, starting soon after a quiet Thanksgiving at Hyde Park, where, in a rare connubial interlude, only the frequently absent Eleanor joined him for turkey. In Daisy's eyes, their dining together, just the two of them, was "a remarkable occurrence."

The extended retreat at Warm Springs was originally supposed to be ten days; going easy on himself, the president tacked on eleven more. What's striking about the prolonged stay is that he saw no need to take or summon a single military official or policy adviser to be nearby. Admirals Leahy, his military chief of staff, and Brown, his naval attaché, had been on constant call at the Baruch plantation. So had General Watson. This time he was content to deal with them long-distance, occasionally by phone or over a signal corps wire but mainly through the daily pouch that arrived by air from Washington with the latest war bulletins and diplomatic notes, accompanied by drafts of responses he might wish to sign or amend. This time he brought along three secretaries, Tully, Brady, and Hassett, to manage the traffic, the constant back-and-forth. He didn't imagine he could take a holiday from inescapable responsibilities. It was the need to confer with officials in person, the parade of familiar old faces as well as any new ones, from which he now sought relief. When Bob Hannegan showed up in Warm Springs, Bill Hassett harrumphed in his diary that it was "another manifestation of insensitivity," given that the visit had been "unrequested" (meaning, by Roosevelt). Hannegan stayed for more than two hours. "The more I see the Pres. the more convinced I am that *the only way he can live* is by having shorter sessions," Daisy wrote in her diary, underlining the key phrase.

The ostensible reason for the sojourn in the spa town was his continued devotion to the foundation he'd established there for polio sufferers. On his first night there, he spoke informally at his foundation's annual dinner for staff, leading townspeople, and more than one hundred patients then in residence. Segregation still reigned, so the guest list was uniformly white, but entertainment was furnished by a black man, a navy petty officer named Graham Jackson who played the piano and accordion and coaxed his audience into a sing-along. The gathering was crashed by the film actress Bette Davis, who managed to squeeze in next to the president. "We suppressed all the pictures," wrote curmudgeonly Hassett.

Roosevelt had a less obvious, deeper motive for journeying to Warm Springs, one that may have played into his wish to postpone the summit until after the inauguration. That became apparent on his third evening there with the arrival of Lucy Rutherfurd and her daughter, Barbara, who'd driven over from the Rutherfurd estate in South Carolina horse country, a distance of more than two hundred miles.

The president's modest cottage, built in 1932 and called the Little White House after he moved into the big one, had unfluted columns out front supporting a small pediment and a large semicircular sundeck beyond the French doors in the living room. But the interior, with paneling of Georgia pine throughout, no painted plaster, gave it the feel of a hunter's cabin in the woods. It conveyed no hint of an interior decorator's touch. Most of the furniture came from a small workshop Eleanor had supported at Val-Kill near Hyde Park. The prevailing motif was naval, a motley mix of hand-me-down seascapes and ship models for which the president had a weakness. A large stone fireplace dominated the main room, off which there were three simple bedrooms, one of which was adjacent to Roosevelt's, separated by only a shared bathroom.

Daisy Suckley was installed in that one for the first two days. Polly Delano, another cousin, occupied the other. No one could know it then, but in an eerie foreshadowing Roosevelt had assembled very nearly the same retinue of devoted female friends, assistants, and attendants that would be with him four months later on his final trip to Warm Springs when he'd meet his end. Now, with Lucy's arrival, Daisy and Polly were asked to move to the guest cottage, which had only fireplaces for heat. Lucy was given the bedroom next to the president's. "I feel very badly to have been the cause of evicting you," she wrote to Daisy a week later, "but you can imagine how very wonderful it was for me to feel myself under the same roof and within the sound of the voice we all love, after so many, many years."

By then, the two women had bonded over their shared feelings for their host and their fear, seeming to deepen from day to day, that he was losing his grip on life. "I try so hard to make myself think he looks well, but he doesn't . . . He looks ten years older than last year . . . he knows it himself," Daisy wrote in her diary before Lucy's arrival. One evening, they found themselves "literally weeping on each other's shoulder."

Lucy stayed two nights. On the one sunny day they had together, Roosevelt took her to a hilltop called Dowdell's Knob, his favorite picnic spot in the vicinity, about eight miles from the Little White House, over dirt roads then. Today that hilltop is part of a state park, but the open view across a wide, largely wooded valley to hills turning purple at a distance of maybe ten miles is much as it was then and strikingly similar to another vista he cherished, the one across the Hudson valley from yet another presidential hideout, his Top Cottage near Hyde Park. Apart from the paved roads leading to the site, the one conspicuous addition is a bronze sculpture of a seated FDR wearing his braces on the outside of his trousers as he'd done on an early visit to Dowdell's Knob.

Months later, Lucy would tell his daughter, Anna, that their long pause on the hilltop turned into "the most fascinating hour I ever had." Anna would later recount what she remembered of that conversation to a Roosevelt biographer. This, according to Anna, was Lucy's fond and grateful recollection: "He just sat there and told me some of what he regarded as the real problems facing the world now." It's intriguing to imagine an unguarded Roosevelt laying out his hopes and fears to his old flame on a Georgia hilltop, on subjects like the coming summit, Stalin, and the likely shape of the postwar order, saying more, perhaps, than he would to his advisers. But all that can be known is that he unburdened himself to some degree as he had in June the day before declaring his candidacy. Lucy's validation, it seems, had become important to him.

Two days before he was finally ready to leave Warm Springs, Roosevelt was examined by Dr. Bruenn and Dr. Robert Duncan, a chest specialist from the naval hospital in Bethesda. Although the story has come down that he never asked his doctors about their findings, the president once again confirmed to Daisy, as he had at Hobcaw, that he had a "cardiac condition" and, in words she underscored in her diary entry for December 15, *that his muscles are deteriorating and they don't know why.*

Daisy's grasp of medical information is hardly more dependable than her understanding of geopolitics. But if that's a fair approximation of what Roosevelt himself believed in these days when he was sealing his decision to make the arduous trip by rail, sea, air, and car to Yalta in the age of the propeller plane (covering a distance, round-trip, that would finally add up to 13,842 miles), it suggests that he was putting his life at risk as knowingly as any GI advancing against an enemy position.

On the surface, it's also a more telling account of Roosevelt's condition than Howard Bruenn later managed to draw from the old jottings he salvaged for the "Clinical Notes" in 1970. There he reported that the patient's "general condition remained essentially unchanged" while he was at Warm Springs, a phrase that begs the question of what exactly it then was. Loss of weight was said to be the main concern, even though all restrictions on his diet had been lifted following the election; daily helpings of eggnog had been laid on as a supplement. The dosage of digitalis, used originally to reverse congestive heart failure, now had to be reduced out of concern that it might be suppressing his appetite; anorexia could be one of the drug's worrisome side effects. Roosevelt continued to complain he couldn't taste his food. His weight, 188 pounds a year earlier, now dropped below

165. Initially, he'd boasted of his new leanness, his "flat tummy." Now Daisy noted that the weight problem bothered him. Roosevelt tried swimming in the soothing waters that gave Warm Springs its name; long ago, he'd invested half his fortune in the dream that those healing waters might help him—and countless others—to walk again. But this time, his few swims led to an "alarming rise" in his blood pressure, sending it up to 260/150. "Further swimming was definitely discouraged," Bruenn noted. If he was going to be able to stand in his braces at his inauguration, he'd need some other exercise to restore a small measure of muscle tone to his hips and wasted legs. "He thinks he can do it by lying flat on a board with his legs hanging, to stretch the front hip muscles," Daisy wrote.

The calm of the Little White House during the president's penultimate stay was conspicuously ruffled by Eleanor, who remained behind in Washington, pressing her husband via the mail pouch in her role as his liberal conscience. She'd been less than overjoyed by his appointment of Stettinius and liked even less his readiness to rubber-stamp the new secretary's promotion of a lineup of starchy assistant secretaries whom Roosevelt himself regarded as "Old Dealers." Only the poet Archibald MacLeish, named an assistant secretary, was spared Eleanor's disapproval. "I can hardly see that the set-up will be very much different from what it might have been under Dewey," she wrote in a tart letter that reached the president at the end of the first week, warning him also, on the basis of something she'd heard about Yugoslavia, that "if we really want Russian influence to be paramount, we are going about it in the right way." A couple of days later, she dispatched another missive going over the same ground. "All of the newspapers which were agin you and all of the people which were agin you in the election are now loudly praising the State Department set-up." For once, Roosevelt didn't try to conceal his irritation from Daisy.

"I had forgotten," Eleanor would write, years later in a memoir, "that Franklin was no longer the calm and imperturbable person who, in the past, had always goaded me to vehement arguments when questions of policy came up. It was just another indication of the change which we were all so unwilling to acknowledge."

However, if he showed irritation in this period, it was mainly with his importunate wife. In his transatlantic correspondence with Churchill, he still managed to remain imperturbable and calm, responding coolly to a crescendo of complaints from 10 Downing Street over perceived American slights on matters that weren't all as urgent as the aggrieved prime minister made them out to be. Underlying them was the nagging question—nagging Churchill, not Roosevelt—of whether the Anglo-American partnership was going to remain one of equals. (Put another way, whether the United States was writing Britain off as an imperial power.) In the twenty-one days the president was at Warm Springs, Churchill fired off twenty messages to him, nearly all marked "Personal and Top Secret" (with the words "Private and Confidential" added on in one instance for good measure).

The prime minister's offended pride regularly leaps out of these cables, no matter the issue. Assailing an American push to open up the competition for commercial aviation after the war, he told Roosevelt that his negotiators were seeking to "dominate and virtually monopolize" the traffic at Britain's expense. His lamentation concluded in the fourteenth numbered paragraph on a note of sustained pathos. "You will have the greatest navy in the world . . . the greatest air force . . . the greatest trade. You have all the gold." Couldn't Roosevelt see the justice of reasonable protectionist measures by Britain? Days later, he took offense at a State Department statement saying a newly established government in liberated Rome should be set up without outside interference. Britain had been maneuvering there to preserve the monarchy, in Athens as well. Churchill regarded State's "stricture" as "a public rebuke to His Majesty's Government." He was personally "hurt" and felt "sure such things have never been said about Russia when very harsh communications have been received and harsher deeds done."

Most of all, he was nervous about the military situation on the western front. Small wonder. Hitler's new V-2 rockets had been smashing into London at the rate of several a day for two months, reprising the terror from the earlier V-1s. His generals had been complaining again about Eisenhower's lack of "strategic vision." His recently promoted field marshals, Alan Brooke and Bernard Montgomery, privately agreed that the supreme commander was "completely and utterly useless." Churchill knew better than to belittle Ike by name but wrote on December 6, "We have completely failed to achieve the strategic object which we gave to our armies five weeks ago. We have not yet reached the Rhine in the northern part and most important sector of the front and we shall have to continue the great battle for many weeks."

He'd have been even more nervous if he could have foreseen the major reversal in Allied fortunes on that sector, just around the corner, only two weeks away, when he wrote to implore Roosevelt to send his chiefs of staff to London for consultation with Eisenhower and British commanders "as soon as possible." Given "the destruction of all hopes" for a three-power summit before the year's end or a bilateral meeting between him and the president, another military talkathon struck him as an urgent stopgap. Between the lines, ever so respectfully, he seems to be implying that the president's latest rest cure, if that's what it was, had become an impediment to sound strategy.

Managing the correspondence from the Little White House in rural Georgia, Roosevelt volleyed smoothly and patiently with his British partner, salving the raw irritation, giving no ground. The drafts went back and forth by wire and Teletype as well as pouch. Roosevelt's instructions were terse, his editing usually light or invisible, but somehow he got the tone he wanted, at once familiar yet firm, consistently optimistic. To Churchill's complaint that the British Empire was being asked to open all its airports to other nations, he replied, "Of course it is. Would you like to see a world in which all ports are closed to all ships but their own?" On Italian politics, he was quick to "deplore" any offense given to Churchill personally, but the British had intervened without consultation with their ally, acting in a way that was "quite contrary to the policy we have tried to follow in Italy." So, of course, the American position had to be made clear.

On the slowness of the Allied advance to the Rhine, he masterfully redrafted a severe reply concocted by Marshall and Leahy, making it chatty and personal but also sharper. "Because in the old days I bicycled over most of the Rhine terrain," he reminisced, "I have never been as optimistic as to the ease of getting across the Rhine with our joint armies as many of our Commanding Officers." Still the trend was clear: "A decisive break in our favor is bound to come." When winter turned to spring, "we will know a lot more than we know now." He was saying don't panic, time is on our side. So there's no need for a strategic review. "My Chiefs of Staff are devoting all their abilities and energies in directing their organizations toward carrying out the plans we have made." He couldn't allow them to "leave their posts" to fly to London. They would all meet soon, he suggested in closing, probably in the Mediterranean en route to the Black Sea. He might have been rusticated in Georgia, but, as usual now, he had the last word.

Churchill had little choice but to be mollified. He recognized, at least sometimes, that his government's influence was declining as the U.S. contribution to the Allied effort on the western front in Europe increasingly outweighed Britain's. "The dwindling of the British Army in France," he wrote to Montgomery, "will affect our right to express our opinion on strategic and other matters." Early in his stay in Warm Springs, Roosevelt scrawled a greeting for the prime minister's seventieth birthday on the back of an envelope, warmly recalling the sixty-ninth, celebrated with Stalin in Tehran. It was duly transmitted via the Map Room in the White House, and Churchill messaged back, "I cannot tell you how much I value your friendship or how much I hope upon it for the future of the world, should we both be spared."

Just before leaving Warm Springs, Roosevelt tried yet again to deal with the political stalemate on Poland. Here he was not acting on his own as he had in June when he'd wooed and cajoled Stanisław Mikołajczyk over several days at the White House. For once, he was following the lead of the State Department, where his messages to Stalin were being drafted by Chip Bohlen, now officially the liaison between the White House and Foggy Bottom, shuttling back and forth between offices on the seventh floor at the State Department, near the secretary's, and Hopkins's cubby at the White House. (With his arrival, the new secretary of state now got copies of Roosevelt's correspondence with Stalin and Churchill. Hull had usually been left in the dark.)

While Roosevelt was in Warm Springs, Premier Mick—still in the president's view, the great Polish hope—had quit his position as titular head of the exile government in London, frustrated over his inability to frame a territorial compromise with the Russians that his inflexibly nationalist colleagues would consider for even a moment. For Roosevelt and Churchill, this was a serious setback, making it easier for the

Kremlin to do what it was doing anyway: prepare the ground for the recognition of its stooges, the so-called Lublin Committee, as a provisional government. The Red Army was less than a month away from crossing the Vistula to take Warsaw and what remained of Poland. Playing what could prove to be his last card in the run-up to Yalta, Roosevelt was advised to write to Stalin, urging him not to do anything rash in the short time remaining before they were due to meet again: specifically, not to grant official recognition to the Lublin gang his own secret police, the NKVD, had brought into being.

The draft Roosevelt approved on December 16 seemed designed to test the dictator's personal goodwill to himself. Nothing should be done, it said, "which would render our discussions more difficult." Stalin's response on December 29 was at once slippery and cogent. Brazenly dishonest in its claim that the Kremlin was being guided by the popular will of the Polish people, it offered a faintly plausible military rationale: that the Red Army was "bearing the brunt of the battle for liberation of Poland" and its success against the Germans was "dependent on the presence of a peaceful and trustworthy rear in Poland." This the Lublin outfit guaranteed (unlike the forces still adhering to the exile regime in London, who showed, in Stalin's view, that they couldn't be trusted by pointedly refraining from giving the Red Army any advance word of their August rising against the Nazis). If his stooges now declared themselves a provisional government—Stalin pretended the decision wasn't up to him—Moscow would recognize it for the sake of the Allied cause. Roosevelt's plea for a delay was thus brushed aside, effectively dismissed.

The president returned to Washington two days before Stalin received his first letter, stopping en route in Atlanta to pick up Lucy Rutherfurd, who then rode with him in the privacy of the *Ferdinand Magellan* all the way back to the capital. By the time he received the dictator's notably unresponsive response, the tide of battle on the western front had suddenly taken a wicked turn against the Allies. The outcome would remain unclear for a dozen tension-filled days. Operation Autumn Mist, Hitler's huge gamble—a massive counterattack through the dense Ardennes forest in Belgium—had surprised and staggered the Allied command, creating the rearward bulge in the American forward line that would give this fierce showdown struggle its name. At its deepest penetration, the German thrust had traveled nearly fifty miles, overrunning outnumbered units of the U.S. First Army—some exhausted and depleted, others green and untested—piling up heavy American casualties, taking prisoners by the thousands, massacring some (notoriously, more than eighty at a Belgian village called Malmédy on the first afternoon). Military censorship helped mask the severity of these losses. At Roosevelt's first press conference after his return to the White House, on December 19, reporters were evidently told he'd not be taking questions on what was already shaping up as the biggest battle of the war; none were asked.

When the president was given the horrifying details of the Malmédy massacre—of prisoners of war lined up and executed—his reaction was cold-blooded but not out of character. "Well," he remarked to Secretary Stimson, "it will only make our troops feel towards the Germans as they have already learned to feel about the Japs."

The completeness of the surprise Hitler engineered stands out in a starkly wide-of-the-mark intelligence report the Office of Strategic Services addressed to the president in Warm Springs on December 16. It said "direct control of affairs" was slipping from the grasp of an ailing führer who was reported to be ensconced in his underground bunker in Berlin, cut off from the military leadership. In fact, Hitler had left Berlin on the evening of December 10 and moved his headquarters close to the western front, at a place called Ziegenberg, in preparation for the final desperation assault he'd been plotting and assembling since September. The same day the OSS report was transmitted, 200,000 seasoned troops and a thousand tanks started to roll through the Ardennes.

The intelligence report didn't mention Ziegenberg. If it had, the name (which means "Goat's Hill") might have rung a bell with Roosevelt, who'd indeed biked nearby in his boyhood, for Hitler's combat headquarters was close to Bad Nauheim, the spa where the president's father took the waters to extend his life in the 1890s, just as Roosevelt had hoped to do himself half a century later at Warm Springs.

Within a week, the Battle of the Bulge forced its way into the president's correspondence with Stalin. Between the two letters on the political dispensation in Poland—Roosevelt's asking for a hold on any new moves, Stalin's brush-off—he found it necessary to write to the dictator on December 23 to beseech him to receive officers from Eisenhower's headquarters for a briefing on the new situation on the western front. The supreme commander believed that Wehrmacht, Panzer, and SS units had been transferred from the east to bolster forces that had sent his own armies reeling. He sought assurances that the seemingly stalled offensive by the Red Army was about to be launched. Between the lines, the president was urging Stalin to hasten his invasion of Poland days after he'd implored the dictator to halt for the time being any new political moves there. Of necessity, he was operating on two parallel planes at once. In such complexity, he was often at his best.

By the time Eisenhower's officers finally reached Moscow, Hitler's counterattack in the west had faltered and the Russian offensive was already under way in East Prussia and Poland. "You may rest assured," Stalin then told his visitors, "that we shall do everything possible to render assistance to the glorious forces of our Allies." The dictator could also operate on two planes.

George Marshall later testified that the president displayed no nervousness, no tendency to second-guess, during the crisis that began with the German thrust into the Ardennes. The chief of staff meant it as high praise when he said, "Roosevelt didn't send a word to Eisenhower nor ask a question. In great stress, Roosevelt was a strong man." Instead, in a radio address on January 6 summarizing what would prove to be his last State of the Union message to Congress, he offered praise: "General Eisenhower has faced this period of trial with admirable calm and resolution and with steadily increasing success. He has my complete confidence." The language had actually been suggested by Marshall and passed on by Secretary of War Stimson at a meeting in Roosevelt's bedroom on the last day of the year. Their intention was to snuff out "agitation" in London for the appointment of a British deputy commander who'd make up for Ike's supposed shortcomings as a strategist. Roosevelt "fully and vocally agreed," Stimson wrote in his diary.

He thought the president "seemed very well and in good condition." Such impressions of the commander in chief continued to seesaw from day to day, one diarist to another. The difference wasn't simply in the eye of the beholder. It was also related to how much rest Roosevelt had had in the preceding twenty-four or so hours. He could change in a matter of hours, Frances Perkins would say, "from looking pretty well to looking very badly." On Christmas Day, a week before Stimson's audience, Bill Hassett had confessed in his diary for the first time that he was now worried: "To me the President seemed tired and weary—not his old self as he led the conversation. I fear for his health despite assurances from his doctors that he is O.K." Two months earlier, when Roosevelt the candidate allowed himself to be drenched touring New York in the rain, the secretary had rejoiced in his display of stamina. As always, Daisy Suckley's prognosis swung like a pendulum. On one of his last days in Warm Springs, she wrote in her diary that he looked "remarkably well." Back in Washington four days later, she was again in a panic, writing, "He can *not* keep up the present rate—he will kill himself if he tries, and he won't be so very useful to the world then." All the while he was processing on a daily basis the latest diplomacy on Poland, the latest bulletins from the salient, or bulge, where Hitler's forces were advancing and then, finally, once again, losing ground.

It was Stimson who'd given the cabinet its first briefing on the Battle of the Bulge. Hitler's aim was to shut down the vital port of Antwerp, key to any advance into the Rhineland, which the Allies had, finally, just reopened. The president, who'd been receiving battle updates and estimates and visiting the Map Room on a daily basis, sometimes more than once a day in the early stages of the struggle, appears not to have said much. "I don't think we're scared," Stimson said, according to Ickes's diary notes.

The proof of Roosevelt's steadiness in this unsettling period was the sharp letter he sent Stalin on the Polish situation three days after clearing the way for Ike's briefing officers. Secretary of State Stettinius, not yet a full month in his job, described in the diary he kept Roosevelt's close involvement in the editing of Bohlen's draft. He "asked a good many questions which Mr. Bohlen answered. The president finally initialed the cable with the additional sentence added." It said, "I can't from a military angle see any great objection to the delay of a month."

Pronouncing himself "disturbed and deeply disappointed," Roosevelt told Stalin—with what he pointedly called "a frankness equal to your own"—that there was no chance that the United States would follow Moscow in recognizing the provisional government Stalin seemed bent on promoting. He then took apart the dictator's argument that the Lublin Committee represented the popular will of most Poles. How can that be known, he asked, when most Poles are still under Nazi rule? Altogether it was a tough response, but it gave Stalin no pause. Two days later, the Lublin group got the formal recognition from the Kremlin he'd foreseen.

The Soviet Union was now recognizing one Polish government, the United States and Britain another. Ever since Tehran, Poland had loomed as the ultimate litmus test for relations between Moscow and the West. With the war nearing its end, Stalin seemed to be telling his allies not to count on a face-saving compromise. If pressed, he seemed ready to show that control of Poland was more important to him than the pending Dumbarton Oaks accord, the United Nations, or the survival of the alliance itself. A little more than a month before Yalta, that doubt over Stalin's basic commitment to the alliance lodged in Roosevelt's mind. The dream of the partnership that would sustain the new security organization—of the great powers, the Four Policemen operating in concert—now seemed troubled. The effect was to make the organization itself even more significant in Roosevelt's eyes as a fruit of victory and a mechanism for engagement.

"The key to many of the actions and decisions of the President," Anne O'Hare McCormick, the *New York Times* foreign affairs columnist, had written earlier in the year after a not-for-quotation interview with Roosevelt, "lies in his desire to win the confidence of Stalin and draw Russia into full partnership in the peace." That had still seemed to be his ambition in November, at least according to the impression left with Averell Harriman, who dictated a "secret and personal" memorandum of conversations he'd had at the White House soon after the election. "The President still feels he can persuade Stalin to alter his point of view on many matters I am satisfied Stalin will never agree to.

"I have tried to impress on the President," the ambassador went on, "that our principal interest in Eastern Europe is to see that the Soviets do not set up puppet governments . . . I do not believe that I have convinced the President of the importance of a vigilant and firm policy."

Stalin's first letter of the New Year to the president might have brought his ambassador's warning back to mind. The dictator had earlier told Harriman that Roosevelt was "a first-class politician on a world scale." Now, in his letter of January 1, he was superficially cordial, basically brusque. He claimed to be "powerless to fulfill your wish" because the Supreme Soviet had already acted, taking the matter out of his hands. He then used the word "powerless" a second time, inviting Roosevelt to believe he'd have liked to be helpful. This was not a response a first-class politician could be expected to swallow. It seemed almost to parody Roosevelt's excuse that he needed to keep in close touch with Congress. Neither man had a clear sense of the political context in which the other operated. Stalin saw Roosevelt's America through a Marxist prism. However successful it had been in the war, its capitalist system was crisis prone, riddled with contradictions. The Great Depression had shown that; the world war could prove to be an interlude. Roosevelt, for his part, couldn't allow himself to consider the dictator's ideology a leading factor in his thinking; that would undermine the hypothetical premise on which he'd been working: that the wartime alliance could evolve into a peacetime security system, more or less smoothly. Stalin's letter of January 1, 1945, about Poland's new government strongly suggested it would be less rather than more.

The dearth of candor wasn't all one way. On the morning of December 31, a day before the dictator's New Year's letter was dispatched, Roosevelt chatted in his bedroom with Henry Stimson about the advisability of briefing Stalin on the secret project known at the War Department as S-1: the atom bomb. ("I told him," the secretary said in a diary note that day, "that I knew they were spying on our work but that they had not yet gotten any real knowledge of it, and I believed it was essential not to take them into our confidence until we were sure to get a real quid pro quo from our frankness . . . He said he thought he agreed with me.") The issue of Poland was left to simmer some more, until Yalta. The same couldn't be said of the actual country. The

Red Army finally occupied Warsaw on January 17, three days before Franklin Roosevelt's fourth inauguration.

In these last weeks of his third term, first weeks of 1945, he found ways to manifest his own sense of onrushing time. Gestures to those closest to him can seem over this distance in time to take on a prophetic status as intimations of his own mortality. They could also have been afterthoughts. His posterity, if not an imminent demise, was obviously on his mind when he asked that each of his thirteen grandchildren be in attendance for the inauguration. To Grace Tully, he dictated a note bequeathing to her "in the event of my death" a print of a sailing ship that hung in his study. Her assistant, Dorothy Brady, was told she'd get a portrait of John Paul Jones hanging over his desk. Back in May, he'd given his aide Jonathan Daniels a verbal account of his talks with Stalin, saying it was "something you ought to write should I pop off." In July, it had occurred to him to tell Sam Rosenman about an idea he'd had for the location of a "small memorial" to himself in Washington if one were wanted. But then his handwritten instructions for his own funeral, found in his bedroom safe only after the obsequies had occurred, were dated December 26, 1937. On the morning of his fourth inauguration, he's said to have spoken to his son James about that will and asked him to serve as an executor. He also bequeathed to him a family ring.

So it's clear he had valedictory thoughts in the final year of his life and earlier. Who doesn't? He might even have known episodes of depression. It's not clear that morbid thoughts were becoming a preoccupation, weighing him down. Though recurrent, they could have been fleeting; he could seldom have been left alone with them for long.

He was still open to desperate hope as well as dark reflection. In the White House log for the first week of 1945, his most frequent visitor wasn't the chief of staff or secretary of war. The name Harry Setaro crops up four times in eight days. Harry, also known as Lenny, was a former professional boxer and handler who now made his living in Philadelphia as a massage therapist. He professed to believe he had a "gift" from God. Daisy Suckley, desperate to find something, anything, to reverse the president's physical decline, had persuaded him to give

Lenny a try. Lieutenant Commander George Fox, Woodrow Wilson's onetime night nurse who had massaged Roosevelt's legs throughout his presidency, was temporarily sidelined when Lenny came on the scene, left to serve as a chaperone. After one session, the president reported he could move a big toe for the first time in years. Later he spoke of unaccustomed tingling sensations in his legs and hips. Lenny told him he would soon be doing "a buck dance." But there was no miracle. The amateur diagnoses of those who got to see the president at close range became more explicitly dismal and anxious. Ed Stettinius would record his impression: "It seemed to me that some sort of deterioration in the President's health had taken place between the middle of December and the inauguration on January 20."

At the White House, he was buffered by Sis, his daughter, Anna, whose innate ability to read his moods and wishes had become a safeguard, one on which his equanimity and comfort increasingly depended. Apart from furnishing reliably cheerful company at his lunches and dinners, she enforced the rest schedule his doctors had long since decreed, mainly by filtering the flow of paper and people that came his way ("using all the tact and ingenuity I can muster," as she would later say, "to try to separate the wheat from the chaff") and making sure, as best she could, that he wasn't overscheduled. Because Anna held no formal position, officials couldn't know for sure whether she was privy to matters they came to discuss or how much could be said in her presence. Back in November, Secretary Stimson came to brief the president on a highly sensitive report on army failures at the time of the Pearl Harbor attack, which Roosevelt was already inclined to suppress, on the recommendation of the navy. (Stimson was prepared to name names of errant commanders who reacted poorly; Admiral King wasn't.) "I couldn't go ahead with my report," he wrote, noting that it had cost him four weeks of work. "So during the luncheon I sat quiet and listened to the chitchat that went on."

At some point after settling on Yalta as a destination, Roosevelt told his wife that he'd not be taking her with him to the summit there. Instead, he'd be taking Anna. This required a fresh rationalization and some juggling of old excuses. Eleanor had expressed a fervent wish to accompany him to Tehran late in 1943, only to be told by the president it was impossible because female passengers were prohibited on all navy ships. Now, it turned out, the commander in chief had the authority to command an exception for his daughter. He couldn't do it for his wife, she wrote, passing along his latest excuse to Joe Lash because "it would only add to the difficulties as everyone would feel they had to pay attention to me." Anna's case was different, the president claimed, because Churchill would be bringing his daughter Sarah.

Loyal trooper that she was, the First Lady swallowed any wifely disappointment or maternal envy she may have felt. The only concern she expressed was for her husband. "I'm not really happy about this trip," she confessed to an English friend, "but one can't live in fear, can one?"

Soon after the election, Roosevelt let it be known that his fourth inauguration would be an austere, scaled-down affair, held on the South Portico of the White House instead of the steps of the Capitol. He didn't say that the usual celebration and hoopla would be inappropriate in wartime, but that was the implied message. Asked by a reporter at his first postelection press conference whether there would be a parade, he replied, "No. Who is there here to parade?" Twelve million Americans were in the armed forces, nearly ten million of them overseas, and as casualties mounted, military commanders were complaining of a manpower shortage that was making the task of mustering replacements ever more difficult.

A light snow had fallen overnight, underfoot for the several thousand shivering onlookers who didn't have the status to be seated on the portico itself along with cabinet members, top generals and admirals, congressional leaders, and the Supreme Court or admitted to a roped-off area where a tarpaulin had been rolled out for standees with the right kinds of passes. These included governors, diplomats, congressmen, and members of the Democratic National Committee, as well as fifty wounded veterans from Walter Reed Hospital, some in wheelchairs. Somewhere nearby, Lucy Rutherfurd sat with a special detail of Secret Service men in a discreetly positioned auto that afforded her a fine view of the speaker's stand on the second story of the mansion.

JANUARY 20, 1945. Fourth inaugural speech from the
South Portico of the White House.

The Marine Corps band, in white caps and scarlet dress jackets, offered the national anthem and "Hail to the Chief." Vice President Wallace swore in his successor, the man from Missouri Harry Truman. Then Franklin Roosevelt, leaning on his eldest son, James—a marine colonel in uniform, summoned from the Philippines to stand by his father as he had at three previous inaugurations—was somehow maneuvered to the front of the portico to take the oath from Chief Justice Harlan F. Stone. A seventeenth-century Dutch Bible, a family heirloom used on those earlier occasions, was open as it had always been then, to the thirteenth chapter of First Corinthians, which includes the verse "And now abideth faith, hope and charity; these three; but the greatest of these is charity."

Virtually all in this audience were huddled in overcoats. The president wore nothing over his dark suit, not even his favored navy cape.

For what would prove to be the last time in his life, he was encased in the steel braces that made it possible for him to stand erect so long as he kept a grip on the lectern. There's no reason to think the memory crossed his mind, but he was positioned near where he'd stood twenty-four years earlier when, as a vice presidential candidate, he and the head of the doomed ticket, James Cox, had called on the ailing Woodrow Wilson. It might have crossed the mind of Wilson's widow, Edith Bolling Wilson, now seated nearby. Later, she'd remark to Frances Perkins, "He looks exactly as my husband looked when he went into his decline."

The next day, however, *The New York Times* described his voice as "clear and emphatic." Only once, the newspaper said, was there a trace of hoarseness. Rosenman, Sherwood, and MacLeish had submitted drafts of the speech. Roosevelt dictated some paragraphs of his own and, according to Rosenman, then spliced together the final version himself, which proved to be unusually short, the shortest on record, only 573 words, lasting no more than five minutes. Nothing in it suggests it was intended as a final testament.

Wallace and Stettinius both thought they saw the president undergoing some sort of seizure, one that sent shivers through his arms and upper body before he started to speak. "His whole body shook, and especially his right arm, which grasped the rail of the reading stand," the now former vice president wrote in his diary. "He was a gallant figure—but also pitiable—as he summoned his precious strength."

"You will understand," the president began when he got possession of himself, "and, I believe, agree with my wish that the form of this inauguration be simple and its words brief." He was brief but not terse. His words had their customary amplitude. They spoke of striving and strove themselves to convey a complex vision of the test America was facing and would face at war's end as it tried to build "a just and honorable peace, a durable peace." Mistakes may be made, he said, "but they must never be mistakes which result from faintness of heart or abandonment of moral principle."

The basic lesson war had taught—learned "at a fearful cost"—was that America couldn't go it alone. It was part of a human community. Its well-being depended on that of "other nations, far away." He quoted Emerson: "The only way to have a friend is to be one." That led to a reflection that came across as platitudinous but actually, at its core, was a personal vow. Only a few would have caught its specific reference to the long trip he was about to undertake in secret across the Atlantic and the Mediterranean to the Black Sea: "We can gain no lasting peace if we approach it with suspicion or mistrust—or with fear. We can gain it only if we approach it with the understanding and the confidence and the courage which flow from conviction."

As on D-Day, he then ended in a prayerful vein. Almighty God, he said, had given the country "a faith which has become the hope of all peoples in an anguished world." He now prayed for "the vision to see our way clearly." He spoke of God's will and peace on earth. For a reinaugurated, now rededicated, yet nearly spent president, these pieties weren't empty. On some level of his being, he took them as a command to go forth.

On a more immediate and basic level, he now needed to get off his feet. After the benediction, Jimmy and a Secret Service man maneuvered him into his wheelchair, then back into the mansion. When they were alone in the Green Room, a relatively small parlor, preparing to face a skimpy buffet luncheon in the State Dining Room through which eighteen hundred persons would pass, the president said, so the son later remembered, "Jimmy, I can't take this unless you get me a stiff drink . . . You better make it straight."

Two and a half days later, he secretly boarded the *Ferdinand Magellan* at his customary station beneath the Bureau of Engraving and Printing for an overnight ride to Newport News, Virginia. There, by the dawn's early light, he was transferred without ceremony to the USS *Quincy,* a year-old heavy cruiser that had seen action on D-Day off Normandy and later in the invasion of southern France. Preferring the starboard side, the commander in chief chose to be installed in the captain's cabin. Anna was given the even more spacious flag cabin, normally reserved for an admiral. The only woman aboard could hardly be expected to sail belowdecks. Their destination was Malta. It would take ten days to get there. On January 30, with the big ship having entered the Mediterranean, the president was presented with five cakes marking his sixty-third birthday; the fifth, conceived as a joke, was the smallest. It was said to represent a fifth term.

Chip Bohlen, who'd seen Roosevelt at the White House less than two weeks earlier, was startled by his appearance after catching up with him once he'd sailed in splendor into the Maltese capital of Valletta. "His condition had deteriorated markedly," Bohlen would write years later in a memoir. "He was not only frail and desperately tired, he looked ill. I never saw Roosevelt look as bad as he did then, despite a week's voyage at sea, where he could rest. Everyone noticed the President's condition."

In the days to come, as an adviser and interpreter, Bohlen would spend more time with Roosevelt than any other American official. The diplomat would always insist that the president was "mentally sharp," that "his mental and psychological state was certainly not affected" at Yalta.

The talks in Valletta dismayed the British, Churchill in particular. Roosevelt had allowed less than a day for them and avoided, as he had before Tehran, any serious discussion of major issues that would have to be faced when, finally, they were across the table from Stalin: the future of a defeated Germany, the Pacific war, the new international organization, and, what continued to be the most intractable, Poland. The next morning, in the early hours of February 2, would come the seven-hour night flight to the Crimea, with six P-38 fighters in formation assigned to guard the president's sleek new plane, a custom-outfitted C-54 nicknamed the *Sacred Cow*—a propeller-driven ancestor of a whole lineage of Air Force One jets—which he boarded for the first time using a built-in elevator to lift him and his wheelchair to its cabin. He fell asleep before it took off but "slept rather poorly on the plane," his cardiologist would later write, "because of the noise and vibration."

CHAPTER 10

At the Czar's Palace

THE NAME OSCAR MANN didn't appear on the roster of officials accompanying Franklin Roosevelt to Yalta. But it's mentioned more frequently than that of Harry Hopkins in letters the president's daughter sent home to her husband in pouches bound every morning for the White House. Only when Anna has recourse to initials does a light go on in the dim recesses of a researcher's mind. "OM," it becomes clear, is code for "old man." Oscar Mann is Anna's father. "We are having to watch OM very carefully from the physical standpoint," she confided at the end of the conference's fourth day. "He gets all wound up, seems to thoroughly enjoy it all, but wants too many people around, and then can't go to bed early enough." Her job was "to keep the unnecessary people out of OM's room and to steer the necessary ones in at the best times."

That plural "we" refers to Anna and Roosevelt's two attending physicians, Admiral McIntire and Howard Bruenn, who were "both worried because of the old 'ticker' trouble—which, of course, no one knows about but those two and me." Bruenn had confided that "it's far more serious than I ever knew. And the biggest difficulty in handling the situation here is that we can, of course, tell no one." The cardiologist even warned her not to tell McIntire that she knew. This is evidence that someone, almost certainly Roosevelt himself, had put the subject strictly off-limits. There's no hint that she attempted to raise it with her father.

"It's truly worrisome—and there's not a helluva lot anyone can do about it," Anna wrote, adding a parenthetical instruction she may have meant to be taken literally: "Better tear off and destroy this paragraph."

Anna's contemporaneous testimony leaves little doubt that the strain of the trip had already taken its toll: the seven-hour flight from Malta in the brand-new but rumbling C-54 traveling at one-third the speed of future Air Force Ones, quickly followed by a five-hour drive in a Lend-Lease Packard over a winding, war-mangled road to the summer palace of Nicholas II, the last czar. Built in 1911 in white limestone in a style usually described as Italianate, with a semidetached Moorish annex, the palace had fifty rooms but, notoriously, only three bathrooms for the seventy-five Americans due to be quartered there. The Livadia Palace, as it was called, sat 150 feet above the sea, about two miles from the once fashionable resort town of Yalta. It had been used only four times by the royal family before Nicholas II abdicated in March 1917 in a futile attempt to save the imperial system. The last czar imagined he'd be able to keep Livadia as a refuge for his family. Instead, the Romanovs were moved to Siberia, then to the Urals, where they were already being held captive when the Bolsheviks seized power in October. There, finally, they were massacred, never having made it back to their summer palace in the south. The Germans turned the Livadia into a headquarters; in retreat, they'd looted its furnishings, down to the doorknobs. The Russians had less than a month to make it suitable for the president and to refurbish only slightly less regal mansions for Churchill and Stalin, hauling in furniture, dishware, linens, mostly from Moscow hotels—all loaded on freight cars (more than fifteen hundred of them, so it's said) bound for the Crimea.

Anna had been told by the cardiologist in no uncertain terms that her father was failing. But she was unable to shed much light on his performance at the conference itself, except to say it got him "all wound up." Like the doctors, she wasn't a witness when it came to the summit's working sessions. The Big Three leaders had eight of those on as many consecutive days, adding up to more than thirty hours, not counting their bilateral one-on-one encounters; trilateral working meetings of their top diplomats and generals on which they had to be consulted; and three elaborate state dinners, replete with banter, serious conversation, and formal toasts (forty-five, by the official U.S. count in the case of the last and most sumptuous, hosted by a beaming, unfailingly cordial—for that night, anyway—Joseph Stalin). Roosevelt missed none of this. In the view of the scholars who have followed most closely and thoughtfully the twists in the multilayered negotiations, he came away with most of what he wanted, just about all he could reasonably have expected. That's one narrative. In a competing one, kept alive in conservative circles over the decades, a moribund president, misled by dubious advisers of dubious loyalty, sells out Poland and the rest of Eastern Europe.

A point of intersection between the two narratives shows up in the formal photographs of the three leaders posing side by side on the Livadia terrace, their labors nearly done. In all these images, the president, seated in the middle, looks tired and gaunt. In most, he appears animated and engaged; in others—the ones that made the deepest impression over time—he looks not just gaunt but unfocused, a little lost. In the one that appeared on the front page of *The New York Times* as the centerpiece of its coverage on the day the Yalta accords were published over the names of the three leaders, he seems to be bantering with Churchill and Stalin, both of whom look amused. That image was printed on February 13. Two months later, he was in his casket in the East Room of the White House. Thereafter, the other photos, invested retrospectively with heavy foreboding by the fact of his death, were typically chosen by picture editors over those "taken seconds before or after in which he appeared relaxed, presidential and good-humored," in the judgment of the one American photographer on the scene, a low-ranking technical sergeant named Robert Hopkins who had received his privileged assignment directly from the president his father had long served.

A less noticed point of contact between history as it has generally been written and scathing posthumous critiques may be found in Howard Bruenn's "Clinical Notes" published twenty-five years after the fact, with the personal encouragement of the president's daughter. If the cardiologist is taken as a reliable witness, an episode of alarm over Roosevelt's condition at Yalta—never revealed in his lifetime—might have had its origins in the diplomatic impasse over Poland. In his medical journal article, Bruenn described the president emerging from an "arduous" and "emotionally disturbing" session at Yalta "worried and upset" about the trend of the discussion on Poland, even more fatigued than he'd been on arrival in the Crimea. A gray

shadow spread across his countenance (a sign, by now familiar, of a deficiency of oxygen in his blood); his chronically high blood pressure readings revealed for the first time a dangerous condition called *pulsus alternans* (in which every second heartbeat is weaker than the preceding one), a warning signal from an overworked heart. Roosevelt's hours of work had already been limited on a daily basis. Now, at a possible turning point of the conference, according to the doctor who treated him, those hours had to be restricted even further. This, presumably, is when the cardiologist took it upon himself to level with Anna. "His hours of activity were rigidly controlled so that he could obtain adequate rest," Bruenn wrote. "No visitors were allowed until noon."

According to Bruenn, Roosevelt was "much better" two days later. His mood and appetite were again "excellent." The *pulsus alternans* had vanished, though it's not clear why. The doctor's chronology doesn't neatly mesh with the schedules, agendas, and transcripts of the Yalta Conference published in a weighty State Department compendium in 1955. Bruenn gives February 8 as the date of the "arduous" session that upset his patient, leading to rigorous controls on his activities. Yet that same evening, the president attended Stalin's banquet, which started at 9:00 and ran on past midnight. Stettinius's diary has the secretary returning to his chambers at 1:30. None of the accounts mention an early exit by Roosevelt. Stettinius later recalled the president suffering a long "coughing fit" during the banquet. "Something due to nerves," he told himself. For all that, Bruenn's recollection that the president found the negotiations on Poland "emotionally disturbing" can be accepted as valuable testimony. From everything we know, it's highly plausible.

The questions of how well Roosevelt prepared for Yalta, how effectively he functioned there, have persisted as matters of controversy over the decades. Harry Hopkins was quoted as saying, after the president's death, he doubted that Roosevelt "had heard more than half of what went on round the table." Churchill would say his comrade-in-arms "really was a pale reflection almost throughout." Eden considered his dinner conversation "vague and loose and ineffective." Lord Moran, the prime minister's physician, in his diary gave "him only a few months to live," reasoning that the president "has all the symptoms of hardening of arteries of the brain."

Neither the White House consigliere nor these Britons were advised about heightened health concerns as the conference wore on. Lord Moran attributed to Roosevelt's daughter and doctors the view that "he is not really ill" at a time when Anna had already made it clear in her letters home that the opposite was the case. Obviously, she was putting up a brave front. Their own diminished access to the president was taken as evidence that he was losing his grip. Churchill's frustration over the president's lack of interest in consulting him on tactics comes through like a choked cry in a note his secretary sent to a Roosevelt aide on the eve of the first session: "The Prime Minister would be glad to know what arrangements the President contemplates for tomorrow." Hopkins—himself a virtual invalid, confined to his bed in the Livadia Palace in between the full-dress afternoon sessions—tried then to intercede with Roosevelt's daughter on behalf of the prime minister, throwing a small tantrum when Anna told him her father might not be able or willing to see Churchill in the morning.

The adviser hadn't been used to having to go through an intermediary, even a daughter, to discuss such a matter directly with the president. It may have felt like a demotion. Anna left a verbal sketch of this encounter. She'd set aside a pledge she'd once made to her father about not keeping a diary on what she saw from her privileged vantage point. Her typed notes portray an out-of-control, possibly inebriated Hopkins making "a few insulting remarks to the effect that FDR had asked for the job and now, whether he liked it or not, he had to do the work."

Jimmy Byrnes, drafted into the Yalta delegation by Roosevelt for his political acumen, also wondered about how hard the president was managing to work. Later he'd speculate that because of illness, Roosevelt hadn't boned up on the bound volumes of position papers the State Department had meticulously prepared for his use. "I am sure that only President Roosevelt, with his intimate knowledge of the problems," he would write in a backhanded paean, "could have handled the situation so well with so little preparation."

State's position papers, presented in black binders, analyzed problems that weren't new to Roosevelt and summarized policies he'd been shaping and reshaping for months. Maybe he went over them closely as Anna later maintained; maybe he merely skimmed them. Chip Bohlen, in the first draft of his memoir, found it "doubtful that President Roosevelt even glanced at the black books before the Yalta meeting." He'd have found nothing really new or surprising. The task before him at Yalta wasn't to take a series of previously scripted stands. It was to weigh one declared priority against another: crucially, as the negotiations unfolded, his aim of getting the UN established and Russia engaged in it against a showdown on self-determination for a Poland already under Soviet occupation. As chair of the formal sessions, he was usually able to determine the order in which issues were taken up and when to cut off discussion. In the estimate of respected historians, far from being a passive and inattentive onlooker, he skillfully deployed that privilege, emerging as "the central figure" of the conference. On the American side, he remained the indispensable decision maker.

Roosevelt's confidence in his ability to sway or at least influence Stalin had been rattled at the turn of the year when the dictator brushed aside his appeal to delay recognition of the handpicked, housebroken Lublin gang. In January, a week after that rebuff, the president acknowledged in a meeting with seven members of the Senate Foreign Relations Committee that he hoped, at best, to "ameliorate" the situation in Eastern Europe after the Nazis were driven out by Soviet arms and that a break with Moscow was unthinkable at this final stage of the war. By the date of that White House meeting, the Red Army was on the western side of the Vistula River, the Polish side, less than a week from sweeping into a depopulated, ruined Warsaw.

All through January, in the weeks leading up to Yalta, its rapid advance in Poland had registered on the walls of the Map Room. It had also registered on the sensitive mental apparatus Roosevelt turned to the world, playing on the politician's constant recalibration and fine-tuning of what he thought he knew, raising new considerations he then factored into his reading of his own country's expectations and mood. Where once he counted on the continuation of the wartime alliance in the postwar world, he now brooded on the role the new security organization might play in restraining the Soviet Union, gradually involving the most powerful wartime ally of the United States in a scheme, maybe someday a habit, of global cooperation. Speaking at the White House to the seven senators on January 11, he listed several ifs at the front of his mind when it came to such cloudy prospects: "if the machinery could be set up, if the Russians could be brought in and [if they could] acquire confidence in it." Almost in spite of himself, circumstances were turning him back into a Wilsonian, making the establishment of the international organization his top priority.

Three weeks later, by the evening of February 3, when Roosevelt was finally settled in Nicholas II's ground-floor bedroom in the Livadia Palace with a warm blaze crackling in the fireplace, the Red Army had taken practically the whole of western Poland. (In the same tumultuous period, scarcely a week earlier, it had entered the most infamous of the Nazi extermination factories, the Auschwitz-Birkenau complex. What it discovered there wouldn't be mentioned, as far as we know, at any point in the conference that was about to convene.) By the time the president broached the subject of Poland in the gathering's third formal session in the czar's former ballroom on February 6, General Georgi Zhukov's forces had already gained a small foothold on German soil, on the western bank of the Oder River, about forty miles east of Berlin. The nearest Anglo-American forces had yet to cross the Rhine. They were still 250 or so miles west of Berlin. Before he said a word, therefore, there was little left in Poland to concede, much to ameliorate.

He was half-apologetic opening the discussion on Poland by yet again making his pitch for a Soviet handover of Lwów (alias Lviv), half-apologetic because he knew from their discussion at Tehran and later correspondence how little he could expect from Stalin. He framed it as a "concession," seeming almost to plead when he said, "It would make it easier for me at home if the Soviet government could give something to Poland." Then, before Stalin could respond, Roosevelt tried to cut through the impasse with a proposal: that the new Soviet-sponsored "provisional" government be replaced by a temporary government of national unity that the United States and Britain could both recognize along with the Soviet Union, pending an election. It would be made up of the chiefs of the five biggest Polish parties. A torrent of Churchillian eloquence carried the same points forward, expressing them more broadly. A Soviet concession on Lwów would be "an act of magnanimity" that would be "applauded and admired," but more important, the prime minister said, was the sovereignty and independence of Poland, the cause that had brought Britain into the war, making it now a question of "honor" for him and his countrymen.

This provoked a fierce, skillfully argued response from Stalin, a thick, short figure pacing in his polished boots and plain tunic where Nicholas II's daughters once danced, back and forth along the perimeter of the circular conference table. Russians had nothing to do with conceiving the border on which he was now insisting, he pointed out in a low-pitched, controlled voice. It had been drawn in 1919 by a British foreign secretary (Curzon, after whom it had come to be named) and a French premier (Clemenceau) and, in fact, had been rejected by Lenin, who later, after fighting between Poland and Russia, had to accept an even more disadvantageous treaty at Riga in 1921. Ceding Lwów now would make him "less Russian" than those two imperialists.

Never responding directly to Roosevelt, he turned his fire on Churchill. For Russia, said Stalin, "it was not only a question of honor but of life and death." Neither Churchill nor Roosevelt was so indiscreet as to allude to the Nazi-Soviet Pact of 1939 or its secret protocols, which licensed the ensuing Soviet invasion of the fungible multilingual, multiethnic territory that was then eastern Poland; had previously been Russian; and further back, Polish; and now was being incorporated by force into Ukraine as a part of the Soviet Union. How, Stalin asked, could the Big Three take it on themselves as a group to replace the government that had just been set up in Warsaw—a tricky line of reasoning since it had been set up, essentially, by himself.

"I have been called a dictator and not a democrat," he cleverly argued, "but I have enough democratic feeling to refuse to create a Polish government without the Poles being consulted." Perhaps, he ventured, some of the formerly Lublin, now Warsaw, Poles could be invited to Yalta.

Roosevelt seized on that cue in a letter to Stalin he ordered up that evening in the vain hope that further prodding might stimulate a more promising response. The same tactic—a personal appeal on Poland, to what might be considered the dictator's better nature or, more aptly, his less paranoid side—had failed miserably five weeks earlier. Chip Bohlen, who drafted both letters with Hopkins, bluntly laid out the situation later: "We were up against a simple fact: the Red

Army held most of the country; Stalin had the power to enforce his will. But the President would not give up so easily."

The hard kernel of Roosevelt's letter stood out clearly once the diplomatic bubble wrap in which it was cushioned—words of reassurance, pledges of mutual understanding—had been stripped away. It said the inflexible Soviet stand on Poland was putting the future of the alliance in question. "The world would regard it as a lamentable outcome of our work here," it said, "if we parted with an open and obvious divergence on this issue." The American public would be left wondering "how can we get an understanding on even more vital things in the future" if "there was no meeting of minds when our armies were converging on the common enemy." (One of the "more vital things," the letter can be read as hinting, could be a Soviet bid for a major infusion of capital and equipment from the United States, along the lines of Lend-Lease, to promote postwar reconstruction of a devastated land. In a meeting at the Kremlin on January 3, Foreign Minister Molotov had tossed out the figure of $6 billion for the industrial credits he had in mind. Large Soviet orders would help the United States avert another depression, he suggested. In return for this favor, the United States wouldn't require Moscow to make any payments until the tenth year of what would be a thirty-year pact.)

The solution on Poland, the president's letter argued, was to invite a broader cross section of leaders from inside the country and abroad— a list on which his own favorite, former premier Mikołajczyk, figured prominently—to create the truly national government for which he'd been pressing hours before. Roosevelt was standing on principle, arguing for the need to reach out beyond Stalin's chosen Poles. But his letter could be read another way: as a lesson in the fine art of keeping up appearances. If there had to be a "divergence," the self-anointed "realist" also might be understood to be asking, did it really have to be so "open and obvious"? If genuine agreement wasn't yet within reach, couldn't words be found to keep the discussion going, to portray the outcome as still open—at least not closed—after Yalta adjourned?

He'd always recognized that the Soviet Union would be able to dominate Poland at the end of the war. His letter now said as much: "The United States will never lend its support to any provisional government in Poland that will be inimical to your interests." All he asked was a decent respect for appearances, a measure of flexibility and finesse, which in his mind included "the holding of free elections in Poland at the earliest possible date." Did this all-American pragmatist realize there might be a contradiction here, that a free election was hardly likely to produce a Polish government friendly to the Soviet Union, that he might be asking the impossible? Such questions probably occurred to Stalin. They may be what he had in mind when he pressed Andrei Gromyko, the young diplomat he'd sent to Washington as his ambassador, for a personal assessment of the president. "Tell me, what do you think of Roosevelt? Is he clever?" the dictator asked later during the conference. Stalin's subordinates invariably tried to give him the answer they sensed he wanted. In this case, the right answer turned out to be affirmative.

Roosevelt followed up on his letter the next afternoon, February 7, with an unusual burst of straight talk, stripped of diplomatic circumlocutions, on what was really needed to resolve the Polish question. Opening the fourth session, he wrote off both the exile government in London, still formally recognized by the United States and Britain, and the so-called provisional government in Warsaw set up by the Russians:

> There hasn't really been any Polish government since 1939. It is entirely in the province of the three of us to help set up a government—something to last until the Polish people can choose. I discard the idea of continuity. I think we want something new and drastic—like a breath of fresh air.

That was hardly what Stalin wanted. The dictator's next move had a certain brilliance, shrewdness at least, like that of a chess master sacrificing a knight or castle in order to protect his queen. Saying he needed more time to study Roosevelt's overnight letter, he announced that Foreign Minister Molotov had something new to say on two issues that had snagged agreement on the new international organization: the Soviet request for sixteen votes in the General Assembly, one for each of its so-called republics whose supposed autonomy, as everyone knew, existed mainly on paper; and its demand for an absolute veto on what could be brought up for discussion in the Security Council. If Stalin stuck to those stands, it seemed at the time that the successor to the discredited League of Nations could be stillborn, for all the weeks of arduous give-and-take the preceding summer and fall at Dumbarton Oaks.

Yet now the usually dour Molotov turned compliant and constructive. Three, even two, extra votes in the assembly (for Belorussia, Ukraine, perhaps Lithuania) would be sufficient, and the American proposal on the veto—promising open discussion on all issues—had just as suddenly ceased to pose any difficulties. Overnight, it had become entirely acceptable to the Soviet Union.

These well-timed concessions seemed very important at the time, not only in themselves, but also as a token of Soviet good faith. They secured one of Roosevelt's paramount goals—the new organization soon to be launched as the United Nations. The next step, the president said, would be to summon a conference to set up the world organization, within four weeks if possible, by the end of March at the latest. Churchill hailed the Soviet concessions as "a great step forward" that would "bring joy and relief to the peoples of the world" but raised a host of doubts about the possibility, even the desirability, of pressing ahead to an early conference while the war in Europe still raged. "This is rot," Roosevelt wrote in a note to Hopkins. He then crossed out "rot," replacing it with the words "local politics." His adviser agreed. "I am quite sure he is thinking about the next election in Britain," Hopkins wrote back. Agreement was reached the next afternoon on April 25 as the date for the conference; it took two more days to settle on San Francisco as the place. Roosevelt had ruled out Washington, Stettinius wrote in his diary, "so that he can travel to open and close the meeting."

By the time Poland came up again for discussion, on February 8, Roosevelt had secured another of the major goals on his Yalta to-do list in a bilateral session with Stalin lasting little more than thirty minutes. That was all it took for the president to signal his approval of the dictator's terms for Soviet entry into the Pacific war following a Nazi surrender. The terms were no surprise. Stalin had disclosed them at a December meeting at the Kremlin with Ambassador Harriman, who reported directly to the president. Roosevelt then had more than a month to consider the dictator's demands, which weren't modest. They involved the restoration of islands in the northern Pacific—the Kuriles and a portion of Sakhalin Island—and privileges in warm-water ports in Manchuria lost by imperial Russia four decades earlier, after its defeat in the Russo-Japanese War. Stalin also opposed any change in the status of Outer Mongolia, then a Soviet satellite. Roosevelt said he hadn't yet cleared these concessions with his ally Chiang Kai-shek, then made that sound like a formality best deferred. The Nationalist regime in Chungking (now Chongqing) couldn't keep a secret; anything conveyed to it, he remarked dismissively, was "known to the whole world within twenty-four hours."

He was acting on a top secret memorandum from his Joint Chiefs, delivered January 23, the day he sailed from Newport News. "Russia's entry at as early a date as possible, consistent with her ability to engage in offensive operations," the document declared, "is necessary to provide maximum assistance to our Pacific operations." Not yet in a state of war with Japan, Stalin said it would take three months after a Nazi surrender in the west to shift sufficient Soviet armies and arms out of Central and Eastern Europe to undertake offensive action against Japan proper and the Japanese puppet state in Manchuria, called Manchukuo. None of this could be announced—the Soviet Union still had a nonaggression pact with Japan—so Stalin wanted it in writing. Roosevelt didn't fuss over the draft of the secret annex Molotov later presented detailing all that the president had pledged in exchange for the Soviet promise to join the war in the east. "This meeting of the three leaders has already carved the seeds of the Third World War," an embittered Chiang would write in his diary when he got a whiff of what had gone on behind his back.

Not only Chiang was left out. It took two days before the Americans got around to telling the British what had transpired. Treated as junior partners, Churchill and Eden fumed. On that very morning of February 8, even before Roosevelt and Stalin got together, the American and Soviet chiefs of staff had sat across a table from each other without the British, for the first time in the war, going over together a wish list the Joint Chiefs had included in their memo to the president detailing the support they were seeking from the Russians. For one morning at least, the Soviet generals seemed to be extending themselves to behave like actual allies. In preliminary discussions, they'd spoken of moving thirty divisions, men and armor, plus two to three months' worth of supplies and ammunition over vast distances on the Trans-Siberian Railroad. The Americans would be expected to pony up much of the supplies. In return, the Russians would be asked to furnish bases for as many as two hundred U.S. B-29s that would be shifted to Siberia from Europe after the air war there ended, for offensive strikes against Japan. They also wanted to establish weather stations in Siberia and Mongolia.

The president then mentioned two Asian territories that hadn't been discussed in his State Department briefing books but had been on his mind. These were Korea and Indochina, scenes of wars yet to come, as yet unimaginable. Roosevelt could sometimes be "almost clairvoyant" (as Frances Perkins would say), but his intuitions about the future went only so far. In this case, he thought both Korea and Indochina would benefit by being placed under trusteeship by the new international organization. Stalin asked whether foreign troops would be involved. "The President replied in the negative," Chip Bohlen's notes say. Intriguing in hindsight, it was an inconclusive exchange, leading nowhere.

The obstacle was Churchill, Roosevelt said. He'd be offended if the British weren't invited to participate in a trusteeship over Korea. "He would kill us," Stalin affably agreed. The president knew better than to float past Churchill an idea he tried out on Stalin: that the British Crown Colony of Hong Kong be put under a United Nations trusteeship too after it was recovered from Japan.

Their ally, they understood, was sure to view any attempt to dismantle the French colonial empire as a dangerous precedent, a potential threat to his own. De Gaulle, Roosevelt added, had been pressing for ships to carry French troops back to Indochina. So far, speaking wryly, the would-be anticolonialist said, he'd been "unable to find the ships."

Four months later—seven weeks after Franklin Roosevelt's funeral—the State Department would send President Truman a report declaring flatly, "The United States recognizes French sovereignty over Indochina."

· · ·

State's Yalta briefing books had come with a memorandum from Secretary Stettinius marked "Top-Secret" listing "United States Political Desiderata in Regard to the Forthcoming Meeting." In the State Department's view, there had been ten key points. Soviet entry into the final stage of the Pacific war wasn't among them. That was a military desideratum, left to the Joint Chiefs. Once agreement on that was wrapped up by Roosevelt in his session with Stalin, his chief of naval operations, Admiral King, was overheard to exult, "We've just saved two million Americans."

The president himself wasn't ready to celebrate. If he glanced down the list of desiderata, most were now accomplished or moving ahead in technical discussions, or so it seemed: the zones to be occupied by the Allies in Germany following a Nazi surrender; the commissions that would jointly administer these and other occupied or liberated areas; the economic and political policies they'd pursue. Other pressing issues that hadn't risen to the rarefied level of State desiderata were also under discussion: a Soviet demand for $10 billion in German reparations; agreements on the exchange and treatment of prisoners of war; the prosecution and punishment of war criminals; the status of France, whether it should be confirmed as an occupying power in Germany and a permanent member of the Security Council; lesser ones too such as heading off a civil war in Yugoslavia. But on the list of key State Department points, one still stood out as stalled. Point five had called for "the emergence of a free, independent and democratic Poland."

Finally, on the afternoon of the fifth session, immediately following his private talk with Stalin, the president bumped up against a firm Soviet rejection of his proposal for a new Polish government of national unity, which he'd now advanced three times: at the conference table on February 6, by letter the next day, and as a formal diplomatic proposal at a meeting of foreign ministers. Initially, the dictator had Molotov respond as softly as possible. The Soviet minister's task was to make it sound like something other than a rebuff, a step toward accommodation. Addressing Roosevelt, Molotov did his best to present it as a more practical way of getting to the shared goal of free elections. He claimed deep popular support for the Soviet-sponsored figures already installed in Warsaw. "It would be better to talk on the basis of the existing situation," he said.

Roosevelt didn't give ground that afternoon. But his response was less than forceful. He advanced no argument, dangled no fresh inducements. The patchwork of incomplete minutes taken by several State Department hands—primarily Bohlen, who also served as the president's interpreter—makes it appear that he has retreated to the sidelines. Possibly he was reassessing his tactics, his ideas about how the conference could be steered to an outcome on the issue that would, at least, have the appearance of being positive. Possibly he was experiencing the obscure cardiac setback that Howard Bruenn would disclose years later, connecting it to the president's distress over the course of the discussion on Poland. Perhaps physical and intellectual reactions were occurring simultaneously. In any event, he spoke only a few times more at that fifth session, never at length, leaving it to Churchill and Stalin to debate the future of a beleaguered land.

The president's impatience comes through in a note he passed to Stettinius just as Churchill began a lengthy intervention. "Now we're in for ½ hour of it," he wrote in tiny, crabbed letters. The note seemed to say he knew where his old comrade was headed before he began, knew already that it would be useless.

Saying the conference was now at its "crucial point," the prime minister mentioned Britain's moral obligation to the 150,000 Polish troops who had fought honorably alongside its own forces. When Stalin's turn came, he almost succeeded in making a slippery claim sound plausible: that the whole course of Polish-Russian history had been completely reversed in the few weeks since the Red Army took Warsaw, that Poles were now rallying en masse to Soviet troops as their liberators. "For many years, the Polish people had hated the Russians, and with reason," Bohlen's notes have him saying. "Now old resentments have disappeared and good will has taken their place."

Stalin concluded by making his personal rejection of Roosevelt's proposal for a new government explicit, unmistakable. "Molotov is right," he said flatly. This was enough to deflate whatever remained of Roosevelt's waning hopes for a real accord on Poland. Searching for a path forward, he then asked how long it would take to hold an election. "About a month," Stalin instantly replied. In the event, it would take more than two years.

Anthony Eden, the British foreign secretary, recounted an exchange with Harry Hopkins at one of the Yalta sessions, without being specific about which one. It might have been February 8, the one eventually cited by the cardiologist Bruenn. "The President's not looking very well this afternoon," Hopkins said, in Eden's version.

"We'd better adjourn now before we get into serious trouble," Eden said he replied.

The date may be hard to pin down on the basis of the official record, but Andrei Gromyko offers an account in a memoir published decades later of an otherwise unrecorded bedside visit Stalin made to the ailing president on what would appear to be that same afternoon: "We sat with him for maybe twenty minutes, while he and Stalin exchanged polite remarks about health, the weather and the beauties of the Crimea. We left him when it seemed that Roosevelt had become detached, strangely remote, as if he could see us, yet was gazing somewhere into the distance."

Gromyko tells the story to reflect on the dictator's seldom-seen capacity for sympathy. On leaving the room, he has Stalin saying softly to himself, "Why did nature have to punish him so?"

Overriding the medical edict denying him visitors before noon, Roosevelt summoned Secretary Stettinius to his chambers first thing on the morning of February 9 to give him new instructions. He'd evidently concluded the previous afternoon, or overnight, that it had become pointless to go on pressing his proposal for a committee of the leading Polish parties to form a national unity government. So the secretary was told to drop the original American proposal and replace it with a new one that would find softer, more presentable language for what would amount to an acceptance of Molotov's insistence on keeping, not replacing, the existing stooge regime as the core of the government that would organize the promised election; at best, it would be expanded by an unspecified number of politicians from non-Communist parties.

At the sixth formal session that afternoon, the president recast his retreat on this issue as a compromise. "It is now largely a question of etymology—of finding the right words," he said. An early election in Poland had become for him the key point. It could be a model, an exemplar of what the struggle had been all about. "I want this election in Poland to be the first one beyond question," he said. By "first one," he meant the first to be held according to standards for self-determination laid down in the Atlantic Charter and now amplified in a new Declaration on Liberated Europe that the American delegation had been circulating at Yalta, holding out a promise that the continent's liberated peoples would have the opportunity "to create democratic institutions of their own choice."

"It should be like Caesar's wife," the president said of the election, which would come, if it came at all, with the imprimatur of the Big Three, Stalin's Russia included. "I did not know her but they said she was pure."

"They said that but in fact she had her sins," Stalin commented dryly, warning in effect that appearances weren't everything.

Intent on making his own point, Roosevelt let the dictator's cynical aside slide by. "I don't want the Poles to be able to question the Polish elections," he said. "The matter is not only one of principle but of practical politics." He was suggesting that the discussion could continue after Yalta, that the outcome there might not be the last word.

Not explicitly but between the lines, some kind of understanding may have passed between Stalin and Roosevelt in this exchange: Whatever was said about Poland at the conclusion of the conference would mirror the American stand; whether it influenced what happened on the ground there was another question, one still to be addressed. At Yalta, a crafty Stalin may still have calculated that the Soviet Union and its Eastern European allies might be able to make the machinery of democratic elections work in their favor. As the journalist and historian Anne Applebaum has pointed out, this was not yet seen as a goal beyond reach.

It would have been better to put the United Nations at risk than compromise on the principle of self-determination for Poland, Anthony Eden argued. That wasn't Roosevelt's view. That morning, he'd instructed his secretary of state to tell the meeting of foreign ministers that failure to reach a settlement of the Polish issue at Yalta "might jeopardize American participation in the world organization."

As always, he was intuiting and seeking to forestall mood swings at home that could undermine the international role he meant all along to be shaping for the United States.

The new language on Poland, negotiated word by word over the next two days, painted a far more optimistic picture of its "liberation" from Nazi tyranny than anything that could be read into Molotov's tightfisted opening remarks. Thus the final version of the Yalta statement spoke of the Polish government being "reorganized on a broader democratic basis" rather than merely "enlarged," as Molotov had wanted. "Reorganized" could be taken to mean replaced, even if it didn't in this instance. The existing Provisional Government would then be renamed "the Provisional Government of National Unity" as Roosevelt had suggested, even if it wasn't anything of the kind. The words sounded promising, appropriate to a real agreement; their practical consequences remained obscure. On paper, it would seem that the Russians had indeed given way. This would be the interpretation of a *New York Times* editorial on February 13 following the document's release. Stalin, the newspaper said, "has consented to the creation of a new government merging all political factions and pledged to free elections, which should insure Poland an independent government." In fact, the dictator had done nothing of the kind. In his own view, he'd merely signed a statement.

The details wouldn't be nailed down at Yalta as Roosevelt had hoped when he called for "something new and drastic"; they'd be left for a commission in Moscow that would "consult" with unspecified Polish leaders over an unspecified period of time. Molotov would be on the commission along with the British and American ambassadors. Nothing was said about their access to the actual country, now occupied by Soviet forces. The final statement promised "free and unfettered elections as soon as possible," the date to be determined by the reorganized government that would somehow emerge from the consultation. It omitted a sentence from the American text that sought to insure the right of British and American diplomats to supervise the voting. With great cynicism, Molotov said that would be offensive to the Poles. Determined to depart Yalta on his own schedule, Roosevelt brooded overnight on the latest Russian demand and all that it implied, then reluctantly went along with that deletion, vowing he'd continue to insist on access for his diplomats.

"Mr. President," Admiral Leahy, as crusty and conservative as he was loyal to Roosevelt, remarked once he'd read the final text of the supposed accord on Poland, "this is so elastic that the Russians can stretch it all the way from Yalta to Washington without ever technically breaking it."

"I know, Bill, I know it," the "realist" replied. "But it's the best I can do for Poland at this time."

Thirty years later, long after Stalin's death and his own fall from power, an octogenarian Molotov described for an interviewer the dictator's reaction to the impressively principled but toothless Declaration on Liberated Europe, upon reading the American draft that sought to advance the idea of national self-determination. By his own testimony, the foreign minister said as he handed the document to Stalin, "This is going too far."

"Don't worry," the dictator replied, "work it out. We can deal with it in our own way later. The important thing is the correlation of forces."

He meant, the old apparatchik explained, "it was to our benefit to stay allied with America. It was important." Roosevelt's wary pursuit of Stalin as a potential postwar ally had by this time, after all the months of maneuvering on Poland, become warier. If he could have eavesdropped on that exchange as the Russians eavesdropped on him, he might have taken it as confirmation that his pursuit hadn't been altogether hopeless, that he might yet be able to make something of the strictly verbal commitments Stalin had made.

Poland was by far the knottiest and most time-consuming issue Roosevelt confronted at Yalta. In doctoring the accord's language, he appeared to have extracted concessions from the Russians that could be called promising, at least not unpromising. This left some Americans with a sense that the conference was headed for a successful outcome, one that could be presented at home and to the world as positive and hopeful. The feeling of forward movement comes across in a note on an issue involving German reparations that Harry Hopkins scrawled and passed to the president at the seventh and penultimate session on

February 10. "The Russians have given in so much at this conference," it said, "that I don't think we should let them down."*

In the concluding volume of his World War II memoir, Winston Churchill would characterize Poland as "the most urgent reason for the Yalta conference" and "the first of the great causes which led to the breakdown of the Grand Alliance." But when the foreign ministers put the agreements in their final form late on the evening of February 11, after the three leaders had packed up and gone their separate ways from Yalta, Poland ranked only sixth as a subject among nine accords they were reported to have reached. Fifth was the Declaration on Liberated Europe to which Joseph Stalin had casually affixed his signature after only a few minutes of discussion. Also published over their signatures, as if it were a logical deduction from the declaration, the statement on Poland affirmed their "common desire to see established a strong, free, independent and democratic Poland." The formula was precooked, lifted from the State Department's briefing paper on Poland, but only someone on the inside of the negotiations would have detected the loopholes in the document, which seemed to promise, in confident affirmations, everything Roosevelt had actively sought and not secured.

On his return to the House of Commons, Churchill would give a more glowing account of Soviet intentions than any Roosevelt would ever utter. "The impression I brought back from the Crimea," he said then, "is that Marshal Stalin and the Soviet leadership wish to live in honorable friendship and equality with the Western democracies. I feel also that their word is their bond." Eight years later, when the Cold War had become something darker than a cloud on the horizon, Churchill the memoirist felt compelled to offer up a rationalization for the exuberant hope he more than once voiced after Yalta. "I felt bound to express my confidence in Soviet good faith in the hope of procuring it," he wrote. Roosevelt would have understood

---

* On the table at that instant was the question of whether the final communiqué had to endorse the $10 billion figure as a fair share for the Soviet Union of any reparations to be extracted from a defeated Germany. Mindful of how steep reparations imposed at Versailles after World War I had undermined the Weimar Republic, Churchill argued passionately against the proclamation of any specific figure. Heeding Hopkins, Roosevelt backed Stalin on the issue, which was then quietly referred to a commission on reparations. There the unfulfilled promise of $10 billion languished for a year, until finally it resurfaced in a secret annex.

and approved the thought, for it had been the crux of his own Soviet policy all through the war. If he failed at Yalta, it wasn't because of his physical or mental capacity. Had he been at a peak of vigor, the results would have been much the same. Like Churchill, who would soon face an election, Roosevelt had his own compelling reasons as the war entered its final phase for putting the best possible face on what had been accomplished. Stalin had committed himself to supporting the United Nations and dispatching mighty armies to the Far East. Seen in that context, it was no time for a break.

In the immediate aftermath of the conference, the issue of Poland's future—that of the rest of Eastern Europe, too—was overshadowed by the announcement of far-reaching plans for the impending peace: for an occupation of a defeated Germany by the Big Three—plus France—that would root out every last vestige of Nazism; and for the international organization, promising a brave new world of global peace and security, which would have its inaugural conference in San Francisco in less than three months. ("It is not our purpose to destroy the people of Germany," the communiqué declared, "but only when Nazism and Militarism have been extirpated will there be hope for a decent life for Germans, and a place for them in the comity of nations.")

Among the first to hail the Yalta agreements was Herbert Hoover, now twelve years removed from the White House, still rare as a Republican ready to express reverence for Woodrow Wilson the peacemaker (if not for the man by whom he himself had been ousted). The agreements, he told his party's Lincoln Day dinner at the Waldorf, offered "a strong foundation on which to rebuild the world."

The world press, completely banished from Yalta, hadn't even been told until the conference was half over that it was taking place, or where. An official statement, the first to be issued from Yalta, said merely that it was being held "somewhere in the Black Sea area." Only at its conclusion were the three American wire service reporters assigned to the president cleared to leave Washington to catch up with his party. They were then told they could meet him in Algiers, a port he wouldn't reach for yet another week.

On February 10, after seven nights in the Livadia Palace, Roosevelt had Stettinius pass the word to the British and the Russians that he planned to depart the next afternoon and therefore needed all Yalta documents made ready for final agreement and signature. Churchill and Stalin both protested that this was more than could be accomplished overnight, that there was still work to be done. Roosevelt wasn't persuaded. Evidently, he felt that there was little if anything more that could still be accomplished on the issues he regarded as central. He may also have been concerned about further Soviet backtracking. Besides, he had appointments in the Middle East.

After the final dinner at a palace called the Vorontsov Villa that Churchill and his party had occupied, the president chatted about his travel plans. Without consulting the prime minister, into whose presumed sphere of influence he'd be venturing, he'd set up a meeting of potentates—himself and the ruler of Saudi Arabia, founder of the royal house of Saud, King Abdulaziz, known also as Ibn Saud, who'd be traveling beyond the borders of his kingdom for the first time in fifteen years. In preliminary encounters, he'd also be meeting separately with Farouk of Egypt and Haile Selassie of Ethiopia. Ibn Saud, the protector of the Muslim holy sites, was the one who really counted in his view.

The president's self-assigned mission was to smooth the way for a Jewish homeland in Palestine. Remarking that he considered himself a Zionist, he posed a question Stalin had probably never before been asked: Was he a Zionist too? According to Bohlen's notes, "Marshal Stalin said he was in principle but he recognized the difficulty." The conversation didn't stay serious. Stalin wondered what gifts Roosevelt would have for the Saudi king. The president said he could offer Ibn Saud the six million American Jews. According to Bohlen, he said it "with a smile."

The cadaverous Harry Hopkins, said to have shed eighteen pounds during the conference, was euphoric when he eventually described its outcome to Robert Sherwood: "We really believed in our hearts that this was the dawn of the new day we had all been praying for and talking about for so many years. We were absolutely certain that we had won the first great victory of the peace." It was a sweeping conclusion for a man who'd spent the better part of the nine days in a sickbed. It's not clear that the adviser's use of the first-person plural included the president, whose preparation and alertness he openly, sometimes acerbically, called into question during the conference in a way that finally begs a further question: If it had been such a monumental success, what credit did the adviser attribute to Franklin Roosevelt, who'd usually acted on tactical advice in notes Hopkins passed along at the negotiating table but no longer was available for the long, confidential strategy sessions that had formerly characterized their collaboration?

The adviser's "we" also didn't embrace key military figures such as Admiral Leahy or the influential chief of the U.S. military mission in Moscow, General John R. Deane, whose accounts of the chronic mistrust he encountered in Soviet military circles made an impression on his superiors, notably Marshall and Stimson. The general was a disciplined officer but, on the basis of frustrating experiences in Moscow, clearly considered his commander in chief grievously misguided in his entreaties to the Soviet dictator. "No single event of the war," he'd later write, "irritated me more than seeing the President of the United States lifted from wheel chair to automobile, to ship, to shore, and to aircraft, in order to go halfway around the world as the only possible means of meeting J. V. Stalin."

The assessment of the one man who was at Roosevelt's side in every encounter he ever had with the Soviet dictator still seems trustworthy. Chip Bohlen was no apologist. He didn't find Roosevelt "a likable man." But notwithstanding the president's undeniable physical decline, his dwindling energy, he remained "mentally sharp" in the diplomat's view. "Our leader was ill at Yalta, the most important of the wartime conferences," Bohlen wrote, "but he was effective."

Roosevelt's own view should count for something. Writing to Eleanor, he expressed it without self-congratulation: "We have wound up the conference—successfully, I think. I am a bit exhausted but really all right."

The president's restraint found expression in other ways that would have registered with Stalin. Their discussion of Soviet entry into the Pacific war could have been the moment to unwrap the secret of the atom bomb as he'd considered doing. He'd been advised that Soviet espionage had made the dictator aware of the bomb's potential. Perhaps he considered it an inopportune time to bring up the matter with Churchill, who would have taken any revision of their agreement on keeping the nuclear duopoly to themselves as yet another slight. Or maybe he lacked the confidence in the postwar future of the alliance that such openness on the bomb might have demanded.

Similarly, the reparations discussion could easily have led to a side conversation on the Soviet request for $6 billion in credits. But Roosevelt sidestepped that too. Here he might have been anticipating a congressional backlash or calculating that the revival of the discussion of postwar aid might be more useful later as a sweetener when Soviet behavior needed sweetening.

The fact that he played neither card may say something about his weariness. Or it may be ascribed to his often cautious, almost mystical sense of timing. It may also suggest that he considered Yalta part of an ongoing process, not a final testament.

After bidding a ceremonious farewell to Stalin that included a presentation of gifts to officers of the ubiquitous NKVD, Roosevelt took a three-hour detour through the ruined city of Sevastopol, home to the Russian navy since the era of Catherine the Great. German bombing and shelling had left thousands of buildings with only a wall or two standing like gravestones. Just six structures in the entire city, the president was told, remained in habitable condition, relatively unscathed. Even if that was hyperbole, his passage through the Crimean port provided the starkest firsthand encounter he would have with the war's devastation. At the port itself, he boarded a converted cargo ship, the USS *Catoctin,* which had been berthed there throughout the conference, handling all radio transmissions between Yalta and Washington. That night, it began encoding and moving the Yalta agreements as Roosevelt tried to sleep in an overheated cabin. "The President had a ghastly night and I think it affected his health," Averell Harriman would say. Before 7:00 a.m., he departed on another three-hour drive for the airfield at Saki, where he'd landed in the Soviet Union ten days earlier. By mid-afternoon, on February 12, he was in Egypt, back aboard the USS *Quincy,* preparing to meet the first of three monarchs, Egypt's Farouk. Over lunch the next day, the king invited the president's daughter to spend a night at his palace. Thirty years later, Anna told the historian Frank Freidel that she was "petrified," given the reputation of the young monarch. Alert enough to intervene, her father expressed gratitude on her behalf but said he couldn't spare her.

By that time, rave reviews of the Yalta accords started pouring in. One from *The Washington Post* was typical: "The President is to be congratulated on his part in this all-encompassing achievement." Meanwhile, Jimmy Byrnes was telling a news conference in Washington that "every American should be proud of the role played by the President [whose] tact, patience and good humor . . . more than once . . . brought about decisions."

Two hours after Farouk departed, Haile Selassie, "the Conquering Lion of the Tribe of Judah," according to the first of his many honorifics, arrived on the deck of the *Quincy* for tea. The next morning, the Saudi king sailed into the Great Bitter Lake aboard an American destroyer, which had been incongruously transformed, at Saudi insistence, into a simulacrum of the sort of tent the monarch might inhabit in the Arabian desert. Precious rugs covered the deck. Large Nubian guards in embroidered robes, armed with drawn scimitars and submachine guns, flanked an enthroned Ibn Saud, whose party of forty-eight included a brother, two sons, an astrologer, an imam, a chief server of the royal coffee, the server's assistant, and "miscellaneous slaves," according to the manifest. Sheep grazed on grassy feed scattered on the fantail. Several had already been slaughtered there for the king's repasts. "Whole party was a scream!" Roosevelt wrote to Daisy Suckley a couple of days later.

Compared with Ibn Saud, Stalin had been a pushover. Roosevelt had nurtured the idea that generous offers of American technology and aid, on top of his own persuasive powers, would be enough to soften the old warrior's heart. He soon learned otherwise. The president launched into a detailed narrative of Jewish suffering under Hitler, then asked the king what he thought could be done for them. "Give the Jews and their descendants the choicest lands and homes of the Germans who oppressed them," Ibn Saud replied. But they consider Palestine a homeland, Roosevelt said. "Amends should be made by the criminal, not by the innocent bystander," the king countered, suggesting that surviving victims could also be distributed among the victors in the war. "Arabs would choose to die rather than yield their land to Jews," he concluded.

Bohlen, who was present, called the Saudi's tone "calm and reasoned." Roosevelt was more affected by the conversation than his guest. Ad-libbing in his final speech to Congress a couple of weeks later, he'd say, "On the problem of Arabia, I learned more about that problem—the Muslim problem, the Jewish problem—by talking with Ibn Saud for five minutes than I could have learned in the exchange of two or three dozen letters."

"The thought must have popped into his head at just that moment," said Sam Rosenman.

The royal guest, who walked with a limp from an old combat wound, departed after four hours, taking with him one of Roosevelt's armless wheelchairs, which he'd admired. The president also gave him a C-47 transport plane.

"Well, Mr. President," said Admiral Leahy a couple of hours later while his chief mixed cocktails in the captain's cabin on the *Quincy*, "the King sure told you, didn't he?"

"What do you mean, Bill?" Roosevelt asked.

"If you put any more kikes in Palestine, he is going to kill them," the admiral said. Roosevelt laughed, so Chip Bohlen noted in the first draft of his memoir, in a passage that never saw print.

The *Quincy* weighed anchor at the Great Bitter Lake twenty minutes after the Saudi king disembarked and set sail through the Suez for Alexandria, where, the next day, Franklin Roosevelt and Winston Churchill met over lunch for what would prove to be the last time. Between the summits in Tehran at the end of 1943 and Yalta at the start of 1945, their buoyant partnership had survived considerable rough weather. It had been tested by tensions among their generals over strategy and command; by Roosevelt's persistent evasions of the prime minister's requests for meetings; by Churchill's readiness to go behind the president's back to negotiate with Stalin on the political fate of Greece and the Balkans as he had the previous October; by the Briton's impassioned determination to keep the sun from setting in the postwar era on an empire that his ally believed to have already outlived its allotted life span; and by an unstated suspicion on both sides that they were no longer equals. Looking back on this final encounter nearly eight years later, Churchill makes it sound as if he recognized at the time that it would be their last. "The President seemed placid and frail," Churchill wrote, seeking to connect with his feelings about that lunch. "I felt he had a slender contact with life . . . We bade affectionate farewells."

Shortly thereafter, however, rumors started to circulate that the president might visit London in June, after the Nazis had been defeated and the United Nations launched. Churchill himself would press the invitation in a letter written a month after Yalta. "I shall be looking forward to your long-promised visit," he wrote.

Other partings were in store as the cruiser left the Egyptian port and headed west for Algiers, at the start of its long voyage home. The two White House aides who'd been with Roosevelt longer than any others among those who went to the Crimea were already belowdecks, each deathly ill. One was Harry Hopkins, the other Major General Edwin "Pa" Watson, the bluff military attaché who'd served him for twelve years, becoming his appointments secretary, always described as jovial, sometimes as discerning and influential. All through the war, he'd been among the first at Roosevelt's bedside every morning as "the Boss" plotted the day ahead. Now he too was under the care of the cardiologist Bruenn, diagnosed with the same hypertensive heart failure with which the president, two years his senior, had earlier been stricken. Against doctor's advice, Watson insisted on making the trip to Yalta. He took a turn for the worse there following a clash on the second day with Hopkins that turned nasty. Without notice, the general had been told that the adviser was requisitioning his bedroom in the Livadia Palace, that he had to clear out immediately so Prime Minister Churchill could take a postprandial nap. Barely repressed resentments quickly surfaced. Hopkins supposedly threatened to tell Roosevelt the general was being obstructive. In the court of an ailing ruler, two ailing courtiers were jousting pathetically for position. Out of consideration for the president, an angry Pa gave way. By the time he reached the *Quincy*, he was in the sick bay in serious condition but conscious. Soon after leaving Alexandria, he was comatose, paralyzed by a stroke.

Hopkins may have taken Watson's stroke as a warning. In failing condition himself, dreading the long sea voyage, he resolved to leave the *Quincy* in Algiers, rest in Marrakesh, then fly home. Roosevelt, protesting that he needed the adviser's help on the speech on Yalta he planned to deliver to Congress on his return to Washington, dispatched Anna to change his mind. "Tell your father to call Sam Rosenman in," Hopkins told her, according to an account Anna appears to have related toward the end of her life to the writer Jim Bishop.

"He won't budge," Anna told her father, in this version.

"Let him go," the president supposedly said.

Rosenman had been in London, not the Crimea, and had seen only the Yalta communiqué when he boarded in Algiers. Chip Bohlen, who planned to accompany Hopkins home, dictated a long memorandum and spent two hours with the adviser and the speechwriter going over the documentary record. Once the two men were gone, Admiral Leahy was the only person left on the *Quincy* besides the president who'd actually attended the Yalta sessions.

"Dad was in a grouchy mood as we took the launch into the port of Algiers," Robert Hopkins wrote. "It was only after we arrived that Dad remembered that he had not said goodbye to the President." Robert himself had thought to say farewell. It's hard to believe that the father's failure to do so was a simple oversight. Better than anyone, he knew how Roosevelt's inherited sense of entitlement blended with his almost regal sense of the duty owed his office and understood that his chief would now feel abandoned, that he could expect no gratitude for his efforts or best wishes for his recovery. So the president and his sometime confidant, his closest wartime collaborator, were both sulking when they parted, never to meet again.

Pa Watson breathed his last the morning after the *Quincy*, pointing westward, completed its passage through the Strait of Gibraltar. Knowing the general had contemplated converting to Roman Catholicism, Roosevelt had arranged for him to receive last rites from a chaplain. The president was just waking up when Admiral McIntire brought him the tidings. "Ross told us that father had taken it in his stride," Anna wrote in a diary note that day. This "was typical of him," she added, "but it is apt to hide much in the way of inside turmoil."

"All in all," wrote Rosenman, "it was a sorry ship."

A full week intervened between Pa Watson's death and the cruiser's return to Newport News. For the first five and a half of those days, Rosenman toiled on the speech, with some help from Leahy, but hardly any from Roosevelt, who seemed unwilling to plunge into their customary working sessions. The president read in the mornings, lunched in his cabin, spent chunks of his afternoon basking in the sunshine on the top deck with Anna, mostly silent, studying the sea, staring at the horizon. Evenings began with his ceremonial mixing of cocktails in his cabin, marking the start of light, animated conversation that only intermittently touched on the negotiations at Yalta. Movies followed. The evening of Hopkins's departure, the president and his party watched *Phantom Lady,* a film about a depressed man who meets a mysterious woman in a bar. Two nights later, after Pa's death, they saw *Frenchman's Creek,* involving a seventeenth-century noblewoman, in flight from a tyrannical husband.

"The President rested continuously through the day and went to the movies at night," Rosenman wrote, summing up the crossing. The speechwriter had no doubt that he was "deeply depressed" by the loss of Watson but didn't speculate further, didn't ask whether the brooding president found in this latest loss any prefiguring of his own end, whether he had fallen into a more general state of depression as his daughter seems to have feared.

The day before he was due to land, he finally pulled himself together and focused on Rosenman's efforts. That evening, he skipped the movie and worked over three of the speechwriter's drafts, returning them with his revisions. Three hours after Roosevelt returned to the White House from his five-week trip, he sat in a limousine at Arlington National Cemetery close to the grave into which Pa Watson was being lowered in the rain. The rest of that first day and evening back were devoted to turning out and polishing three further drafts of his speech, with John Boettiger, the former newsman, pitching in, working at the big table in the cabinet room.

By the next morning, when the president headed to the Capitol to deliver what would prove to be his final address to Congress, he'd spent only three nights in the White House since the inauguration. He'd left in January; it was now March. Given his long absence, that first week back can be viewed, in a political sense, as the delayed start of his fourth term. Until that morning, no member of Congress had heard his voice in all that time, nor had the nation at large. "Dear Alben" Barkley was the first, sitting on "a certain functional stool" in the president's bathroom while Roosevelt attempted to shave and, simultaneously, regale his guest with Yalta yarns, not incidentally bringing himself up to date on the political scene.

Talking about his diplomatic marathon in private conversations, he still displayed his uncanny ability to adjust the pitch of his words and views to the mind-set or function of his listener. After his sessions on Yalta with Roosevelt, Sam Rosenman could write that he was "certain that it had paved the way for the kind of world that he had been dreaming, planning and talking about." It would have served no purpose, after all, to have his speechwriter afflicted by doubts; the speech had to serve as a sales job for a leading American role in the emerging international order. At this late stage, with the war continuing in two theaters, it couldn't be an alarm, a renewed call to arms.

In that same week, the protean president presented an essentially antithetical view to Adolf Berle, a charter member of the New Deal brain trust, later a senior State Department official, who early on had become convinced that the Soviet Union meant to be dominant in Europe, that therefore the Yalta venture was a mistake. "He was obviously unhappy about certain of the settlements he had to make at Yalta," Berle wrote in his diary, "but saw no escape from the facts of the situation."

Throwing up his arms, in Berle's depiction, Roosevelt resurrected the line he'd earlier used with a skeptical Admiral Leahy back at the czar's palace. "Adolf," he said, "I didn't say it was good. I said it was the best I could do."

The political leader who faced Congress and the nation on the morning of March 1, just thirty hours after his return to Washington, spoke in yet another vein. He was careful neither to oversell the Yalta accords, nor to sow fresh doubts that could undermine them at home or abroad. Roosevelt was protean because he was a master of the overview, able to look at most issues from all sides. Leadership for him remained an exercise in cautious optimism. Weary as he was, he still felt he could lead.

In fact, he had six weeks left.

CHAPTER II

Almost to Victory

AS HE APPROACHED the start of what was supposed to be his thirteenth year in office, Franklin Roosevelt did something he'd never done before. He appeared in public in his wheelchair and not just in public but before a joint session of Congress. Secret Service men wheeled him down the aisle to the well of the House of Representatives and helped him shift into a straight-backed armchair cushioned in red velvet, set behind a table festooned with microphones. There he sat at the base of the podium where he'd stood uncomfortably erect through all his prior addresses in the chamber, propped in his braces. Photographers who might have been tempted to test the long-standing ban on wheelchair pictures were either barred from the gallery until he was seated or warned not to hoist their cameras. Five months earlier, he'd delivered his slashing Fala speech to the Teamsters from a seated position. This time, after all these years, he allowed himself to mention his disability, casually and openly, before a national radio audience. That was the real first.

"I hope that you will pardon me for the unusual posture of sitting down during the presentation of what I want to say," he began in a conversational tone, "but I know that you will realize that it makes it a lot easier for me not to have to carry ten pounds of steel around on the bottom of my legs; and also because of the fact that I have just completed a fourteen-thousand-mile trip." A wave of applause swept the chamber, whether for his candor or the long trip in this pre-jet age it's now hard to say, for his stalwartness in either case.

Frances Perkins had known him before he was crippled and

MARCH 1, 1945. Delivering his final speech to Congress.

throughout his public life. She could write with authority that this was "the first time he mentioned his affliction or asked any quarter for it." She thought he carried it off without a trace of self-pity or strain. In her judgment, "it was one more spiritual inner victory for him in his long adjustment."

Soon attentive onlookers noticed that he seemed to be losing his way in his text and filling in with unscripted remarks until he found his place. He said he'd returned "refreshed and inspired." Then, a moment later, he said it again. In between, he insisted with less than total accuracy, "I was not ill for a second until I returned to Washington" and caught up with the latest rumors about his health (prompted, as he'd have known, by his washed-out appearance in the images from the Big Three photo op at the czar's palace). Walter Lippmann didn't think he protested too much. The president said he was "much refreshed," the columnist noted warmly, and "manifestly he was."

Belle Roosevelt—widow of Teddy's son Kermit—watched from the gallery. "He looked well and handsome," she wrote in her diary. "The impression was that the President was rendering a carefully considered report and that the report was being carefully appraised by the House."

"He is looking pretty well—much better than he looked in the pictures that were taken during the trip," Secretary Stimson noted in his.

The New York Times agreed that "refreshed" was the right word. "The President looked the part," it reported, "as he sat tanned and glowing under a battery of floodlights." His numerous interpolations into his prepared text added up to more than seven hundred words, the newspaper calculated. Occasionally, these off-the-cuff departures showed how determined he was to come across as measured, ambitious in his goals, but cautious in his claims. Instead of saying his journey had been fruitful, for instance, he said at the start that it had "so far" proved fruitful. Elsewhere the text called the Yalta accords "a good start on the road to peace" and "the beginnings of a structure of peace upon which we can begin to build." A start, a beginning, not a sure thing.

It would be up to Congress and the American people to follow through. On occasion, he allowed himself to go overboard. Where his text had him saying that the conference in the Crimea had been "a turning point in American history," he couldn't keep himself from adding, "And therefore in the history of the world." In that he was asking the country to shoulder responsibilities in an international order it had failed to take up in Woodrow Wilson's day, the first claim might have been justified; the second had a touch of triumphalism he elsewhere held to a minimum. He meant to dwell more on the prospects for peace than victory, which now seemed assured. The path ahead would be burdensome. "Responsibility for political conditions thousands of miles away can no longer be avoided by this great nation," he warned in a line that can now be read as prophetic, more than a little ominous as well. "Certainly I do not want to live to see another war," he explained.

The combination of cautious hedging and broad vision was charac-teristic. In this case, it reflected oscillations in the political tactician's own thinking in the aftermath of Yalta. Keeping an eye on a distant horizon all through the war years, he'd been trying to imagine and pre-pare the ground for an international organization that would maintain the peace. That stood for a destination of a kind, however indistinct. But hard realities intruded, bringing inconsistencies and course cor-rections in their train. So now, addressing Congress, he found himself pointing awkwardly—deceptively, in fact—to "the solution reached on Poland," citing it as an "outstanding example of joint action by the three major Allied powers in the liberated areas." Already that was a dubious proposition as he knew all too well. Ad-libbing again, he felt a need to qualify the words as soon as they left his mouth. "Everybody does not agree with us, obviously," he acknowledged.

His final attempt to explain where matters now stood came with built-in escape clauses. "I am convinced that the agreement on Poland, *under the circumstances*, is the most hopeful agreement *possible* for a free, independent, and prosperous Polish state [emphasis added]." This was his way of saying, yet again, it was "the best I could do," that he hadn't given up, would go on wrestling with the problem.

In a speech only a few minutes short of an hour, nearly all of it confined to the Yalta accords, he mentioned Stalin and Churchill by name only once in passing. The leaders now had "a greater facil-ity in negotiating with each other that augurs well for the peace of the world," he said. The words could be taken as implying that they trusted each other more, but he stopped short of saying that. Another omission, obviously calculated, became conspicuous before the end of the month once the *Herald Tribune* broke the story of what Secretary Stettinius called in his diary "the X-matter." This was Stalin's claim for two extra seats in the General Assembly, which Churchill had sup-ported at Yalta and Roosevelt had finessed in order to close the overall deal on the United Nations, in effect pledging that the United States wouldn't oppose the extra votes (might even make claims of its own) if the matter could be deferred some months until the world organi-zation actually came into being. The *Trib*'s story ignited speculation about other side deals that might still rise to the surface and specula-tion, which has never quite stopped, that the ailing president had been outwitted.

But that was later. This address, scarcely a day after his return, didn't immediately arouse such second-guessing. It had been a stirring occasion but, the consensus seemed to be, not a stirring speech. "A pretty good report of reports already reported," one Republican called it. "It was a long, rambling, rather lifeless affair," the reporter Allen Drury wrote in his journal, "delivered in a rather rambling and lifeless fashion. He just talked along." By the oratorical standards of our own day, it might be considered slightly better than that. But Roosevelt's effort from the well of the House was being held up to his own high standard, which encouraged expectations of an aria, graced by wit and memorable phrases. The young Drury, then covering the Senate for a wire service, was in a pack of quote-seeking reporters surrounding the new vice president. "One of the greatest ever delivered," Harry Truman said of the address, laughing heartily with what could be taken as a wink. The pack, Drury wrote, laughed with him. Giving and receiving, they were doing their jobs.

Another young reporter in the gallery, the future TV anchor and commentator David Brinkley, judged the speech one of Roosevelt's "poorest." But the response, as he recalled it, was sustained and generous: "It seemed the applause would never end. As Roosevelt was wheeled out, those near him thought they saw tears in his eyes. He was home, the victorious leader of a victorious nation."

Even if no actual tears were shed, he could have felt he was nearing the completion of his mission, though his new term had only just begun. The softened mood of the occasion might have been expressed best by an antagonist, the reliably anti-Roosevelt columnist for New York's *Daily News*, John O'Donnell, who wrote that the president's acknowledgment of his infirmity had "reawakened even in his grimmest political foes their honest appreciation of the undoubted personal courage and fighting heart of the man who was about to tell them what he had done in the name of the Republic ... It didn't change many political ideas or give birth to personal affection which hadn't existed before. But it blew away some of the fumes of personal bitterness."

Pravda the next day devoted its front page to Roosevelt's speech. It was an encouraging sign, becoming rarer as the action-packed days and weeks since Yalta raced by, that the Kremlin still placed a positive value on the alliance and the vaunted unity of the victors, to which the Big Three had recently renewed their vows. Contradictory signs, crude indications of an opposing trend, also were piling up, fast becoming dominant. These started within two weeks of the Yalta accords with a crackdown by the Red Army and the NKVD in the streets of the Romanian capital of Bucharest, leading to the installation of a Communist-dominated government. There was no way to read this as a rogue operation. An ultimatum sealing the takeover was personally delivered to the Romanian monarch by Andrei Vyshinsky, who'd been at Molotov's side at Yalta (the same Vyshinsky who'd played the sinister role of chief prosecutor at the Moscow trials of the 1930s). Ambassador Harriman twice protested to the Soviet foreign minister that the Bucharest coup violated the principles of the recent accords, not to mention the Atlantic Charter; protested futilely, of course.

All this was old news by the time Roosevelt boarded his secret train for Hyde Park two days after his speech to Congress. When he returned to the White House on March 8, he was faced with a Churchill cable alerting him to "liquidations and deportations that are going on" in Poland. "If we do not get things right now," the prime minister warned, "it will soon be seen by the world that you and I by putting our signatures to the Crimea settlement have under-written a fraudulent prospectus." Churchill had to concede that he was ill-placed to complain about what the Russians were doing in Romania, because back in October, on his visit to Moscow, he'd all but conceded that Balkan chip to Stalin, along with Bulgaria, in exchange for the dictator's pledge to keep hands off Greece. So now he was attempting to pass off the Romania issue to Roosevelt, who'd never seen a role for the United States in the Balkans. At the same time, he implored the president to take the lead on Poland as well by firing off a firmly worded message to Stalin.

Five days later, the prime minister pressed even harder. "A month has passed since Yalta and no progress of any kind has been made," he said. Soon he'd be forced to tell Parliament that "We are in the presence of a great failure and an utter breakdown of what was settled at Yalta." He'd hate to "reveal a divergence between the United States and British Governments," he wrote to Roosevelt with unconcealed petulance, but he'd have to acknowledge that Britain couldn't do more if the Americans declined to play their part. The implied threat was easily brushed aside.

Harriman's reports from Moscow were similarly troubled. The three-man commission of Molotov, himself, and the British ambassador was mired, getting nowhere on the national unity regime for Warsaw seemingly promised at Yalta. The Soviet foreign minister had swung back to his original, stingiest interpretation of what the Yalta accords' call to "reorganize" the Polish government "on a broader democratic basis" really meant, saying no Poles outside the new ruling group in Warsaw could be added without its explicit approval; not just that, Molotov now maintained, Moscow's chosen Poles had a sovereign right to block the admission of American and British observers even if he himself had promised such access. The Soviet definition of self-determination was becoming clear; it meant determination by the faction whose strings it pulled. Stalin's offer of an election in about a month similarly evaporated. George Kennan, who accompanied Harriman to meetings on Poland with Molotov and Vyshinsky, would write in his memoir of his "boredom and disgust" through "many hours of unreal, repetitious wrangling." The Yalta accords, with all their fine phrases about democracy, were being shown up as "the shabbiest sort of equivocation," in his view.

Bohlen, who drafted most of the president's replies, later wrote that Roosevelt's powers of concentration were "slipping." But the messages that went out over his name still reflected his thinking. The reply to Churchill's latest fulmination calmly discarded any idea of a "breakdown" over goals between Whitehall and Washington in their response to Soviet intransigence. There were only disagreements on tactics, the letter said. He continued to feel that protests should be exhausted at the ambassadorial level before he raised the stakes by writing directly to Stalin. The prime minister's next cable sounds contrite. "Your friendship is the rock on which I build for the future of the world as long as I am one of the builders," he wrote.

Someone had to be shaping the responses that came out of the White House. It's not likely, for various reasons, to have been Leahy (politically tone-deaf) or Bohlen (insufficient rank) or Stettinius (insufficient stature); Hopkins remained at the Mayo Clinic in Minnesota (entirely out of the loop). It could only have been the president, whose final stretch of consecutive days there, from March 8 to March 24, encompassed such long-distance discussions on issues of Soviet behavior and questions of how to respond. At about the middle of this period, he had a revealing side conversation with Senator Arthur Vandenberg of Michigan, a former isolationist undergoing conversion to the internationalist faith. Roosevelt had made a deliberate point of naming a bipartisan delegation for the San Francisco conference, intending to avoid a fatal oversight by Wilson, who took no Republicans to Versailles. Vandenberg, who figured to be the most influential Republican member, represented many voters of Polish descent; he'd recently been outspoken on Polish issues. If that made him an embarrassment, he told the president, he'd "break a leg" so he could be replaced on the delegation. "Just between us, Arthur," Roosevelt replied, according to the senator, "I am coming to know the Russians better, and if I could name only one delegate to the San Francisco conference, you would be that delegate."

About a week later, before departing on his final trip to Hyde Park, he's supposed to have allowed himself a rare outburst of pessimism over lunch with Anna Rosenberg, his favored gadfly. "We can't do business with Stalin. He has broken every one of the promises he made at Yalta," she quoted him as saying.

Diplomatic exchanges were still unfolding behind the scenes, providing a distracting sideshow to the crescendo of advancing armies and overwhelming airpower on all fronts. In Roosevelt's last days in the White House, George Patton's Third Army battled its way across the Rhine, south of Cologne, and plunged into the industrial Ruhr. On the other side of the globe, the fierce and costly struggle for Iwo Jima raged on, with deeply dug-in Japanese defenders fighting practically to the last man. General Curtis LeMay organized the incendiary bombing of Tokyo from low-flying B-29s that would kill more people and destroy more structures than the atomic weapons yet to be assembled. Forces gathered for an imminent invasion of Okinawa, the final stepping-stone to Japan's home islands.

On March 15, the president had a long lunch with Henry Stimson, who needed to bring him up to date on progress of the S-1 project—the A-bomb—and remind him of pertinent issues they'd already discussed but not resolved. The secretary now argued that Roosevelt ought to decide before the first "projectile" was dropped how nuclear weapons would be managed in the future: whether their secrets could be bartered to the Russians in exchange for the easier, more trusting relationship the president had sought, which now seemed to some advisers to be receding as a prospect. Roosevelt left Stimson, as he left most importuning visitors, with the impression that he'd taken the point. But, also characteristically, he vouchsafed no decisions in what would turn out to have been their final meeting.

If he'd lived to make them, the decisions on the issues the secretary of war was raising—how to use the weapon, whether then to put it under international controls—would have been among the most momentous of his presidency. Stimson's notes betray no second thoughts or anxieties about the president's ability to engage such truly epochal questions. Five days earlier, however, a seasoned American diplomat had come away with the opposite impression from what was meant to be an important audience with Roosevelt in his private upstairs study following a dinner to which he'd been urgently summoned. This was Robert Murphy, a troubleshooter slated to become the top American civilian official in occupied Germany after the inevitable collapse of the Third Reich. Instead of the trenchant discussion of problems he might face with the Russians that Murphy had anticipated, he was served the same golden oldie impressions of the German character left over from Roosevelt's boyhood that the president had trotted out at Quebec and Yalta, seemingly whenever the subject came up.

"The man who sat across from me that night was unable to discuss serious matters," the ambassador would later write. "He talked for an hour, but aimlessly." It may be that Roosevelt was stonewalling due to second thoughts about the role he'd foreseen for the ambassador, or that he'd stayed up past his prescribed bedtime as he was doing most evenings now. Murphy, who hadn't seen him in six months, came away convinced that the problem went deeper, that hardly a month after Yalta the president had lost the capacity to do his job. A State Department veteran, he now thought he knew why important political decisions were being made at the recently completed Pentagon.

Two nights later, Roosevelt kept William Lyon Mackenzie King, Canada's longest-serving prime minister, up almost to midnight in another one-way conversation, this one wandering from the Crimea to San Francisco to the trip he was now hoping to make to London and beyond in June, when the war in Europe would be over. He would stay at Buckingham Palace, ride through London with King George VI in an open car, address Parliament at the Palace of Westminster, and visit Churchill at Chequers, then maybe drop in on American troops still in France and Queen Wilhelmina at The Hague. The Canadian is a tireless diarist and stays on for days as a houseguest, dictating his impressions for up to an hour at a shot. His copious notes, adding up to more than fifty single-spaced pages in the Canadian archive, are of interest not because the visitor is especially perceptive or because Roosevelt is unusually candid talking to a fellow head of government. They're of interest because they allow us to see Roosevelt in his final days as a man still making short-term plans, still eager for engagement.

Mackenzie King's Roosevelt is more alert and better informed than Ambassador Murphy's. He has familiar Roosevelt traits, for instance: "He is fond of talking continuously. He does listen and takes in points quite keenly, but links everything to a personal point." In other words, to himself. He repeats his stories, a sign, Mackenzie King concludes, that his memory is failing. "He has lost a certain merriment, looks older and wearier but has a certain firmness, which might carry him along for some time."

The meaning of "firmness" in this context isn't clear. It's not weight, of which he had obviously shed a lot, too much. Roosevelt had been complaining about his lack of appetite, saying he couldn't taste his food. In the course of a year, he had lost more than twenty-five pounds. Mackenzie King is struck by his thinness, especially in the lower part of his face. ("He is consolidating into a man of a different size and shape, looking more like President Wilson," the diarist imagines.) In context, then, "firmness" seems to translate as something extracorporeal like presence or determination, a trait in any case more of habit and character than physical strength or stamina.

Roosevelt might have been experiencing private doubts about the trustworthiness of Stalin and Soviet Russia, but he still maintained his accustomed optimistic tone speaking to his neighbor from the north. Stalin at Yalta, in this account, had been full of good humor, friendly in manner to Churchill but especially to himself. He liked Stalin's directness, liked his company, and didn't see any particular reason to fear him. So he now told Mackenzie King.

This post-Yalta Roosevelt continued to dream aloud about the international security system he had been assembling and reassembling in his mind for months and years, going so far as to say he'd welcome an early outbreak of hostilities between two smaller countries in order to test-drive the new peacekeeping machinery now on the drawing boards before "making too many treaties."

How far Mackenzie King was from getting beneath the surface of his host's honeycombed mind, or following his often whimsical flights of imagination, was revealed on a more personal level at his second White House dinner. Eleanor had been present for the first, then left on a late train for a busy program in North Carolina, where she was due to address the legislature and a conference on "Education in the Mountains." At the second dinner, "a very delightful family-like affair" three evenings later, the prime minister was introduced to "another relative, Mrs. Rutherfurd." By this time, he had been let in on the secret of the atom bomb but not the secret of Lucy's relationship to Franklin. The Canadian guest, later revealed by his diary to have been a spiritualist who sought contact with his own relatives on "the other side," thought he could discern an "exceptionally fine character" in this latest "relative of the President."

The former Lucy Mercer had been to the White House the previous evening for dinner with Roosevelt and Anna and her husband. On March 14, the day following the dinner with the Canadian prime minister, she'd returned for lunch with Anna and the president as well as for dinner; on that occasion, Lucy and Roosevelt dined alone before withdrawing to his upstairs study, where they remained for more than two hours. In a short time span, Roosevelt was seeing more of Lucy than he normally saw of his wife. Eleanor, by now the only member of the household who knew nothing of such comings and goings by her onetime secretary whom she hadn't seen in a quarter of a century, was back not long after dawn the next morning.

The evening of the following day, Saturday, March 17, Eleanor and her husband marked their fortieth wedding anniversary with a dinner for eighteen in the State Dining Room. Two days later, the First Lady returned to North Carolina, this time for a symposium on "The Returning Black Serviceman," and Roosevelt again took advantage of her absence to invite Lucy back to the White House for dinner. The next day, Lucy spent half an hour with him over tea in his upstairs study. He also went "motoring" with her that week, once, probably twice, in the Virginia countryside, with a Secret Service car following and a glass partition between passengers and the driver in the president's limousine shielding the privacy of their conversation.

His calendar was too crowded for him to find time for Lucy on the two evenings remaining before his planned departure for Hyde Park. On March 22, he had to face the all but mandatory social ritual of the annual White House Correspondents Dinner at the Statler Hotel; the next evening, there was a state dinner for another visitor from Canada, the governor-general. Roosevelt spoke to the correspondents with what Allen Drury called "a fair semblance of his earlier self." He told this gathering of puffed-up newspaper types and their bosses that he'd give them a word. That word was "Humanity." What he gave them was a riff.

"We all love Humanity," he said. "You love Humanity, I love Humanity. Humanity's with me all the time. I go to bed and I dream of Humanity. I get up and I eat breakfast and there's Humanity. Humanity follows me around all day." It was hard to know what to make of this. Was it presidential improv? Satire seemed to mix with self-mockery, which seemed to acknowledge the impossibility of the job, or at least of the expectations it aroused. Leaving that message for his baffled or tickled listeners to decipher, he began his departure to cheers and laughs, shifted by his security men from his dais seat, and wheeled toward the ballroom's exit, waving and flashing his trademark grin as he went. The route brought him past the table where a frequent antagonist, Arthur Krock of *The New York Times,* sat. "If ever death was written on a human countenance," Krock would write years afterward, "it seemed to me I saw it that evening."

"Cheer up, Arthur," the president said with perfect aplomb, literally in passing. "Things have seldom been as bad as you said they were."

On March 28, 1945, another anniversary occurred, one it's hard to imagine anyone mentioning out loud in Roosevelt's hearing. It was exactly a year since Howard Bruenn first examined the president and came to the conclusion that his new patient was suffering from congestive heart failure as a result of chronic high blood pressure. Anna, who provoked that checkup, was informed only sketchily of the diagnosis before her conversation with Bruenn at Yalta. Her mother wasn't

MARCH 29, 1945. On his final day at the White House.

informed at all. ("If they had said he had hypertension, it would have meant very little to her," the daughter told Joseph Lash.) It could hardly be said that her father had been in robust health during that year—though Admiral McIntire would always say it when asked—but he had done his job, maybe not perfectly but more or less convincingly in an unusually demanding time: through D-Day, his renomination and selection of a new running mate, the rendezvous with MacArthur in Hawaii and the Quebec conference, the decisions on the bomb, the campaign leading to another reelection, the Battle of the Bulge, and Yalta.

No one, of course, knew it at the time, but March 28, 1945, would also be the last day of his life at Hyde Park. March 29 would be his last day at the White House. He returned to Washington in secret on the presidential train that morning and departed in secret late that afternoon for Warm Springs. By then, the usual division of amateur diagnosticians among his visitors and associates on whether he looked well or unwell seems to have been resolved. No one said he looked well. Grace Tully, his secretary, had the impression (as later related by her literary ghost) that he had "failed dangerously" between morning and afternoon. It wasn't the first time that such a change had come over him so fast. "His face was ashen, highlighted by the darkening shadow under his eyes," her memoir would say, explaining what moved her to beg him to give up on a pile of unanswered mail into which they'd been burrowing. Senator Barkley, who saw him at the White House that same day, later claimed to have remarked to a colleague, "I'm afraid he'll never return alive."

Still he managed to function in those final Washington hours. Looking back, Chip Bohlen would write that Roosevelt "was in no mood, the last time I saw him, to take further violations of the Yalta accord lying down." The last day Bohlen saw Roosevelt happens to have been this same March 29, the day of his departure for Warm Springs.

In previous days, the correspondence between Roosevelt and Stalin had taken a distinct turn for the worse, reflecting new friction and mistrust between the supposed allies. There was the continuing impasse on Poland, of course, getting more touchy and intractable by the day. And there were two new issues: one having to do with the fate of American prisoners of war liberated by the Red Army from German camps, only to be held in miserable conditions in Soviet camps to which American officers were routinely denied access; the other, even more sensitive, involving tentative feelers from the Waffen-SS commander in northern Italy to the chief agent of the Office of Strategic Services in Bern, the Swiss capital.

As we've seen, Roosevelt statecraft not infrequently involved a conscious attempt to work around or play down problems rather than confront them head-on, on the theory that confrontation tends to exacerbate, that given time, some problems recede. The diplomatic historian Warren Kimball labels this approach "creative procrastination." But Roosevelt could be blunt. On March 17, he approved a sharp cable to Stalin on the POWs matter, showing his readiness to call in his chits. "Frankly I cannot understand your reluctance to permit American officers and means to assist their own people," he said. "This Government has done everything to meet each of your requests. I now request you to meet mine."

On the secret contacts between the SS general and the OSS station chief—the future director of Central Intelligence Allen Dulles—Roosevelt's first letter tells Stalin that he has got the facts all wrong. These are exploratory talks about whether surrender negotiations are feasible, not actual negotiations, he insists. Stalin's replies are brusque, largely stripped of diplomatic soft-pedaling. The American POWs in Russian camps are being treated better than Russian POWs in American camps, he blasts back. As for the contacts with the Nazis, these have already made it possible for the Germans to shift divisions from northern Italy to the Soviet front. He comes close to suggesting that his allies are on the brink of collusion with the enemy. "This circumstance is irritating the Soviet command and creating grounds for mistrust," the dictator writes. That letter headed the president's agenda on that final day in the White House.

A couple of hours after his return, five hours before his departure, he called in six of his top State Department advisers, including Stettinius and Bohlen, the only Soviet specialist in the group. For a president who had improvised his own foreign policy throughout the war, often neglecting to tell the State Department where he was headed or why, it was a telling climax, revealing both his need now for support and his recognition that the terrain of global politics could be shifting.

"Roosevelt was furious," Bohlen would write. "It was one of the few times that I saw him angry. He was seated at his desk at the White House, his eyes flashing, his face flushed, outraged that he should be accused of dealing with the Germans behind Stalin's back." The cable that went out that day was firm and to the point; the one that ricocheted back from Moscow after Roosevelt was already at Warm Springs brought clouds of free-floating Russian suspicion, thrusts of outright accusation. The Germans were no longer battling the Americans and the British, Stalin asserted; they were concentrating their forces on the Russians "as a result of these separate negotiations in Bern or in some other place."

This time it was an indignant Roosevelt who blasted back:

It would be one of the great tragedies of history if at the very moment of victory now within our grasp, such distrust, such lack of faith should prejudice the entire undertaking after the colossal losses of life, materiel and treasure involved. Frankly I cannot avoid a feeling of bitter resentment toward your informants, whoever they are, for such vile misrepresentations of my actions or those of my trusted subordinates.

That cable was dispatched on April 4. It's not impossible that the words were set down by Chip Bohlen or some other professional empowered to stand in as presidential ventriloquist. But it's obvious who furnished the emotion behind them, their force. Even at that late date, a waning Franklin Roosevelt still appears to be in command. The signal corps maintained a direct line from the unpretentious living room in the Little White House, with its big stone fireplace and walls of unpainted pinewood planking, to the executive mansion in Washington. Once again he'd traveled south without any military or diplomatic advisers, but he could always speak to them when he felt the need. White House phone logs show he was calling in regularly from Warm Springs. They say simply, "The President called," without specifying whom.

At some point before Roosevelt entrained for Warm Springs on March 29, the Secret Service increased the security it assigned to Vice President Truman. Someone high in the government—it's not clear who or on what basis—had reached the conclusion that the recently reelected president could collapse and die at any time. So, at least, *Time* magazine would deduce after the succession had actually occurred. That premonition wasn't passed along to the members of the First Family. Eleanor and Anna stayed in Washington, as did Admiral McIntire, who'd long since turned over day-to-day care for the president (excepting only his sinuses) to Dr. Bruenn. On the train heading south therefore were Bruenn; three secretaries (Tully, Brady, and Hassett); Mike Reilly, longtime head of the Secret Service detail; George Fox, the medical orderly and masseur; Daisy Suckley and cousin Laura Delano, called Polly—a femme fatale past her prime, now sporting blue hair—who'd been brought along to provide company on the president's previous Warm Springs sojourn in November; and two old friends with Warm Springs ties, early backers of the center for polio treatment he'd established there. Taken together, this entourage would furnish an audience for Roosevelt once absence from Washington restored, as it always had, his seldom suppressed impulse to entertain over drinks and dinner, to perform before company. Lucy Rutherfurd was expected to join the scaled-down presidential party in little more than a week.

As usual, the president's whereabouts were off the record, not for publication. Shortly after he arrived in Warm Springs on March 30, he received a military intelligence report signed by General Marshall forecasting the "utter defeat" of the Nazi regime by the end of April. "For all practical purposes, a central German political authority will have ceased to exist about May 1," it said. Roosevelt never got to celebrate V-E day, but he knew it was coming.

At his arrival in Georgia, he still had the worn, ashen look that had struck Grace Tully the previous afternoon. The Secret Service man Reilly noticed for the first time that Roosevelt didn't have enough strength in his arms and shoulders to offer assistance as he always had when being shifted into a car; he was "absolutely dead weight," Reilly said. Roosevelt would usually drive his custom-made, hand-operated Ford convertible to the Little White House himself; this time, Daisy noted, he rode in the passenger seat. That evening his traveling secretary, Bill Hassett, in a state of distress, sought out the cardiologist Bruenn for a confidential chat. "He is slipping away from us and no earthly power can keep him here . . . To all the staff, to the family and with the Boss himself I have maintained the bluff," Hassett said, "but I am convinced there is no help for him." The doctor acknowledged that the president's condition was parlous, touch and go, but said it might not be "hopeless," if only he could be protected from mental strain and emotional upset. That wasn't possible, Hassett knew. When they parted, he came away with the conviction that although he couldn't admit it, "the doctor shared the layman's point of view."

Roosevelt's changeable moods in his final weeks and days were even more under wraps than his whereabouts or the state of his health. He'd been seriously depressed a month earlier on the way back from Yalta following Pa Watson's death, which seems likely to have forced him to contemplate, however fleetingly or deeply, his own limited lease on life. Within days of his return, however, he was indulging in elaborate dreams of future travel, telling Mackenzie King about the triumphal tour he'd soon be making to London and beyond once the Nazis capitulated and, days later, surprising a skeptical Eleanor with an imaginative flight to the Middle East, where he said they might eventually spend a couple of years inspiring efforts to make the deserts bloom.

"When we get through here," his wife quoted him as saying, "I believe I'd like to go and live there . . . I believe I could help to straighten out the Near East."

"Can't you think of something harder to do?" she asked. "Well yes," he replied, ignoring the sardonic edge to her question. "It's going to be awfully hard to straighten out Asia."

He could dream about the future, but in these last days he had next to no patience for Eleanor's urgent interventions on behalf of one good cause or another. "On her side," Anna would say years later, "she pressed more abruptly and with less tact than she had in the past. The nerves of both of them were raw."

One evening at Warm Springs, according to Howard Bruenn, she kept him on the phone for forty-five minutes as she detailed the needs for supplies and arms of anti-Nazi partisans in Yugoslavia as related to her by sympathizers in the United States. Patiently, he explained that our armed forces weren't positioned to deliver help. She found the explanation insufficient and carried on. His patient explanations turned impatient. When the conversation finally ended, the veins in his forehead were visibly elevated. Dr. Bruenn had taken his blood pressure not long before the call came through. He took it again when it ended. The reading had shot up by fifty points, the cardiologist later said. The episode helps explain why his admirable, unrelenting wife wasn't among those Roosevelt wanted by his side when he traveled south to replenish his vanishing stamina.

Eleanor understood this too. She wrote of her husband's need for a "real rest" and the sort of undemanding "companionship" Daisy and Polly could provide. Lucy was not yet on her mind. "I say a prayer daily that he may be able to carry on till we have peace & our feet are set in the right direction," she wrote to a friend in a letter that surfaced the concern she seldom allowed herself to express, her fear that he might pass from the scene, felt not just for his sake or her

APRIL 11, 1945. On the last full day of his life.

own but for his mission as a peacemaker, which she saw herself as supporting. In her last letter to her husband in Warm Springs, dated April 7—the last letter that would ever pass between them—she allowed her hopes to outweigh her fears. "You sounded cheerful for the first time last night," she wrote, "& I hope you'll weigh 170 pounds when you return."

Of all his reveries in his final days, the most revealing and touching were described by Daisy Suckley, in passages written in his last week that she later crossed out of her diary but left legible. To stoke his failing appetite, she and cousin Polly had taken to serving him cups of oatmeal—"gruel," she called it—as he rested before dinner and later in the evenings at what was supposed to be his bedtime. This had developed into a game. Franklin Roosevelt, generally deemed the most powerful person on the planet, pulled his covers up to his chin and "relapsed into babyhood," indicating that he wanted to be mothered and fed. In Daisy's words, he "put on his little act of helplessness! It amuses him to be fed, and I love to feed him," she told her diary. "On paper it sounds too silly for words and it *is* silly—but he's *very* funny and laughs at himself with us." On April 7, he halts the game when he's only half-finished with his gruel, sits up, and lights a cigarette. Then he talks earnestly about the San Francisco conference and the prospects for peace. He says that he can probably resign in a year once the world organization is "well-started." Then he stubs out his cigarette and finishes his gruel. "I kissed him goodnight & left him relaxed and laughing," Daisy wrote. This was on the fifth night before his death.

Getting the United Nations "well-started" meant continuing to strive for some kind of understanding on an armed peacekeeping system with Stalin. Or so he still thought, with an inevitably clouded sense of the postwar world, of how it might be transformed by the decolonization he favored, by new movements, conflicts, and realignments. Even after the Soviet regime landed in Trotsky's "dustbin of history" decades later, cooperation with Vladimir Putin's Russia on matters of international security would remain minimal, at best. The world doesn't much notice, but more than one hundred nations nowadays dispatch troops in blue helmets and berets to scattered "peacekeeping" operations on several continents. The United States underwrites one-quarter of the costs, sometimes provides logistic support, but furnishes few bodies. Its larger military adventures (Vietnam, Iraq, Afghanistan) have involved the UN only marginally, or not at all—a far cry from Roosevelt's original idea of the Big Four (or Five) standing together under the UN aegis to maintain a peaceful world order, imposed mainly through overwhelming airpower. Faced with many-sided civil wars, involving what are now called "violent non-state actors," with terrorism and mass migration spilling across regions and borders, they seldom stand together. At the end of his days, Roosevelt concluded it was better to have a United Nations than not to have one. But in his bag of nostrums, there was no answer to the question of how it could be made to work.

Just before leaving Washington for Warm Springs, the president finally agreed to dispatch the cable to Stalin over Soviet backsliding on Poland for which Churchill had been impatiently pressing. The flat, uninspired message, drafted by Admiral Leahy and left unrevised by Roosevelt, dutifully rehashed previous arguments and appeals—found, for instance, in the February 6 letter to Stalin at Yalta covering the same issues—without sharpening them in any obvious way. This latest approach made little or no apparent impression on the dictator but helped restore Roosevelt's strained relationship with Churchill, which may have been its basic purpose in the mind of its supposed author, the inscrutable realist who now saw little real chance for the progress on Poland about which he'd allowed himself to boast in his speech to Congress just a month earlier. "I'm delighted with our being in such perfect step," the prime minister wrote approvingly.

On April 11, the last full day of his life, Franklin Roosevelt sent off two cables designed to "minimize"—his word—recent arguments with Stalin: in other words, to treat the alliance as a going concern even where wear and tear had shown it to be threadbare. To Stalin, he wrote about the need to avoid "minor misunderstandings" like the dictator's suspicions over possible talks with the Germans in Bern. Ambassador Harriman, who was supposed to deliver the cable, held it up, "respectfully" arguing that the word "minor" didn't apply. "I must confess that the misunderstanding appeared to me to be of a major character," he wrote. The reply that went out in Roosevelt's name sounded regal. It said it was the president's "desire to consider the Bern misunderstanding a minor incident." In the same vein, writing to Churchill in what appears to have been the last message he himself had a hand in drafting, he said, "I would personally minimize the general Soviet problem as much as possible because these problems, in one form or another, seem to arise every day and most of them straighten out as in the case of the Bern meeting."

It concluded, "We must be firm, however, and our course thus far is correct."

Coming from a president who only a week earlier had expressed his "bitter resentment" to Stalin over the "vile misrepresentations" that the dictator had credited in this same "misunderstanding," these last words of guidance on relations with Russia are not easily tracked, revealing the characteristic zigzagging with which he pursued his higher goals: in this case, an ordered world, free from war. They say that right up to the end he was still relying on his own intuitions in managing the relationship, still hoping that the birth of the United Nations, with himself and Joseph Stalin as godparents, would make it possible for him to discern a way forward. Getting to San Francisco without another serious clash had thus become a short-term end in itself. "He was looking to inauguration of the San Francisco conference as the crowning act of his career," wrote Anne O'Hare McCormick, a *New York Times* columnist who'd interviewed him on a not-for-attribution basis days before he left Washington. "No one ever accused Franklin Roosevelt of having a single-track mind," she wrote shortly after his death, "but for once he hardly deviated from his subject. And he developed it from every aspect with a clarity and vigor that belied his look of weariness."

In the last day or two of his life, he set the itinerary for his travel by train to the Golden Gate: He'd leave Warm Springs on April 18, pause for a day at the White House, and then head west, arriving in San Francisco in time to deliver his speech on April 25, leaving immediately thereafter. The next task he set for himself at the Little White House was to start dictating that speech.

Historians have speculated ever since about how relations between the two powerful wartime allies might have unfolded had a vigorous Roosevelt remained at the helm in Washington. Those who believe that the Cold War couldn't have been avoided cite his "bitter resent-ment" cable of April 4. Those who think his finesse, his patience, and his "artistry" might have muted future clashes point to the cable to Churchill one week later stressing the need to "minimize the general Soviet problem." To the end of his days, it seems fair to conclude, the president was still trying out different approaches, feeling his way, and improvising as he'd done on most major issues all through his long presidency.

Roosevelt was so eager to see Lucy Rutherfurd that he had the Secret Service drive him to Macon, Georgia, a distance of eighty miles, and back. This was the road she was expected to use on April 9 as she traveled from her South Carolina home to Warm Springs. Lucy was heading his way in a not inconspicuous white Cadillac convertible with New York license plates belonging to Elizabeth Shoumatoff, a successful society portrait artist of aristocratic Russian origins from whom Lucy had commissioned a life-size watercolor of the president, which she meant to give her daughter. Roosevelt and Lucy had been talking by phone through the White House switchboard and had agreed to meet up at four in the afternoon in Macon; the ladies were an hour late. With the sun sinking, the presidential car eventually turned back. Heading at dusk into a hamlet close to Warm Springs, the two women noticed a small crowd gathered around a limousine. Inside sat the president of the United States sipping a Coca-Cola. He invited Lucy and Shoumie, as Madame Shoumatoff was some-times called, into his limo. Self-effacing Daisy Suckley, not altogether immune to jealousy, got the small folding seat. "The drive was too long, and F was chilly and looked tired all the evening and his blood pressure was up when he went to bed. However," her diary entry for the day concludes, "he took his gruel."

The next afternoon, Roosevelt kept his bevy of four females enter-tained at the lunch table, cheerfully spinning stories, then went off for a nap. "He came out at five, looking more tired than ever," Daisy wrote, "and went out for a drive" with Lucy and Fala, taking her back to his favorite lookout, Dowdell's Knob, which he'd first shown her five months earlier. "They sat in the sun, talking, for over an hour, & he came back with a good tan," according to Daisy, who wasn't, it seems, invited. On the way back in the open Ford coupe with a Secret Service car trailing, they came upon a rider on horseback. That was Merriman Smith, a fixture over the years at the White House for his wire service, United Press, who would cover a more violent termination of a presidency in Dallas on November 22, 1963. Here's how the journalist described the encounter:

> Mr. Roosevelt bowed majestically to me. The car was moving slowly and the President spoke. His voice was wonderful and resonant. It sounded like the Roosevelt of old . . . Roosevelt hailed me with: "Heigh-O Silver!" As far as I was concerned, those were his last words.

On the morning of Wednesday the eleventh, Dr. Bruenn checked up on Roosevelt and departed with the words, as transcribed by Daisy, "Keep lazy, Sir!" But the president had some work to do, putting finishing touches, perhaps, on his cable to Churchill about minimizing the Soviet problem and revising Robert Sherwood's draft of an address he was due to deliver by radio on Friday night to his party's annual Jefferson Day dinners across the land. The last line of the undelivered speech, written on the draft in his own hand, is frequently quoted. Had he lived, it might not have drawn such notice. But given that he didn't get to speak the words, it has been accepted as a last testament by biographers. An earlier passage, reflecting Sherwood's reading of his mind, possibly then reworded by the president, is generally overlooked but may register as more poignant:

> Let me assure you that my hand is steadier for the work that is to be done, that I move more firmly into the task, knowing that you—millions and millions of you—are joined with me in the resolve to make this work endure. The work, my friends, is peace. More than an end to this war, an end to the beginnings of all wars . . . to this impractical, unrealistic settlement of the differences between governments by the mass killing of people.

There was an obvious fallacy here: His hand wasn't steadier. But his resolve may have been. At a time when forces he commanded were engaged in mass killing of their own, when he faced a decision about the use of a terrible new weapon, his inclination wasn't to justify the mayhem by dwelling on the wickedness and atrocities of enemies. It was to stay focused on the future. The line from this speech that's usu-

APRIL 11, 1945. Lucy Mercer Rutherfurd
in Warm Springs.

ally quoted, the one in his own hand, would have ended his remarks
on a typically challenging, inclusive note. "Let us move forward," he
intended to exhort, "with firm and active faith." Which was his sense,
at least, of the course he'd set for himself.

Henry Morgenthau Jr., his Treasury secretary and Hudson valley
neighbor, stopped by for dinner that night. Roosevelt, sitting at the
card table where he worked during the day, signaled that the time had
come to open a can of caviar he'd been saving since Stalin presented
it to him at Yalta. As he poured his last round of cocktails, his hands
trembled so badly the visitor had to hold the glasses. After a second
drink, the president seemed steadier, Morgenthau noticed. Dinner, as
Madame Shoumatoff recalled it, "was unusually tasteless dry meat-
balls and waffles with thick chocolate sauce." Lucy sat on Roosevelt's
right. "He seemed constantly to be addressing himself to her," the
portraitist recalled. Before departing, the secretary then had a private
session with the president that he'd requested to press his case for the

systematic deindustrialization of a defeated Germany, the so-called Morgenthau Plan. Months earlier, Roosevelt had backed the idea enthusiastically, then distanced himself when it met resistance from Stimson and Stettinius, leaving the issue to Allied negotiators and the administrators who'd be responsible for the occupation. Without his active backing, the "plan" withered on the policy vine. Now, as usual, he was full of reassurance. "Henry, I am with you 100 per cent," he said.

Once Morgenthau departed, Roosevelt sat by the fireplace with the four women gathered around him, his two cousins, Madame Shoumatoff, and Lucy, listening to the artist's rendering of a ghost story that had something to do with Catherine the Great's necklace of black pearls. "The President listened with that particular expression of complete attention he always gave to those who talked to him," she later wrote. This counts for something. As a portrait painter, she was, after all, a student of facial expressions.

On the morning of the twelfth, he was presented with his last roundup of military news. It said the U.S. Ninth Army had reached the Elbe below Magdeburg, placing it about sixty-five miles from Berlin; the First Army was twenty miles from Leipzig; the Third had reached Halle. Daisy noted in her diary, "F woke up with a slight headache and a stiff neck." Dr. Bruenn massaged the neck, then ordered a hot water bottle. Everyone agreed, however, that Roosevelt was looking especially well when he moved to his favorite living room chair. "He looked smiling & happy & ready for anything," Daisy would write in her diary. No longer gray, his face had a slightly rosy glow, a misleading sign of well-being, which may actually have pointed to an incipient cardiovascular event. Madame Shoumatoff had spent her first two mornings at the Little White House arranging for photographic portraits of the president she could study and use as cue cards, positioning his chair so it faced the light streaming in from the veranda rather than, as usual, the room, and settling on the best pose and background. Thinking his double-breasted gray suit hung too loosely on his diminished frame, she'd arranged to sketch him in his familiar navy cape. All her preparations made, she was now finally ready to begin painting, starting with the eyes. Unlike oil paints, watercolors could not easily be painted over. While she worked, so did her subject, signing letters and documents Hassett laid before him, then spread around the room so the ink could dry; his "laundry," the president called it.

"Here's where I make a law," he trumpeted in a lighthearted way as he signed a bill sustaining the Commodity Credit Corporation. Shortly before one o'clock, a Filipino steward, Joe Esperancilla, began setting the table for lunch. "We have fifteen minutes more to work," the president said. Those fifteen minutes were nearly up when suddenly, according to Madame Shoumatoff, "he raised his right hand and passed it over his forehead in a strange jerky way." Daisy thought she heard him, in a low, hardly audible voice, declare distinctly, "I have a terrific pain in the back of my head." The portrait painter didn't register any words. He pitched forward toward the card table. Daisy and Polly tried to tilt him back. Arthur Prettyman, his valet, and Esperancilla carried him the fifteen feet or so to his small bedroom and laid him on his simple pinewood bed with the women trailing. Daisy loosened his tie; Polly tried to fan him. His eyes opened but didn't appear to focus. Within a few minutes, he lost whatever consciousness he'd retained.

It took maybe fifteen minutes for Dr. Bruenn to be fetched from the swimming pool at the polio center. Immediately upon examining the patient, he diagnosed a hemorrhage in the brain. Brain damage and further paralysis could be part of the picture, but the outlook in this case was worse. That the stricken man had pitched forward with a rigid neck, having complained of blinding pain there; that he quickly lost consciousness; that he had a history of high blood pressure all pointed to a type of stroke known as a subarachnoid hemorrhage in which blood fills the space between the brain's surface and one of its protective membranes—likely caused by the bursting of a blood vessel in the brain or the rupture of an aneurysm, a congenital defect. Roosevelt was doomed from the instant he was stricken.

For the next two hours, the dying man's stertorous breathing and gasps reverberated in the nearby living room. Various therapeutic methods were tried to little avail—heat applied to his chest, several drugs administered including shots of aminophylline and nitroglycerine, later artificial respiration, finally, as a desperation move, a shot of adrenaline injected directly into the heart muscle after his breathing stopped. In less than two and a half hours after his collapse, the longest-serving president was pronounced dead, aged sixty-three.

It wasn't until midnight that Daisy managed to record the moment of his passing. "*3:35 p.m.*," she wrote in her diary, underscoring the words, "*Franklin D. Roosevelt, the hope of the world, is dead.*"

Anna had been at the naval hospital in Bethesda visiting her son Johnny, suffering from a persistent gland infection, when she was told she needed to return to the White House. She knew her father had been stricken, not that he'd died. In the jumble of anxious thoughts that assailed her as she rode down Wisconsin Avenue in an official car, she later recalled, the example of a stricken Woodrow Wilson popped into her mind. It would be "the Wilson thing all over" if the president was incapacitated, she worried, "with demands for his impeachment." That was his biggest fear; it was now hers. She'd been the last member of the family to speak to her father. He'd called the previous evening to see how his grandson was getting on, mentioning a barbecue he was due to attend the next afternoon in Warm Springs but not the fact that Lucy Rutherfurd had been with him for two days.

A distraught Lucy, meantime, was on her way back to her South Carolina estate in the portrait painter's convertible. Once she understood that the president had lost consciousness, she realized her presence at the Little White House could become an embarrassment to his family and herself. "We must pack and go," she cried out to Madame Shoumatoff. Passing through Macon, they saw a flag at half-staff. A weeping hotel operator told them why.

Eleanor was present in the cabinet room to watch Harry Truman, standing before a portrait of Woodrow Wilson, take the oath of office as her husband's successor, not quite three hours after he died. The widow then flew to Warm Springs with Admiral McIntire, who'd subsequently argue that his patient's sudden death from a stroke, not a heart attack, proved he'd always been right to downplay any suggestion that the president might have heart disease, as if the brittleness of blood vessels in his brain could have nothing to do with cardiovascular disease, or cardiovascular disease had nothing to do with the heart. After being forced into retirement, the admiral would assert in his ghost-written memoir that Roosevelt's "stout heart" never failed (omitting any mention of congestive heart failure) and that his blood pressure was "not alarming at any time," which if not a flat-out falsehood at least raises the question of what it would have taken to alarm him. By the time his book was published in 1946, Roosevelt's medical file had disappeared from the safe in which it was kept at the naval hospital in Bethesda. As surgeon general, McIntire was one of only several people who had access to that safe, the only one with an obvious motive to remove a record that would likely have shown the emptiness of the reassurances he'd fed the press and the public over the years, whenever questions arose about the president's health.

Recognizing that her grief was also the nation's, the straight-backed, dry-eyed widow bore herself stoically, perfectly, reciprocating expressions of sympathy. Her dutiful tone was set in the telegrams she sent her four sons in their various war zones. "Father slept away," they said. "He did his job as he would want you to. Love, Mother." The now former First Lady didn't reach the low point of her long day until she arrived at the Little White House at about midnight. Then, in response to her question about her husband's last moments, Laura Delano all too eagerly and not without cruelty let her know that he'd been sitting for a portrait by a friend of Lucy Rutherfurd's, that Lucy had been there for three days. Later, so Anna was told, Laura let Eleanor know that Lucy had been to the White House, with Anna, at her father's request, serving as hostess on more than one occasion. Grief and bitter fury were folded tightly together in a large knot as Eleanor stepped into her husband's bedroom to view his remains in private. It wasn't until Saturday morning, hours before the funeral service in the East Room of the White House, that Anna had to confront her mother's anguish, her feelings of betrayal. Many years later, after Eleanor's own death, Anna would say that they remained estranged for only two or three days and that, thereafter, neither mother nor daughter mentioned the subject again. But she believed her mother never quite forgave her for heeding her father's wishes, then guarding his privacy.

"That Lucy Mercer was there when father had his stroke was devastating to her," Anna said. She took it as a verdict not only on her husband but on herself. Ultimately, she was harder on herself.

APRIL 15, 1945. Eleanor at end of burial service in the Hyde Park Rose Garden with daughter Anna facing camera.

· · ·

The searing family drama didn't come to light for more than twenty years. The public drama, the abrupt end to the Roosevelt years as the world conflict neared its climax, easily overshadowed it. At train station after station, crossing after crossing, men, women, and children lined the tracks, many weeping openly, as the funeral train, traveling in secret no longer, bore Roosevelt's remains and his stony-faced widow north to Washington. The scene was repeated on Pennsylvania Avenue as six white horses pulled the caisson bearing the flag-draped coffin on his final trip to the White House. By Sunday afternoon, with the new president, old cabinet, commanders, and congressional leaders bearing solemn witness, he'd been laid to rest beside a hedge in the Hyde Park garden near the grand house on the Hudson where he had his sheltered boyhood, to which he regularly returned as president.

The *New York Post*, a liberal paper then, headed its roster of military casualties that weekend with a boldfaced entry: "Roosevelt, Franklin D., Commander-in-Chief, wife, Mrs. Anna Eleanor Roosevelt, the White House." Secretary Stimson attempted to sort out his feelings and assessment in a personal diary entry that was not without criticism of Roosevelt's eccentric, sometimes haphazard approach to administering a rapidly expanding government. Stimson's private conclusion, nevertheless, was that Roosevelt had been "without exception the best war president the United States has ever had." His vision, the lifelong Republican judged, "has always been vigorous and quick and clear and guided by a very strong faith in the future of our country and of freedom, democracy and humanitarianism throughout the world."

Among the most striking and generous of the public tributes that poured from the offices of politicians of all stripes, at all levels, was one that crossed party lines, from a senator who'd built his reputation on steadfast opposition to Franklin Roosevelt and virtually all his works, foreign and domestic. This was Robert A. Taft of Ohio—eldest child of President William Howard Taft, called "Mr. Republican" by his admirers—a past and future contender for the office his father once held.

"The President's death," Senator Taft said, "removed the greatest figure of our time at the very climax of his career, and shocks the world to which his words and actions were more important than those of any other man. He dies a hero of the war, for he literally worked himself to death in the service of the American people."

No liberal, no Democrat, no New Dealer, said it better. For a brief time, the Roosevelt haters and those dedicated to rolling back his programs, however long it took, were stilled as the nation took his measure and weighed its loss.

In His Wake

IT TOOK the Twentieth Amendment to the Constitution to shorten the four-month waiting period between the election of a new president and the inauguration. The last to be held in March was Franklin Roosevelt's first on March 4, 1933. Had it been in January, as it has been ever since, he'd have been sworn in ten days before the demonic leader of a mass movement bent on absolute power was confirmed through parliamentary maneuvering and thuggish threats as chancellor of a Germany that was still nominally a republic. Later, in its last legislative act, in 1942, an obedient single-party Reichstag would formally recognize Adolf Hitler's word as the supreme law of the Third Reich. By then, this was news to no one. Hitler's Germany had conquered most of Europe, and Roosevelt was the leader of an alliance sworn to roll it back and vanquish it. This, the "rendezvous with destiny" he'd vaguely prophesied, was unfolding as he died. The demented tyrant, who'd come to power a mere thirty-three days before him, would yet outlast him by another eighteen.

Outlast him, in the depths of the reinforced, bombproof bunker sunk fifty feet below the garden of the partially bombed-out Reich Chancellery where he'd reigned in his manic glory days. Carpeted, with its own generator, diesel-powered ventilation system, and water supply, the *Führerbunker,* as this vertical apartment and suite of offices was called, was easily double the size of the unpretentious airy hillside lodge in a pine forest in southwestern Georgia that went by the name Little White House. When an exultant Joseph Goebbels reached his führer there near midnight on April 12 with news of the death in

Warm Springs of his American nemesis, Hitler is said by Albert Speer to have cried out, "Here we have the great miracle I have always foretold. Who's right now? The war is not lost. Read it! Roosevelt is dead!"

The führer's imagination had long been inflamed by the coincidence that he and the American president gained power in the same season of the same year. His speech on December 11, 1941, declaring war on the United States dwelled on it derisively, contrasting in a long tirade Roosevelt's weakness with his strength. "I understand only too well that a worldwide distance separates Roosevelt's ideas and my ideas," he said. The president hailed from a capitalist class that allied itself with Jews and Bolsheviks. "The diabolical meanness of Jewry rallied around this man, and he stretched out his hands." He'd allowed himself to be surrounded by "parasites."

Three and a half years later, the death of Roosevelt was the first welcome news to penetrate the gloom of the bunker since the führer moved in, following the failure of his strategic gamble in the Ardennes in January. It would also prove the last. In the ruins of the Third Reich, it could flare for an instant as a good omen, be hailed as a kind of fulfillment. Goebbels compared it to a turning point in the Seven Years' War when the death of a czarina presaged victory for Frederick the Great. But the illusion quickly crumbled. The next day, the Red Army took Vienna. Within a week, Russian tanks entered the outskirts of Berlin. On the last day of the month, the führer, seated on a sofa next to an already poisoned Eva Braun, his mistress for years and bride for days, put a pistol to his head.

Red banners with black borders—official mourning flags—flew from the Kremlin and other public buildings in Moscow the day after Roosevelt's death. Official expressions of grief struck Americans as heartfelt, unofficial ones even more so. The American embassy had to lay on extra operators to handle all the condolence calls. It was past one in the morning when the first bulletins arrived. Ambassador Harriman phoned Foreign Minister Molotov to relay the news. Molotov insisted on coming to Spaso House, the ambassador's residence, at that late hour to pay a sympathy call. There was nothing perfunctory about the visit. "He seemed deeply moved and disturbed . . . I have never heard Molotov talk so earnestly," Harriman would say. The next evening, when Harriman called on Stalin at the Kremlin, the dictator grasped his hand and held eye contact for half a minute, without at first speaking. "I personally feel deep sorrow at the loss of a trusted friend," he would say in a cable to Harry Hopkins.

Pravda said the flowering of friendship between the United States and the Soviet Union would be a fitting monument to the departed leader. A commentary in *Red Flag,* the army newspaper, saluted him as "a leader in the cause of guaranteeing security to the world." Taking advantage of such sentiments, Harriman urged Stalin to reverse a peremptory earlier notice that Molotov would be too busy to attend the conference in San Francisco for which the late president had pressed. In one of his last messages, Roosevelt had protested, to no avail, that "Mr. Molotov's absence will be construed all over the world . . . as a lack of [real] interest in the great objectives of this conference on the part of the Soviet government." Now what had been impossible a couple of weeks earlier almost instantly became a sure thing. Molotov and a retinue of high Soviet officials showed up at a memorial service at the American embassy on the day Roosevelt was to be buried in Hyde Park.

His passing in the final stages of the war fixed his place in the firmament of Soviet historiography. He had been the president who conferred diplomatic recognition on the Soviet Union, who later extended Lend-Lease assistance, who acknowledged the great power status of his Communist ally. Had he lived to see and participate in further deterioration in relations between the two powers, the exalted standing the party line now conferred on him might have buckled. Dying when he did, he was transfigured into an enduring symbol of the alliance at its best and most dependable.

Harry Truman never acknowledged that a premonition crossed his mind when he was summoned from the Capitol to the White House late on the afternoon of April 12. "I thought I was going down there to see the President," he later said. "I wouldn't allow myself to think anything else." Speaker Sam Rayburn, who was standing next to him when he took the call from Steve Early, had a different recollection, which he passed on in an off-the-record chat with a *Time* correspondent the next day. "Truman knew exactly what to expect," the Speaker said. The vice president was visibly shaken. Color drained from his face. "Jesus Christ and General Jackson," he muttered in a choked voice.

The thought Truman tried to shove out of his mind still had to be uttered by someone else. Ushered upstairs to the family quarters when he arrived nearly breathless at the White House, he found Early, who'd just stepped aside as press secretary, waiting for him with Eleanor Roosevelt, her daughter, and son-in-law. It was Eleanor who spoke. "Harry, the President is dead," she said. For a moment, the man from Missouri was speechless, according to both his account and hers. Then he found his voice and asked, "Is there anything I can do for you?" The new widow replied, "Is there anything we can do for *you*? You are the one in trouble now."

Later that same evening—president for less than an hour—Truman had a brief session with Henry Stimson at the war secretary's urgent request. Stimson needed to lift the curtain on the atomic bomb. Not going into details, he promised the neophyte commander in chief the full briefing on the secret project Truman had never received as vice president. It wasn't the first time the matter had come up between them. The two men had touched on this most sensitive of subjects twice before. That was back in March 1944, when Senator Truman, as chairman of an investigative committee charged with exposing misuse of military appropriations—the role in which he gained the stature and respect that made him a plausible candidate for vice president—insisted that the war secretary explain the mysterious S-1 project to an investigator from his committee. It was an invisible footnote to the budget, a black hole into which vast sums poured for purposes on which no member of Congress had been briefed in any detail. Apparently, Truman had signed a huffy letter some time after that initial conversation in which he'd accepted the secretary's private assurances on the supreme importance of the project. An offended Stimson replied stiffly, saying that the president had set the ground rules for the unusual secrecy in which the project was wrapped, that its nature had been disclosed to the fewest possible outsiders, civilian or military. In his diary, later that day, he called Truman "a nuisance and a pretty untrustworthy man" who "talks smoothly" but "acts meanly." Now the untrustworthy nuisance whom he'd summarily rebuffed would be the one to determine the new weapon's use.

Of the missteps in his waning months at the end of the war and his life that have been posthumously blamed on Roosevelt, the one judged most severely has been his failure to confide in his understudy on subjects like the bomb and Yalta. Truman himself would tell his daughter, Margaret, that the president "never did talk to me confidentially about the war, or about foreign affairs, or what he had in mind for peace after the war." One scholar, in a study of the Truman succession, calls that lapse "disgraceful." The oversight cannot be defended. But it may be pointed out that it was thoroughly in accord with Roosevelt's character and the customs of the office.

Taking the vice president into his confidence on the most sensitive matters would have demanded a greater willingness to face his own mortality than he'd so far shown. It would also have represented a departure from the arm's-length relationship presidents always had with their mandated successors until then. For a century and a half, vice presidents had been classified as spectral, hybrid creatures more habituated to the legislative branch than the executive, spending their time, insofar as anyone noticed or cared, at the Capitol rather than the White House. It wasn't until 1947, with the establishment of the National Security Council, that the vice president was given a statutory national security role and not until the Carter years in the late 1970s that a vice president was permitted to occupy an office in the West Wing or placed on his president's schedule as a regular lunch partner. Besides, in the eighty-two days that Roosevelt's abbreviated final term lasted, he and his new vice president had both been in Washington simultaneously on only twenty-one. They met twice with congressional leaders in those days; there's no record of their meeting alone.

What all this proves is that while Roosevelt knew he was mortal and getting weaker, he wasn't planning to die just then. He didn't take Truman into his confidence, because, like virtually all his predecessors and most of us, he didn't care to be reminded of the hovering Reaper. Also, creative procrastinator that he was, he hadn't settled on a plan for use of the new weapon that he might conceivably have passed along. And he was still feeling his way with Stalin. His oversight is revealing of his state of mind and customary practice, but it's hard to make a convincing argument that it mattered in the end. When the time came for decisions on the bomb and the Russians, he was gone.

Various theories have been offered about what Roosevelt might have done about the bomb had he lived, starting with one by the official historian of the U.S. Navy, Samuel Eliot Morison, who speculated that the president might have seized on a suggestion by the then undersecretary of state, Joseph C. Grew, a former ambassador to Japan, as a way of averting its use. "It is possible that if President Roosevelt had lived another six weeks longer, he would have taken [Grew's advice] to give public assurance that if Japan surrendered 'unconditionally,' she could keep her Emperor."

On two occasions, Roosevelt may have allowed himself to speculate about the possibility of allowing the enemy to witness a test of the bomb in all its destructive power. But had he asked for it, he'd have gotten the same advice from George Marshall and Henry Stimson that they gave to such suggestions in the weeks following his death. With the Battle of Okinawa raging, they worried that Japanese militarists would interpret any gesture over the fate of the imperial order as a sign of "war weariness" on the part of the Americans, that it might then have the perverse effect of stiffening their resistance. The idea of inviting the Japanese to a military test was discussed and dismissed. There was an outside chance, it was reasoned, that the first A-bomb to be assembled and tested could turn out to be a "dud" due to some undetected miscalculation or flaw.

A systematic canvassing of such issues hadn't yet begun when Stimson called on the new president less than two weeks after his predecessor's death to lead him through the comprehensive briefing he'd promised. With him was General Leslie Groves, the crusty administrator of the Manhattan Project, who had zero interest in finding a way around using the bomb. Before calling Groves into the room, the secretary began the tutorial by reading aloud from a memorandum that put the stakes in the starkest terms. The new weapon couldn't be monopolized for long, it said. Once unleashed, it could eventually destroy "modern civilization."

Having set the scene with that chilling preamble, he then called in Groves and asked the president to read in their presence a detailed document on the status of the project. Truman had already been told by Byrnes that it had the potential of "wiping out entire cities and killing people on an unprecedented scale." Roosevelt's "creative procrastination" had the effect of leaving responsibility for the big decision where it now had to be, in his successor's hands.

Out of that White House meeting came Truman's approval for the appointment of two secret panels to sort out the issues in an orderly way, one opaquely called the Interim Committee, the other with a more straightforward name—the Targets Committee. Bearing the realization that he'd soon possess the power to vaporize whole cities, Truman then left for San Francisco to fulfill the task Roosevelt had assigned himself, that of blessing the new international organization designed to secure the peace. It was a complicated, if not contradictory, bequest that his predecessor had left him.

On June 1, steered by Byrnes, the Interim Committee reached a conclusion that went beyond its deliberately vague mandate: "that the bomb should be used against Japan as soon as possible, that it be used on a war plant surrounded by workers' houses, and that it be used without prior warning." That conclusion was ultimately accepted by Truman, who retained final authority. On July 16, a prototype of a plutonium bomb designated for use in Japan, called Fat Man, was successfully tested at Los Alamos in New Mexico, three months after Roosevelt's death. On August 6, a uranium-fission bomb called Little Boy was dropped on Hiroshima. On August 9, the second Fat Man was released over Nagasaki. In between those two dates, Soviet forces crossed into Manchuria, fulfilling Joseph Stalin's promise to Franklin Roosevelt of Soviet intervention in the Pacific war. Estimates of the number of Japanese killed by the two bombs, including those who died from radiation in the first year, approach 200,000, a high proportion women and children, but that was still fewer than the 260,000 said to have been killed in the firebombing of Tokyo and other Japanese cities.

On August 14, Japan finally succumbed, having received a signal that the emperor could be retained after its "unconditional" surrender. Most Americans have believed ever since that the atom bombs ended the war. Some authors and scholars speculate that Soviet entrance into the Pacific war might have inspired even greater trepidation in the Japanese war cabinet. Others think the signal on the emperor was decisive. Still others have argued that Japan was in such a general state of collapse—all but cut off from sources of raw materials, its navy destroyed, effectively blockaded—that it was likely to have surrendered, even without the bombs, before the invasion of U.S. ground forces planned for November.

Truman said his preeminent consideration was to end the war as soon as possible with the fewest American casualties. That's a standard Franklin Roosevelt—visionary, strategist, politician, and inveterate hoarder of his own options—would have recognized and embraced. "It was our common purpose, throughout the war, to be the first to produce an atomic weapon and use it," Stimson would later reflect. Of course, the race to build the bomb had been understood to be against Nazi Germany. And that had ended before the decision to use the weapon against Japan was taken.

Four and a half months after Franklin Roosevelt's death, the Japanese foreign minister in top hat, morning coat, and white gloves and the chief of the Japanese general staff with a chest full of medals and a soft army cap resembling a beanie boarded the battleship USS *Missouri* in Tokyo Bay with a small delegation to sign the surrender instruments under the solemn gaze of General MacArthur, Admiral Nimitz, their top officers, and other Allied commanders. With World War II now officially ended, the President then addressed the nation, pronouncing the name Roosevelt only once, in a single-sentence tribute simultaneously reverential and spare, showing that his predecessor was already receding into history.

After an additional eighteen months, another kind of epilogue was written to the age of Roosevelt by the first Republican Congress since the Hoover years. In the new House of Representatives, the first order of business was swift passage of a constitutional amendment limiting future presidents to two terms. Every Republican and enough anti-Roosevelt Democrats, mostly from the South, went along with it to insure the two-thirds vote needed to send the proposed amendment to the Senate. There'd been no public hearings and only two hours of actual debate on the House floor. A freshman Democrat from Massachusetts voted with the Republicans. Representative John F. Kennedy later said that his vote had been influenced by a conversation with Dr. Frank Lahey two months before Roosevelt's death. The surgeon told the young Kennedy that Roosevelt's doctors should have warned the president not to run again.

Its Republican sponsors argued that the proposed amendment simply buttressed a worthy political tradition honored from the time of

George Washington. To show their motives were untainted by partisanship, they made a tactical decision to avoid casting aspersions on the man responsible for the recent breaches of that tradition. Roosevelt loyalists, now distinctly a minority, nevertheless called it a mean-spirited act of political revenge, "a pitiful victory," one of them said, "over a great man now sleeping on the banks of the Hudson."

The amendment and the debates on Capitol Hill attracted remarkably little press coverage and commentary. The speeches were appropriately laden with citations to founding fathers and the Constitutional Convention, where the issue of mandatory term limits was debated at length, then left unaddressed in the written document. In Philadelphia in 1787, it seems, the nays had it. Once again, the views of Hamilton (against) and Jefferson (for, once he ascended to the job) were considered; also debated was the question of whether citizens could be trusted to come to their own conclusion or whether inserting term limits into the fundamental law after a century and a half of trying would tend to weaken a reelected president in a second term by turning him (in 1947, no one thought to say "her") into a lame duck sooner than necessary. The debate was supposed to be about fundamentals, about the Constitution and democracy, to be beyond partisanship. But, inescapably, it was also about Franklin Roosevelt and his record after he engineered a "draft" and stood for a third term in the weeks following Dunkirk, the fall of Paris, and Vichy France's capitulation to the Nazis.

"Who can say," a Kentucky Republican asked during the House debate, "that some other great American, Democrat or Republican, could not have handled the affairs of the nation from 1940 to 1945 equally as well as President Roosevelt? To take any other view is to assume that we have and do produce in this country indispensable men . . . My sincere prayer is that we shall never live to see the day when this great republic becomes so bankrupt of leadership and patriotism that we accept the principle of the indispensable man."

Once the amendment moved to the Senate, a Florida Democrat, Claude Pepper, turned the question around and asked whether "an inexperienced man" would have had the "courage and genius" to conceive Lend-Lease or put vast, unlimited funds behind a secret project to build a bomb more powerful than any previously imagined. It was the difference between victory and defeat, he argued, and only Roosevelt could have managed it. Soon the passions of 1940 were stirred into issues of the present. "If the Republicans had prevailed then and we had let the Germans eat up Russia, we would not be in the predicament we are in now," an unreconstructed isolationist from Illinois actually argued. "It was not Lend-Lease, it was giving away, and nothing has come of it."

The Twenty-Second Amendment couldn't change the outcomes of past elections, but in the eyes of its supporters it would be the next best thing. First it had to be ratified by three-quarters of the states, a tall order. The states were given seven years to act after it was officially sent to them on March 27, 1947. Five with Republican legislatures didn't dally, ratifying it in the first week. Maine, which Roosevelt four times failed to carry, completed its deliberations on the first possible day. A freshman legislator from the town of Waterville named Edmund Muskie—later a governor, senator, nominee for vice president, presidential candidate, and, finally, secretary of state—asked why the haste. So Maine could be first, a sponsor said.

By the end of the year, another thirteen states had followed; eighteen more were still needed. There, halfway to the required thirty-six, the amendment stalled. Franklin Roosevelt had been dead for nearly six years when the ratification exercise was finally completed in February 1951. In recognition of the occasion, an Illinois Republican named Noah Mason rose on the House floor and reeled off a checklist of setbacks to America that wouldn't have occurred, in his own peculiar reading of history, if the magic balm of term limits had been applied twenty or so years earlier:

"A sick President would not have gone to the Yalta conference . . .

"We would not have spent hundreds of millions of dollars on the Berlin airlift . . .

"We would not have spent $100 billion on the so-called cold war . . .

"We would not be in Korea today . . .

"World War III would not now be threatening . . .

"We would not now have Senator Harry Truman for President."

The amendment, in the view of this obscure representative from the heartland, was a time machine traversing, if not reversing, recent history, tidying up in Roosevelt's wake. Such wallowing in far-fetched hypotheticals was "ridiculous" in the view of a second termer from Minnesota, a former Benedictine novice and future presidential candidate.

Eugene McCarthy said Roosevelt was a great American leader, "not perfect but a man who served his country well . . . Men who broke political bread with him and his Republican enemies accuse him. What do they accuse him of? Principally that he did not solve for them, and for us, all problems.

"The very men who say that all the good which was accomplished during his administration was accomplished despite him, rather than because of him, blame him for everything that was not accomplished while he lived and for every failure and disappointment following his death."

The American people, he concluded, "are not like jackals who gather to feast on the flesh of the fallen lion."

That proved to be the last word in the debate on the Twenty-Second Amendment. Presidential term limits came into force and have survived. So has Roosevelt's reputation. With the new check, a new balance came into being. Today the amendment limits Republicans and their super PACs as well as Democrats and theirs. Circumstances under which it might be seriously challenged have yet to arise. Given the difficulty of amending the Constitution, they probably never will. What Roosevelt decried as "government by organized money" prevails.

Although he has now been dead longer than he was alive, the conflict between those who blessed him and his actions in peace and war and those who loathed him has, similarly, yet to end. And maybe never will.

ACKNOWLEDGMENTS

This book is an attempt to trace the shifting patterns of Franklin Roosevelt's thinking through the climactic stages of his presidency, a world war and, ultimately, his life. He resisted self-disclosure, biding his time, shuffling his priorities. Not easily pinned down in life, he's not easily pinned down now, despite the trove of 17 million documentary pages left behind at the presidential archive he established at Hyde Park. Roosevelt didn't foresee a day when the most important of these could be summoned online in a matter of minutes, even seconds, to a laptop or smartphone screen anywhere. These are helpful up to a point when read in conjunction with his day-by-day appointment schedules and logs, also online, and with diaries kept by significant figures from his era (three Henrys, for instance—Stimson, Wallace, and Morgenthau). Taken together with the more personal diary left behind by his distant cousin and regular companion Margaret Suckley, they begin to limn the contours of Roosevelt's mental map.

I'm indebted to members of the staff at the Roosevelt Library, especially Virginia Lewick for introducing me to FRANKLIN, a search engine that opens the digitized portion of the collection to online browsing. My research mainstay has been Connor Gaudet, a recent product of the archive studies program at New York University, who roamed a vast virtual library on my behalf to retrieve documents, texts and articles I sought on a broad range of topics, assembling them over a period of three years in several dozen plastic binders. Thus a digital semiliterate and graduate school dropout was able to operate as if he'd mastered basic skills an up-to-date scholar needs. Philip Herrington, a graduate student at the University of Virginia, made similar searches on my behalf through the papers of Roosevelt's last secretary of state, Edward Stettinius Jr. I received useful guidance from James Wilson in the Office of the Historian at the State Department. Dennis Frank, a librarian at St. Bonaventure University near Allegany, N.Y., made it possible for me to go through interview notes for the 1974 book by the popular journalist Jim Bishop, *FDR's Last Year.* June Hopkins, a granddaughter and biographer of Roosevelt's closest wartime adviser, kindly loaned me a manuscript copy of an unpublished Hopkins biography by James Halsted, the third husband of Anna Roosevelt.

Occasionally I contacted historians who have labored in this vineyard and invariably received prompt and thoughtful guidance. These included Robert H. Ferrell, Frank Costigliola, Warren Kimball, and David Nasaw. I also compared notes with Avis Bohlen, who, emulating her father, had a distinguished career in the foreign service and now is at work on his biography. Lilia Fontana, director of the Gold Coast Railway Museum in Miami, guided me through the *Ferdinand Magellan,* Roosevelt's special rail car, which is preserved there. I was toured through the Hobcaw Barony, Bernard Baruch's plantation near Georgetown, South Carolina, used by an ailing Roosevelt as a retreat in the spring of 1944, by Lee Brockington of the Belle W. Baruch Foundation, which now manages this large coastal holding as a nature preserve and research center.

I visited Dr. Harry S. Goldsmith, a surgeon and super-sleuth among doctors who have made an avocation of explorations into Roosevelt's medical history, at his home near Lake Tahoe. The first of the doctors I consulted, he told me he no longer held to the thesis with which he started—that the president's life was cut short by melanoma. He also recounted his long legal struggle with the Lahey Clinic north of Boston to recover a memo dictated by its founder, Dr. Frank Lahey, dated the day before Roosevelt finally declared that he'd seek a fourth term. Dr. Lahey, who'd been consulted in the case, wanted to leave a record that he took a dim view of Roosevelt's chances of surviving four years. At the Lahey Hospital & Medical Center, as it's now known, I was at first told that the founder left behind no archive. Eventually, having been cleared by Dr. Howard Grant, its chief, I was given the run of some forty storage cartons stuffed with Lahey's correspondence, travel records, memos, and other effects. These contained an apparently complete record of his government service and travels during the war. There was no evidence that I could find that he ever suggested surgery for the president. I'm especially grateful to Dr. John A. Libertino, James E. Thompson, and Trish Rick at Lahey.

Among other doctors I consulted were a retired cardiologist, Marvin Moser, who subsequently died; Dr. Gyatri Devi, a neurologist who gave me a tutorial on the characteristics of hypertensive strokes and aneurysms; and Dr. Larry Norton, a senior oncologist at the Memorial Sloan Kettering Cancer Center who discussed the diagnostic factors that, in the absence of any direct evidence, made the melanoma thesis plausible. Drs. Henry S. Lodge and David Sherman, both on the faculty of New York–Presbyterian Hospital, affiliated with Columbia University, were kind enough to read my pages alongside Dr. Howard Bruenn's "Clinical Notes," published twenty-five years after his patient's death, and thus backstop this layman's summaries of medical fundamentals. Neither had delved into the Roosevelt case before; neither can be held responsible in any way for what appears here.

After perusing the material I gave him, Dr. Sherman, himself a cardiologist, hit upon a striking coincidence. He asked a senior colleague in the Park Avenue suite of offices where he practices whether he'd ever heard of Dr. Bruenn. As a matter of fact, the colleague said, Bruenn had worked in the same suite after the war; not just that, before his retirement, he'd used the same rooms Dr. Sherman now occupies. Later, unpacking a closet, the colleague came upon an old portable EKG machine in a handsomely crafted wooden case with the name Howard G. Bruenn engraved on a brass plate—old enough to have been carried to Honolulu, the Aleutians, Yalta, and Warm Springs in Roosevelt's last months.

Geoffrey C Ward, the author of three Roosevelt books and compiler of the invaluable Suckley diary, was a generous sounding board during the time I was attempting to organize and set down my thoughts. Later he gave my manuscript a close reading. Brenda Wineapple, an accomplished biographer, took time from her current study of Andrew Johnson's impeachment to do the same. My third reader was my brother David, a bona fide scholar in another field, who caught me in some glaring anachronisms, some of which I removed. I'm grateful to each of them for constructive suggestions and moral support. Also, as always, I'm indebted to Andrew Wylie, a peerless literary agent, and to Jonathan Segal, a stalwart editor while a book is taking shape and later when it's launched into the world. Thanks to them I've more or less managed to reinvent myself as a writer in the years since I had to turn my back on the fast-paced team sport known as daily journalism. Finally, I should mention Peter Andersen at Knopf who's responsible for the book's design, Julia Ringo who monitored its production schedule, and Catherine Talese who rounded up permissions for the photographs we selected and acquired usable prints. Steven Rattazzi was a one-man emergency squad on whom I relied to keep me backed up and retrieve my words when they were sucked into some digital cavern.

Janny Scott, a delightful hostage—maybe not the right word but "companion" seems too casual and passive for what we have—has been an inspiration. Over my desk in what we call "the bureau" she hung a World War II poster with an image of Franklin Roosevelt's head set against a flag's red and white stripes and gold tassels. LOST GROUND CAN ALWAYS BE MADE UP—LOST TIME NEVER! it admonishes. When I raise my eyes from my keyboard, they fall on a half dozen words in smaller characters at the bottom of the poster: *Avoid time off! Avoid time out!*

What was intended for war workers decades ago is suitable for writers today—more so those classed as seniors. But then time out with Janny is never lost.

NOTES

ABBREVIATIONS

FDRL   Franklin Delano Roosevelt Presidential Library

LOC   Library of Congress

PSF   President's Secretary's File

PPF   President's Personal File

CC   Ward, Geoffrey C., ed. *Closest Companion: The Unknown Story of the Intimate Friendship Between Franklin Roosevelt and Margaret Suckley*. Boston, 1995.

C&R   Kimball, Warren F., ed. *Churchill and Roosevelt: The Complete Correspondence*. Princeton, N.J., 1984.

FRUS   United States Department of State. *Foreign Relations of the United States Diplomatic Papers. The Conferences at Cairo and Tehran, 1943; The Conferences at Malta and Yalta, 1945*. Washington, 1961, 1955.

PPA   Rosenman, Samuel L., ed. *The Public Papers and Addresses of Franklin D. Roosevelt, 1944–1945*. Vol. 4. New York, 1950.

PC   Roosevelt, Franklin D. *The Complete Presidential Press Conferences of Franklin D. Roosevelt*. Vols. 22–25. Cambridge, Mass., 1972.

PROLOGUE: PLAINTIVE

3 "He is just *too* tired": *CC*, 249.

3 contemplate stepping down: Edward Flynn, the Democratic boss of the Bronx and an old political sidekick, later claimed to have urged Roosevelt to consider stepping down. That appears to have been in mid-June 1944. Flynn, *You're the Boss*, 179.

4 "You're getting picayune": Roosevelt press conference no. 929, Dec. 28, 1943, in *PC*, 22:252.

4 "Completely in the dark": Harold Ickes diary, Dec. 19, 1943, Harold L. Ickes Papers, LOC.

4 "Oh": Hassett, *Off the Record with FDR*, 229.

4 "Open me up": Dr. James Halsted, chap. 13, ms. of unpublished biography of Harry Hopkins in the possession of June Hopkins.

5 "Rooseveltian ideas": "Memorandum Concerning the Fourth Term," 3, Benjamin V. Cohen Papers, LOC.

5 "Dear Ben": FDR to Ben Cohen, March 13, 1944, Cohen Papers, PPF, folder 3509, FDRL.

6 In just two months: Overy, *Russia's War*, 212.

6 in the range of twenty-seven to thirty million: Timothy Snyder in *Bloodlands*, 335, asserts that losses on the Soviet side were disproportionately non-Russian, Belarusian, Ukrainian, and, tallying civilians, Jews.

6 "We would lose this war": Eubank, *Summit at Teheran*, 348.

6 "the fight against Nazi": Katznelson, *Fear Itself*, 17.

7 "the post-war settlement": British Foreign Office notes quoted in Reynolds, *From Munich to Pearl Harbor*, 109.

7 "rather touchy": Quoted by ibid.

8 predicted it never would: Adams, *Witness to Power*, 294.

8 "the withering effect": Editorial in *New York Herald Tribune*, Jan. 24, 1944.

8 Edwin Johnson: Pogue, *Organizer of Victory*, 277.

8 in his grave: *New York Herald Tribune*, March 31, 1944.

9 Polls made that point: For instance, see Mark Sullivan's analysis in *New York Herald Tribune*, Jan. 30, 1944, sec. 2; report on Gallup poll, *New York Times*, March 25, 1944. A *Fortune* poll in May 1943 showed 64.8 percent favoring Roosevelt if the war were still on at the time of the next election and 59.2 percent opposed to his seeking a new term if it were to end. Public Opinion polls, PSF, FDRL.

9 "All the boys who went down": Jonathan Daniels, *White House Witness*, 73.

9 "would do anything for a change": Conant, *Irregulars*, 134.

10 "Don't ever say anything": Draft of *Roosevelt and Hopkins*, chap. 7, dated May 8, 1948, Robert E. Sherwood Papers, Houghton Library, Harvard University.

10 "has lost its sense of direction": *New York Herald Tribune*, March 28, 1944.

10 "round generalities": *Time*, Jan. 3, 1944.

11 "The United States has no": *New York Times*, April 6, 1944.

11 "To Roosevelt's Gladstone": Berlin, *Washington Despatches*, 453.

12 medical historians and sleuths: Books and articles along these lines include Goldsmith, *Conspiracy of Silence*; Lomazow and Fettmann, *FDR's Deadly Secret*; Park, *Impact of Illness on World Leaders*; Evans, *Hidden Campaign*; Ferrell, *Dying President*; L'Etang, *Pathology of Leadership*; David Owen, *In Sickness and in Power*; Alan J. Salerian and Gregory M. Salerian, "A Review of FDR's Mental Capacity During His Fourth Term," *Forensic Examiner* (Spring 2005): 31–38; Ray W. Gifford, "FDR and Hypertension: If We'd Only Known Then What We Know Now," *Geriatrics* (Jan. 1996): 29; Baron H. Lerner, "Revisiting the 'Definitive' Accounts of Franklin D. Roosevelt's Terminal Illness," *Bulletin of the History of Medicine* (Summer 2007): 386–406.

12 "What is most striking": Freidel, *Rendezvous with Destiny*, 600.

13 "He won't live a year": There were many people at that time, Roosevelt later said when Smith's remark was repeated to him, "who believed I was headed for a tombstone." Morgan, *FDR*, 292. Also in Ward, *First-Class Temperament*, 788; PPF 5872, FDRL.

13 secret envoy: Rosenman, *Working with Roosevelt*, 464.

13 idea of resigning: Roosevelt talks to Daisy Suckley about leading a new international peace organization as early as April 1943. The word "resign" comes up in this context in February 1944. *CC*, 207, 257, 277. Senator Pepper's remark was in an AP dispatch dated Feb. 19, 1944. See New York *Daily News*, Feb. 20, 1944, 87.

15 "feminine": Reminiscences of Henry Agard Wallace, oral history, 1951, 3200, Butler Library, Columbia University.

15 "almost clairvoyant": Reminiscences of Frances Perkins, oral history, 1955, 7:561, Butler Library, Columbia University, cited by Costigliola, *Roosevelt's Lost Alliances*, 186, 365.

15 "a conjuror": Eden, *Reckoning*, 433.

15 "His mind does not": Henry Stimson diary, Dec. 18, 1940, Henry Lewis Stimson Papers, Sterling Memorial Library, Yale University, cited by Persico, *Roosevelt's Secret War*, 17.

15 "almost an egomaniac": Transcription of a taped comment made by Eisenhower as president in a political conversation in his office on January 7, 1955, as released by the Eisenhower Library in Abilene, Kansas, on March 14, 1997, cited by Ferrell, *The Dying President*, 168. In his memoir *Crusade in Europe*, Eisenhower said Roosevelt fulfilled all that could possibly be expected of him as "leader of a nation at war," 452.

15 "by far the most enigmatic": Keegan, *Second World War*, 537.

15 "You know, I am a juggler": Kimball, *Juggler*, 7.

16 "splendid deception": Gallagher, *FDR's Splendid Deception*, p. xiv.

16 "He was a helpless cripple": Reilly, *Reilly of the White House*, 15.

17 "absolute edict": Wilson Brown, galleys of "Aide to Four Presidents," *American Heritage*, Feb. 1955, Wilson Brown Papers, FDRL.

17 "Here is a picture": Stephen Early to Ross McIntire, Aug. 13, 1937, Box 11, Stephen T. Early Papers, FDRL.

18 scepter or magic wand: Jonathan Daniels, *White House Witness*, 102.

18 Washington bureau chief: His name was Byron Price. The office he headed was officially called the Office of Censorship. His correspondence can be found in the Early Papers.

18 "Now don't let the engineer": Reilly, *Reilly of the White House*, 226. Reilly, the agent in charge of Roosevelt's Secret Service details, says that the president was especially concerned to have the trains travel at slow speeds at night. Bob Withers, in *The President Travels by Train*, 132, makes the opposite case, writing, "Roosevelt ordered his trains to travel slowly during the day."

18 "somewhere in the South": *New York Times*, April 13, 1944.

19 told him "frankly": Stimson diary, Nov. 4, 1943.

19 "The trouble now": Ibid., Oct. 28, 1943.

19 "Very confidentially": Early to Joseph E. Davis, Feb. 4, 1942, Early Papers.

20 "whether Roosevelt": Ickes, *Lowering Clouds*, 269. This is probably the earliest reference to the idea of a Roosevelt resignation, leaving open two questions: Did it originate with Roosevelt himself? Was it ever serious, or a way of fending off health questions at a time when there was no constitutional procedure in the event of incapacity of a president?

20 "a very slight heart attack": Bullitt, *For the President, Personal and Secret*, 398.

20 "excellent": Bohlen, *Witness to History*, 142.

20 "magnificent shape": As quoted by Belle Willard Roosevelt, diary, Dec. 18, 1943, Kermit Roosevelt and Belle Roosevelt Papers, LOC.

20 "He looked robust and well": Rosenman, *Working with Roosevelt*, 411.

20 "Just as we of the cabinet": Henry Stimson diary, Dec. 17, 1943.

21 "heartfelt prayers": Buhite and Levy, *FDR's Fireside Chats*, 275.

22 "His stamina is far": *New York Times*, Jan. 29, 1944.

22 promoted to rear admiral: *New York Herald Tribune*, Feb. 3, 1944.

22 spoken the truth: In 1954, the admiral responsible for Roosevelt's health showed how much of a politician he'd become in his White House years by running—unsuccessfully—for Congress from a district in San Diego where he might have expected more votes from retired naval officers like himself than he evidently got.

22 "robust health": *New York Herald Tribune*, Jan. 29, 1944.

22 Arthur Prettyman: Bishop, *FDR's Last Year,* 353, 721. The book has no footnotes. A search of Bishop's manuscript and what remains of his research materials in an archive at St. Bonaventure University in Olean, New York, revealed no source for his assertion on this point. He did not list Prettyman, who died in 1957, among the people he interviewed. Bishop did claim to have interviewed Secret Service agents on duty in that period.

22 "sleeping sickness": *CC,* 330.

23 "wonderfully well": Kelly to Robert Hannegan, Hannegan Papers, Harry S. Truman Library; Kelly to Harry Hopkins, Oct. 20, 1944, Harry L. Hopkins Papers, 1928–46, Georgetown University Archive.

24 traces his "stoicism": Ward, *Before the Trumpet,* 145.

24 "queer" sensations: *CC,* 295.

24 "amazingly reticent": Jonathan Daniels, *White House Witness,* 3.

24 "heavily forested interior": Sherwood, *Roosevelt and Hopkins,* 9.

CHAPTER I   UNCLE JOE IN TEHRAN

25 openly discussed: This suggestion was first made by Charles E. Bohlen in *Witness to History,* 157. It was repeated by Ted Morgan in his biography, *FDR,* 701, and by Jean Edward Smith in his identically titled volume, 591.

25 six or seven million: According to Susan Butler in her *Roosevelt and Stalin,* 124, this was an overcount. She puts the number of Polish-Americans at "just under two million" in 1940.

25 never go to war over the Baltics: Bohlen, *Witness to History,* 157. Subsequently, he was quoted as saying in an off-the-record interview with one journalist, Marquis Childs, that he would never go to war over Poland. This was in April 1944. Marquis Childs Papers, Wisconsin Historical Society.

26 bypassed by his president: Butler, *My Dear Mr. Stalin,* 63. Later, Hull would complain that he was never shown the minutes of the Tehran sessions, nor told about the atomic bomb.

26 "old maids": Interview with Charles E. Bohlen, Jan. 14, 1947, Sherwood Papers.

26 "I know that you": Cited in Roberts, *Masters and Commanders,* 126.

27 "near our common border": letter from Roosevelt to Stalin, April 11, 1942, in Butler, *My Dear Mr. Stalin,* 64.

27 "The whole question": Diary note by Henry Morgenthau Jr. quoted in Blum, *Years of War,* 84–85.

27 "in some secure place": Roosevelt to Stalin, Dec. 2, 1942, in Butler, *My Dear Mr. Stalin,* 101.

27 "either on your side": Roosevelt to Stalin, May 5, 1943, in Butler, *My Dear Mr. Stalin,* 129.

27 denying he'd suggested: Eubank, *Summit at Teheran,* 98–99.

27 "A meeting between": Churchill to Roosevelt, June 25, 1943, cable, in *C&R,* 2:278.

28 "get-at-able": Sherwood, *Roosevelt and Hopkins,* 799.

28 "the big question": Eden, *Reckoning,* 432.

31 "Russia is so necessary": Burns to Hopkins, Aug. 10, 1943, memo, Hopkins Papers, FDRL.

31 "Roosevelt's World Blueprint": Forrest Davis, "Roosevelt's World Blueprint," *Saturday Evening Post,* April 10, 1943.

33 "The attack on Poland": Lash, *Eleanor and Franklin,* 584.

33 Anna Louise Strong: Ibid., 591.

34 "with the identical confidence": Sherwood, *Roosevelt and Hopkins,* 322.

34 "the questions he asked": Ibid., 343–44.

34 "Mr. Stalin spoke": Ibid., 327.

34 "I am a confirmed optimist": Harriman to Roosevelt, July 5, 1943, W. Averell Harriman Papers, LOC.

35 "the fatal vice": Bullitt to Roosevelt, Jan. 29, 1943, in Bullitt, *For the President, Personal and Secret,* 576–90.

36 "Harry says he's not": Brownell and Billings, *So Close to Greatness,* 293.

36 drunken binge: The 1940 incident is recounted in the following books: Welles, *Sumner Welles;* Brownell and Billings, *So Close to Greatness;* Irwin F. Gellman, *Secret Affairs* (New York, 1995); Morgan, *FDR,* 678–86.

37 second incident on a train: Mentioned in Gellman, *Secret Affairs,* 308.

37 "Bill, you've tried to destroy": Welles, *Sumner Welles,* 345.

37 "The P. never wants to see": *CC,* 244.

37 "a very superficial man": Bullitt, *For the President, Personal and Secret,* xiv–xv; Kimball, *Juggler,* on criticism of Roosevelt being "foolish and naïve rather than Machiavellian" in his dealings with Stalin, 18. See also Kennan, *Memoirs,* where he writes: "I could only feel there was something frivolous about our action in this Polish question. I reflected on the lightheartedness with which great powers offer advice to smaller ones in matters affecting the vital interests of the latter," 209.

38 "despite his distrust": Henderson, *Question of Trust,* 539.

38 *Mission to Moscow:* On DVD in the Warner Bros. Archive Collection. The screenplay is reprinted in Culbert, *Mission to Moscow.* Dwight Macdonald's letter, signed by Edmund Wilson and Alfred Kazin among others, is quoted there on p. 33.

39 "a man of great sagacity": Roberts, *Masters and Commanders,* 278.

39 "Stalin the Great": Eubank, *Summit at Teheran,* 344.

39 "hard, tenacious driving mind": Willkie, *One World,* 64.

39 "I found in Marshall Stalin": Hull, *Memoirs,* 2:1315.

40 "Moscow was a real": Roosevelt to Lippmann, Nov. 8, 1943, Walter Lippmann Papers, Sterling Memorial Library, Yale University.

40 "U.J. is to meet him": *CC,* 255.

40 "impossible": Roosevelt to Stalin, Oct. 21, 1943, cable, in Butler, *My Dear Mr. Stalin,* 178.

40 "bad heart": Hopkins quoted in Sherwood, *Roosevelt and Hopkins,* 671.

41 "I am not in any way considering": Roosevelt to Stalin, Oct. 21, 1943, cable.

41 put off to the spring: Eubank, *Summit at Teheran,* 123.

41 trial run: Reilly, *Reilly of the White House,* 172.

41 "Arthur! Arthur!": Rigdon, *White House Sailor,* 64. The torpedo incident is further described in the official log of the trip. PSF, box 7, FDRL.

42 "Assume that *all* rooms": Undated memo from Colonel Richard Park Jr., top officer in the White House Map Room, in briefing papers distributed to U.S. delegates, FDRL.

42 "to realize the psychological benefits": Stimson diary, Nov. 4, 1943.

42 "out of his shell": Harriman and Abel, *Special Envoy*, 216.

43 "Do they know": Beria, *Beria, My Father*, p. 93.

43 "great sympathy and respect": Ibid.

43 "Stalin is quick": Leahy diary, Nov. 30, 1943, 65, LOC.

43 "It was a beautiful": Bohlen, *Witness to History*, 144.

43 "turned green": Ibid., 149.

44 agreed "100%": *FRUS: Cairo and Tehran*, 485.

44 "Stunted" and "hopeless": Roberts, *Masters and Commanders*, pp. 138, 311.

45 "with all his lip service": Stimson diary, Oct. 28, 1943; subsequent entry of Nov. 4, 1943; Stimson to Hopkins, Nov. 10, 1943, Stimson Papers.

45 "This conference is over": Remark by Sir Alan Brooke quoted in Moran, *Churchill*, 143.

45 "If that is unknown": Eubank, *Summit at Teheran*, 304.

46 "I should like to know": Ibid., 309; *FRUS: Cairo and Tehran*, 339.

46 "in a quasi-jocular fashion": Bohlen, *Witness to History*, 152.

46 Sir Owen O'Malley: Paul, *Katyn*, 305; *C&R*, 2:389–99.

46 "I should like to have it back": Churchill to Roosevelt, in *C&R*, 2:388. The full text of the O'Malley letter follows in the same volume, 389–99.

47 "I thank the Lord": Stimson diary, Dec. 5, 1943.

47 "The ice was broken": Perkins, *Roosevelt I Knew*, 81–82, 365.

48 "showed himself more prescient": Churchill, *Closing the Ring*, 321.

48 "If the Japanese": *FRUS: Cairo and Tehran*, 531.

49 "This was hardly calculated": Eden, *Reckoning*, 496.

49 At the penultimate dinner: Bohlen, *Witness to History*, 155–56; *FRUS: Cairo and Tehran*, 469, 582–85.

49 "If there was any supreme peak": Sherwood, *Roosevelt and Hopkins*, 799.

49 "He believed intensely": Rosenman, *Working with Roosevelt*, 411.

50 "by far the biggest man": Stimson diary, Dec. 16, 1943.

50 "He always had a wider point of view": Bland, *Marshall Interviews and Reminiscences*, 331.

50 "A man has a great": Ibid., 330.

51 "In effect you say": Roosevelt to Marshall, Sept. 23, 1941, PSF, war folder, FDRL.

51 "We fail to see": Bland, *Marshall Interviews and Reminiscences*, 622; also p. 593, cited in Roberts, *Masters and Commanders*, 203.

51 "The best way I can": Pogue, *Organizer of Victory*, 273–74.

52 "of all our combined forces": Hopkins note to Roosevelt, Oct. 4, 1943, cited by Roll in *The Hopkins Touch*, 299.

52 "will not occur while I hold": Churchill, *Closing the Ring*, 271.

53 "It is dangerous to monkey": Eisenhower, *Crusade in Europe*, 224.

53 "matchless power": Stimson diary, Dec. 17, 1943.

54 "The President never thinks": Larrabee, *Commander in Chief*, 644, cited by Goodwin, *No Ordinary Time*, 190.

54 "I didn't feel": Pogue, *Organizer of Victory*, 321.

54 Truman's daughter, Margaret: Margaret Truman, *Harry S. Truman*, 169.

54 strong candidate: Ickes diary, Dec. 19, 1943.

54 role for Truman: Pauley to Hannegan, Dec. 9, 1943, Correspondence Book II, box 1, Hannegan Papers.

54 "I would call him": Press conference no. 927, Dec. 17, 1943, in *PC*, 22:217. FDR's complete press conferences are also available on the FDRL Web site.

54 "perhaps the poorest": *Time*, Jan. 3, 1944.

55 "international relationships": Buhite and Levy, *FDR's Fireside Chats*, 277–78.

55 "Fourth-Term": *New York Herald Tribune*, Jan. 2, 1944.

55 "The President, now": Walter Lippmann, *New York Herald Tribune*, Dec. 23, 1943.

55 "tired, as usual": *CC*, 280.

56 "sitting around his bed": Rosenman, *Working with Roosevelt*, 418.

56 "the most radical": Brands, *Traitor to His Class*, 754. See also Burns, *Soldier of Freedom*, 425–26.

CHAPTER 2 WILSON'S SHADOW

58 "or it would break the heart": Lash, *Eleanor and Franklin*, 234.

59 "wished a leading role": Josephus Daniels, *Wilson Era*, 255.

59 "rattle the sword": Ward, *First-Class Temperament*, 308.

59 "We've got to get into this war": Cited by Burns in *The Lion and the Fox*, 61.

60 "Neither you nor I": Ward, *First-Class Temperament*, 346.

60 "horrified to find": Belle Willard Roosevelt diaries, July 13, 1943, LOC.

63 "Woodrow Wilson had reached the zenith": Hoover, *Ordeal of Woodrow Wilson*, 69.

63 "FDR persona non grata": Cited by Ward in *First-Class Temperament*, 481.

63 "I committed enough illegal acts": Ibid., 477.

63 "fell out of bed": Ibid., 481.

64 "Mr. Cox, that fight": Gene Smith, *When the Cheering Stopped*, 165.

64 Boston Common: *Springfield Republican*, Sept. 15, 1920, *Boston Herald*, Sept. 16, 1920, Roosevelt Papers for 1920, series 4, box 9, newspaper clippings, FDRL.

65 "generous labors": Wilson to Roosevelt, April 30, 1922, Woodrow Wilson Papers, Princeton University.

65 "Plan to Preserve World Peace": Eleanor Roosevelt, *This I Remember*, 353–66, app. 1, discussed on p. 24. Roosevelt's plan was apparently submitted in a contest sponsored by a publisher, Edward Bok, who offered a prize called the America Peace Award along with $100,000 for the best plan to involve the United States in the pursuit of world peace. It was not a winner.

65 "to agitate the question": Dallek, *Franklin D. Roosevelt and American Foreign Policy*, 17.

65 "The League of Nations today": Ibid., 19.

66 "created something akin to panic": Freidel, *Franklin D. Roosevelt*, 69.

66 "She hasn't spoken to me": Conversation with Agnes Leach of the League of Women Voters cited by Lash in *Eleanor and Franklin*, 347.

66 "effective international organization": Hoopes and Brinkley, *FDR and the Creation of the UN*, 38.

67 "For heaven's sake": Divine, *Second Chance*, 49.

67 "categorical repudiation": Hoopes and Brinkley, *FDR and the Creation of the UN*, 39, 64.

67 "Winning the war": Sumner Welles, "Two Roosevelt Decisions," *Foreign Affairs*, Jan. 1951, 188.

67 "How does this fit": Welles, *Sumner Welles,* 149.

67 "The P. remembers": *CC,* 19.

67 "will turn again": Divine, *Second Chance,* 45.

68 "Woodrow Wilson's whole career": Roosevelt Remarks, Staunton, Va., May 4, 1941, American Presidency Project, www.presidency.ucsb.edu/ws.

68 "virile, a reality": MacMillan, *Paris, 1919,* 88.

68 "I am not a Wilsonian idealist": Quoted by Kimball in *Forged in War,* 201.

68 "of asking two different people": Rosenman, *Working with Roosevelt,* 104.

69 "The President was unusually serious": Welles, *Sumner Welles,* 337–38.

69 Leo Pasvolsky: See Stephen C. Schlesinger, *Act of Creation: The Founding of the United Nations,* 33–57.

70 "I pray that the P.": *CC,* 311.

70 fifth term in 1948: New York *Daily News,* May 31, 1944, March 13, 1944.

71 "The Most Important Event": Divine, *Second Chance,* 170.

71 "The dream of a world": *Wilson,* directed by Henry King, produced by Darryl F. Zanuck, available on DVD.

71 "By God, that's not going to happen to me": Bruenn, "Clinical Notes," 587, quoted by Black, *Champion of Freedom,* 494.

CHAPTER 3   HIS "ENORMOUS" HEART

73 never got to see the president: Jonathan Daniels, *White House Witness,* 62.

73 down to 128 pounds: *CC,* 275. Also, Halsted, "Severe Malnutrition in a Public Servant of the World War II Era."

74 "Well, you are not in uniform": Boettiger, *Love in Shadow,* 238.

74 "I crave you": Anna Boettiger letter, April 4, 1944, John R. Boettiger Papers, box 6, FDRL.

75 He'd lost ten pounds: First reported in *New York Times,* Jan. 19, 1944. There is no consistent month-to-month record on Roosevelt's weight fluctuations from this point until his death. His normal weight was around 188 pounds. At his death, it was said to be about 165 but might have been less. Weight losses and marginal gains were indicated in this period in various accounts. Sometimes the loss was said by Admiral McIntire to be deliberate for the sake of his health, meaning his heart, although concern about his cardiovascular condition was never publicly acknowledged until after his death. In his last months, his physicians sought to reverse his weight loss by giving him eggnog; see McIntire, *White House Physician,* 183.

75 "Of what was inside him": Roosevelt and Shalett, *Affectionately, F.D.R.,* cited by Gallagher in *Roosevelt's Great Deception,* 183.

75 "He was really incapable": Quoted by Gallagher, *Roosevelt's Great Deception,* 128, citing Oursler, *Behold This Dreamer.*

75 old leather valise: This was discovered upon her death in 1991. The Wilderstein Mansion in Rhinebeck, New York, has been preserved as a historic trust. Daisy Suckley's complete papers, generously excerpted in Geoffrey Ward's *CC,* are archived there.

76 "He puts so much of himself": *CC,* 272.

76 "He was the perfect picture": John O'Donnell, New York *Daily News,* Feb. 2, 1944.

77 "I said, 'Winston'": *PPA,* 70–72.

77 "I'm either Exhibit A": *CC,* 201.

77 "He needs to have": Ibid., 277. See also pp. 197 and 201 for comparable quotations pointing to his loneliness.

77 "The P. felt feverish": Ibid., 281, for March 2 entry and 283–84 for March 8.

78 "looked quite rested": Henry Wallace diary, Feb. 18, 1944, 3074–76, Oral History Collection, Butler Library, Columbia University.

78 "The P. is tired": *CC*, 271, 277, 280, 281, 283, all allude to his thoughts about resigning at some future date.

79 "politically and emotionally stingy": Breitman and Lichtman, *FDR and the Jews*, 210.

79 antilynching bill: Alan Brinkley, *End of Reform*, 166–67.

79 "Do you want to be": Wallace diary, March 10, 1944, 3183.

79 "a man with a conception": Kimball, *Forged in War*, 112. Professor Kimball is writing here about Roosevelt's hesitation on intervention in the war in the months leading up to Pearl Harbor.

80 "he intends to get the Jews": Wallace diary, March 6, 1944, 3151.

80 "It makes you feel": Roosevelt to Churchill, Jan. 5, 1944, in *C&R*, 3:650.

80 "may be most useful": Churchill to Roosevelt, Jan. 7, 1944, in *C&R*, 3:651.

81 "essential unity": Roosevelt to Churchill, Feb. 7. 1944, in *C&R*, 2:706.

81 "No reply necessary": Butler, *My Dear Mr. Stalin*, March 15, 1944, 212.

81 "hardening": Churchill to Roosevelt, March 18, 1944, in *C&R*, 3:54.

82 "I don't take him": *CC*, 274.

82 "It is not a tax bill": Grace Tully treats the phrase "not for the needy but the greedy" as Roosevelt's own. *FDR, My Boss*, 224. Jim Bishop attributes it to Ben Cohen in *FDR's Last Year*, 31.

82 "had the instinct of a virtuoso": Barkley, *That Reminds Me*, 144.

83 "perhaps imperiling whatever ambitions": *New York Herald Tribune*, Feb. 24, 1944.

84 "WITH PRESIDENT ROOSEVELT": *New York Times*, Feb. 25, 1944.

84 Fiorello La Guardia wondered: Ibid. Same point made in Ickes diary, Feb. 26, 1944.

84 "more than any other event": Barkley, *That Reminds Me*, 169.

84 "bitter, vindictive": Rosenman, *Working with Roosevelt*, 430.

85 Marvin McIntyre: Jonathan Daniels, *White House Witness*, 132.

85 "the simple facts": *Louisville Courier-Journal*, Feb. 25, 1944.

85 "People who are looking": *Louisville Courier-Journal*, Feb. 27, 1944.

86 "generous and manly statement": *New York Herald Tribune*, Feb. 25, 1944.

86 "Most of the Democrats": *New York Times*, Feb. 27, 1944.

86 "When he gets off": Jonathan Daniels, *White House Witness*, 126. The insider was Marvin McIntyre.

86 "Alben must be suffering": Hassett diary, Feb. 23, 1944, 235.

86 blinking: Wilson Brown, unpublished memoir, 133, FDRL.

87 "It doesn't make sense": Hassett, *Off the Record with FDR*, 235–36.

87 "The thing for you to do": Byrnes, *All in One Lifetime*, 211–12.

87 "surrounded by a ring of children": *CC*, 280.

88 Daisy called it "our house": See John G. Waite Associate Architects, *President as Architect*, 7; also *CC*, 35–36.

88 "This flare-up": *CC*, 280.

88 "is more philosophical": Lash, *Eleanor and Franklin*, 696, citing a Feb. 24, 1944, letter to himself from Eleanor Roosevelt.

89 "I have been worrying": Roosevelt to Churchill, Feb. 29, 1944, in *C&R*, 2:766–67.

89 "Underneath one detects": Drury, *Senate Journal*, 108.

90 overseeing a system: Figures cited by Gallagher in *FDR's Splendid Deception*, 179.

90 "to keep Russia": Hull, *Memoirs*, 2:1657–59.

90 "Every morning": Hassett, *Off the Record with FDR*, 239.

91 "Roosevelt represents a textbook case": Marvin Moser, "Historical Perspectives on the Management of Hypertension," *Journal of Clinical Hypertension* (Aug. 2006): 15–20.

92 "Now that you have got": Lahey to McIntire, Dec. 20, 1944, Lahey Papers, Lahey Clinic, Burlington, Mass.

92 consulting role: Dr. Frank Lahey to Dr. Louis Hopkins, March 16, 1944, Louis Hopkins Collection, Grinnell College.

93 "Ross is one of the few men": Ickes diary, July 9, 1944.

93 "I didn't think McIntire": Anna Roosevelt quoted by Asbell, *Mother and Daughter*, 177.

93 "McIntire was annoyed": *CC*, 288.

93 first mentioned: Article by Walter Trohan, *Chicago Tribune*, Aug. 6, 1944.

93 medical journal: Bruenn, "Clinical Notes."

93 seven interviews: Bernard Asbell, Jim Bishop, Geoffrey Ward, Robert Ferrell, Brenda L. Heaster, Jan K. Herman, and Doris Kearns Goodwin. The biographer James MacGregor Burns corresponded with Bruenn and read the draft of his clinical notes.

93 "'Lord Moran' book": Note dated March 8, 1967, Halsted Papers.

94 "The wholesale extermination": *PPA*, 4:105.

95 "Sincerely yours": Lucy Mercer Rutherfurd Papers (1926–28), box 1, FDRL.

95 "with the distinct impression": Associated Press report on the basis of the *Atlanta Journal* article were reprinted in *New York Times* and *Chicago Tribune* on March 26, 1944.

96 shown quarters: Press conference no. 948, May 6, 1944, in *PC*, 144. Eleanor Roosevelt, *This I Remember*, 320.

96 "Cuba is lousy with anarchists": quoted by Rigdon, *White House Sailor*, 97.

96 "I am very angry": Roosevelt to Churchill, March 20, 1944, in *C&R*, 4:60.

97 Some writers: See Lomazow and Fettmann, *FDR's Deadly Secret*, 101.

97 "God awful": Bruenn interview with Jim Bishop (notes are archived at St. Bonaventure University) and interview with Jan K. Herman in "The President's Cardiologist," *Navy Medicine: A Magazine of Service*, March–April 1990, 6–13.

98 "Under fluoroscopy": Bruenn Folder, Small Collections, FDRL.

98 The cardiologist had to explain: Goodwin, *No Ordinary Time*, 494.

99 "as a brake": Bruenn's incomplete notes show the phenobarbital was discontinued on April 23. It was resumed in the last month of his life.

100 "Rest! With perhaps two": Bruenn folder, Small Collections.

100 "McIntire was appalled": Goodwin, *No Ordinary Time*, 495.

100 "told him I literally": Bruenn notes in Bruenn Papers, FDRL.

101 "Still looking tired": New York *Daily News*, March 29, 1944.

CHAPTER 4   SOMEWHERE IN THE SOUTH

102 "The President spoke": Marquis Childs notes, April 7, 1944, Childs Papers, Wisconsin Historical Society.

103 "a quitter": *CC*, 276.

103 "simplify things": Roosevelt to Churchill, Feb. 29, 1944, in *C&R*, 2:767.

103 "The habit of power": Childs notes, April 7, 1944.

104 "When I entered": Catledge, *My Life and "The Times,"* 146. The White House logs show that Catledge had another session with the president on July 11, 1944.

105 "I forgot to tell you": *CC*, April 17, 1944, 295.

105 "the diastole and systole": *CC*, 296.

106 two such conversations: The first was at Hobcaw, which Anna visited only for a day, on April 25, 1944. It's described by Goodwin, *No Ordinary Time*, 499. The second conversation would be at Yalta.

106 George Fox: Ferrell, *Dying President*, 72.

107 avoiding the tunnels: Explained by Withers, *President Travels by Train*, 132.

107 "I'm in no hurry": Ibid., 131.

108 "She was Barney Baruch's girl": Jonathan Daniels, *White House Witness*, 49; also *CC*, 295.

108 "No family should object": *America Magazine*, Dec. 1942. The wedding dinner was on Dec. 16, 1942. This material resides in the Hopkins Papers, Georgetown University Archives.

109 felt ill-used: Described by Sherwood, *Roosevelt and Hopkins*, 700; and by Baruch himself, *Public Years*, 314–17.

109 "I am girding myself": Baruch to Watson, July 5, Nov. 11, and Dec. 5, 1944, in Watson Papers, archive of the University of Virginia.

110 It held them fine: Rigdon, *White House Sailor*, 98.

110 global network: Reilly, *Reilly of the White House*, 34.

110 Hull used the telegraph: Hull, *Memoirs*, 2:1659.

111 whose guest: Ickes diary, April 29, 1944. Admiral McIntire told him.

111 spilled the beans: Stimson diary, April 17, 1944.

111 "The President felt miserable on arrival": Rigdon, *White House Sailor*, 98. Hugh Gallagher, in *FDR's Splendid Deception*, makes a strong, though circumstantial, argument that he was actually suffering from depression.

112 nightly stakeouts: See Miller, *Baroness of Hobcaw*, 120–27. The Baruch estate survives as a nonprofit foundation, home of an institute of coastal ecology and forest science.

113 No photographs: At least none survive. On YouTube, one can call up a film clip of the president fishing in the ocean during his stay. He's shown only from the back.

113 "a full report": Clark, *Calculated Risk*, 336.

115 "almost oppressive": Leahy diary, April 9, 1944.

115 never touched the stamps: Comment made to Secretary Ickes; noted in Ickes diary, May 13, 1944.

115 "You have to lead": Roosevelt to Hopkins, May 18, 1944, PSF, box 133, FDRL, cited by Roll, *Hopkins Touch*, 338.

115 "The conversation was animated": Bruenn, "Clinical Notes," 583.

116 "If he asks": Roosevelt to Churchill, April 23, 1944, in *C&R*, 3:109.

116 "The program of rest": Bruenn, "Clinical Notes," 589.

117 didn't have any "pep": Bishop, *FDR's Last Year*, 37.

117 meeting the president: *New York Times*, April 19, 1944.

117 "He said that Roosevelt": General Alan Brooke diary, in Bryant, *Triumph in the West*, 137, cited by Roberts in *Masters and Commanders*, 481.

117 ration coupons: Goodwin, *No Ordinary Time*, 500.

117 almost certainly knew: Cary Grayson, Wilson's doctor and a close friend of Baruch's,

saw the young Ms. Mercer and the assistant secretary of the navy together on more than one outing in the summer of 1917.

118 "I am an American first": quoted in Knox obituary, *New York Times,* April 29, 1944.

118 "bronzed and obviously": *New York Times,* April 29, 1944.

118 "After a restful four weeks": Leahy, *I Was There,* 237.

119 sixty thousand tons: *New York Times Week in Review,* April 30, 1944.

119 The report on the 771 bombers: Map Room File, FDRL. See War Department briefing for April 30, 1944.

120 "Don't let the boys": in Francis Biddle, *In Brief Authority,* 320–21.

120 "Tanned, refreshed": *New York Times,* May 8, 1944.

120 "brown as a berry": Hassett, *Off the Record with FDR,* 241.

120 "much snappier": Stimson diary, May 17, 1944.

120 brought back a rumor: Jonathan Daniels, *White House Witness,* 223.

121 "Under his tan": *CC,* May 4, 1944, 294.

122 "I can't live out": Jim Bishop scrapbook, 10. The author's notes for his book *FDR's Last Year* are archived at St. Bonaventure University. The typed notes on his interview with Anna were remounted in a scrapbook, as was much of his material, apparently for his convenience in composition. The page with this quotation is marked with the number "57." Neither the approximate date nor the context of the remark is made clear in the notes.

122 "I am really practically": Roosevelt to Churchill, May 20, 1944, in *C&R,* 3:139.

122 "Bill, I just hate to run": Leahy diary, May 15, 1944, 37.

123 "lack of interest": Flynn, *You're the Boss,* 179.

123 no evidence that she tried: Lash, *Eleanor and Franklin,* 708.

123 "All of us knew": Eleanor Roosevelt, *This I Remember,* 329.

123 "I haven't even decided": *CC,* May 22, 1944, 301–2.

124 "I don't think it will be": Rosenman to Roosevelt, PSF, box 140.

124 "It seemed that he had": Ickes diary, May 20, 1944.

124 "Here we are": *CC,* June 20, 1944, 311.

CHAPTER 5 GOING AFTER "BIGGER COINS"

126 "that this is the time": Roosevelt to Churchill, May 18, 1944, in *C&R,* 3:134.

126 "taking into consideration": Stalin to Roosevelt, May 26, 1944, in Butler, *My Dear Mr. Stalin,* 233.

126 "our Allied forces": Buhite and Levy, *FDR's Fireside Chats,* 296.

127 6,483 vessels, including 3,372 landing craft: These numbers look precise, but they vary slightly in the many different histories of the landings, including official histories. The first of these figures was found in Keegan, *Second World War,* 378; the second in Burns, *Soldier of Freedom.*

127 he knew already: Roosevelt press conference no. 954, June 6, 1944, in *PC,* 23.

127 "Rommel asparagus": Hastings, *Overlord,* 64.

127 "He sat up in bed": Goodwin, *No Ordinary Time,* 509.

128 4,649 killed: As in the tallies of ships and landing craft, the counts on D-Day casualties in various reputable histories are not perfectly consistent. This figure comes from Keegan, *Second World War,* 387.

128 "there were men crying, men moaning": Quoted in Atkinson, *Guns at Last Light,* 86; Roosevelt D-Day press conference no. 954, June 6, 1944, in *PC,* 23.

128 "a welder or something": Roosevelt press conference no. 954, June 6, 1944.

128 "struggle to preserve": Text in Rosenman, *Working with Roosevelt,* 434.

128 understated editorial: *Washington Post,* June 7, 1944.

129 "the self-anointed apostle": John O'Donnell column, New York *Daily News,* June 8, 1944.

129 "Every movement": Tully, *FDR, My Boss,* 265.

130 offered his own good offices: Butler, *My Dear Mr. Stalin,* 237.

130 "An independent Poland": Lippmann column, *New York Herald Tribune,* Jan. 25, 1944.

131 "in ten or twenty years": Gannon, *Cardinal Spellman Story,* 223–24.

131 "He said that in view": Stimson diary, March 18, 1944.

131 "in all probability": Harriman Papers, Jan. 29, 1944.

132 "This is entirely German propaganda": Paul, *Katyn,* 317–18. The ambassador with whom Roosevelt was corresponding was George Howard Earle, a special envoy to the Balkans.

132 Mick by some: Davies, *Rising '44,* 37.

132 "ringing condemnation": Mikołajczyk, *Rape of Poland,* 10.

133 "We mustn't forget": Ibid., 59–60.

134 "not allow any petty considerations": Roosevelt to Stalin, personal letter, June 17, 1944, in Butler, *My Dear Mr. Stalin,* 237–38.

134 the only Polish leader: Roosevelt to Stalin, Dec. 29, 1944, in Butler, *My Dear Mr. Stalin,* 289.

134 "made one of the most tasteful": Stimson diary, June 7, 1944.

134 On July 22: See the account in Davies, *God's Playground,* 2:413.

135 "To President Franklin D. Roosevelt": Stalin to Roosevelt, June 7, 1944 (via Harriman), in Butler, *My Dear Mr. Stalin,* 235.

135 "This is the first friendly talk": Harriman to Roosevelt, cable, Map Room File, box 31, FDRL.

135 "In all our dealings": Mikołajczyk, *Rape of Poland.*,60; *CC,* July 3, 1944, 316.

136 "ticklish" affair: Dallek, *Franklin D. Roosevelt and American Foreign Policy,* 440.

136 "Absolutely. Yes.": Press conference no. 951, May 26, 1944, in *PC,* 23.

136 "the highest American quarters": Forrest Davis, "What Really Happened in Teheran," pts. 1 and 2, *Saturday Evening Post,* May 13 and 20, 1944.

137 Azores and Hawaii: Hull, *Memoirs,* 2:1681.

137 "did not want an over-all international organization": Ibid., 1683.

138 taking ownership: Divine, *Second Chance,* 206.

138 "The maintenance of peace": *PPA,* 179–80.

138 couple of secretaries: *CC,* April 3, 1943, and June 4, 1944, 207, 308.

138 with Roosevelt's backing: Warren Kimball attributes the idea to Roosevelt. Woolner, Kimball, and Reynolds, *FDR's World,* 99.

139 "our American veto": Vandenberg, *Private Papers of Senator Vandenberg,* 96.

139 "no less historic": Editorial, *New York Times,* June 17, 1944.

139 "a plan in soft focus": Emmet Crozier commentary, *New York Herald Tribune,* July 18, 1944.

139 "a convenient venue": Woolner, Kimball, and Reynolds, *FDR's World,* 99.

140 "Churchill is the kind": Djilas, *Conversations with Stalin*, 61.

140 "obviously a candidate": Jonathan Daniels, *White House Witness*, 229.

140 "nowhere to go": Atkinson, *Guns at Last Light*, 100–101.

140 "Tobey certainly has not": June 14, 1944, memorandum marked "private" from Roosevelt to James F. Byrnes, PSF, box 168, FDRL. In his autobiography, *All in One Lifetime*, p. 215, Byrnes quotes the memo in full (omitting only Tobey's name), then writes: "I leave it to the reader to judge whether this reply is that of a sick man who has lost his grip on affairs!"

141 "secondary metabolic encephalopathy": See Park, *Impact of Illness on World Leaders*, 227.

141 "My expectation": Ickes diary, May 28, 1944.

141 "I don't know. No one": Ibid., June 24, 1944.

141 "after November": Jonathan Daniels, *White House Witness*, 224.

142 "the men in the White House": Bishop, *FDR's Last Year*, 92.

142 Gallup poll: Richard Norton Smith, *Dewey and His Times*, 421.

142 "apt to disappear": Press conference no. 950, May 16, 1944, Leahy diary entries, May 15–16, 1944.

143 "godfather": Persico, *Franklin and Lucy*, 252.

143 always been a Märtha: Lash, *Eleanor and Franklin*, 677.

143 "never knows when to leave": In an unpublished portion of Margaret Suckley diary, Sept. 25, 1944, in the archive at Wilderstein Preservation, Rhinebeck, N.Y., JE 87.

143 inconvenient evening guest: Roosevelt made two visits to Princess Märtha's rented estate, Pooks Hill, in Maryland in May and June 1944. He also brought her to Hyde Park in mid-June on his special train.

143 "The time from the middle": Bruenn, "Clinical Notes," 584.

143 "I noticed that he sits": *CC*, 311–12. Roosevelt was evidently referring to the tendency of his blood pressure to record its highest levels in the mornings rather than the evenings, the reverse of the normal pattern.

144 "If you want to finish the journey": McIntire, *White House Physician*, 187–88; Paullin to McIntire, June 24, 1946, McIntire Collection, FDRL.

144 "political observers": Walter Trohan column, *Chicago Tribune*, May 28, 1944. Trohan later wrote a memoir in which he tacitly acknowledged that John Boettiger, his old colleague and Roosevelt's son-in-law, was one of his sources. See Trohan, *Political Animals*, 133.

144 release of a memorandum: The document was uncovered after a prodigious pursuit by Dr. Harry Goldsmith, a surgeon, who tracked down Frank Lahey's former business manager Linda Strand, to whom Lahey had bequeathed it for safekeeping. The memorandum passed into the possession of a Boston law firm, Herrick and Smith, as part of a settlement between Mrs. Strand and the Lahey Clinic following Frank Lahey's death. With Harry Goldsmith's encouragement, Mrs. Strand sued to have the memorandum returned to her so she could fulfill her late employer's wishes. This drawn-out and winding sequence of steps is recounted by Dr. Goldsmith in his book *A Conspiracy of Silence*. Goldsmith provides the complete Lahey memorandum, now archived at FDRL. Curiously, the original copy of the document was never returned to Mrs. Strand by Herrick and Smith, although it was ordered by the Massachusetts high court to do so, and Mrs. Strand had been the firm's presumptive client. Mrs. Strand received only a photocopy after the ruling was handed down in 1986.

146 dated "Monday July 10, 1944": Archival records at the Lahey Clinic that I was permitted to inspect confirm that the surgeon traveled by train from Boston to Washington on the previous Friday, returning Saturday evening. In another letter a few
days later, he speaks of spending part of Saturday afternoon with Admiral McIntire.
So there can be little doubt of the memorandum's authenticity, notwithstanding one
conspicuous error in what Dr. Lahey wrote: a reference to Roosevelt's "activities in
his trip to Russia." It seems obvious, in context, that he means the Tehran journey in
November 1943. Roosevelt would not go to Russia until six months after the date on
the Lahey memorandum, when he met Stalin for a second time at Yalta. I consider
this error a mental slip by the surgeon, who was thinking of Roosevelt's principal
interlocutor, not the place. (The only alternative explanation would be that he composed and backdated the memorandum following the president's death. That seems
to me far-fetched.) All in all, the document says little for the clarity of Lahey's prose.

146 "I have never voted for you": The words attributed to Dr. Lahey can be found in the
manuscript of an unpublished, never completed history of the Lahey Clinic by Dr.
David Boyd, a noted cardiovascular surgeon who died in 1989. The manuscript, preserved in the clinic's archive, contains a passage from a privately published history of
a country club on Lake Winnipesaukee in New Hampshire, to which Frank Lahey
belonged, the Bald Peak Colony Club, relating a conversation between a man called
Howard and the president. Lahey, who was known by his middle name, Howard,
was the obvious source.

146 "Dear Ross": Letters in the archive of the Lahey Clinic.

146 "that his chances": McIntire, *White House Physician*, 194.

147 "He is, I *think*, rather uncertain in his mind": *CC*, July 5, 1944, 317.

148 "No sons of Iowa farmers": Quoted in Pogue, *Organizer of Victory*, 400.

148 "It was by light touches": Quoted in Black, *Champion of Freedom*, 958.

148 "President" of the Provisional Government: Leahy diary, July 6, 1944.

149 "I still found": Halsted Papers, box 84.

150 "I know one should be proud": Anna Roosevelt Halsted papers, box 70.

CHAPTER 6   THE GREAT TANTALIZER

151 "I think you ought": Wallace diary, March 13, 1944, 3198.

151 "a quart of milk": Ibid., 2267. Wallace attributes the remark to the president of the
National Association of Manufacturers and denies he ever said anything of the kind.

152 "Never has one man": Macdonald, *Henry Wallace*, 102.

152 "I think people": Wallace diary, 3.

153 "passion for manipulation": Biddle, *In Brief Authority*, 364.

153 out of touch: Wallace diary, May 18, 1944, 3331.

153 "that I would like to have him": Rosenman, *Working with Roosevelt*, 440. In 1940,
Roosevelt had threatened to withdraw as head of the ticket if he could not have his
chosen running mate, Wallace.

153 "I have no interest": Ibid., 441.

154 "You are not nominating": Pauley to Jonathan Daniels, memorandum, White House
Confidential Files, box 30, Truman Library.

154 "that almost any minute": Pauley, "Life and Times," chap. 2, p. 14.

154 more of a paper trail: In addition to the two previous documents, there are separate

oral histories at Truman Library and Columbia University, the latter conducted by the historian Allan Nevins, who found him "transparently candid."

155 "great tantalizer": Pauley, "Life and Times," chap. 2, p. 20.

155 detective story: *CC,* June 25, 1944, 323.

155 "sincere in wanting me": Byrnes, *All in One Lifetime,* 221.

155 Ickes recorded their comments: Ickes diary, June 2, 1944, 8948, also June 4, 1944, 8958.

156 "worse than Don Quixote": Cited in Bruce Allen Murphy, *Wild Bill,* 218. The quotation is from Corcoran's unpublished memoir in the Thomas G. Corcoran Papers, LOC.

156 "The President had his eye on him": Sherwood, *Roosevelt and Hopkins,* 882. It's not clear how Hopkins, who was absent from the White House for the first half of 1944, would have known this. Possibly the observation is based on a conversation after the selection was made. Hopkins also claimed to be "certain the president made up his mind on Truman months before the convention." Cited by Margaret Truman, *Harry S. Truman,* 190, originally in Sherwood notes on file at Houghton Library, Harvard.

156 "I doubt if there are a half dozen senators": Cited by Ferrell, *Choosing Truman,* 17. From an interview Truman gave during his brief time as vice president, on file in the Truman Library.

156 "original idea": Flynn, *You're the Boss,* 183.

156 chairman couldn't believe: Ibid., 181.

156 "Roosevelt would seldom express": Walker, *FDR's Quiet Confidant,* 152. Subsequent Walker quotation is also on p. 152.

157 "Franklin says I must": Lash, *Eleanor and Franklin,* 708.

157 Hannegan and Ellis Arnall: Hannegan spoke of Roosevelt's thoughts about resignation in an interview with Robert Sherwood in the Sherwood Papers. The reference to Arnall can be traced through the diary of Henry Morgenthau, who writes that Steve Early, White House press secretary, said "the Georgia governor spoke of it to newspapermen. Steve said that if that got around it would be terrible." See Blum, *Years of War,* 280.

158 "Long have I been aware": Cited by Culver and Hyde, *American Dreamer,* 135.

158 nominated Roerich for the Nobel: Ibid., 141.

158 They weren't used then: Some of the letters were to Frances Grant, an American woman who ran the Roerich Institute in New York. Told about these during the 1940 campaign, the president is said to have asked whether the relationship was purely spiritual. "We can handle sex, but we can't handle religion," he supposedly joked. Quoted in ibid., 232.

158 "Oh, you are talking": Cited by Ferrell, *Choosing Truman,* 20, from a 1948 entry in the diary of Max Lowenthal, recounting a conversation with Philip Murray, president of the CIO. Lowenthal is described as a friend of Truman's. His diary is in the University of Minnesota Archive.

159 "Three simultaneous presidents": Roosevelt to James L. Rowe, Feb. 15, 1941, PSF, FDRL.

159 "Those who were around": Sherwood, *Roosevelt and Hopkins* 741.

159 "essentially pragmatic": Davis, "What Really Happened at Tehran," May 20, 1944.

159 "on very high authority": Wallace diary, May 11, 1944, 3330.

160 "the Soviet Union would be": Ibid., March 20, 1944, 3222.

160 "I'm as sure of this as anyone": Wallace to Roosevelt, Aug. 29, 1941, PSF, box 170, FDRL.

161 "That was my cue": Bush, *Pieces of the Action,* 292.

161 Byrnes in: The July 12 entry in the diary of Admiral Leahy says Hopkins told him this. In fact, the previous evening, in a White House meeting with Democratic leaders, Roosevelt appeared to come close to eliminating Byrnes from consideration.

161 actually a long shot: Between the Hopkins breakfast on July 6 and the Rosenberg appointment, the president had a conversation with Ed Flynn, who was strongly opposed to Byrnes. Rosenberg filled Byrnes in on her talk. Byrnes, *All in One Lifetime,* 221.

162 "If I were a delegate": Wallace diary, July 10, 1944, 3364.

162 "As I shook hands": Ibid., July 10–13, 1944, 3373.

162 "You are the best": Byrnes, *All in One Lifetime,* 222.

162 "A simple pattern": Freidel, *Rendezvous with Destiny,* 531.

162 "Think of the cat-calls and jeers": Wallace diary, July 10–14, 1944, 3365.

163 "Even though they do": Ibid., 3373.

163 vice president's loyalty: Byrnes, *All in One Lifetime,* 222.

163 counting on it: This suggestion is made by Ferrell, *Choosing Truman,* 32.

164 "The quesiton of": Lippmann column, *New York Herald Tribune,* July 11, 1944. According to Pauley, the Democratic National Committee distributed the column at the convention before voting on the vice presidential nomination began, even though it plainly implied that the head of the ticket was a goner.

164 assassination attempt: He was referring to the incident in Miami shortly before his first inaugural in which the mayor of Chicago, Anton Cermak, was killed by a gunman aiming at the president-elect. The summary of the dinner conversation is based on Pauley, "Life and Times," chapter 2, 40.

164 "All that is within me": The texts of the Hannegan and Roosevelt letters were read out by the president at his 961st press conference, July 11, 1944, available online at the FDRL Web site or in PC, 24: 21–25. Steinbeck's role is detailed by Cliff Lewis in "Steinbeck: The Artist as FDR Speechwriter," in Britch and Lewis, *Rediscovering Steinbeck,* 199.

165 "Is that news?": Quoted in Berlin, *Washington Despatches,* 385.

165 left the church: Roosevelt saw Spellman in June 1944, but the conversation about Byrnes, as he recounted it, seems to have taken place four years earlier before the 1940 convention when the "assistant president," then a senator, was also under consideration. According to Jonathan Daniels in *White House Witness,* 232, "Spellman denied that he had given FDR any such advice."

165 "with a wave and a laugh": The summary of Roosevelt's various remarks is based on Pauley, "Life and Times," chap. 2, pp. 43–48.

166 "Bill Douglas has a nice": In the Pauley account, Truman Library. See also Robert H. Ferrell, *Choosing Truman,* 13.

166 Each then believed: Flynn, *You're the Boss,* 181.

166 "Boys, I guess": Walker, *FDR's Quiet Confidant,* 140. In another variant, Roosevelt is quoted as saying to Hannegan, "Bob, I think you and everyone else here want Truman." Ted Morgan, *FDR,* 728. That version leaves his own stand less certain.

167 "Bob, I think Truman": David McCullough in his biography, *Truman,* says "several accounts" tell of this note (301). He doesn't, however, offer documentation in his notes.

167 "part of the game": Walker, *FDR's Quiet Confidant,* 142. It's unclear whether Walker is quoting or paraphrasing Roosevelt.

167 not a good politician: Lash, *Eleanor and Franklin*, 708.

168 "hurt, angry": Walker, *FDR's Quiet Confidant*, 142.

168 "I would like to know": Byrnes, *All in One Lifetime*, 222.

168 "Mr. President": Ferrell, *Choosing Truman*, 30, based on a "log" or journal kept by a Byrnes aide, Walter J. Brown, in the James F. Byrnes Papers, Clemson University.

169 "I can't call the President a liar": Ferrell, *Choosing Truman*, 32.

169 Jim Bishop: Bishop, *FDR's Last Year*, 101–3. The redoubtable Robert Ferrell points out the discrepancy between Bishop's account and the official White House log in *Choosing Truman*, 108.

169 "We have to be damned": Byrnes, *All in One Lifetime*, 224.

170 Hannegan had her reverse: Tully, *FDR, My Boss*, 275–76.

170 the chairman's son: Interview with Bill Hannegan by the former senator Thomas F. Eagleton and Diane L. Duffor for their article, "Bob Hannegan and Harry Truman's Vice Presidential Nomination," *Missouri Historical Review*, April 1996, esp. 275–78.

171 "I am of the opinion": Letter to a constituent dated March 21, 1942, Truman Library.

171 "Well, you know Jimmy": Byrnes, *All in One Lifetime*, 226. See also Ferrell, *Choosing Truman*, 38.

172 "The Communists are now": Cited in Morgan, *FDR*, 708. Late in the campaign, a cartoon in the *Chicago Tribune* portrayed Hillman with a hammer and sickle emblazoned across his chest.

172 "political liability": Quoted in Robertson, *Sly and Able*, 358. Author is depending on the Walter J. Brown "log."

172 "go all out for Truman": Walker, *FDR's Quiet Confidant*, 146.

173 "Well, tell him": In Ferrell, *Choosing Truman*, 61–62, based on Pauley account. "Oh shit" is in McCullough, *Truman*, 314; "Jesus Christ" in Ferrell, *Choosing Truman*, 61.

173 "I don't know": Quoted by Goodwin, *No Ordinary Time*, 528.

174 "in deference": Robertson, *Sly and Able*, 361.

174 "Father turned suddenly": Roosevelt and Shalett, *Affectionately, F.D.R.*, 315. Roosevelt's daughter, Anna (who was not on the train), casts doubt on her brother's account in this ghostwritten memoir in her oral history interview archived at Columbia University. James Roosevelt tells the story as if he and his father were alone on the Pullman car. That was never supposed to happen. There were always two porters, and the Secret Service would have had an agent on duty nearby. Arthur Prettyman, his valet and a Filipino navy steward, would also have been present. If father and son were alone in the president's small sleeping compartment with the door shut, it would have been difficult for him to perform the physical maneuvers James describes. Their reluctance to summon medical help is easier to explain. Given that there were three news agency reporters on the train, the president's absence from the military exercise being held for his benefit on the day he was to be renominated might have been a story too big to keep under wraps, the "voluntary" censorship regime notwithstanding. The footage of the president watching the exercise is available at the FDRL. Competing with footage from the convention and actual war fronts, it appears never to have been used in newsreels shown to the public.

175 "the collywobbles": Ibid.

175 "in the usual partisan, political sense": From one July 11 letter to Robert Hannegan read out on that date to a White House press conference, *PPA*, 197.

176 "the greatest master": *Chicago Tribune*, July 16, 1944.

176 racing like a Thoroughbred: cartoon in the *Chicago Tribune*, July 16, 1944.

176 "In these days": *PPA*, 202.

176 refrained from standing: Daniels, *White House Witness*, 239.

176 newsreel footage: Taken at the same time, July 25, 1944, newsreel can be found at Alexander Street Archives on the following link: http://search.alexanderstreet.com /view/work/1789807. For an August 10, 1944, newsreel, visit www.aparchive.com and search "Roosevelt Stands for 4th Term."

178 banished an AP photographer: See Goodwin's richly detailed account, *No Ordinary Time*, 530.

178 cropped out: The full photograph is reproduced in Ward and Burns, *Roosevelts*, 433.

178 Walter Trohan: His report was published on page 3 of the *Chicago Tribune*, Aug. 5, 1944.

179 "The knockout blow": Littell, *My Roosevelt Years*, 259.

179 "This should be said": Quoted in Richard Norton Smith, *Dewey and His Times*, 417.

179 "Like so many others": Drury, *Senate Journal*, 220.

180 "You made a grand fight": Culver and Hyde, *American Dreamer*, 367.

CHAPTER 7   COMMANDER IN CHIEF

182 "localize" knowledge: Log of the president's inspection trip to the Pacific, 15, Tully Papers, box 7.

182 "delayed": *New York Times*, Aug. 11, 1944.

182 "a modern marvel": *PPA*, Aug. 12, 1944, Bremerton Speech, 219.

182 "a political picture-taking junket": Manchester, *American Caesar*, 364.

183 "If this system,": Pogue, *Organizer of Victory*, 445–46.

184 to send him packing: In a letter dated March 20, 1951, to the Republican leader in the House of Representatives, Joseph W. Martin, MacArthur supported the idea of helping Chinese Nationalist forces cross the Taiwan Strait, thus widening the Korean War. "There is no substitute for victory," he wrote. Manchester, *American Caesar*, 639.

184 "a huge stallion": Ibid., 152.

184 a few "Franklin"s: The familiar address reported both by Forrest C. Pogue in his biography of George Marshall (p. 452) and by a naval historian, E. B. Potter, in his biography of Chester Nimitz, *Nimitz*, 317. The admiral is the likely source.

184 "If the war": Manchester, *American Caesar*, 366.

184 "the overwhelming favorite": MacArthur, *Reminiscences*, 199.

185 "I do not want command": Pogue, *Organizer of Victory*, 440–41.

186 "register most complete resentment": Manchester, *American Caesar*, 369.

186 "at his best": Leahy, *I Was There*, 257.

186 "to take Luzon": Adams, *Witness to Power*, 254.

187 "Someday there will be": Manchester, *American Caesar*, 379.

187 "We've sold it!": Potter, 319.

187 "the President is a man": Manchester, *American Caesar*, 370.

187 "The mark of death": Ibid., 368.

187 "electrify the world": MacArthur, *Reminiscences*, 217–18.

188 "The celerity of movement": Ibid., 249.

188 "smoothed the way": Stimson diary, Aug. 23, 1944, 3.

188 being canceled: Adams, *Witness to Power*, 255.

188 "He had known": Rosenman, *Working with Roosevelt*, 458–59.

189 "It sounds like a little bit": Roosevelt press conference no. 962, July 29, 1944, in *PC*, 24:35.

189 "I look forward": Adams, *Witness to Power*, 256.

189 twenty-eight enemy troops: Dear and Foot, *Oxford Companion to World War II*, 27.

190 "From these islands": Log of trip to the Pacific, 32, Tully Papers.

190 "unknown and unknowable": Ward, *First-Class Temperament*, 712.

191 half the income: Roosevelt's son James put his name to two ghosted memoirs. In the second of these, he says his father deliberately left the will unchanged after Missy's death, even though the provision wouldn't apply, saying, "If it embarrasses mother, I'm sorry. It shouldn't, but it may." James Roosevelt, *My Parents*, 108. In an interview, James Roosevelt subsequently told Doris Kearns Goodwin that the provision in the will for Missy would have had the effect of cutting out Roosevelt's five children as beneficiaries. *No Ordinary Time*, 246, also 668.

191 six-day fishing excursion: Roosevelt to LeHand, Aug. 11, 1943, Franklin D. Roosevelt Papers, subseries 3, Tully Papers, box 11.

192 "Yes, poor Missy": Asbell, *FDR Memoirs*, 404, also 263–65. Also Goodwin, *No Ordinary Time*, 534–35.

193 largely razed: See Kershaw, *Hitler 1936–1945*, 717.

193 "This seems to me": Churchill radiograms of July 29 and Aug. 10, in *C&R*, 3:262–69. Once again, "U.J." stands for "Uncle Joe."

194 "These men are bloated with power": Harriman and Abel, *Special Envoy*, 341.

194 "over our inability": Roosevelt to Churchill, Sept. 5, 1944, *C&R*, 3:313.

195 "Though he held the strongest": Davies, *Rising '44*, 628.

195 "There can be no real": George Orwell, "As I Please," *Tribune*, Sept. 1, 1944, reprinted as appendix to *Rising '44*, 671–73.

195 "the outcome in Poland": Bohlen, *Witness to History*, 168–69.

196 "The speech had nothing to say": Rosenman, *Working with Roosevelt*, 461.

196 "May I point out": Early to Roosevelt, Aug. 10, 1944, radiogram, Early Papers.

198 "substernal oppression": Bruenn, "Clinical Notes," 586. Geoffrey Ward quotes Bruenn as saying Roosevelt said he had "one hell of a pain in my chest that lasted half an hour," *CC*, 321. In his published article, he said fifteen minutes.

198 "This was the first time": Interview with Dr. Howard Bruenn, *Navy Medicine*, March–April 1990.

198 "It scared the hell out of us": *CC*, 321. After publication of his article in a medical journal, Bruenn had at least seven interviews with writers; see note, p. 357.

198 "in fine spirits": Hassett, *Off the Record with FDR*, 264.

198 "in better physical form": Stimson diary, Aug. 23, 1944, 2.

199 "the old master": In a note by Rosenman in *PPA*, 228.

199 campaign portrait: The photograph can be seen online at the Web site of the FDRL by going to an interactive feature, FDR Day-by-Day. The calendar takes the viewer to specific days. At Aug. 20, 1944, you find the portrait taken by a Philadelphia portrait photographer, Leon Perskie.

199 "I really was shocked": Blum, *Years of War*, 347.

199 "His face in repose": Mary Bingham in a Sept. 4, 1944, letter to her husband, cited by Freidel in *A Rendezvous with Destiny*, 741, is in the Bingham Papers at the Radcliffe Institute's Schlesinger Library.

199 two or three times: Margaret Truman in her biography of her father, *Harry S. Truman*, 203, says he saw Roosevelt only twice, on Aug. 18 and Sept. 6. But the White House log records his presence at a second lunch on Sept. 9.

199 "a haggard old man": McCullough, *Truman*, 327.

200 "One of us has to stay alive": Margaret Truman, *Harry S. Truman*, 203.

201 valedictorian: Ibid., 246.

201 possible source: Other sources could have been the newspapermen with whom Georgia's governor, Ellis Arnall, had an off-the-record conversation in July. The rumor had been in circulation all year since Florida's senator Claude Pepper first mentioned it. In each case, it was traceable to Roosevelt himself.

201 "I told him": Lahey to McIntire, Sept. 12, 1944, McIntire Papers, FDRL.

201 "brilliant presage of total victory": *PPA*, 241.

202 "Do you think I will": Bush, *Pieces of the Action*, 277.

203 "worried him to death": Rhodes, *The Making of the Atomic Bomb*, 516.

203 "startled": Ibid., 538.

203 Churchill had a veto: Bernstein, *Atomic Bomb*, 98.

203 with his son Aage: Rhodes, *Making of the Atomic Bomb*, 536.

204 own intelligence reports: See Bird and Sherwin, *American Prometheus*, 286.

204 alerted for a year: Bernstein, *Atomic Bomb*, 99, 156.

205 "FDR had only fleeting": Hershberg, *James B. Conant*, 207.

205 "The better I get to know": Quoted in Roberts, *Masters and Commanders*, 463.

205 "Bohr ought to be confined": Rhodes, *Making of the Atomic Bomb*, 537–38.

205 "the prophetic voice": Burns, *Soldier of Freedom*, 459.

206 "Nuclear fission": Rhodes, *Making of the Atomic Bomb*, 538.

207 "If you still press": Cited here are Churchill messages of June 28, 1944, and July 1, 1944, and Roosevelt message of July 1, in *C&R*, 3:219–24.

207 "most passionate": Reynolds, *In Command of History*, 449.

207 "Winston is very bitter": Sir Alan Lascelles, cited in Roberts, *Masters and Commanders*, 500.

207 "wanting to fight": Bryant, *Triumph in the West*, 168.

207 "If we take this lying down": Roberts, *Masters and Commanders*, 501.

207 "I appreciate deeply": Roosevelt message of July 1, 1944, in *C&R*, 3:232.

207 "The Americans now begin": Brooke in Bryant, *Triumph in the West*, 168.

207 he didn't hear a shot: Moran, *Churchill*, 180.

208 "She came on the train": *CC*, 323.

208 "frame-up": Bryant, *Triumph in the West*, 202.

209 "No sooner offered": Adams, *Witness to Power*, 258; Potter, 324; Dear and Foot, *Oxford Companion to World War II*, 829.

210 "70 million shepherds": Black, *Champion of Freedom*, 988.

210 "A Program to Prevent": Cited in Morgan, *FDR*, 734.

210 "Semitism gone wild": Stimson diary cited by ibid., 235.

210 "Germany should be allowed": Blum, *Years of War*, 352.

210 "The English people": Moran, *Churchill*, 190.

210 "I have never had": Blum, *Years of War*, 369.

211 added to, revised, and rewritten: See discussion in Reynolds, *Command of History*, 372, 520–22.

211 "wonder how far": Moran, *Churchill*, 192.

211 "in flowery language": Colville, *Fringes of Power*, 514.

212 "I sat on the President's": In Bryant, *Triumph in the West*, 204.

212 "stress the President's age": McIntire, *White House Physician*, 204.

CHAPTER 8   STAYING ON THE JOB

213 "like a boiled owl": *CC*, Sept. 4 and 6, 1944, 325.

213 "He just doesn't seem": Sherwood, *Roosevelt and Hopkins*, 820–21.

213 "Fourth-termites": Richard Norton Smith, *Dewey and His Times*, 404, 410.

214 "all a speaker": Richard Strout in the *New Republic*, also *TRB: Views and Perspectives*, cited by Weintraub, *Final Victory*, 126.

214 "You ought to hear him": Sherwood, *Roosevelt and Hopkins*, 821.

214 "defeatist" attitude: Roosevelt press conference no. 969, Sept. 22, 1944, in *PC*, 24:122.

214 "scraps": Ibid., 125.

215 "Don't leave the task": *PPA*, 286.

215 "my little dog, Fala": Ibid., 290.

215 ladle against a silver tray: Richard Norton Smith, *Dewey and His Times*, 421.

216 "a return to the best": Berlin, *Washington Despatches*, 427.

216 "much gusto": *C&R*, 3:341.

216 "It was a speech": Dewey text, *New York Times*, Sept. 26, 1944.

218 "I am deeply convinced": Dewey text, *New York Times*, Sept. 9, 1944.

219 "took pains": Richard Norton Smith, *Dewey and His Times*, 427. For treatment of Marshall's approach, see pp. 425–30 in that volume, also Pogue, *Organizer of Victory*, 471–73.

220 "After sixty-three days": Dispatch by Sydney Gruson from London, *New York Times*, Oct. 4, 1944.

220 "the bulk of our business": *C&R*, 3:343.

220 "I wish you every success": Ibid.

221 "relieved when Hopkins": First draft of Charles E. Bohlen's memoir, 263, LOC.

222 "You, naturally, understand": Butler, *My Dear Mr. Stalin*, 263.

222 "complete freedom of action": Harriman and Abel, *Special Envoy*, 353.

222 "so directly related": *C&R*, 3:344. The passage goes on to say that it matters to opinion in Britain and all the United Nations, but the emphasis, with the election looming, is really on U.S. opinion.

222 "set a good example": Roosevelt press conference no. 971, Oct. 3, 1944, in *PC*, 24:152.

223 "the results of the private": *New York Times*, Oct. 8, 1944.

224 "Communism does not fit the Poles": Mikołajczyk, *Rape of Poland*, 100.

225 "I wash my hands of this": Ibid., 98; see also Harriman and Abel, 360.

225 "felt helpless to do anything": Harriman and Abel, *Special Envoy*, 366.

225 "The President does a lot": Ibid., 372.

226 flattering profile: *Life*, July 31, 1944.

226 "sweated blood": Richard Norton Smith, *Dewey and His Times*, 432.

226 "Let's not be squeamish": New York *Sun*, Oct. 13, 1944.

226 "In view of Mr. Roosevelt's": *Chicago Tribune*, Oct. 28, 1944.

227 "a complete disregard": Bruenn, "Clinical Notes," 587.

227 "I know more about": Roosevelt press conference no. 973, Oct. 17, 1944, in *PC*, 24:181.

227 "the most spectacular campaign": Freidel, *Franklin Roosevelt*, 563.

227 "It looks like rain": Roosevelt press conference no. 974, Oct. 20, 1944, in *PC*, 24:187.

227 The Democratic chairman: Nasaw, *Patriarch*, 574–76.

228 "best smile": Hassett, *Off the Record with FDR*, 279.

229 some later writers: For instance, the historian Robert Ferrell in *The Dying President* and the popular columnist Jim Bishop in *FDR's Last Year*.

229 "The President has sought": *Herald Tribune*, Oct. 29, 1944.

230 "He smoked only two": *Time*, Oct. 30, 1944.

230 "we are fighting with": *PAA*, 4:344. Rosenman, in *Working with Roosevelt*, 362, relates how the president insisted on retaining a passage on Russia in the text his aides wanted to remove.

231 "again and again and again": Ibid., 399.

233 "undercut" Stilwell: Bland, *Marshall Interviews and Reminiscences*, 375.

233 "adopted the tone": Tuchman, *Stilwell and the American Experience in China*, 629.

234 "I handed this bundle": Stilwell, *Stilwell Papers*, 305.

234 "most severe humiliation": Bernstein, *Atomic Bomb*, 45.

234 "just one of them things": Roosevelt press conference no. 977, Oct. 31, 1944, in *PC*, 24:205.

234 "to assume responsibility": Pogue, *Organizer of Victory*, 479.

235 "bloodlands": I use Timothy Snyder's term here.

235 "a world of awakened peoples": In Boston, Nov. 4, 1944, *PPA*, 4:406.

236 "I am in the middle": Quotations in this paragraph are meant to serve as a collage of his campaign themes. They can be found in *PPA*, 361, 369, 384–87, 399.

236 "without serious support": Stalin's speech was reprinted in *New York Times*, Nov. 7, 1944.

237 "It looks like I will": *PPA*, 414.

238 "Enable us to grant": Ibid., 412. The bishop was Angus Dun of the Washington, D.C., diocese.

238 "I still think": Hassett, *Off the Record with FDR*, 294.

238 "fourscore years": Ibid., 295.

239 "the outstanding symbol": Entries for Nov. 10, 1944, are held in the Oral History Collection at Columbia University's Butler Library, 3518–21.

240 "May I be the first": Roosevelt press conference no. 979, Nov. 10, 1944, in *PC*, 24:221.

CHAPTER 9   GALLANT, AND PITIABLE

241 "We shook hands": *CC*, 229.

241 end of November: Harriman Papers, box 175.

242 doctor's orders: *FRUS: Yalta*, 4. Harriman to President, Sept. 24, 1944, cited by Dobbs, *Six Months in 1945*, 33.

242 "I am still hoping": Roosevelt to Harriman, Dec. 6, 1944, PSF, box 20, FDRL.

242 "dysentery and Bubonic plague": Harriman and Abel, *Special Envoy*, 368.

242 "I can, under difficulties": Roosevelt to Stalin, Nov. 18, 1944, in Butler, *My Dear Mr. Stalin*, 267.

244 "I should be where you are": Hull, *Memoirs*, 2:1715–21.

244 "Of course I want you": Ickes diary, Dec. 12, 1944.

244 "absolutely" wanted: Stimson diary, Dec. 12, 1944.

244 "It goes without saying": Roosevelt to Winant, Dec. 3, 1944, PSF, box 20, FDRL.

244 "you can't go now": Perkins, *Roosevelt I Knew*, 377.

244 "a decent man": Bohlen, *Witness to History*, 173.

244 "a nice enough lad": Freidel, *Rendezvous With Destiny*, 569.

244 "a good clerk": Roll, *Hopkins Touch*, 351.

244 "perhaps greater than": Quoted in ibid., 348.

244 "becoming frightening": Ickes diary, Dec. 9, 1944, 9390.

244 Hopkins told Harriman: Harriman and Abel, *Special Envoy*, 372.

244 "too independent": Quoted in George McJimsey, *Harry Hopkins: Ally of the Poor and Defender of Democracy* (Cambridge, Mass., 1987), 347. The source is not clearly stated there. See the similar quotation in Robertson, *Sly and Able*, 379.

245 "remarkable occurrence": CC, 346.

245 occasionally by phone: Secretaries Stettinius and Stimson were reached by phone in his Warm Springs stay. See Stimson diary, Nov. 30, 1944, 61.

246 "another manifestation of insensitivity": Hassett diary, in *Off the Record with FDR*, 305.

246 "The more I see the Pres.": CC, 364.

246 "We suppressed all the pictures": Hassett diary, 302. Bette Davis's presence is mentioned by Theo Lippman Jr. in *The Squire of Warm Springs*, 14.

247 "I feel very badly": CC, 358.

247 "I try so hard": Ibid., 348.

247 "literally weeping": Ibid., 353.

247 "the most fascinating hour": Interview with Anna Roosevelt Halsted, formerly Anna Boettiger, in Asbell, *FDR Memoirs*, 413.

248 *"that his muscles are deteriorating"*: CC, 363.

248 "general condition": Bruenn, "Clinical Notes," 587.

249 "He thinks he can": CC, 355.

249 "Old Dealers": Hassett diary, 304–5. Term may be Hassett's rather than Roosevelt's.

249 "I can hardly see": Quotations from Eleanor's letters are in Lash, *Franklin and Eleanor*, 713.

249 "I had forgotten": Eleanor Roosevelt, *This I Remember*, 343, cited by Lash in *Franklin and Eleanor*, 716.

250 "sure such things": Various quotations from Churchill letters are in *C&R* on air traffic issue, 3:419–24, on Italy, 3:437–39.

250 "completely and utterly useless": Montgomery in correspondence with Brooke, who doesn't take issue, quoted by Atkinson, *Guns at Last Light*, 383.

250 "We have completely failed": Churchill to Roosevelt, Dec. 6, 1944, in *C&R*, 3:434–36.

252 "The dwindling of the British Army": Quoted by Atkinson, *Guns at Last Light*, 407.

252 "I cannot tell you": Churchill to Roosevelt, Dec. 3, 1944, in *C&R*, 3:429.

253 "which would render our discussions": Roosevelt to Stalin, Dec. 16, 1944, in Butler, *My Dear Mr. Stalin*, 215. See also *FRUS: Yalta*, 214–23.

254 none were asked: PC, Jan. 2, 1945, no. 986, 24:259–71.

254 Malmédy massacre: See Atkinson, *Guns at Last Light*, 422–23. In all, just under twenty thousand Americans were killed in the Battle of the Bulge, twenty-three thousand taken prisoner.

254 "it will only make our troops": Quoted in Stimson diary, Dec. 31, 1944, 144.

254 moved his headquarters: Kershaw, *Hitler, 1936–45*, 742.

254 OSS report: PSF, box 151, FDRL.

255 beseech him to receive: Roosevelt to Stalin, Dec. 23, 1944, in Butler, *My Dear Mr. Stalin*, 277.

255 "You may rest assured": Pogue, *Organizer of Victory*, 504.

255 "Roosevelt didn't send a word": Ibid., 486.

255 "General Eisenhower has faced": *PPA*, 508.

255 "agitation": Stimson diary, Dec. 31, 1944.

256 "from looking pretty well": Frances Perkins Oral History at Columbia University. Cited by Goodwin, *No Ordinary Time*, 570.

256 "To me the President": Hassett diary, 307.

256 "He can *not* keep up": *CC*, Dec. 15 and 19, 1944, 362, 367.

256 "I don't think we're scared": Ickes diary, Dec. 24, 1944, touching on Dec. 22 cabinet meeting. See also Bishop, *FDR's Last Year*, 301.

256 "asked a good many": Stettinius diary, 209.

257 "disturbed and deeply disappointed": Roosevelt to Stalin, Dec. 29, 1944, in Butler, *My Dear Mr. Stalin*, 282.

257 "The key to many": Anne O'Hare McCormick, Abroad column, *New York Times*, June 26, 1944.

257 "The President still feels": Averell Harriman, "Memorandum of Conversations with the President," marked "Secret and Personal," 8, Harriman Papers.

258 "a first-class politician": Harriman Papers, box 175, dated Oct. 17, 1944.

258 "powerless to fulfill your wish": Stalin to Roosevelt, Jan. 1, 1945, in Butler, *My Dear Mr. Stalin*, 284.

258 "I told him": Stimson diary, Dec. 31, 1944, 143.

259 Gestures to those closest: Bishop, *FDR's Last Year*, 332; Goodwin, *No Ordinary Time*, 517.

259 "something you ought to write": Jonathan Daniels, *White House Witness*, 220.

259 "small memorial": Goodwin cites Rosenman as saying Roosevelt thought it might be situated at the intersection of Constitution and Independence Avenues. *No Ordinary Time*, 517.

259 family ring: Freidel, *Rendezvous with Destiny*, 574.

259 Harry Setaro: *CC*, 369–78.

260 "a buck dance": Ibid., 371.

260 "It seemed to me": Stettinius, *Roosevelt and the Russians*, 73.

260 "using all the tact": Anna to John Boettiger, Feb. 5, 1945, Yalta, Boettiger Papers, Halsted Papers, box 6.

260 "I couldn't go ahead": Stimson diary, Nov. 21, 1944, 39. Eventually, after lunch, the secretary got to make his report. Stimson Papers.

261 "it would only add": Lash, *Franklin and Eleanor*, p. 716.

261 "I'm not really happy: Ibid.

261 "No. Who is there here to parade?": Press conference no. 980, Nov. 14, 1944, *PC*, 24:231.

263 "He looks exactly as my husband looked": Frances Perkins oral history at Columbia University, cited by Goodwin, *No Ordinary Time*, 573.

263 "clear and emphatic": *New York Times*, Jan. 21, 1945.

263 "His whole body shook": Wallace diary, Jan. 20, 1945, 3623–33. Jim Bishop, *FDR's Last Year*, 356, asserts that Roosevelt was having an angina attack similar to the one he'd experienced in the Bremerton shipyard five months earlier. He offers no source

or basis for this conclusion; neither do his notes in the archive at St. Bonaventure University. James Roosevelt, in the first of two ghostwritten memoirs, claims his father had an attack similar to the one he'd had near Camp Pendleton the previous July, which was presumed by father and son to have been intestinal. Dr. Bruenn, who was candid about the Bremerton episode, never mentioned a seizure at the inauguration in his "Clinical Notes" or printed interviews.

263 "You will understand": Inaugural speech, Jan. 20, 1945, in *PPA*, 523–25.
264 "Jimmy, I can't take this": Roosevelt and Shalett, *Affectionately, F.D.R.* 318.
265 "His condition had": Bohlen, *Witness to History*, 178.
265 "slept rather poorly": Bruenn, "Clinical Notes," 588.

CHAPTER 10   AT THE CZAR'S PALACE

266 "We are having to watch": Anna to John Boettiger, Feb. 5, 1945, John Boettiger Papers, box 6. It's not certain that all Anna's letters to her then husband, John Boettiger, were saved and preserved in the archive. Later, in an oral history, recorded as part of Columbia University's project in 1975, shortly before her death, Mrs. Halsted, as she'd then become following her third marriage, maintained she'd "never heard him [Dr. Bruenn] discuss father's health at all, so I had absolutely no idea." (Page 39 of the transcript at Columbia.)

268 view of the scholars: Studies by Diane Shaver Clemens, S. M. Plokhy, Fraser J. Harbutt, David Reynolds, Robert Dallek, Susan Butler, and Herbert Feis are listed in the bibliography. In addition, the author relied on *Foreign Relations of the United States: The Conferences at Malta and Yalta, 1945,* a documentary compendium published by the State Department in 1955.

268 "taken seconds before or after": Robert Hopkins, *Witness to History,* 154.
270 *pulsus alternans:* Bruenn, "Clinical Notes," 589.
270 "Something due to nerves": Oct. 10, 1948, interview in the Stettinius Papers, cited in Butler, *Roosevelt and Stalin,* 403.
270 "had heard more than half": Remark by Harry Hopkins reported to have been made in Washington to the British ambassador, Lord Halifax, quoted by Reynolds in *In Command of History,* 473. Churchill removed the quotation, drawn from a Halifax cable of April 16, 1945, from his memoir, Reynolds says.
270 "really was a pale reflection": Ibid.
270 "vague and loose": Eden, *Reckoning,* 593.
270 "him only a few months to live": Moran, *Churchill,* 242.
271 "The Prime Minister": J. M. Martin to Charles Bohlen, Feb. 3, 1945, Bohlen Papers, LOC.
271 "a few insulting remarks": Anna Boettiger, Yalta Diary, 18, Halsted Papers, box 84.
271 "I am sure": Byrnes, *Speaking Frankly,* 23.
272 Anna later maintained: See Anna Roosevelt Halsted to James L. Snell (historian at Tulane University), Dec. 30, 1955. "I do know my father did a great deal of study of papers and documents given to him by the State Department and other experts in preparation for the Yalta meeting. This study was done, however, in the privacy of his own quarters." Anna Roosevelt Halsted Papers, box 85.
272 first draft of his memoir: Bohlen Papers.

272 "the central figure": Both Clemens in her pioneering *Yalta*, iii, and Harbutt in his more recent *Yalta 1945*, 309, describe him in those terms.

272 break with Moscow: The meeting with the senators is described in Campbell and Herring, *Diaries of Edward M. Stettinius*, 214–15, cited by Dallek, *Franklin D. Roosevelt and American Foreign Policy*, 508.

273 "It would make it easier": *FRUS: Malta and Yalta, 1945*, 677.

273 five biggest Polish parties: Bohlen, *Witness to History*, 197. According to Bohlen, the proposal Roosevelt advanced was originally drafted by Stanisław Mikołajczyk.

274 "I have been called a dictator": *FRUS: Malta and Yalta*, 669–70.

274 failed miserably: See page 253 in chapter 9.

274 "We were up against": Bohlen, *Witness to History*, 197. Eden claims to have stiffened Roosevelt's note. *Reckoning*, 598.

275 "The world would regard": *FRUS: Malta and Yalta*, 728.

275 tossed out the figure of $6 billion: Harriman and Abel, *Special Envoy*, 384.

276 "Tell me, what do": Gromyko, *Memoirs*, 89, cited by Plokhy, *Yalta*, 216.

276 "There hasn't really been": *FRUS: Malta and Yalta*, 718. Quotation comes from minutes taken by H. Freeman Matthews, director of Office of European Affairs, in the State Department. In addition to Bohlen and Matthews, a third official kept a set of notes on the formal sessions. This was Alger Hiss, who was convicted in 1950 of perjury for denying he spied for the Soviet Union. Studies of Yalta usually find it necessary to note that he never had a private meeting there with President Roosevelt. Hiss, then in State's Office of Special Political Affairs, specialized on issues involving the establishment of the UN.

277 a great step forward": Ibid., 713.

277 "This is rot": Ibid. covers the UN discussion on 713–14, 722–28. Also see Campbell and Herring, *Diaries of Stettinius*, 203–6, 249.

278 "known to the whole world": *FRUS: Malta and Yalta*, 789.

278 "Russia's entry": Ibid., 396.

278 "This meeting of the three": Quoted by Mitter, *China's War with Japan*, 360.

278 moving thirty divisions: Deane, *Strange Alliance*, 247. At Yalta, Stalin spoke of twenty-five, not thirty, divisions. *FRUS: Malta and Yalta*, 769.

279 "He would kill us": *FRUS: Malta and Yalta*, 770.

279 "The United States recognizes": Logevall, *Embers of War*, 89.

280 "Top-Secret": *FRUS: Malta and Yalta*, 43.

280 "We've just saved two million Americans": Admiral Ernest J. King recalled decades later by Katherine Harriman in interview with Jon Meacham in *Franklin and Winston*, 317, 440.

280 "It would be better": *FRUS: Malta and Yalta*, 786–87.

281 "Now we're in for ½ hour of it": Stettinius, *Roosevelt and the Russians*, 185.

281 "For many years": *FRUS: Malta and Yalta*, 780.

281 "Molotov is right": Ibid., 790.

282 "We'd better adjourn": Eden, *Reckoning*, 594.

282 "We sat with him": Gromyko, *Memoirs*, 98.

282 new instructions: Campbell and Herring, *Diaries of Stettinius*, 223, cited by Plokhy, *Yalta*, 243.

282 "It is now largely": *FRUS: Malta and Yalta*, 851.

283 "to create democratic institutions": Ibid., 972.

283 "It should be like": Ibid., 854.

283 work in their favor: Applebaum, *Iron Curtain*, 194.

283 Eden argued: Eden, *Reckoning*, 609.

283 "might jeopardize": Campbell and Herring, *Diaries of Stettinius*, 223.

284 continue to insist: Stettinius, *Roosevelt and the Russians*, 252.

285 "Mr. President, this is so": Plokhy, *Yalta*, 251, citing Leahy, *I Was There*, 315–16.

285 "This is going too far": Resis, *Molotov Remembers*, 51.

286 "The Russians have given": *FRUS: Malta and Yalta*, 920.

286 "the most urgent": Churchill, *Triumph and Tragedy*, 366.

286 "common desire": *FRUS: Malta and Yalta*, 973.

286 "I felt bound": Churchill, *Triumph and Tragedy*, 400.

287 now twelve years removed: *New York Times*, Feb. 13, 1945.

287 "somewhere in the Black Sea area": Levin, *Making of FDR*, 407.

288 "Marshal Stalin said": *FRUS: Malta and Yalta*, 924.

288 "with a smile": Bohlen, first draft of his memoir, 212, LOC.

288 "We really believed": Sherwood, *Roosevelt and Hopkins*, 870.

289 called into question: Moran, *Churchill*, 243, attributes to Hopkins the view that "the President seems to have no mind of his own." This is presented as a self-evident proposition on which the two gossips agreed, not a quotation.

289 "No single event": Deane, *Strange Alliance*, 160.

289 but he was effective: Bohlen, *Witness to History*, 179; his comment that Roosevelt wasn't likable is on page 219.

289 "We have wound up": Letter dated Feb. 12, 1945, to Eleanor Roosevelt in Elliott Roosevelt, *Rendezvous with Destiny, Roosevelt Letters*, 3:526, cited by Freidel, 592.

289 bomb's potential: Truman eventually told Stalin about the bomb at the Potsdam Conference. Molotov confirms that Stalin had been well briefed. "Before and during the war, our intelligence worked quite well. We had a fine group in America," he said in Resis, *Molotov Remembers*, 56.

290 the ubiquitous NKVD: Reilly, *Reilly of the White House*, 214. The visit to Sevastopol is also described on p. 35 of the official White House Yalta log.

290 "The President had a ghastly night": Harriman and Abel, *Special Envoy*, 417.

291 "The President is to be": Official Yalta log, 39. Byrnes's news conference was covered in *New York Times*, Feb. 14.

291 The king's repasts: This account is derived from the Bohlen, Reilly, and Rigdon memoirs; also the official log.

291 "Amends should be made": Holden and Johns, *House of Saud*, 137–38.

291 "calm and reasoned": Bohlen, *Witness to History*, 213.

292 "On the problem": Rosenman, *Working with Roosevelt*, 528.

292 "the king sure told you": Bohlen, draft of memoir, 249, Bohlen Papers.

292 "The President seemed placid": Churchill, *Triumph and Tragedy*, 397.

293 visit London in June: Roosevelt mentioned such reports in a detached way in his press conferences 992 and 993 on February 23 on the *Quincy* and March 2 back at the White House.

293 "I shall be looking forward": Churchill to Roosevelt, March 17, 1945, in *C&R*, 3:574.

293 requisitioning his bedroom: Accounts of this argument are in Rigdon's memoir and Bishop, *FDR's Last Year*. The journalist has Hopkins and Watson fighting face-to-face. As usual, he cites no source. Lieutenant Rigdon says the fight transpired in verbal messages that he carried from one man to the other.

293 as a warning: Robert Hopkins, the photographer son, visited "Pa" Watson on the *Quincy* and presumably kept his father informed of his condition. See Robert Hopkins, *Witness to History*, 169.

294 "Tell your father": In Bishop, *FDR's Last Year*, 606–7. David L. Roll in *The Hopkins Touch* draws the conclusion that Bishop based his account on an interview with Anna Roosevelt Halsted. Robert Sherwood in *Roosevelt and Hopkins* has the adviser going to the president to exchange terse farewells.

294 accompany Hopkins: Bohlen wrote in his memoir that he had no idea that the president wanted him to stay on the ship or was annoyed by his departure. *Witness to History*, 214.

294 never to meet again: Roosevelt's calendar as edited and preserved in the FDRL at Hyde Park has the two men dining at the White House, on February 28 and March 2. Roll convincingly explains the mistake in *Hopkins Touch*, 463n. He accepts an archivist's suggestion that the original notation of "HH" denoted "household," not Harry Hopkins, in this instance. Hopkins was in the Mayo Clinic on those dates. It appears he was still there when Roosevelt died.

294 "Ross told us": Halsted Papers, box 84.

294 "All in all": Rosenman, *Working with Roosevelt*, 522.

295 state of depression: This conclusion is drawn by Gallagher, *FDR's Splendid Deception*, 199, and Freidel, *Rendezvous with Destiny*, 595. Freidel hints that he might have gotten guidance on this point from Anna, whom he interviewed. He does so by indirection in a footnote on p. 661, saying it was not Howard Bruenn who spoke to him of Roosevelt's depression. The daughter would seem to be the only other person aboard the *Quincy* in a position to draw that conclusion.

295 "a certain functional stool": Barkley, *That Reminds Me*, 191.

296 "certain that it had paved the way": Rosenman, *Working with Roosevelt*, 526.

296 "He was obviously unhappy": Berle and Beal, *Navigating the Rapids*, 476–77. Berle saw the president on March 5.

CHAPTER 11   ALMOST TO VICTORY

297 "I hope that you will pardon": Address to Congress, March 1, 1945, *PPA*, 570.

298 "the first time he mentioned": Perkins, *Roosevelt I Knew*, 379.

299 "much refreshed": Lippmann column, *Herald Tribune*, March 3, 1944.

299 "He looked well and handsome": March 12, 1944, Belle Willard Roosevelt diary, Kermit Roosevelt and Belle Roosevelt Papers.

299 "He is looking pretty well": Stimson diary, March 1, 1945.

300 "the solution reached on Poland": March 1 to Congress, in *PPA*, 581.

300 "the X-matter": *Diaries of Stettinius*, 305.

301 "A pretty good report": Representative Charles Halleck, quoted by Berlin in *Washington Despatches*, 521.

301 "It was a long, rambling": Drury, *Senate Journal*, 373.

301 "It seemed the applause": David Brinkley, *Washington Goes to War*, 267.

301 "reawakened even in": John O'Donnell, New York *Daily News*, March 2, 1945.

302 crackdown by the Red Army: See Dobbs, *Six Months in 1945*, 115–25.

302 "liquidations and deportations": Churchill to Roosevelt, March 8, 1945, cable, in *C&R*, 3:547–49.

302 "We are in the presence": Churchill to Roosevelt, March 13, 1945, in *C&R*, 3:565.

303 "boredom and disgust": Kennan, *Memoirs*, 212.

303 "slipping": Bohlen, *Witness to History*, 216.

303 disagreements on tactics: Roosevelt to Churchill, March 15, 1945; Churchill to Roosevelt, March 17, 1945, in *C&R*, 3:562, 574.

304 "Just between us, Arthur": Vandenberg, *Private Papers of Senator Vandenberg*, 155.

304 "We can't do business with Stalin": Cited in Harriman and Abel, *Special Envoy*, 444.

305 how nuclear weapons would be managed: Stimson diary, March 15, 1945; Rhodes, *Making of the Atomic Bomb*, 621.

305 "The man who sat across": Robert Murphy, *Diplomacy Among Warriors*, 247.

306 "He is fond of taking": *Diaries of William Lyon Mackenzie King*, entries starting March 9, 1945, Canadian Archive, p. 238 of original manuscript (available online). Also see pp. 223, 249.

307 "Education in the Mountains": Persico, *Franklin and Lucy*, 325.

307 "The Returning Black Servicemen": Reference in Goodwin, *No Ordinary Time*, 592.

308 "a fair semblance": Drury, *Senate Journal*, 390.

308 "We all love Humanity": In Morgan, *FDR*, 759.

308 "If ever death": Krock, *Memoirs*, 219.

309 "If they had said": Anna Roosevelt Halsted interviewed by Joseph Lash, Lash Papers, box 44, folder 2, FDRL.

310 "failed dangerously": Tully, *FDR, My Boss*, 357.

310 "I'm afraid he'll never return alive": Barkley, *That Reminds Me*, 193.

310 "was in no mood": Bohlen, *Witness to History*, 223.

310 "creative procrastination": Warren Kimball, editorial note in *C&R*, 3:630.

311 "Frankly I cannot": Roosevelt to Stalin, March 17, 1945, in Butler, *My Dear Mr. Stalin*, 300.

311 collusion with the enemy: See Susan Butler's discussion in *Roosevelt and Stalin*, 439–42; also p. 246 of *Mackenzie King Diary*, summarizing a March 13 conversation with the president in which Roosevelt blames Churchill for being too forthcoming with the Russians on the negotiation over Italy.

311 "Roosevelt was furious": Bohlen, *Witness to History*, 218.

311 "as a result of these": Stalin to Roosevelt, April 3, 1945, in Butler, *My Dear Mr. Stalin*, 312–13. Roosevelt response on April 4, 313–15.

312 *Time* magazine would deduce: April 23, 1944, issue.

313 "utter defeat": Marshall memo, April 2, Map Room File, FDRL.

313 "absolutely dead weight": Reilly, *Reilly of the White House*, 227.

313 "He is slipping away": Hassett, *Off the Record with FDR*, 327–28. (Original manuscript is in Box 22 of Hassett Papers at FDRL.)

313 seriously depressed a month earlier: See endnote in previous chapter citing Freidel, *Rendezvous with Destiny*, 661.

314 "When we get through": Lash, *Franklin and Eleanor*, 719.

314 "On her side": Lash notes on interview with Anna, Lash Papers, box 44, folder 2.

314 shot up by fifty points: Bruenn appears to have related this anecdote at least three times in later years. Doris Kearns Goodwin locates Eleanor's persistence on Yugoslav partisans in the president's December trip to Warm Springs. *No Ordinary Time*, 564. Freidel locates it in March, relying on notes made by Dr. James Halsted, Anna's third husband. See *Rendezvous with Destiny*, 604.

314 "I say a prayer": Lash, *Franklin and Eleanor*, 719.

316 developed into a game: *CC*, 408, 410, 412, 416.

316 scattered "peacekeeping" operations: See summary by Rick Gladstone, *New York Times*, July 29, 2015.

317 "I'm delighted": Churchill to Roosevelt, April 1, 1945, in *C&R*, 3:602.

317 "respectfully" arguing: Butler, *My Dear Mr. Stalin*, 322.

318 "I would personally minimize": Roosevelt to Churchill, April 11, 1945, in ibid., 321, also in *C&R*, 3:630.

318 "He was looking to": Anne O'Hare McCormick, *New York Times Magazine*, April 22, 1945.

319 life-size watercolor: The painting now hangs in a memorial museum adjacent to the Little White House in Warm Springs, both part of a historic site maintained by the State of Georgia.

319 "The drive was too long": *CC*, 413.

320 "Mr. Roosevelt bowed": Smith, *Merriman Smith's Book of Presidents*, 202. Roosevelt was echoing the farewell cry of the Lone Ranger, hero of a popular radio serial, a fighter for justice in the Wild West, which would have been familiar to most radio listeners, children especially, in that era. Now in their dotage, those who survive can be found arguing on the Internet about whether "Heigh-O" should be transcribed "Heigh-O," "Hi-ho," or "Hi Yo." Silver was the Lone Ranger's horse.

320 "Keep lazy, Sir": *CC*, 414.

320 "Let me assure you": *PPA*, 615–16.

321 "was unusually tasteless": Shoumatoff, *FDR's Unfinished Portrait*, 111.

322 "Henry, I am with you": Blum, *Years of War*, 419.

322 "He looked smiling": *CC*, 417.

323 "Here's where I make a law": Freidel, *Rendezvous with Destiny*, 603.

323 "he raised his right hand": Shoumatoff, *FDR's Unfinished Portrait*, 117.

323 "I have a terrific pain": *CC*, 418.

324 "the Wilson thing all over": Anna Roosevelt interview, Lash Papers, box 44, folder 22.

325 "not alarming at any time": McIntire, *White House Physician*, 239.

325 never quite forgave her: Interview in Lash Papers.

327 "without exception the best": Stimson diary, April 15, 1945, 5–6.

327 "The President's death": Cited by Goodwin, *No Ordinary Time*, 606.

EPILOGUE   IN HIS WAKE

329 "Here we have the great miracle": Kershaw, *Hitler, 1936–1945*, 791.

329 "He seemed deeply moved and disturbed": Harriman and Abel, *Special Envoy*, 441.

330 "I personally feel": Butler, *Roosevelt and Stalin*, 467.

330 "a leader in the cause": Dispatch by C. L. Sulzberger, *New York Times*, April 14, 1945.

330 "Mr. Molotov's absence": Roosevelt to Stalin, March 24, 1945, in Butler, *My Dear Mr. Stalin*, 302–3.

330 "I thought I was going": McCullough, *Truman*, 341–42.

331 "Jesus Christ and General Jackson": Truman's exclamation never appeared in print in the magazine. It shows up in an account of Rayburn's conversation in a collection of *Time* "files"—field reports by correspondents—at Harvard University's Houghton Library, on microfilm, Box 14. This background memo was filed by the

Washington bureau chief, Frank McNaughton, for the April 23 cover story on the new president.

331 "Is there anything": Harry Truman, *Year of Decisions*, 5. The exchange is paraphrased in Eleanor Roosevelt, *This I Remember*, 344.

331 "a nuisance": Stimson diary, March 13, 1944.

332 "never did talk to me": McCullough, *Truman*, 355.

332 "disgraceful": Miscamble, *From Roosevelt to Truman*, 311.

332 habituated to the legislative branch: Henry Wallace was briefly given responsibilities in the executive branch at the start of the war—notably, as chairman of the Board of Economic Warfare—but by mid-1943 the board was renamed and refashioned without him (as discussed in chapter 7).

333 "It is possible": Morison, "Why Japan Surrendered," 42.

333 On two occasions: In his conversations with the Canadian prime minister, Mackenzie King, and Alexander Sachs, a financier who made sure that the letter from Albert Einstein warning of the potential and menace of nuclear power reached Roosevelt. If the point came up with King, it would have been on March 9 after dinner at the White House. The passage in King's diary is ambiguous at best. Sachs gave an account to *Look* magazine (March 14, 1950, issue), but the scholar Barton J. Bernstein writes him off as "not fully reliable," in his collection *Atomic Bomb*, 101.

333 "wiping out entire cities": Rhodes, *Making of the Atomic Bomb*, 625, citing Truman memoir.

334 "that the bomb should be": Ibid., 651.

334 260,000 said to have been killed: Dear and Foot, *Oxford Companion to World War II*, 531, 546, 773; Keegan, *Second World War*, 576.

335 "It was our common purpose": Cited in Bernstein collection, *Atomic Bomb*, 4, citing Stimson, "The Decision to Use the Atomic Bomb," *Harper's*, Feb. 1947.

335 The surgeon told the young Kennedy: Burns, *John Kennedy*, 96.

336 "a pitiful victory": Speech by Representative Adolph Sabath of Illinois as recorded in the *Congressional Record* for Feb. 6, 1947, 841. (The congressional practice, then as now, was to allow members of Congress "to extend and revise" their remarks for the sake of the record, which does not distinguish words actually spoken on the floor from such afterthoughts.)

336 "Who can say": Speech by Representative John Robsion of Kentucky, Cong. Rec., Feb. 6, 1947, 850.

337 "If the Republicans": Speech by Senator Charles Brooks of Illinois, Cong. Rec., March 12, 1947, 1968.

337 completed in February 1951: The amendment to limit presidential terms had explicitly exempted the incumbent at the time of its passage by Congress. But Republican strategists calculated it would have symbolic force, making it more difficult for Truman to seek reelection in 1952.

337 "A sick President": Cong. Rec., Feb. 27, 1951, 1604.

338 hypotheticals: The *Los Angeles Times*, July 13, 1949, then staunchly conservative, hypothesized in a wry, backhanded editorial that Roosevelt might still be alive had term limits kept him from seeking a fourth term.

338 "not perfect but a man": Cong. Rec., Feb. 27, 1951, pp. 1606–7.

BIBLIOGRAPHY

BOOKS AND ARTICLES

Adams, Henry H. *Witness to Power: The Life and Fleet of Admiral William D. Leahy.* Annapolis, Md., 1985.

Applebaum, Anne. *Iron Curtain, 1944–1956.* New York, 2012.

Asbell, Bernard. *The F.D.R. Memoirs.* Garden City, N.Y., 1973.

———, ed. *Mother and Daughter.* New York, 1988.

Atkinson, Rich. *The Guns at Last Light.* New York, 2013.

Barkley, Alben. *That Reminds Me.* Garden City, N.Y., 1954.

Baruch, Bernard. *My Own Story.* New York, 1957.

———. *The Public Years.* New York, 1960.

Beria, Sergo. *Beria, My Father: Inside Stalin's Kremlin.* London, 2001.

Berle, Beatrice Bishop, and Travis Beal Jacobs, eds. *Navigating the Rapids: From the Papers of Adolf A. Berle.* New York, 1973.

Berlin, Isaiah. *Washington Despatches, 1941–1945: Weekly Political Reports from the British Embassy.* Edited by H. G. Nicholas. Chicago, 1981.

Bernstein, Barton J. *The Atomic Bomb: The Critical Issues.* Edited by Barton J. Bernstein. Boston, 1976.

Bernstein, Richard. *China 1945: Mao's Revolution and America's Fateful Choice.* New York, 2014.

Biddle, Francis. *In Brief Authority.* New York, 1962.

Bird, Kai, and Martin J. Sherwin, *American Prometheus.* New York, 2006.

Bishop, Jim. *FDR's Last Year.* New York, 1974.

Black, Conrad. *Franklin Delano Roosevelt: Champion of Freedom.* New York, 2003.

Bland, Larry I., ed. *George C. Marshall Interviews and Reminiscences for Forrest C. Pogue.* Lexington, Va., 1996.

Blum, John Morton. *Years of War, 1941–1945: From the Morgenthau Diaries.* Boston, 1967.

Boettiger, John R. *A Love in Shadow.* New York, 1978.

Bohlen, Charles E. *Witness to History.* New York, 1973.

Brands, H. W. *Traitor to His Class.* New York, 2008.

Breitman, Richard, and Allan J. Lichtman. *FDR and the Jews.* Cambridge, Mass., 2013.

Brinkley, Alan. *The End of Reform.* New York, 1995.

———. *Franklin Delano Roosevelt.* New York, 2010.

Brinkley, David. *Washington Goes to War.* New York, 1988.

Britch, Carroll, and Cliff Lewis. *Rediscovering Steinbeck.* Lewiston, N.Y., 1989.

Brown, Walter J. *James F. Byrnes of South Carolina: A Remembrance.* Columbia, S.C., 1992.

Brownell, Will, and Richard N. Billings. *So Close to Greatness: The Biography of William C. Bullitt.* New York, 1987.

Bruenn, Howard G. "Clinical Notes on the Illness and Death of President Franklin D. Roosevelt." *Annals of Internal Medicine* 72 (April 1970): 579–91.

Bryant, Arthur. *Triumph in the West.* New York, 1959.

Buhite, Russell D., and David W. Levy, eds. *FDR's Fireside Chats.* Norman, Okla., 1992.

Bullitt, Orville H., ed. *For the President, Personal and Secret: Correspondence Between Franklin D. Roosevelt and Orville H. Bullitt.* Boston, 1972.

Burns, James MacGregor. *John Kennedy: A Political Profile.* New York, 1960.

———. *Roosevelt: The Lion and the Fox.* Boston, 1956.

———. *Roosevelt: The Soldier of Freedom.* Boston, 1970.

Bush, Vannevar. *Pieces of the Action.* New York, 1970.

Butler, Susan. *Roosevelt and Stalin: Portrait of a Partnership.* New York, 2015.

———, ed. *My Dear Mr. Stalin: The Complete Correspondence of Franklin D. Roosevelt and Joseph V. Stalin.* New Haven, Conn., 1995.

Byrnes, James F. *All in One Lifetime.* New York, 1958.

———. *Speaking Frankly.* New York, 1947.

Campbell, Thomas M., and George C. Herring, eds. *The Diaries of Edward M. Stettinius, Jr., 1943–1946.* New York, 1975.

Catledge, Turner. *My Life and The Times.* New York, 1971.

Churchill, Winston. *Closing the Ring.* Vol. 5 of *The Second World War.* Boston, 1951.

———. *Triumph and Tragedy.* Vol. 6 of *The Second World War.* Boston, 1953.

Clark, Mark W. *Calculated Risk.* New York, 1950.

Clemens, Diane Shaver. *Yalta.* Oxford, 1971.

Colville, John. *Fringes of Power.* London, 1985.

Conant, Jennet. *The Irregulars: Roald Dahl and the British Spy Ring in Wartime Washington.* New York, 2008.

Cooper, John Milton, Jr. *Woodrow Wilson: A Biography.* New York, 2009.

Costigliola, Frank. *Roosevelt's Lost Alliances.* Princeton, N.J., 2011.

Culbert, David, ed. *Mission to Moscow.* Madison, Wis., 1980.

Culver, John C., and John Hyde. *American Dreamer: The Life of Henry A. Wallace.* New York, 2000.

Dallek, Robert. *Franklin D. Roosevelt and American Foreign Policy, 1932–1945.* New York, 1979.

Daniels, Jonathan. *White House Witness, 1942–1945.* Garden City, N.Y., 1975.

Daniels, Josephus. *The Wilson Era.* Chapel Hill, N.C., 1946.

Davies, Norman. *God's Playground: A History of Poland.* Vol. 2. New York, 1979.

———. *Rising '44.* New York, 2003.

Deane, John R. *The Strange Alliance: The Story of Our Efforts at Wartime Cooperation with Russia.* New York, 1947.

Dear, I. C. B., and M.R.D. Foot, eds. *Oxford Companion to World War II.* New York, 1995.

Divine, Robert A. *Second Chance: The Triumph of Internationalism in America During World War II.* New York, 1967.

Djilas, Milovan. *Conversations with Stalin.* London, 1967.

Dobbs, Michael. *Six Months in 1945.* New York, 2012.

Drury, Allen. *A Senate Journal, 1943–1945.* New York, 1963.

Eden, Anthony. *The Reckoning: The Memoirs of Anthony Eden, Earl of Avon.* Boston, 1965.

Eisenhower, Dwight D. *Crusade in Europe.* Garden City, N.Y., 1948.

Eubank, Keith. *Summit at Teheran: The Untold Story.* New York, 1985.

Evans, Hugh E. *The Hidden Campaign: FDR's Health and the 1944 Election.* Armonk, N.Y., 2002.

Feis, Herbert. *Churchill, Roosevelt, Stalin: The War They Waged and the Peace They Sought.* Princeton, N.J., 1957.

Ferrell, Robert H. *Choosing Truman.* Columbia, Mo., 1994.

———. *The Dying President: Franklin D. Roosevelt, 1944–1945.* Columbia, Mo., 1998.

Flynn, Edward. *You're the Boss.* New York, 1947.

Freidel, Frank. *Franklin D. Roosevelt: A Rendezvous with Destiny.* Boston, 1990.

Gallagher, Hugh. *FDR's Splendid Deception.* New York, 1985.

Gannon, Robert L. *The Cardinal Spellman Story.* Garden City, N.Y., 1962.

Goldsmith, Harry. *A Conspiracy of Silence: Impact on History.* Bloomington, Ind., 2007.

Goodwin, Doris Kearns. *No Ordinary Time.* New York, 1994.

Gromyko, Andrei. *Memoirs.* New York, 1990.

Halsted, James A. "Severe Malnutrition in a Public Servant of the World War II Era: The Medical History of Harry Hopkins." Undated reprint from Department of Medicine, Albany Medical College; also, an unpublished biography of Harry Hopkins, in the possession of June Hopkins.

Harbutt, Fraser J. *Yalta, 1945: Europe and America at the Crossroads.* Cambridge, U.K., 2010.

Harriman, Averell, and Elie Abel. *Special Envoy to Churchill and Stalin, 1941–1946.* New York, 1975.

Hassett, William D. *Off the Record with FDR, 1942–1945.* New Brunswick, N.J., 1958.

Hastings, Max. *Overlord.* New York, 1984.

Henderson, Loy W. *A Question of Trust: The Origins of U.S.-Soviet Diplomatic Relations: The Memoirs of Loy W. Henderson.* Stanford, Calif., 1986.

Hershberg, James G. *James B. Conant: Harvard to Hiroshima.* Palo Alto, Calif., 1993.

Holden, David, and Richard Johns. *The House of Saud.* London, 1983.

Hoopes, Townsend, and Douglas Brinkley. *FDR and the Creation of the UN.* New Haven, Conn., 1997.

Hoover, Herbert. *The Ordeal of Woodrow Wilson.* New York, 1958.

Hopkins, Robert. *Witness to History.* Seattle, 2002.

Hull, Cordell. *The Memoirs of Cordell Hull.* Vol. 2. New York, 1948.

Ickes, Harold L. *The Lowering Clouds, 1939–1941.* Vol. 3 of *The Secret Diary of Harold Ickes.* New York, 1953.

Katznelson, Ira. *Fear Itself: The New Deal and the Origins of Our Time.* New York, 2013.

Keegan, John. *The Second World War.* New York, 1989.

Kennan, George. *Memoirs, 1925–1950.* New York, 1967.

Kershaw, Ian. *Hitler, 1936–1945: Nemesis.* New York, 2000.

Kimball, Warren F. *Forged in War.* New York, 1997.

———. *The Juggler: Franklin Roosevelt as Wartime Statesman.* Princeton, N.J., 1991.

———, ed. *Churchill and Roosevelt: The Complete Correspondence.* Princeton, N.J., 1984.

Krock, Arthur. *Memoirs.* New York, 1968.

Larrabee, Eric. *Commander in Chief.* New York, 1987.

Lash, Joseph P. *Eleanor and Franklin: The Story of Their Relationship Based on Eleanor Roosevelt's Private Papers.* New York, 1971.

Leahy, William D. *I Was There.* New York, 1950.

L'Etang, Hugh. *The Pathology of Leadership: A History of the Effects of Disease on 20th Century Leaders.* New York, 1970.

Levin, Linda Lotridge. *The Making of FDR: The Story of Stephen T. Early.* Amherst, N.Y., 2007.

Lippman, Theo, Jr. *The Squire of Warm Springs.* Chicago, 1977.

Littell, Norman M. *My Roosevelt Years.* Seattle, 1987.

Logevall, Fredrik. *Embers of War: The Fall of an Empire and the Making of America's Vietnam*. New York, 2012.

Lomazow, Steven, and Eric Fettmann. *FDR's Deadly Secret*. New York, 2010.

MacArthur, Douglas. *Reminiscences*. Annapolis, Md., 2001.

Macdonald, Dwight. *Henry Wallace: The Man and the Myth*. New York, 1947.

MacMillan, Margaret. *Paris, 1919: Six Months That Changed the World*. New York, 2002.

Manchester, William. *American Caesar*. Boston, 1978.

McCullough, David. *Truman*. New York, 1992.

McIntire, Ross T. *White House Physician*. New York, 1946.

Meacham, Jon. *Franklin and Winston*. New York, 2003.

Mikołajczyk, Stanisłav. *The Rape of Poland*. New York, 1948.

Miller, Mary E. *Baroness of Hobcaw: The Life of Belle W. Baruch*. Columbia, S.C., 2006.

Miscamble, Wilson D. *From Roosevelt to Truman*. New York, 2007.

Mitter, Rana. *China's War with Japan, 1937–1945*. London, 2014.

Moran, Charles McMoran Wilson. *Churchill: Taken from the Diaries of Lord Moran: The Struggle for Survival, 1940–1965*. Boston, 1966.

Morgan, Ted. *FDR: A Biography*. New York, 1985.

Morison, S. E. "Why Japan Surrendered." In *The Atomic Bomb: The Critical Issues*. Edited by Barton J. Bernstein. Boston, 1976.

Murphy, Bruce Allen. *Wild Bill: The Legend and Life of William O. Douglas*. New York, 2003.

Murphy, Robert. *Diplomacy Among Warriors*. Garden City, N.Y., 1964.

Nasaw, David. *The Patriarch*. New York, 2012.

Oursler, Fulton. *Behold This Dreamer*. Boston, 1964.

Overy, Richard. *Russia's War: A History of the Soviet War Effort, 1941–1945*. New York, 1998.

Owen, David. *In Sickness and in Power: Illnesses in Heads of Government During the Last 100 Years*. Westport, Conn., and London, 2008.

Park, Bert Edwards. *The Impact of Illness on World Leaders*. Philadelphia, 1986.

Paul, Allen. *Katyn: Stalin's Massacre and the Triumph of Truth*. New York, 1991.

Pauley, Edwin W. "Life and Times of Edwin W. Pauley." Unpublished autobiography, manuscript at Truman Library.

Perkins, Frances. *The Roosevelt I Knew*. New York, 1946.

Persico, Joseph E. *Franklin and Lucy*. New York, 2008.

———. *Roosevelt's Secret War*. New York, 2001.

Plokhy, S. M. *Yalta: The Price of Peace*. New York, 2010.

Pogue, Forrest C. *Organizer of Victory, 1943–1945*. Vol. 3 of *George C. Marshall*. New York, 1973.

Potter, E. B. *Nimitz*. Annapolis, Md., 1976.

Reilly, Michael F. *Reilly of the White House*. New York, 1947.

Resis, Albert, ed. *Molotov Remembers*. Chicago, 1993.

Reynolds, David. *From Munich to Pearl Harbor: Roosevelt's America and the Origins of the Second World War*. Chicago, 2001.

———. *In Command of History*. London, 2005.

———. *From World War to Cold War*. Oxford, 2006.

———. *Summits*. New York, 2007.

Rhodes, Richard. *The Making of the Atomic Bomb*. New York, 1987.

Rigdon, William M. *White House Sailor*. Garden City, N.Y., 1962.

Roberts, Andrew. *Masters and Commanders*. New York, 2009.

Robertson, David. *Sly and Able: A Political Biography of James F. Byrnes.* New York, 1994.

Roll, David L. *The Hopkins Touch.* New York, 2013.

Roosevelt, Eleanor. *This I Remember.* New York, 1949.

Roosevelt, Elliott, ed. *The Roosevelt Letters.* Vol. 3. London, 1952.

Roosevelt, Franklin D. *The Complete Presidential Press Conferences of Franklin D. Roosevelt.* Vols. 22–25. Cambridge, Mass., 1972.

Roosevelt, James. *My Parents.* London, 1977.

Roosevelt, James, and Sidney Shalett. *Affectionately, F.D.R.* New York, 1959.

Rosenman, Samuel L. *Working with Roosevelt.* New York, 1952.

Schlesinger Jr., Arthur M. *The Imperial Presidency.* Boston, 1973.

Schlesinger, Stephen C. *Act of Creation: The Founding of the United Nations.* Boulder, Colo., 2003.

Sherwood, Robert E. *Roosevelt and Hopkins.* New York, 1948.

Shoumatoff, Elizabeth. *FDR's Unfinished Portrait.* Pittsburgh, 1990.

Smith, A. Merriman. *Merriman Smith's Book of Presidents.* New York, 1972.

Smith, Gene. *When the Cheering Stopped.* New York, 1964.

Smith, Jean Edward. *FDR.* New York, 2007.

Smith, Richard Norton. *Thomas E. Dewey and His Times.* New York, 1982.

Snyder, Timothy. *Bloodlands: Europe Between Hitler and Stalin.* New York, 2010.

Stettinius, Edward R. *Roosevelt and the Russians: The Yalta Conference.* Garden City, N.Y., 1949.

Stilwell, Joseph W. *The Stilwell Papers.* London, 1949.

Stimson, Henry L. "The Decision to Use the Atomic Bomb." In *The Atomic Bomb: The Critical Issue.* Edited by Barton J. Bernstein. Boston, 1976.

Strout, Richard. *TRB: Views and Perspectives on the Presidency.* New York, 1995.

Trohan, Walter. *Political Animals.* Garden City, N.Y., 1975.

Truman, Harry. *Year of Decisions.* Vol. 1. of *Memoirs of Harry S. Truman.* Garden City, N.Y., 1955.

Truman, Margaret. *Harry S. Truman.* New York, 1973.

Tuchman, Barbara. *Stilwell and the American Experience in China.* New York, 1972.

Tully, Grace. *F.D.R., My Boss.* New York, 1949.

United States Department of State. *Foreign Relations of the United States Diplomatic Papers: The Conferences at Cairo and Tehran, 1943 (FRUS).* Washington, D.C., 1961.

Vandenberg, Arthur H., Jr. *The Private Papers of Senator Vandenberg.* Boston, 1956.

Waite, John G. Associates Architects. *The President as Architect: Franklin D. Roosevelt's Top Cottage.* Albany, N.Y., 2001.

Walker, Frank C. *FDR's Quiet Confidant.* Edited by Robert H. Ferrell. Niwot, Colo., 1997.

Ward, Geoffrey C. *Before the Trumpet: Young Franklin Roosevelt.* New York, 1985.

———. *A First-Class Temperament: The Emergence of Franklin D. Roosevelt, 1905–1928.* New York, 1989.

———, ed. *Closest Companion: The Unknown Story of the Intimate Friendship Between Franklin Roosevelt and Margaret Suckley.* Boston, 1995.

———, and Ken Burns. *The Roosevelts.* New York, 2014.

Weintraub, Stanley. *Final Victory: FDR's Extraordinary World War II Presidential Campaign.* Boston, 2012.

Welles, Benjamin. *Sumner Welles: FDR's Global Strategist.* New York, 1997.

Willkie, Wendell. *One World.* New York, 1943.

Withers, Bob. *The President Travels by Train: Politics and Pullmans.* Lynchburg, Va., 1996.

Woolner, David B., Warren F. Kimball, and David Reynolds, eds. *FDR's World: War, Peace, and Legacies.* New York, 2008.

MULTIMEDIA AND DIGITAL RESOURCES

Alexander Street Archives. alexanderstreet.com.
The American Presidency Project. A collaboration between Gerhard Peters and John T. Woolley at the University of California, Santa Barbara. www.presidency.ucsb.edu /ws.
Associated Press Multimedia Archive. www.aparchive.com.
Foreign Relations of the United States. Digital Facsimiles. UW-Madison Libraries Digital Collections. http://digital.library.wisc.edu/1711.dl/FRUS.
Mission to Moscow. DVD Warner Bros.
Wilson. Directed by Henry King. DVD.

ARCHIVAL RESOURCES

FDRL

John Boettiger Papers
Wilson Brown Papers
Stephen T. Early Papers
Anna Roosevelt Halsted Papers
William D. Hassett Papers
Harry L. Hopkins Papers, also at Georgetown University Archives
Joseph Lash Papers
Ross T. McIntire Papers
Franklin Delano Roosevelt Papers
  Map Room File
  President's Personal File
  President's Secretary's File
Small Collections
  Howard G. Bruenn File
Grace Tully Papers

Library of Congress

Charles E. Bohlen Papers
Benjamin V. Cohen Papers
William Averell Harriman Papers
Harold L. Ickes Papers
William D. Leahy Papers
Kermit Roosevelt and Belle Roosevelt Papers

Oral History Collection at Columbia University's Butler Library

Reminiscences of Frances Perkins, 1955
Reminiscences of Henry Agard Wallace, 1951

Yale University, Sterling Memorial Library

Walter Lippmann Papers
Henry Lewis Stimson Papers

Other Repositories

Jim Bishop Papers, St. Bonaventure University Archives, Olean, N.Y.
Marquis Childs Papers, Wisconsin Historical Society
Robert Hannegan Papers, Harry S. Truman Library, Independence, Mo.
Harry L. Hopkins Papers, Georgetown University Library
Louis Hopkins Collection, Grinnell College, Grinnell, Iowa
Frank D. Lahey Papers, Lahey Clinic, Burlington, Mass.
Robert E. Sherwood Papers, Houghton Library, Harvard University
Gen. Edwin Watson and Edward Stettinius Jr. Papers, Archives, University of Virginia

Page numbers in *italics* refer to illustrations.

A NOTE ABOUT THE AUTHOR

Joseph Lelyveld spent nearly four decades as a reporter and editor at *The New York Times,* ending up as executive editor from 1994 to 2001. This is his third book since then, following *Great Soul: Mahatma Gandhi and His Struggle with India* and *Omaha Blues: A Memory Loop.* His earlier book on apartheid, *Move Your Shadow: South Africa, Black and White,* won the Pulitzer Prize for General Nonfiction. He lives in New York.

A NOTE ON THE TYPE

This book was set in a modern adaptation of a type designed by the first William Caslon (1692–1766). The Caslon face, an artistic, easily read type, has enjoyed more than two centuries of popularity in the English-speaking world. This version with its even balance and honest letterforms was designed by Carol Twombly for the Adobe Corporation and released in 1990.

Composed by North Market Street Graphics,
Lancaster, Pennsylvania
Printed and bound by Berryville Graphics,
Berryville, Virginia
Designed by Peter A. Andersen